the
FLORA
Publications Trust

Published by The Flora Publications Trust
c/o Natal Herbarium, Botanic Gardens Road, Durban 4001
Website: www.floratrustkzn.com

Distributed by ABC Bookshop, PO Box 642, Hilton 3245

First edition 2003
Text, maps & drawings ©The Flora Publications Trust
Photographs ©Photographers as indicated

Cover design sponsored by Orange Juice Design
Pre-press by Gundela Haywood
Printed and bound by Fishwicks
Binding of sponsors' editions by Peter Carstens

ISBN 0-620-30222-4 (subscribers' edition)
ISBN 0-620-30221-6 (standard edition)

Cover photograph:
Elands River Falls, near Mont-aux-Sources, northern Drakensberg by Steven Johnson

MOUNTAIN FLOWERS

A Field Guide to the Flora
of the Drakensberg and Lesotho

ELSA POOLEY

Looking north over a snow-sprinkled Giant's Castle, with Cathkin Peak in the distance. *Greig Stewart*

CONTENTS

WARNING
The publisher and author do not assume responsibility for any sickness, death or other harmful effects resulting from eating or using any plant in this book.

Harveya pulchra Tom de Waal *Craterocapsa congesta* David McDonald

Rhodohypoxis milloides Lal Greene *Erica alopecurus* Mike Hirst

Dedicated to

Olive Hilliard & *Bill Burtt*

plant explorers and taxonomists whose work has
enhanced our knowledge and understanding of the Drakensberg flora

Giant's Castle   *Lorraine van Hooff*

THE FLORA PUBLICATIONS TRUST

The peace of the hills and mountains is best sought in the company of flowers. The rarefied but pure air of the Drakensberg stimulates all the senses, breeding a lazy contentment that enables the mind to attune itself to beauty. I have spent some of my happiest mountain days amongst exquisite alpine flowers seeking them out and marvelling at their beauty. Then I have realised that the smallest flower in the smallest cranny of the precipice is as much a part of the unique berg experience as the achievement of its tallest peaks.

Elsa and her dedicated team have once again excelled themselves and I am confident that all those who love the mountains will derive pleasure from this guide for years to come.

The trustees are deeply appreciative of the support of so many individuals, companies and organisations whose financial and personal contributions have made this book a reality.

A.L. Crutchley
Chairman

The Flora Publications Trust was established in 1992 to raise sponsorship for the publication of popular, affordable books on the indigenous plants of KwaZulu-Natal and the Eastern Region, with the object of providing attractive, easy-to-use, authorative works to stimulate greater understanding of our exceptionally rich plant life and environment. All proceeds from sales are used to keep the books in print and to revise them from time to time when necessary.

6

R.A. Knight
Werner Knuffel
Noelline Kroon
Hendrik Krüger
John & Celia Latilla
Nico & Maud Laubscher,
   Stellenbosch
Peter & Val Law
Jean-Marie and Astri Leroy
Dawn Livingstone
George & Kate Lockhart
Peter & Margo Louw
O.J. Mackenzie
Winks & Murray Mackenzie
Mike & Christine Mair
A.E. March, Nkosi Nursery
Keith & Wendy McCall
Tim & Helen McClurg
Gavin McDonald
T.P. McDonogh
Thomas McGregor Vos &
   Lloyd McGregor Vos
Mrs. J.E. McIlrath
Cameron & Rhoda McMaster
Meet Us In Africa Tours
Patsy Millin
Missouri Botanical Gardens
Adéle Moore, Maclear
H.K. Morgan
Jeff W. Morris
Doug & Terri Morton
Tara Munro
M. Murray
R.M. Murray
Bruce & Cilla Nel
Penny Nicholson
Desmond L. Nielsen
Johann & Leigh Nieuwoudt,
   Simply Indigenous Nursery
Mrs. G.A. Nikschtat
Pat & Andy Ochse
Oude Stasie, Wakkerstroom
Rodney & Barbara Owen
Neva Y. Pahler
Parceval (Pty) Ltd.
Merry Park
Elizabeth Parker
Jeff & Bev Parsley
The Pattrick Family
Nigel Paul
Graham Payne
Anne & Anthony Peepall -
   for Belinda & Carolyn
Gareth P.H. Penny, UK
Bianca Pera
Chris & Di Perry
Craig Peter
Dave Peters
Michael Plastow - Earth & Sky
Dr. Ian Player
Francis Potter
Dr. Thomas R. Pray
Catherine Prentice

Pretoria University, Dept. of Botany
M.G. & R.P. Prew
Jenny & John Price
Elizabeth & Martin Prozesky
John Rae
Gary M. & Marie-France Ralfe
D. Randell
Random Harvest Nursery
Dave & Margot Raulstone
Patti & Bernard Ravnö
R.F. Raymond
Suzette Raymond
Dallas Reed
Caroline Reeders, Rhodes
Christopher Reim
Dr. Muriel B. Richter
Keith Roberts
Neal Roberts
Maralyn Robinson
In memory of Brem Ross,
   from Pam, Paul & Illona
Ron & René Rossler
Mrs. Diane L. Rowe
Janet D. Roxburgh - in memoriam
Dr. P. Rush
Dr. M.C. & Mrs. T.B.A. Rutherford
Gray & Samantha Ryder
Marc & Lorna Ryder
H. Sakamoto, Japan
N.T. Salm
Peter & Grace Sandalls
Margaret & Trevor Sandwith
Rod & Rachel Saunders
Errol & Jenny Scarr
Susan M. Schönefeld-Bradshaw
Michael & Karoline Schurr
W.G. Scurr
Ernest & Teresa Seamark
Kiyoyasu Seki
T.J.B. Simons
Geoff & Anne Skelton
Sandy Slater
Dennis & Ansie Slotow
Bill Small – Sani Wildlife Society
Dr. Ant Smith
A.W.H. Smith
Errol & Rosemary Smith
Cecily Smyth
L.C.P. Smyth
Melanie Spear
W.G. Sperryn
Malcolm & Lesley Stainbank
June Stannard
Ines & Basil Stathoulis
Estelle & Lucas Steenkamp
Stellenbosch University
   Library Service
Jan Smuts Collection,
   Stellenbosch University Library
K.P. Stephenson
Michael Stevenson
Terry-Anne Stevenson
Stef & June Steyn

Dorothea Stielau
B. & C. Street
Henriette Stroh
Dr. Dawie Strydom
Gerhard Strydom
Di & Jeremy Stubbs
Andrew & Vanessa Sutherland
Sue Swan
Colin Tedder
Prof. Peter & Mary-Lynne Tennant
Sandy Terreblanche
Grace N. Thompson
Lu & Peter Thompson
Keith Thomson
C.L. Tinley
Roy Trendler
Dave & Jo Trickett
Janine & Duncan Turner
Dr. ing Bob Ursem, The Netherlands
Dr. André vanden Baviere, Belgium
Dr. Erika van den Berg
Bossie & Rosalie van den Bosch
J.H. van der Byl
Dick & Liz van der Jagt
Betsie van der Merwe
Dr. Roelof van der Merwe
Dave & Jill van der Schyff
Peet C.L. van der Walt
Frank & Elspeth van Duuren
Dr. Karl van Laeren
M. & M.A. van Rijswijck
W. van Rÿswÿck
Thomas R. van Viegen
Braam & Elsa van Wyk
Carl Vernon
C.C. Viljoen
Coral & John Vinsen
Richard von Rahden
Vula Environmental Services
Jenny Wainwright-Klein
Christine Walkden
Joan Walker, Tanglewood
Lindsay & Gail Walker
C.J. (Roddy) Ward
Ron & Diana Webb
Ron Wedderburn
Norman & Hantie Weitz
Ilse & Stephan Wentzel
Freda Whipp
Dr. Dave H. White
Vic White, UK
Mark C. Wilkes
Michael & Carol Willetts
Glyn Williams
Rosemary Williams & Waldo Menne
J.B. Withers
B. Nigel Wolstenholme
F. Wood
L.S. Wood
Rob & Janet Wood
Ken & Alida Wray
E. Anne Wyatt-Goodall
Michelle Yates

7

ACKNOWLEDGEMENTS

This book is a tribute to the wonderful plants of the Eastern Mountain Region and to the people who have studied and lived amongst them. My role has been to bring together, in a popular form, as much of the existing knowledge and expertise as could be fitted onto the pages. Plant-loving people have been generous in sharing their knowledge and donating their photographs.

Photographers: All photographs in the book have been donated, an extraordinary contribution without which the costs of publication would have been prohibitive. Particular thanks for their significant collections to: Martin von Fintel, David McDonald, Lal Greene, Neil Crouch, Olive Hilliard and Bill Burtt, Tony Abbott, Peter Linder, Pam Cooke, Mike Hirst and Darrel Plowes.

My appreciation to Lawrence and Sheila Peacock who set up the photographic collection, and to Pam Cooke who took over this responsibility and has been a great colleague, generous with her time during final layouts and proofing.

Steven Johnson donated the cover picture which the Trust has used for promotional purposes.

Editing Olive Hilliard and Bill Burtt have been more than generous in sharing their field knowledge of the flora of the region. They have made time to check the text and to deal with countless queries. Responsibility for any errors and omissions is entirely mine, particularly the decision to keep scientific terms to a minimum.

My thanks to Di Smith, the technical editor whose botanical background has enhanced the work.

My sister, Creina Alcock brought experience, energy and insight to the intricate final stages of publishing and I thank her for making the time to help and for sharing the load.

Mapping: The distribution maps have been drawn from specimens in the Natal, Bews and Killick herbaria and from the NBI PRECIS database. Shernice Soobramoney has brought her considerable skills in managing data to the laborious process of producing the maps. Rob Scott-Shaw (Ezemvelo KZN Wildlife) supervised the input of data from the herbarium search, a demanding task. Thanks too to Kevin Thompson who assisted the process and to Hassina Aboobaker for the endpaper maps.

Drawings: My thanks to Angela Beaumont who brought her combined skills of botanist and botanical artist to the line drawings, working to difficult deadlines with good humour.

Thanks to the artists for drawings from *Trees of Natal, Zululand & Transkei*: Heather Borchers, Jane Browning, Tanza Clark, Trevor Edwards, Anne Haselgrove, Lynne Nichols and Wayne Vos.

National Botanical Institute (NBI): My thanks to Prof Brian Huntley, Chief Executive of the NBI, for making available facilities at Natal Herbarium and, through NBI staff at Kirstenbosch, Durban and Pretoria, assistance with many aspects of the book. Thanks in particular to Gideon Smith and Estelle Potgieter in Pretoria. **Natal Herbarium**: I am really appreciative of the support of Rosemary Williams, immediate past curator, Yashica Singh, curator, and the whole staff, especially Alfred Ngwenya and Helen Noble. They have provided a wonderful supportive working environment for me and my helpers, providing facilities for the data capturers, fielding endless queries, and making the extra effort to identify photographers' specimens. **Precis and Mappit** We are indebted to Trevor Arnold, Carol de Wet and Hannelie Snyman for the essential backup they provided and for patiently and efficiently dealing with all queries and requests.

Bews Herbarium, University of Natal (Pietermaritzburg). My grateful thanks to Trevor Edwards, curator, and Christina Potgieter, senior technician, for all their help and for providing facilities for the map data capturers and the artist.

Specialist Advice: I am indebted to: Kathleen Gordon-Gray for checking the Cyperaceae. Ashley Nicholas for generously providing the extensive research notes on Asclepiadaceae on which the text was based and checking this section of the photographic collection. I am grateful to Rodney Moffett for the considerable time he spent on the grasses and *Rhus* species. Kevin Balkwill, John Burrows, Marie Jordaan, Hubert Kurzweil, Peter Linder, John Manning, Ted Oliver and Braam van Wyk were all valuable sources of information.

Common Names: Dr Sumitra Talukdar, Prof David Ambrose and Khotso Kobisi (The National University of Lesotho) kindly checked the Sesotho names. Their careful comments and corrections are much appreciated. I am grateful to Prof Adrian Koopman (Dept of Zulu, University of Natal) for checking the Zulu names and to Gina Baldo for the Afrikaans.

Repro and printing: To Gundi Haywood, my appreciation for the considerable skills she has brought to this book. She has been generous with her time and support for the project, and a meticulous, committed colleague. Dave Armstrong has handled the scanning and Macintosh advice with patience and enthusiasm. Thanks to Mike Mills for PC backup.

My thanks to the management and staff at Fishwick's, particularly Geoff Scott and Roche Smith.

On the road to Royal Natal National Park, northern Drakensberg

Lorraine van Hooff

Design: To John Charter (formerly of Mathews & Charter) and Kelly Litke (formerly of Orange Juice Design), our thanks for the design of the cover and the sponsor's brochure.

General: I am indebted to Anne Haselgrove who has filled many roles - research assistant, artist and proof reader. She and June Dahle tackled the index with meticulous care.

To the many friends and colleagues who have assisted in a variety of ways over the last few years, my grateful thanks for all your help.

The Trust: My appreciation to the trustees, past and present, for their support throughout the project and special thanks to the Chairman Jack Crutchley and trust secretary Marylynn Grant, who for the past three years have kept this project on track.

The Working Group helped design these field guides and were involved in planning this one. My thanks to Gina Baldo, Trevor Coleman, David and Sally Johnson, Wally Menne, Geoff Nichols, Lawrence and Sheila Peacock, Dennis Slotow and Rosemary Williams.

My husband Tony originally set me on the path of recording plants in paint and print nearly 40 years ago. For the past 10 years he has provided the inspiration that has helped bring three field guides to completion. Words cannot adequately express my appreciation to Tony, Thomas, Simon and Susan, Justin and Joanne, for their unfailing support and for sharing and understanding my quest to make an illustrated record of these plants.

Clockwise:

Dianthus basuticus
David McDonald

Androcymbium striatum
Martin von Fintel

Felicia drakensbergensis
David McDonald

An afternoon thunderstorm in summer, building up around the Devil's Tooth and Inner Tower (Mont-aux-Sources Amphitheatre), photographed from the gap between the Witches and the Sentinel.

Greig Stewart

INTRODUCTION

This book provides a guide to the flora of the highest mountain region of southern Africa, the uKhahlamba-Drakensberg and Lesotho. It is forbidding, awe-inspiring territory caught amongst the mists and clouds of basalt peaks where waterfalls turn to columns of ice in winter. Long familiar to herdsmen and mountaineers, the area is largely inaccessible and still considered *terra incognita* by botanists. The plants may differ with every fold of the mountains, with every change in altitude, aspect, drainage and rock type, from one valley or peak to the next, clinging to cracks in rock faces, taking hold in basalt gravels or floating in shallow rock pools on the summit.

The dramatic broken landscape of the escarpment and the harsh climatic conditions on the highlands of Lesotho account for the remarkable diverse plant life with about 2200 species and almost 400 endemics (plants found only in this area and nowhere else in the world).

The flora of these high mountains has recently been recognised as one of the world's 'hot spots', a centre of plant diversity of global botanical importance.

Lesotho, the Mountain Kingdom, is a highland found entirely above 1000m rising to 3482m at Thabana Ntlenyane, the highest mountain south of Kilimanjaro. Although the interior is exposed and windswept, its marshes, mires and sponges are the watershed of southern Africa, giving rise to rivers that flow to two oceans on opposite sides of the continent, the Atlantic and Indian.

The summit of the Drakensberg, which averages an altitude of 3000m, forms an almost inaccessible boundary between Lesotho and South Africa, with sheer cliffs falling 1200m in places. This beautiful area can be very bleak until the plants respond to rain and warm summer temperatures with a burst of colour, flowers carpeting the sheet rock and marshy ground on the summit.

The grasslands can be transformed into fields of flowers in response to fires, often started as a result of rock falls or lightning (the area has the highest lightning strike rate in southern Africa). People also use fire to bring on new grass for grazing.

Many of the Drakensberg and Lesotho plants are already well known to gardeners in the northern hemisphere. Some were introduced to horticulture in Britain and Europe by intrepid explorers and collectors as long ago as the late 1800s. Although mostly unknown in gardens of southern Africa, many plants such as

Cyrtanthus erubescens Simon Milliken   *Gladiolus microcarpus* David McDonald   *Myosotis semi-amplexicaulis*   Peter Linder

11

Gladiolus flanaganii, the Suicide Gladiolus, found on cliffs near the summit, is named for the difficulties of getting close to it. The long-tubed flowers are specially adapted to pollination by Malachite sunbirds which perch on the sturdy, inclined stems to probe for nectar from above.

▲ *Martin von Fintel*   ▼ *Godfrey Symons*

View of the Eastern Buttress and Devil's Tooth from the south-east. The Sentinel is in the background and the Amphitheatre wall lies inbetween, hidden from view.   *John Hone*

Felicia filifolia   *Darrel Plowes*

Euryops acraeus   *Mike Hirst*   *Rhodohypoxis baurii*   *Darrel Plowes*

Rhodohypoxis species, *Euryops acraeus* and *Delosperma nubigenum* are popular and available to gardeners in Europe, Britain, USA and Japan, while horticultural hybrids and cultivars abound.

A note of caution to both the professional and the amateur plant collector – feast on these plants with your eyes and your senses only. Growing them can be difficult and, more importantly, they are protected by the nature conservation laws of South Africa and Lesotho. You may not collect plants without a permit.

A World Heritage Site
In 2000, the uKhahlamba-Drakensberg area was proclaimed a World Heritage Site for its rich diversity of plant and animal life, spectacular natural landscape and outstanding San (Bushman) rock paintings. Africa's greatest concentration of rock art is to be found in the caves and overhangs of these mountains, with more than 600 recorded sites containing over 40000 images. The area is now recognised as one of the world's few World Heritage Sites that meets criteria for both natural and cultural properties. For more information on an international initiative to conserve the region, the Maloti-Drakensberg Transfrontier Conservation and Development Programme, see page 18.

The 'Maletsunyane Falls near Semonkong in Lesotho, drop nearly 200m. Also known as LeBihan Falls, this is a beautiful, wild place where it takes 3 to 4 hours to hike to the bottom of the falls.

David McDonald

The Eastern Mountain Region

The Eastern Mountain Region or EMR (also known as the Drakensberg Alpine Centre) is centred on the mountains of Lesotho including the Maloti and Thaba Putsoa ranges. It includes the southern and northern Drakensberg in KwaZulu-Natal, the E Cape Drakensberg and Witteberg and several outliers, high mountains which lie away from the main range such as Ingeli, Mahaqhwa and Kamberg.

The emphasis of this book is on those species found above 1800m or 6000ft. However, with the needs of visitors in mind, plants of the Drakensberg foothills are also included.

Climate

The region is alpine in terms of climate rather than vegetation. The average annual rainfall ranges from 635mm in parts of Lesotho to 2000mm on the escarpment. The average temperature of the warmest month is below 22°C. The 'alpine' belt, above 2800m, is cool to hot in summer and cold to freezing in winter. The coldest temperature ever recorded in Lesotho is -20°C (measured at 3050m). Snow can lie on the ground for three months or more and there are daily frosts in winter with mist occurring throughout the year. Winds are extreme on the summit and on the face of the escarpment. This accounts for the summit vegetation – cushion forming dwarf shrubs. Larger woody plants are restricted to sheltered places at lower altitudes. Storms are severe.

Geology

The region was formed by massive volcanic activity in the Jurassic period resulting in basalt lavas covering most of the Lesotho plateau and the upper face of the escarpment with dolerite intrusions. It overlays the softer Cave Sandstone (Clarens Formation) which is exposed as cliffs and overhangs below the escarpment and in great wind-sculpted boulders in the south.

The soils are black, very rich; thin on the summit plateau, deeper on the foothills. In summer the soils on the summit are often waterlogged. In winter they freeze every night. The freeze and thaw heaves the soil and stones making it an unstable habitat for plants. This activity also causes the crescent-shaped scars on mountain slopes lower down.

Moraea inclinata   Clinton Carbutt

Sebaea leiostyla   Mike Hirst   *Nerine bowdenii* David McDonald

13

Tarn at Sehlabathebe National Park, Lesotho   *Neil Crouch*

Geranium drakensbergense   *Darrel Plowes*

Helichrysum nanum   *Martin von Fintel*

Brunsvigia natalensis
Rob Saunders

Schizochilus flexuosus
Neil Crouch

Traditional uses of plants

The traditional medicinal and magical uses of plants are included where space allows. This information has been mostly drawn from the literature and the reader should not attempt to try any remedies or other uses. The demand for plants for traditional medicine is growing, and the volume of the trade is having a considerable impact on wild populations. There has been an explosion of interest and academic research into the subject, documenting existing uses and analyzing the chemical and curative properties of these plants. Some of this research is taking the plants into mainstream western medicine.

Do not try these remedies! As with all medicines or home remedies, incorrect use can result in extreme illness and even death.

Scientific names of plants

Scientific names, unlike common names, are internationally applicable only after strict rules have been followed by the plant taxonomist. The plant enthusiast who becomes familiar with the scientific names is often frustrated by fairly frequent name changes. This is the penalty of having an exciting and still-to-be-explored flora. Southern Africa has over 23000 plant species, the richest temperate flora of any area of comparable size in the world.

New species are still being discovered and, as more information becomes available on plants and the relationships between species and their distribution, scientific name changes will be necessary.

The scientific name is usually derived from Greek or Latin and consists of a genus name eg *Agapanthus* reflecting a group of similar species and a specific name eg *campanulatus* which identifies different species. This two-part name is in turn part of a large family unit eg Alliaceae which groups genera with characters in common. Every name is based on a 'type specimen', the plant upon which the original description of the species was based.

Common names of plants

All local names have been recorded where known. Plant names, like dialects, vary from district to district. Attempting to provide a single common name is difficult. African common names pose problems for the English reader. The Zulu common names, for example, are made up of a prefix (eg um-) and stem (eg -bhendula) and they have been indexed as they are spoken (umbhendula). Names can be found under the following prefixes: um-, m-, isi-,a-, ama-, na, with c, q, x pronounced as clicks. To avoid confusion and because of the difficulty of locating the stem, capital letters have not been used.

On the summit, on the wall of the Amphitheatre, looking south towards the Eastern Buttress, with Lesotho to the west (on the right) and KwaZulu-Natal to the east (on the left). *Kevan Zunckel*

'The friend of nature who wants to get to know the alpine region at its best, must come here high or late summer when the richly coloured splendour of flowers unfolds most abundantly, then, like the Cape Flats in spring, this bleak and melancholy land, too, resembles a lovely garden, a more beautiful one than could hardly be imagined.'

Hans Justus Thode, who explored the high altitude Drakensberg flora in the 1890s.

Jamesbrittenia pristisepala David McDonald

Diascia integerrima   Clinton Carbutt

Cysticapnos pruinosa with *Geranium* and *Senecio* species   Clinton Carbutt

Helichrysum sutherlandii   Neil Crouch

15

Brachystelma perditum   Auriol Batten

Habitat unknown. First collected about 70 years ago - rediscovered in 1976 when plants were obtained from Basotho herd

The meanings of African names can be very evocative. The Sesotho name, *lepata-maoa* for example, can be used for any fern that hangs from damp rocks and means 'the one hiding the caves'. *Merxmuellera macowanii*, a tall, wiry mountain grass is often called *mohlaba-pere* 'the one which pricks the horses'. A single name can refer to any plant of a genus (*moli* in Sesotho can refer to any *Hypoxis* species - plants well known to the Basotho as many are used for plaiting into ropes). Sometimes a name can refer to function. *Toane-ea-loti* is Sesotho for *Helichrysum montanum*, while *toala-ea-loti* is the name for charcoal derived from this plant.

Where to go

The frontispiece map provides names of some parks, resorts and villages. Although there are few roads or footpaths on the escarpment, there are wonderful walks and climbs with camping in caves, huts or tents in the mountains, as well as in comfortable camp sites in the foothills. For those less mobile, one can follow roads up the mountain passes, choosing vehicles suitable to the terrain. Many roads in Lesotho and South Africa are now tarred or gravel in good condition (except in wet and stormy weather). Naude's Nek, for example, is an inspiring destination for plants in mid-summer but requires an off-road vehicle. The jewel of the southern Drakensberg, Sani Pass, is well served by day-tour operators. In Lesotho, pony trekking is a wonderful alternative way of exploring the mountains.

When to go

There will always be interesting plants to see, at all times of the year. The best flowering season is high summer, December to February. Before and after these months flowering can be good but this will depend on rainfall or even snow. The bleakest months are June to August, mid-winter, yet this is a time when the seeding grasses clothe the mountain slopes golden-red, snows fall and

Helichrysum trilineatum   *Erica aestiva*
    John Grimshaw   Martin von Fintel

Sani Pass is perhaps the most outstanding feature of the southern Drakensberg. Pack animals beat out the first rough track between South Africa and Lesotho which is now a road giving access to the summit at 2900m.   Pam Cooke

Didima Gorge is a fine example of a river valley that has incised deep into the mountain range, creating a wide diversity of habitats within close proximity. Subalpine habitats tower above warm temperate ones. Many plant communities can be observed here including the largest example of montane forest in the Drakensberg. This gorge also holds some of the best San paintings in the region.

Martin von Fintel

Aristea cognata
Lal Greene

Cyrtanthus flanaganii
Martin von Fintel

Berkheya circiifolia
Mike Hirst

Hesperantha coccinea
Cynthia Giddy

HOW TO USE THE BOOK

Colour coding provides a quick and easy guide to identifying plants. You will find flowers and/or fruits in one of seven colour sections. This is an artificial system. Flower colour varies considerably. The colour seen in the wild may differ from the photographic reproduction. It is important to check in all related colour sections. The colour coding strips indicate the range of colours to be found in each section.

The distribution maps were compiled using information derived from herbarium records in the Natal Herbarium, Durban, Bews Herbarium (University of Natal, Pietermaritzburg), Killick Herbarium (Ezemvelo KZN Wildlife) and the National Botanical Institute PRECIS database. The maps record the high mountain distribution of these plants and should only be considered as a first guide. The current state of knowledge is very incomplete and it is to be hoped that the book will encourage further work in this area.

Flowering times are taken from herbarium records. However they must be considered approximate because the flora has not been comprehensively collected. There is also great variation in flowering times caused by factors such as fire, drought and unseasonal rainfall.

Technical terms are kept to a minimum. An illustrated glossary (see pg 302) explains those that were unavoidable.

▼ *Kniphofia thodei*
Mike Hirst

▼ *Moraea huttonii*
Martin von Fintel

▼ *Sabaea thodeana*
Rodney Moffett

▼ *Cycnium racemosum*
Martin von Fintel

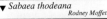

A landscape without borders: The Maloti-Drakensberg mountains straddle the boundary between the Mountain Kingdom of Lesotho (right of picture) and South Africa (left of picture). This aerial view looking south-east from the Mnweni area shows the source of the Senqu/Orange river (right foreground) and the flat-topped Cathkin peak in the background. The two countries share this heritage and the responsibility for its future.

Herman Potgieter

THE MALOTI-DRAKENSBERG TRANSFRONTIER
CONSERVATION AND DEVELOPMENT PROGRAMME

Kevan Zunckel
Project Co-ordinator (South Africa)

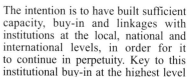

The Maloti-Drakensberg Transfrontier Conservation and Development Programme (MDTP) is the culmination of work by individuals in both South Africa and Lesotho that has been on-going since the early 1980's. These efforts have been driven by the recognition of the fact that this mountain bioregion, divided by both international and provincial boundaries, requires a coordinated approach to the establishment and implementation of appropriate conservation and development plans. Not only does it host globally significant cultural and natural resources and provide essential ecosystem services, i.e. the provision of clean air and water, but also numerous man-induced impacts are threatening its conservation status and integrity.

After the completion of the preparatory phase that lasted from 1999 to 2000, the Programme entered a five-year World Bank funded implementation phase at the beginning of 2003.

The intention is to have built sufficient capacity, buy-in and linkages with institutions at the local, national and international levels, in order for it to continue in perpetuity. Key to this institutional buy-in at the highest level was the historic signing of a Memorandum of Understanding between Lesotho and South Africa that took place at the Sehlabathebe National Park in Lesotho on 11 June 2001. The government representatives on the day were Ms Mathibiso Lepono, the Minister of Environment, Gender and Youth Affairs in Lesotho, and Mr Mohammed Valli Moosa, the Minister of Environment Affairs and Tourism in South Africa.

The Memorandum of Understanding (MoU) formalised the recognition of the importance of cooperative and harmonious management and development of the area. In addition it also officially recognised that:
• Lesotho and South Africa have the right to develop their respective resources;

- Co-operation is required to discourage transboundary threats to the bioregion;
- Peace, economic development and environmental protection are interdependent and indivisible;
- Poverty is both a cause and a consequence of environmental degradation; and,
- The biological and cultural heritage of the bioregion is globally significant.

The Memorandum of Understanding also expressed concern that at the time of signing, the levels of exploitation of the natural resources could be approaching the limits of sustainability. The production of crops and grazing of livestock were seen as the most prolific agents of unacceptable change with the associated destruction of the natural rangelands and wetlands so essential to sustain livelihoods. The following objectives were formulated in response to these concerns:
- Identify and secure the conservation integrity of those portions of the bioregion containing important elements of biological diversity;
- Retain the area as far as possible in its natural state as an undivided ecosystem for the benefit of biological diversity, conservation research, ecotourism and the community at large, with particular focus on those communities who live there and depend on the resources;

- Institute integrated land-use planning and management programmes for the various protected areas and their buffer zones;
- Develop and expand an integrated community based conservation and development programme;
- Facilitate a sustainable nature conservation development and ecotourism investment programme based on the natural, social and cultural resources of the area; and,
- Facilitate cooperation between Lesotho and South Africa regarding sustainable development that is based on the natural resources.

THE PROGRAMME AREA

An outline of the programme area can be found on the frontispiece map. It is important to note that the area includes a number of formally protected areas. Beginning in the north, these are the Golden Gate Highlands and Qwa Qwa National Parks. The imminent amalgamation of these two adjoining but separately managed areas is eagerly awaited. The consolidated area is to be managed by South African National Parks.

Eland herd in the 'Lake District', Cobham area, uKhahlamba Drakensberg Park and World Heritage Site. Eland have roamed these montane grasslands for many thousands of years and were central to the San peoples' food chain and spiritual experience, forming the subject of countless rock paintings.
Greig Stewart

Basotho herdsmen and Angora goats after a summer snowstorm on Kotisephola Pass, Mokhotolong District. Making a difference to the lives of these herders is a key focus of the Project.
Greig Stewart

Free State Nature Conservation manages the Sterkfontein Nature Reserve just to the east of this complex and on the border of KwaZulu-Natal. Ezemvelo KwaZulu-Natal Wildlife manages the Royal Natal National Park, uKhahlamba Drakensberg Park and the Coleford Nature Reserve, and the Ongeluksnek Nature Reserve at the southern tip of the area is managed by Eastern Cape Nature Con-servation.

Besides these formally protected areas, a mosaic of other land uses are present in the area. These are predominantly agricultural of nature and vary from dry land cultivation to extensive livestock grazing. Exotic timber plantations have also been established in the area and have contributed to irreversible land transformation that has impacted signif-icantly on the conservation integrity of the area. Nodes of settlements occur throughout the area and range from upmarket tourism clusters such as the Cathkin node, to densely populated remnants of previous political social engineering such as the city of Phuthaditjhaba, with associated high levels of poverty and unemployment and associated threats to the environment.

As a result of the mosaic of land uses being superimposed on this biologically,

culturally and ecologically important area, the programme is applying a Transfrontier Conservation Area (TFCA) model as opposed to the less complex Transfrontier Protected Area (TFPA) model. The latter is relevant where there are large contiguous areas of formally protected land on either side of the boundaries, whereas the former recognises the mosaic of land uses and respects existing land ownership. Although it is hoped that the protected area network will be expanded and consolidated, this will have to be achieved through successful negotia-tions with landowners who will maintain their ownership but accept responsibility for the conservation status of their land.

It is important for the reader and all involved in keeping this initiative alive, to fully understand the complex nature of the dynamics associated with this programme. While the main objective is biodiversity conservation, conservation strategies will be frustrated and even halted if socio-economic dynamics are not recognised and addressed proactively.

It is in recognition of this fact that the implementation phase was structured to include a significant emphasis on community involvement and sustainable livelihoods.

THE IMPLEMENTATION PHASE

Co-ordination between Lesotho and South Africa is ensured through the existence of a high level Bi-Lateral Steering Committee, while implementation in each country is monitored and guided by Programme Co-ordinating Committees. The latter will remain after the implementation phase has been completed, but country specific Co-ordinating Units were established to drive this phase. In addition to co-ordinator and administration and financial management personnel, the units comprised biodiversity, social, planning, resource-economic, cultural and information management expertise. This diversity of specialists ensured that all relevant information was gathered and collectively analysed to inform the strategic direction of the Programme. As the various conservation agencies will be responsible for maintaining the TFCA after implementation, every effort has been made to carry out every facet of this phase in conjunction with them.

BEYOND THE IMPLEMENTATION PHASE

Critical to the success of the implementation phase is the maintenance of a vision that looks into the future. The programme coordinating units aim to ensure that sufficient institutional capacity has been built to render the units redundant within the timeframe set by the World Bank. The particular challenge is with regard to the continual funding required to establish and maintain a management entity that will be required to monitor implementation, especially with regards to community initiatives.

It is for the lives of children such as these that this initiative needs to make a difference. Photographed in the Sani Pass area, with a wind chill factor of zero degrees Celsius. *Kevan Zunckel*

Within the sustainable livelihoods objective, the idea exists to exploit the 'sale' of the area's ecosystem services to the extent that this will be a source of sustainable funding, not only to support a management entity, but also to ensure that land use management incentives may be disbursed. It would be a major step forward in the fight to secure sustainable land management if water reticulation agencies could reimburse landowners and managers for the implementation of specific strategies aimed at securing the sustained delivery of high quality water from catchments for example. This concept may be taken even further if creative resource economics are applied. Such thoughts currently exist but are insufficiently developed to warrant discussion at the time of publication.

The fence between Sehlabathebe National Park (Lesotho) and the uKhahlamba Drakensberg Park and World Heritage Site (South Africa). The vision is that transfrontier co-operation will lead to shared management policies and the removal of this fence. *Greig Stewart*

Eucomis bicolor

John Grimshaw

MONOCOTYLEDONS Single seed-leaf, parallel veins; flower parts in threes or multiples of three.
COLCHICACEAE Afr, Medit, W Asia, Austr, ±17 genera, ±67 species, 12 genera in SAfr, 2 in this region. *Sandersonia* (named after John Sanderson, 1820-1881, journalist, trader, Natal plant collector) One species, endemic to SA.

Sandersonia aurantiaca Christmas Bells; Geelklokkie (A); ihlamvu lasenhla, umagobongwana, ushayabhici (Z) (*aurantiaca* - between yellow and red, ie orange)

Up to 750mm tall. On margins of forest patches, in *Leucosidea* scrub and in coarse growth along streams, up to 1950m. KZN to Mpum. LEAVES ±90×20mm, tips forming tendrils in the shade. Flowers ±26mm long, bright orange, **only tips of tepals free** (Nov-Jan). GENERAL: Endangered by picking and by loss of suitable damp grassland habitat. Traditionally used as an aphrodisiac and as a protective charm. Developed for horticulture in New Zealand. **Similar species: *Littonia modesta* Littonia; Geelklokkies (A); ihlamvu lehlathi, uhlamvu lwentombazana (Z)** Erect or climbing with leaf tendrils. On forest margins, up to 1450m. E Cape to Limpopo Prov. LEAVES ±130mm long. **Tepals pointed, free nearly to base** (Dec-Jan). GENERAL: Used in traditional medicine to treat infertility. Grown from seed.

ASPHODELACEAE Europe, Asia, Afr, centred in SAfr, particularly *Kniphofia* and *Aloe*, 15 genera, ±780 species, 10 genera in SAfr, 3 in this region. *Kniphofia* - **Red-hot Pokers** (Named after JH Kniphof, 1704-1763, prof. of medicine at Erfurt Univ) Mostly Afr, ±70 species, 47 in SAfr, ±15 in this region. *Kniphofia* species hybridise readily in the wild, making identification difficult at times.

Kniphofia angustifolia [= *K. rufa*] Grass-leaved Poker; leloele (SS); icacane (Z) (*angustifolia* - narrow leaves)

Up to 650mm tall, **solitary or in small groups**. In damp or marshy mountain grassland, up to 2450m. KZN/EMR . LEAVES **grasslike, 2-3mm broad**, dull bluish green, soft, slightly keeled. INFLORESCENCE **loosely arranged, bracts pointed**; BUDS cream, dull yellow to orange-red; FLOWERS 20-30mm long, **creamy white, yellow, salmon, coral to red** (Nov-Apr). **Similar species: *Kniphofia laxiflora* Slender Poker; umathunga (Z)** (*laxiflora* - loose flowers) Up to 1m tall. Solitary or in small groups among rocks, on grassy slopes, up to 2450m. KZN midlands to EMR. LEAVES **6-10mm wide**. INFLORESCENCE elongate, tapering gradually to tip; FLOWERS **24-35mm**, yellow, orange or salmon pink, **not** white or cream, **bracts blunt or rounded** (Nov-Apr). GENERAL: Very variable. Wonderful range of colour in a single colony. Rhizome used in traditional medicine to treat chest ailments.

Kniphofia caulescens Lesotho Red-hot Poker; Basoetovuurpyl (A); leloelele-lenyenyane (SS); icacane, umathunga (Z) (*caulis* - stem, refers to distinct stem of the plant)

Robust, 0.6-1m tall. Often in **large colonies**, in marshes, on wet cliffs, up to 3000m. E Cape, KZN, Les. Rhizome thick, with **simple or branched stem ±300mm long**. LEAVES 450-700×25-50mm, **blue-grey-green**, almost fleshy, V-shaped, margins finely toothed. INFLORESCENCE very dense, buds coral-pink to red; FLOWERS 22-24mm, pale green to creamy yellow, **stamens protruding, 8-13mm** (Jan-Mar). GENERAL: Often grown around rural homesteads as a charm against lightning. Common name is a misnomer because it is also found from E Cape to S KZN Drak.

Kniphofia linearifolia Common Marsh Poker; Vuurpyl (A); icacane, umathunga (Z) (*linearifolia* - narrow leaves)

Robust, up to 1.5m tall. Often in large colonies, in marshy ground, on streambanks, up to 1980m. Widespread. LEAVES 600-1400×12-28mm, **yellow-green**, soft, strongly keeled. INFLORESCENCE **large**, thick, dense, ±160×65mm; BUDS pinkish red to greenish; FLOWERS 25-35mm long, greenish yellow to yellow, **stamens hardly protrude** (Dec-Mar).

Kniphofia ritualis leloele-la-Lesotho, lelutla (SS) (*ritualis* – refers to the fact that this plant is used during initiation rites for girls in Lesotho)

Solitary, on wet grassy slopes or in loose damp soil, 2100-3000m. EMR endemic. LEAVES 400-900×12-24mm, soft, spreading, deeply keeled, **margins finely toothed**. INFLORESCENCE 90-140×40-50mm; BUDS coral or salmon to orange-red; FLOWERS greenish yellow, 25-30mm long (Jan-Mar). GENERAL: Similar to *K. caulescens* which has a branched stem, shorter flowers and markedly exserted stamens. **Similar species: *Kniphofia hirsuta* Hairy Red-hot Poker; leloele (SS)** Resembles *K. ritualis* but leaves **softly hairy**. On rocky slopes or streams, up to 2900m. EMR endemic.

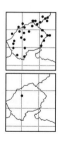

22

Martin von Fintel

Sandersonia aurantiaca

Lal Greene

Littonia modesta

Tom de Waal

Kniphofia angustifolia

Peter Linder

Kniphofia caulescens

Martin von Fintel

Kniphofia laxiflora

Hilliard & Burtt

Kniphofia hirsuta

Peter Linder

Kniphofia caulescens

Martin von Fintel

Kniphofia linearifolia

Martin von Fintel

Kniphofia ritualis

23

Kniphofia evansii Evans' Poker, Cathedral Peak Poker (named after Maurice Evans, 1854-1920, businessman, politician and pioneer plant collector in the Drakensberg)

Dainty, up to 650mm tall, solitary or in small groups. In damp grassy places, 1800-2100m. EMR endemic. LEAVES grasslike, spreading, 600-760×3mm. INFLORESCENCE dense, ±100×4mm; BUDS **same colour as flowers**; FLOWERS 12-15mm long, yellow-orange to coral-red, spreading to hanging (Dec-Feb).

Kniphofia northiae Broad-leaved Poker, Marianne North's Poker; leloele (SS); icacane, umathunga (Z) (named after Marianne North, intrepid Victorian traveller and botanical artist who first illustrated this plant and supplied a live specimen to Kew Gardens in the late 1800s)

A very robust plant, up to 1.7m tall. In mountain grassland, on streambanks, basalt cliffs, seepage lines, up to 3000m. E Cape to KZN. LEAVES **large, recurved**, aloe-like, 500-1500×30-120mm, **not keeled**. INFLORESCENCE dense, up to 220×60mm, flowering stem stout; BUDS pinkish red; FLOWERS whitish or orange-red to yellow, **stamens protruding** (Oct-Dec). GENERAL: The colour varies from E Cape to KZN.

Kniphofia fluviatilis River Poker (*fluviatilis* - growing in running water)

Up to 700mm tall, in groups. **On mountain streambanks**, usually partly in water, up to 2900m. KZN to Mpum. LEAVES erect, firm, dull **blue-green, up to 25mm broad**. INFLORESCENCE ±90×80m, stem stout; BUDS hanging, dark- to orange-red; FLOWERS hanging, yellowish to luminous apricot, **40-50mm long** (Nov-Jan).

Kniphofia thodei Thode's Poker; leloele (SS) (named after Justus Thode, 1859-1932, pioneer plant collector in the Drakensberg)

Up to 500mm, solitary. In moist mountain grassland, up to 2750m. EMR endemic. LEAVES narrow, 2-5mm wide, pale **blue-green**, soft, margins slightly toothed. INFLORESCENCE dense, ±60×50mm; BUDS hanging, dull red to red-brown, tipped white; FLOWERS 25-35mm, white or tinged reddish brown (Nov-Mar).

Kniphofia triangularis subsp. **triangularis** [= *K. macowanii*] Mandarin Poker; leloele-le-lenyenyane, motosi, qaloe (SS) (*triangularis* - 3-sided, refers to fruit)

Up to 600mm tall, solitary or in small groups. On damp grassy slopes, up to 2500m. E Cape to KZN, FS. LEAVES grasslike, soft, curved, up to 600×2-6mm, margins smooth to finely toothed. INFLORESCENCE up to 80×50mm; BUDS hanging; FLOWERS 24-35mm long, coral-red to orange-yellow, open flowers often paler than the buds (Jan-Feb).

Aloe (appears to be derived from an old Greek name for the plant, allied to the Hebrew word 'allal' meaning bitter, although it may also have its origins in an Arabic word 'alloch') Afr, Arabia, Socotra, Madag, ±500 species, ±130 in SAfr, ±10 in this region.

Aloe arborescens Krantz Aloe; Kransaalwyn (A); ikhala, unomaweni (X); inhlaba-encane, inkalane-encane, umhlabana (Z) (*arborescens* - treelike)

Much branched, 1-3.5m tall. On cliffs and rocky places, up to 1800m. One of the most widespread aloes in SAfr, Cape to Malawi. LEAVES narrow, curved, **dull grey to bluish green**, reddish in winter. FLOWERS in 3-4 large racemes, coral-red to salmon-pink (Jun-Jul). GENERAL: Birds attracted to the nectar-laden flowers. Used in traditional medicine, for burns, bruises and grazes. A popular hedging and garden plant. Fairly frost resistant.

Kniphofia caulescens
in Lesotho

David McDonald

Kniphofia fluviatilis

Hilliard & Burtt

Kniphofia thodei

Mike Hirst

Kniphofia evansii

Ray Boardman

Kniphofia northiae

Auriol Batten

Kniphofia triangularis

Cameron McMaster

Kniphofia triangularis

Anne Rennie

Kniphofia northiae

Cameron McMaster

Aloe arborescens

Darrel Plowes

25

Aloe aristata Guinea-fowl Aloe; Tarentaalaalwyn (A); lekhala-le-lenyenyane, lekhalana, sereleli (SS); umathithibala (Z) (aristata - awned, referring to tips of leaves)

Small, dense rosettes of leaves up to 150mm diam, forming tight clumps, flowering stems up to 500mm tall. In moist places, on rocks, cliffs, epiphytic in forest, on mossy rocks, under the drip line of overhangs, up to 2450m. KZN, EMR (on dry sandy flats in E Cape, FS). LEAVES thick, incurved, 80-100mm, green with white spots, **tip a long bristle.** INFLORESCENCE loose; FLOWERS ±40mm long, dull orange-red (Nov-Dec). GENERAL: A popular house plant. Used in traditional medicine to induce pregnancy and as a protective charm against lightning.

Aloe boylei subsp. *boylei* Broad-leaved Grass Aloe; incothobe, isiphukuthwane, isiputhujane (Z) (named after F. Boyle, botanist)

Robust, up to 600mm tall, in colonies. On stony outcrops, around rock sheets, on steep grassy slopes, up to 2400m. Stems branched, up to 200mm long. LEAVES deciduous, **erect, flat, 60-90mm broad, for most of the length, abruptly narrowing to pointed tip**, spotted white near base. INFLORESCENCE **dense, flattish**; FLOWERS **large, ±40mm long, tubular,** salmon-pink, tips greenish (Nov-Jan). GENERAL: Leaves cooked and eaten. Summer flowering garden plant.

Aloe ferox Bitter Aloe; Bitteraalwyn (A); lekhala-le-leholo, lekhala-la-Quthing (SS); ikhala (X); inhlaba (Z) (ferox - ferocious, refers to the spiny leaves)

Sturdy, single-stemmed, 2-3m tall. S Cape, E Cape, Les, FS. LEAVES ± spiny with reddish teeth on the margins. INFLORESCENCE with 5-9 erect spikes; fLOWERS orange-red, inner tepals tipped brown-black (May-aug). GENERAL: Leaves eaten by stock and game in times of drought. Nectar attracts birds, baboons, monkeys, insects and children. Dry leaves are ground for snuff. An essential ingredient in the herbalists's medicine horn. Fresh leaves are used to make the drug 'Cape Aloes'. Withstands some frost. *Aloe candelabrum*, sometimes considered a northern form of *A. ferox*, is found on some steep N-facing slopes in S Drak, up to 1980m. LEAVES, longer, deeply channeled, recurved. INFLORESCENCE with 6-12 spikes; inner tepals white-tipped.

Aloe maculata [= *A. saponaria*] Common Soap Aloe; Bontaalwyn (A); lekhala, lekhala-la-Lesotho (SS); ingcelwane (X); icena (Z) (maculata - spotted or blotched, refers to leaves)

Up to 1m tall. On rocky slopes, often N-facing, up to 2000m. Widespread in SAfr. LEAVES with dull white spots in irregular bands, tips dry, twisted, margins with hard brown teeth. INFLORESCENCE **flat-topped, moplike**; FLOWERS ±45mm long, yellow, orange to red (Jul-Sep). GENERAL: Birds probe the flowers for nectar. Used in traditional medicine to treat colds, wounds and as a protective charm against lightning. Popular garden plant.

Aloe polyphylla Spiral Aloe; Kroonaalwyn (A); kharatsa, lekhala-la-thaba (SS) (polyphylla - many leaves)

Symmetric spiral rosette, up to 600mm tall. On steep mountain slopes, above 2000m. Les endemic. LEAVES up to 300×100mm, grey-green, tips dry, purplish-black. INFLORESCENCE branched low down; FLOWERS ±55mm long, pale red to salmon (Sep-Oct). GENERAL: This is the national plant of Lesotho. It is under threat in the wild from indiscriminate collecting. Unlike most other *Aloe* species, which are successful garden subjects, these plants will not survive for long out of their natural habitat.

Martin von Fintel

Aloe polyphylla

Cynthia Giddy

Aloe aristata

Cameron McMaster

Aloe aristata

Godfrey Symons

Aloe polyphylla

David McDonald

Aloe aristata

Darrel Plowes

Aloe boylei

David McDonald

Aloe polyphylla

Neil Crouch

Aloe maculata

Trevor Coleman

Aloe ferox

27

Aloe pratensis Meadow Aloe; lekhala-la-Linakeng, lekhala-qualane (SS) (*pratensis* - growing in meadows, an inappropriate adjective, it actually grows amongst rocks!)
Up to 600mm tall, plants in small groups. On cliffs, among boulders, up to 1900m. E Cape to KZN. LEAVES grey-green, margins with red-brown teeth, lower surface with **brown spines on white base.** INFLORESCENCE unbranched, **stems covered in large, white, striped, papery bracts**; FLOWERS ±40mm long, red to orange (Sep-Nov). GENERAL: Does not do well in cultivation.

Aloe striatula mohalakane, seholobe (SS) (*striatula* - refers to thin parallel lines on the leaf sheaths)
Robust, much branched, straggling shrub, up to 2m tall. On mountain tops. E Cape to S Les. LEAVES shiny dark green or grey-green at higher altitudes. INFLORESCENCE **dense**; BUDS greenish yellow; FLOWERS yellow-orange (Nov-Jan). GENERAL: The bitter juice is spread on hides to stop dogs from eating them. It is used as a hedging plant in Lesotho. A useful garden plant, it forms large bushes and withstands snow and frost.

ALLIACEAE - Onion Family Subcosmop, ± 30 genera, ± 720 species, 3 genera in SAfr (2 naturalised), 1 in this region. *Tulbaghia* (named after Ryk Tulbagh, Governor of the Cape, 1751-71, who sent specimens to Linnaeus) Flowers with a corona or fleshy ring at mouth of tube. Some plants have an onion or garlic smell. Afr, mostly SAfr, ± 20 species, 5 in this region.

Tulbaghia acutiloba Wild Garlic; Wildeknoffel (A); motsuntsunyane, sefothafotha (SS); ishaladi lezinyoka (Z) (*acutiloba* - sharply pointed lobes)
Up to 300mm tall. In rocky grassland, up to 1800m. E Cape to Limpopo Prov. LEAVES 50-450×3-8mm, soft. FLOWERS nodding, green, **tepals conspicuously recurved,** fleshy ring or corona orange to reddish brown, sweetly scented (Sep-Dec). GENERAL: Very variable. Noticeable after fires. Used as a culinary herb. Plant parts smell of garlic. Used traditionally as a snake repellent.

HYACINTHACEAE Afr, Eurasia, N America ± 46 genera, ± 900 species, 27 genera in SAfr. Popular ornamentals. *Eucomis* (*eucomis* – beautiful hair or topknot) SAfr, ±10 species, ±4 in this region.

Eucomis schijffii Miniature Eucomis (named after prof. of botany, H.P. van der Schijff)
Dwarf, up to 100mm tall. In wet basalt gravel, wet rock faces or against rocks, 2300-3200m. EMR endemic. LEAVES 3-4, **usually prostrate**, purplish below, **veins grooved above**, striped dark green below, margin smooth or minutely crisped. INFLORESCENCE 25-30mm diam, stem 20-70mm long, sometimes spotted purple-spotted; FLOWERS ±20mm diam, **dull dark red or purple, stamens purple** (Nov-Feb). CAPSULE inflated, thin, purplish.

AMARYLLIDACEAE Bulbous herbs. Popular horticultural subjects. Trop and warm regions, ±60 genera, over 800 species, 18 genera in SAfr, 6 in this region. *Scadoxus* (*doxus* – glory or splendour) Leaves thin, with stalks and distinct midrib, **forming a false main stem**. Mainly Afr. 9 species, 3 in SAfr, 1 in this region.

Scadoxus puniceus [= *Haemanthus magnificus, H. natalensis*] Paintbrush, Snake Lily, Blood Lily; Rooikwas, Seerooglelie, Skeerkwas (A); idumbe-lika-nhloyile (Z) (*puniceus* - scarlet, carmine)
Robust, up to 600mm tall. Among rocks, in scrub or forest patches, up to 2100m. S Cape to Trop Afr. LEAVES beside the inflorescence, bases tightly rolled to form **a false stem**, spotted red at base. FLOWERING STEM stout, spotted red towards base, BRACTS green to dark reddish brown; FLOWERS pinkish-red, anthers orange (Aug-Nov). FRUIT round, ±10mm diam, red. GENERAL: Bulb poisonous. Pollen reputed to be poisonous. Birds feed on the nectar. Ripe fruits are eaten by birds and monkeys. Used in traditional medicine to treat coughs, headaches, stomach ailments and as poultices. Excellent garden and container plant.

Brunsvigia (honours the House of Brunswick) SAfr endemic, ±20 species, ±4 in this region.

Brunsvigia undulata (*undulata* - refers to wavy margins of leaves) (see pg 182)

Cyrtanthus (*kyrtos* - curved; *anthos* - flower, refers to the frequently curved flower tube) Mainly SAfr, ±50 species, 9 in this region.

Cyrtanthus falcatus (*falcatus* - sickle-shaped)
In clumps, hanging out of cracks in dolerite and sandstone cliffs, usually below 1800m. EMR endemic. LEAVES leathery, sickle-shaped, ±250×30mm. INFLORESCENCE stem stout, **curving upwards**, 300mm long, **bending sharply downwards at the tip**; FLOWERS greenish coral-red, pendulous, 60-70mm long (Sep-Nov). GENERAL: Suitable for hanging baskets.

Aloe pratensis

Cameron McMaster

Tulbaghia acutiloba

Van Wyk & Malan

Scadoxus puniceus

Godfrey Symons

Eucomis schijffii

Neil Crouch

Scadoxus puniceus

Pam Cooke

Cyrtanthus falcatus

Hilliard & Burtt

Aloe striatula

Mike Hirst

Brunsvigia undulata

Pam Cooke

29

Cyrtanthus epiphyticus Hanging Cyrtanthus; Boomlelie **(A)** *(epiphyticus* - growing on another plant, not parasitic)

Growing in crevices of moist and partially shaded cliffs or large boulders, on mossy branches in forest, 1800-2500m. E Cape, KZN. LEAVES flat, tapering to base and tip, 300-500×10-20mm, with flowers. INFLORESCENCE with 6-15 flowers, stem shorter than leaves; FLOWERS red, 30-35mm long, **tube narrow**, curved, **lobes spreading, recurved** (Nov-Feb). GENERAL: Potential as a hanging basket plant.

Cyrtanthus tuckii Green-tipped Fire Lily; Brandlelie **(A)**; isiwesa **(Z)** (named after William Tuck, 1824-1912, horticulturist and collector)

Up to 450mm. In grassland, up to 1980m. E Cape to KZN and Mpum. LEAVES produced after flowers. INFLORESCENCE with ±15 flowers; BRACTS ±90mm, **green, erect at flowering**; FLOWERS red with green tips, 40-60mm long, **tube curved, lobes straight not spreading** (Sep-Oct, after burning).

IRIDACEAE - Iris Family Temp regions, ±70 genera, ±1800 species, ±32 genera in SAfr, ±12 in this region. *Hesperantha* (*hesperos* - evening; *anthos* flower but only one night-flowering species, *H. tysonii* found in this region) Sub-Saharan Afr, ±75 species, mostly SAfr, 14 in this region.

Hesperantha coccinea [= *Schizostylis coccinea*] Scarlet River Lily; Rooirivierlelie **(A)**; khahlana **(SS)** [*coccinea* - scarlet]

Up to 600mm tall. In clumps, **on streambanks**, often in water, up to 1830m. E Cape to Limpopo Prov. LEAVES ±400×10mm, midrib distinct. FLOWERS **large**, ±65mm diam, **glistening scarlet** (pink), tube ±30mm long, style split (Jan-Apr). GENERAL: This is a strikingly lovely plant in the wild and is also a popular garden plant. Frost resistant and a good cut-flower. (see pg 186)

Dierama - Hairbells, Wand-flowers; Grasklokkies **(A)** (*dierama* - a funnel) Afr, ±44, mostly SAfr summer rainfall region, ±8 in this region. Popular garden plants.

Dierama dracomontanum Drakensberg Hairbell; lethepu **(SS)** (*dracomontanum* refers to the Drakensberg mountains)

In large clumps, up to 1m tall. In grassland, sometimes dominating mountain slopes, 1525-2800m. EMR endemic. LEAVES up to 650×3-6mm. INFLORESCENCE pendulous, with **2-4 branches**, **2-5 flowers each**, bracts solid dark or red-brown, shoulders broad, white or heavily flecked, 5 main veins each side; FLOWERS 19-25mm long, light to dark rose **pink**, **coral** or **red**, sometimes purple pink (Nov-Feb). GENERAL: The leaves are plaited into rope. Used in traditional medicine as a strong enema. Lovely garden plant. (see pg 186)

Dierama latifolium Broad-leaved Hairbell; lethepu **(SS)**; ithembu **(Z)** (*latifolium* - broad leaves)

In large clumps, 1-1.8m tall. In open grassland, up to 2200m. KZN endemic. LEAVES up to 900×**8-13mm**. FLOWERS 22-33mm long, pale pink to wine red; **bracts white to very lightly speckled** (Jan-Mar). GENERAL: Used in traditional medicine. Leaves plaited into rope. Lovely garden plant. (see pg 186)

Tritonia (*triton* - a weathercock, refers to the variable direction of the stamens of the different species) SAfr to Tanz, 28 species, mostly in coastal areas of S Cape, 2 in this region.

Tritonia disticha [= *T. rubrolucens*] Red Tritonia; isidwi esibomvu **(Z)** (*disticha* - in 2 rows)

Up to 300mm tall. In grassland, rock crevices, up to 2300m. E Cape to KZN. LEAVES 8-12mm wide, with strong midvein and marginal veins. FLOWERS 25-30mm, bright red or pink with small yellow blotch on 3 lower lobes (Jan-Feb). GENERAL: Used in traditional medicine to treat stomach complaints in babies. (see pg 188)

Tarn and prominent sandstone boulders, Sehlabathebe National Park, Lesotho, 2400m.

Neil Crouch

Cyrtanthus epiphyticus

David McDonald

Dierama latifolium

Pam Cooke

Cyrtanthus epiphyticus

Darrel Plowes

Dierama latifolium

Hilliard & Burtt

Dierama dracomontanum

David McDonald

Hesperantha coccinea

Rod Saunders

Hesperantha coccinea

Rod Saunders

Dierama dracomontanum

Darrel Plowes

Cyrtanthus tuckii

Darrel Plowes

Tritonia disticha

Martin von Fintel

31

Crocosmia (*krokos* - saffron; *osme* - a smell, refers to the strong smell of saffron when the dried flowers are placed in warm water) Mostly SE Afr, 9 species, 7 in SAfr, 4 in this region.

Crocosmia aurea Falling Stars, Montbretia; umlunge, udwendweni (Z) (*aurea* - yellow)

Up to 1m tall. In forest, up to 2000m. S Cape to Trop Afr. LEAVES soft, 20-30mm wide, in a fan, forming a 'stem' at base. INFLORESCENCE branched, nodding; FLOWERS ±40mm diam, luminous orange and red, tepal lobes spreading (Jan-Mar). FRUIT leathery orange capsule, shiny purplish black seeds. GENERAL: Seeds eaten by birds, corms eaten by bushpigs. Used in traditional medicine. Excellent shade plant, which can become invasive. **Similar species: *Crocosmia pottsii* Slender Crocosmia; umlunge, umdwendwene (Z)** (named after George Potts, 1877-1948, botanist, b. England, d. in Bloemfontein) Slender, up to 1m tall. In stony grassland, on streambanks, up to 1600m. LEAVES narrow. INFLORESCENCE arching; FLOWERS **short**, orange-red, funnel-shaped (Dec-Feb). GENERAL: Used in traditional medicine. Excellent garden plant. A hybrid with this species, possibly a garden escape, is common along streams in KZN midlands.

Crocosmia paniculata [= *Curtonus paniculatus*] Falling Stars, ZigZag Crocosmia; Vallende sterretjies, Waaierlelie (A); khahla-ea-Bokone, moloke (SS); umlunge (Z) (*paniculata* - refers to branched inflorescence)

Evergreen, 1-1.8m tall, **in big clumps**. In moist places in grassland and on forest margins, up to 1500m. LEAVES **pleated**, ±750×6mm. INFLORESCENCE dense, **branches zigzag**; FLOWERS **tubular**, curved, ±75mm long, yellow-orange, tepal lobes short, scarlet-brown (Dec-Feb). GENERAL: Used in traditional medicine to treat dysentery and infertility. Attractive garden plant. Can become invasive in grassland.

Crocosmia pearsii (named after R.O. Pearse, 1900-1995, mountaineer, educator, author of several books on the Drakensberg and he was the first to collect the plant in 1977)

Up to 1m tall, in small clumps. In rocky grassland, 2200-3000m. EMR endemic. LEAVES **pleated**. INFLORESCENCE **held horizontally**, stem straight to slightly zigzag; FLOWERS red-orange, **hooded**, funnel-shaped, tube 70-90mm long (Jan-Feb).

Gladiolus (*gladiolus* - small sword, refers to leaf shape) Hybrids created since the early 1800s have produced the cut-flowers and garden plants popular worldwide. Known as *itembu* (X) 'fruits of the earth' corms are dug up and eaten in rural areas. Afr, S Europe and Middle East, ±260 species, ±165 species in SAfr, ±14 in this region.

Gladiolus dalenii [= *G. dracocephalus, G. natalensis, G. psittacinus*] African Gladiolus; Papegaai-gladiolus (A); khahla-e-kholo (SS); isidwi esibomvu, uhlakahle, udwendweni (Z) (named in 1828 after Cornelius Dalen, Director, Rotterdam Botanic Gardens who introduced the species into gardens in Europe)

Up to 1m tall. In grassland and scrub, up to 2500m. E Cape to Trop Afr, W Arabia. LEAVES erect, ±20mm wide, grey-green, in a loose fan. INFLORESCENCE with up to 7 flowers, bracts green to red-brown, clasping; FLOWERS **large**, ±60×30-40mm, **hooded**, **variously coloured** (Dec-Feb). GENERAL: Pollinated by sunbirds attracted to the copious nectar. Leaves plaited into ropes. Corms used as tops in children's games. Used in traditional medicine, also as good luck charms and in the medicine horns of diviners. Cultivars developed in Europe in the early 1900s are grown worldwide and have become very successful cut-flowers. A popular garden plant.

Gladiolus ecklonii Sheathed Gladiolus; litšoantšoang, mokhabebe (SS) (named after Christian Ecklon, 1795-1868, apothecary, traveller and plant collector who first collected this species)

150-350(700)mm high. In grassland, up to 2250m. E Cape to Bots. LEAVES ±240× 30mm, margins red or yellow, in short, stiff, spreading fan. INFLORESCENCE with 6-14 flowers, **bracts large, 45-60mm, keeled, overlapping**; FLOWERS 40-55mm long, greenish to silvery-white, densely speckled red-brown, chocolate-purple, grey or mauve (Jan-Feb), closing at night to re-open in warm sunlight. GENERAL: Hybridises with *G. crassifolius*, Pollinated by long-tongued bees (*Amegilla* species). Corms eaten raw or cooked. Flowers used as a potherb. Used in traditional medicine.

Gladiolus flanaganii Suicide Gladiolus; Selfmoordgladiolus (A); khahla-ea-Maloti (SS) (named after Henry Flanagan, one of the first to collect plants in the high N Drak who collected the type specimen)

350-600mm long. **Hanging from crevices of wet basalt cliffs**, 2300-3300m. EMR endemic. LEAVES 200-350×7-14mm, firm, veins thickened. FLOWERS large, 70-90 ×40-50mm, **funnel-shaped** with long tube, **deep red with white streak on 3 lower tepals** (Dec-Feb). GENERAL: Adapted for pollination by the malachite sunbird. Common name refers to the difficulties of photographing the species! (see pg 12)

Darrel Plowes

Lal Greene

Crocosmia pearsii

Crocosmia aurea

Rosemary Williams

Gladiolus ecklonii
Martin von Fintel

Peter Linder

Crocosmia paniculata

Gladiolus dalenii

Darrel Plowes

Neil Crouch

David McDonald

Crocosmia pottsii

Gladiolus dalenii

Gladiolus flanaganii

33

Gladiolus saundersii Saunders' Gladiolus, Lesotho Lily; khahla-ea-Maloti (SS) (named after Wilson Saunders who first grew and illustrated the plant in 1870 and employed Thomas Cooper who made the type collection)

400-600mm tall, in colonies. In fairly dry rocky places between 2400-3000m. EMR endemic. LEAVES **sturdy, erect, in a fan**, 15-25mm wide, midrib thickened, veins prominent. INFLORESCENCE erect; FLOWERS **large**, ±60mm wide, **downward facing, strongly hooded**, bright red with broad white mark and speckling on 3 lower tepals (Jan-Mar). GENERAL: Flowers eaten as salad or cooked as a pot herb. Used in traditional medicine to treat diarrhoea.

Watsonia (named after English scientist Sir William Watson, 1715-1787) Mostly SAfr, ±52 species, 1 in Madag, 5 in this region.

Watsonia gladioloides (*gladioloides* - like *Gladiolus*)

Up to 0.5(1)m tall, in clumps. In rocky mountain grassland, 1800-2200m. E Cape to KZN . LEAVES 2, basal, 3-15mm wide, **midrib and margins heavily thickened**, 2 shorter, sheathing stem leaves. INFLORESCENCE closely packed, **bracts dry, brown, clasping**; FLOWERS ±70mm long, **narrowly funnel-shaped, tepal lobes narrow, ±20 mm, deep red** (Dec-Jan).

Watsonia socium [often referred to as *W. pillansii* which was first described from Montagu in the Cape; also, in the past, as *W. meriana*] Orange watsonia; Knolpypie, Lakpypie, Suurknol (A) (*socium* - companion)

Up to 1.2 m tall. **In clumps, in large colonies**, on rocky mountainsides, 1500-2400m. E Cape to KZN. LEAVES 12-18mm wide, slightly twisted, light green, margins translucent yellow, tips usually sharp, dry. INFLORESCENCE with 25-35 flowers, bracts green to reddish, tips dry; FLOWERS ±80mm long, **bright orange** (Sep-Jan). GENERAL: Baboons suck the flowers for nectar. Popular garden plant.

ORCHIDACEAE - Orchid Family Very large family with highly specialized flowers. Cosmop, ±800 genera, ±20 000 species, 52 genera in SAfr. *Disa* (origin unclear, possibly from *dis* - double, referring to the two large wings in the style or *dis* - rich or opulent, referring to the red of the spectacular *Disa uniflora* the first species of the genus described) Median sepal hooded, prolonged into a spur or pouch. **The direction in which the spur points is useful in identification in the field.** Afr, Madag, ±162 species, 131 in SAfr, ±29 in this region.

Disa chrysostachya Torch Orchid; ´mametsana, mohopung (SS); uklamkleshe, umnduze wotshani obomvu, umnduze wotshani ompofu (Z) (*chrysostachya* - golden spots)

Robust, 250-650mm tall. In damp grassland, marshy areas, up to 2400m. E Cape to Limpopo Prov. LEAVES, 3-5 at base, densely overlapping on stem. INFLORESCENCE **tall, very slender, dense**; FLOWERS small, **bright orange** and yellow, tinged pink or red, **spur hanging straight down**, 5-11mm long (Dec-Jan). GENERAL: Like glowing candles, often seen on damp roadsides in the foothills. Pollinated by sunbirds.

Disa porrecta lekholela, ´mametsana (SS) (*porrectus* - extended forwards)

Grasslike, 200-600mm tall. In grassland, up to 2000m. E Cape, Les, FS. LEAVES basal, up to 300mm long, narrow, often persisting as a fibrous sheath. INFLORESCENCE dense; FLOWERS face down, overlapping, bright red (pink) with yellow petals and lip, sepals abruptly narrowed to a hairlike tip ±3mm long, **spur large, pointed up, 20-40mm long** (Jan-Mar).

Disa sanguinea (*sanguis* - blood, refers to the flower colour)

200-400mm tall. On steep grassy mountain slopes, 1800-2300m. E Cape, S KZN. LEAVES reduced and overlapping on stem. INFLORESCENCE a dense thick spike; FLOWERS **small, round, red, spur short, 2-3mm long, pointing up** (Dec-Jan).

Looking southwest from the upper slopes of Royal Natal National Park below Witsieshoek, northern Drakensberg; with part of the Ampitheatre, Eastern Buttress, Devil's Tooth and Inner Tower visible.

David McDonald

Gladiolus saundersii

Rodney Moffett

Watsonia socium

George Lockhart

Gladiolus saundersii

Charles Rostance

Watsonia socium

Tom de Waal

Disa porrecta

Rod Saunders

Watsonia gladioloides

Darrel Plowes

Disa chrysostachya

Lal Greene

Disa sanguinea

Steven Johnson

35

DICOTYLEDONS Two seed leaves, net veins, flower parts in fours, fives or multiples of these.
PAPAVERACEAE - Poppy Family Herbs, with milky or yellow latex; fruit a capsule, opening by pores or slits. Popular ornamentals. Mostly N Hemisp, ±23 genera, ±240 species, 1 genus indigenous to SAfr. *Papaver* (Latin name for the poppy) Herbs. ±80 species, 1 in SAfr.

Papaver aculeatum Orange Poppy; Doringpapawer, Koringpapawer, Wildepapawer (A); sehlohlo (SS) *(aculeatum - with prickles)*

Prickly herb, 0.1-1.5m tall. In rocky places, in scrub, among boulders in riverbeds or along cliffs, in disturbed areas, 1600-2950m. Widespread in SAfr. **Covered in stiff yellow spines and hairs.** LEAVES 120-130mm, deeply lobed, margins toothed. FLOWERS ±50mm diam, orange to red (Oct-Mar). FRUIT ribbed, oval, 10-20mm. GENERAL: Young plants used as a pot herb by the Sotho. Grown from seed.

CRASSULACEAE - Crassula Family (see pg 74, 128) *Cotyledon* (*kotyledon* - cup-shaped hollow, refers to the leaves) Large succulent herbs or shrubs; 5 petals joined to form a tube. Attracts butterflies. SAfr, E Trop Afr, SW Arabian Peninsula, ±9 species in SAfr, 1 in this region.

Cotyledon orbiculata Pig's Ears; Plakkies (A); serelile (SS); ipewla (X,Z) *(orbiculata - roundish)*

Succulent shrublet, up to 800mm tall. On cliffs, rocky steep slopes, 2000-3000m. E Cape to Limpopo Prov. LEAVES 50-100×35-60mm, crowded at base, thick, fleshy, often with whitish bloom. INFLORESCENCE branched; FLOWERS 30-40mm long (Nov-Feb). GENERAL: Leaf shape very variable. Used in traditional medicine. Afrik name refers to its use as a poultice on boils. A popular garden plant, visited by sunbirds.

Crassula (*crassus* - thick, refers to fleshy leaves). (see pg 74, 128)

Crassula alba feko, khato (SS); isidwe, isikhelekhehlane (Z) *(alba* - white, inappropriate because flowers are red or pink in bud)*

Succulent herb, up to 100-500mm tall. On rocky banks, up to 1900m. E Cape to Ethiopia. STEM finely hairy. LEAVES in rosette at base, up to 150×40 mm, in pairs on stem, often with reddish purple markings. INFLORESCENCE ±150mm wide; FLOWERS cup-shaped, **petals erect**, 5-6mm long, **blunt, with distinct appendage at the tip**, white inside, pink or red in bud (Mar). GENERAL: Grown from seed. (see pg 202)

LEGUMINOSAE (FABACEAE) - Pea or Legume Family (see pg 130). *Indigofera* (produces indigo, a blue-dye obtained from several species of this genus) Annual or perennial herbs, shrubs; leaves pinnately 1-9-foliolate, pods cylindrical. Economic potential for forage crops, chemical compounds, insecticides, dyes and horticultural ornamentals. Attract butterflies. Cosmop, ±730 species, ±210 in SAfr, ±12 in this region.

Indigofera foliosa [= *I. vestita*] *(foliosa - leafy)*

Erect tufted shrublet, 600-900mm tall. In grassland up to 3000m. E Cape to KZN. STEMS straight, **densely leafy**. LEAVES ± erect, overlapping, 3-4 pairs leaflets, 8-10mm long, **very narrow**, margins rolled under. INFLORESCENCES shorter than leaves; FLOWERS 3-6, small, ±4mm long, red, tawny hairy behind (Dec-Jan). PODS ±12mm long.

Indigofera hedyantha Black-bud Indigo; Aambeibossie (A); 'musa-pelo-oa-mafika (SS); ilidolo-lendoda, uhlomantethe (oluncane) (Z) *(hedyantha - sweet flowers)*

Shrublet, up to 450×600mm tall. In rocky grassland, on boulder beds, up to 2100m. E Cape to Kenya. Branches covered in short hairs. LEAFLETS in **3-5 pairs**, ±8-12×3mm. INFLORESCENCE **stem longer than leaves**; FLOWERS ±12mm long, **red with darker spot in centre, standard and crowded buds covered in silky golden brown hairs, calyx covered in fine black hairs** (Nov-Feb). PODS ±40×2 mm. GENERAL: Used in traditional medicine and as a good luck charm. A garden plant.

Indigofera hilaris igqokisi, isikhubabende, uhlomantethe (oluncane) (Z) *(hilaris – cheerful, gay)*

Perennial shrublet, stems up to 350mm long, ± prostrate. In grassland, up to 1900m. Widespread, E Cape to Malawi. STEMS covered with silky hairs. LEAVES crowded, 1-4 pairs leaflets, ±8-10×2mm, grey-green, tip a fine point. INFLORESCENCES short, dense, in profusion, stems short, 25-35mm; FLOWERS ±6mm, bright pink, red, silvery hairs on back of standard (Jul-Jan). PODS ±20mm long. GENERAL: Lovely in spring.

Tephrosia (*tephros* - ashen, refers to grey-green or silvery leaves of many species) Herbs or shrubs; leaves pinnate, with **close parallel veins**; pods flattened. Some species used as a fish poison and insecticide. Trop, subtrop, ±400 species, mostly Afr, ±53 in SAfr, ±3 in this region.

Tephrosia marginella isidala (Z) *(marginella* - refers to thickened margin of leaflets)

Slender, tufted, perennial, herb, stems up to 300mm long. In mountain grassland, 1220-2135m. Stems very slender. LEAVES **1-foliolate**, 14-100×12mm, **margins thickened, yellow**, stalks 6-30mm. FLOWERS ±10mm long, orange (Dec-Feb). PODS ±45×3mm.

36

Tephrosia marginella — Tony Abbott

Papaver aculeatum — Mike Hirst

Papaver aculeatum — Pam Cooke

Tephrosia marginella — Lal Greene

Crassula alba — Pam Cooke

Indigofera hedyantha — Pam Cooke

Indigofera hilaris — Rosemary Williams

Cotyledon orbiculata — Peter Linder

Indigofera foliosa — Pam Cooke

37

Sutherlandia (named after James Sutherland, 1639-1719, first Superintendent of Edinburgh Botanical Gardens) Soft-wooded shrubs; leaves pinnate; flowers large, red; pods inflated. Cultivated in Europe since 1683. Endemic, 5 species in SAfr, 1 in this region.

Sutherlandia montana Mountain Balloon Pea; Bergkankerbos, Gansies (A); ´musa-pelo-oa-noka (SS); unwele (Z) (*montana* - growing in mountains)

Soft-wooded shrub, up to 1.5m tall, erect or sprawling, dwarfed at higher altitudes. In boulder beds, on streamside cliffs or in shrub communities, 1500-2500m. E Cape to KZN/Mpum. LEAFLETS 4-10mm, grey-green. INFLORESCENCES small, in leaf axils; FLOWERS ±35 mm long, red (Oct-May). PODS 50-60mm, inflated, papery, **conspicuously stalked beyond calyx lobes**. GENERAL: Browsed by stock. Used in traditional medicine as a tonic, to treat eye ailments, pain, influenza, reputed to delay the spread of cancer. Quick growing, short-lived, hardy garden plant.

Eriosema (*erion* - wool; *sema* - sign, refers to woolly standard) Herbs or shrubs; usually 3-foliolate, terminal leaflet stalked, with resinous dots; inflorescence on stems twice as long as flower cluster. Attracts butterflies. Warm regions, Afr, ±130 species, ±36 in SAfr, ±4 in this region.

Eriosema distinctum Scarlet Eriosema; ubanalala olukhulu (Z) (*distinctum* – distinctive)

100-250mm tall. Often in large colonies in stony grassland, up to 2000m. KZN endemic. LEAVES **large**, stalks short, ±20mm; TERMINAL LEAFLETS ±95×50mm, stalklets ±10mm, stipules large, ±20×5mm. INFLORESCENCES short, on **stems ±180mm long**; FLOWERS ±14mm, light orange or red (Oct-Jan). GENERAL: Unpalatable to cattle, flowering in heavily grazed areas. Used in traditional medicine to treat urinary complaints.

GERANIACEAE - Geranium Family (see pg 206, 236) ***Pelargonium*** (*pelargos* - stork's beak, refers to fruit) Perennial (annual) herbs or soft woody shrubs; leaves usually lobed or divided, often aromatic; flowers asymmetrical. The horticultural varieties, generally (incorrectly) known as Geraniums, have been popular garden and container plants since the 1700s. Attract butterflies. Afr, Asia, Madag, Austr, New Zealand, ± 270 species, ± 219 in SAfr, mostly in W Cape, ± 13 in this region.

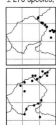

Pelargonium schlechteri Two-tiered Pelargonium (named after Friedrich Schlechter, 1872-1925, eminent German botanist and traveller who collected plants widely in SA)

In rocky grassland, often near streams, up to 2000m. KZN endemic. INFLORESCENCE **2-3-tiered**, petals greenish yellow, each with a purplish-red blotch (Oct-Dec). (see pg 208)

Pelargonium sidoides [= *P. sidaefolium*] Kalwerbossie (A); khoara-e-nyenyane (SS)

(*sidoides* - refers to leaves which resemble those of *Sida rhombifolia*)

Hardy, perennial, aromatic herb, 200-500mm tall. In short stony grassland, 2000-2600m. E Cape to Mpum. LEAVES **in rosette**, ±40mm diam, silvery grey-green, **densely velvety, heart-shaped**, tips rounded, margins toothed, stalks 70-100mm. INFLORESCENCE branched, with 2-4 clusters of 5-7 flowers, petals 5, **very dark reddish purple**, 12-14×2-3mm, honey scented (Oct-Jan). GENERAL: Evergreen in gardens. Easily propagated from seed or cuttings.

EUPHORBIACEAE - Rubber or Euphorbia Family (see pg 256) ***Acalypha*** (*akalephe* - a nettle, refers to the leaves which resemble a nettle) Annual or perennial herbs, shrubs or trees; leaves alternate; male and female flowers usually on separate plants, male flowers in catkin-like inflorescences, female flowers with stigmas greatly elongated. Cosmop, in warmer regions, ±450 species, ±22 in SAfr, ±4 in this region.

Acalypha punctata Sticky Brooms and Brushes; usunundu (Z) (*punctata* - marked with dots)

Perennial herb, up to 500mm tall. On grassy slopes, up to 2100m. E Cape to Trop Afr. Stems stout, sparsely hairy. LEAVES ±70×30mm, margins sharply toothed, **surface with tiny gland dots**. MALE FLOWERS in a spike ±50mm long, stem ±60mm long. FEMALE FLOWERS partly within leaves, stigmas long, red, **bracts gland-dotted** (Sep-Mar). GENERAL: The bracts turn red in autumn and colour the grassland. Used in traditional medicine to treat diarrhoea and chest complaints.

Acalypha schinzii [= *A. depressinervia*] Bearded-leaved Brooms and Brushes (named after Hans Schinz, 1858-1941, Swiss botanist who collect in SA ,1884-87)

Slender perennial herb, up to 500mm tall. On grassy slopes, up to 1980m. E Cape to Mpum. STEMS slender, erect, hardly branched. **Plant covered in long hairs**. LEAVES **narrow**, ±30×5mm, margins entire. Male and female flowers on separate plants. MALE FLOWERS in a spike ±50mm long, stem ±50mm long. FEMALE FLOWERS with long red stigmas (Oct-Mar). GENERAL: Used in traditional medicine to treat diarrhoea.

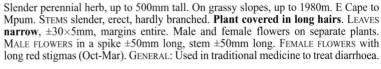

Sutherlandia montana   *Pelargonium sidoides*   *Eriosema distinctum*

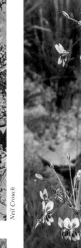

Acalypha punctata ♀

Sutherlandia montana

Pelargonium schlechteri

Acalypha punctata

Sutherlandia montana   *Acalypha schinzii* ♂   *Acalypha schinzii* ♀

39

STERCULIACEAE - Cocoa-Sterculia Family Star-shaped hairs usually present; petals usually twisted in bud. The source of cocoa from the S American tree *Theobroma cacao*. Cosmop, trop, warm regions, ±72 genera, ±1500 species, 7 genera in SAfr. *Hermannia* (named after Paul Herman, 1646-1695, professor of botany in Leiden, one of the first collectors to visit the Cape) Leaves alternate, stipules often leaflike; calyx papery. Attracts butterflies. Afr, Arabia, Austr, S America, ±180 species, ±162 in SAfr, ±10 in this region.

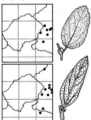

Hermannia woodii moleko, phate-ea-ngaka, seletjana (SS) (named after John Medley Wood, 1827-1915, botanist, founding curator of Natal Herbarium)

Prostrate herb. In grassland, on bare soil, 1300-2000m. E Cape to KZN. LEAVES up to 45×25mm. FLOWERS few, on long stalks, pink, red or creamy yellow (Oct-Feb). GENERAL: Used in traditional medicine to treat colic and diarrhoea, to boost the effectiveness of other medicines and to give them a red colour. Used by diviners. **Similar species: *Hermannia cristata* Crested Hermannia** (cristata - crested, refers to the fruit) Small, **erect herb**, up to 300mm tall. On grassy rocky slopes, 1300-1920m. E Cape to Limpopo Prov. LEAVES 20-65×3-20mm. FLOWERS ±20mm, bright red-orange, calyx segments about 15mm long (Oct-Dec). FRUIT deeply 5-angled with **long crests**.

BEGONIACEAE - Begonia family Often succulent; leaves often with unequal sides; male and female flowers separate on same plant. Popular ornamentals. Trop, mostly Americas, 5 genera, ±900 species, 1 genus in SAfr. *Begonia* (named after Michael Begon, 1638-1710, French governer of San Domingo, patron of botany) About 6 species in SAfr, 1 in this region.

Begonia sutherlandii Wild Orange Begonia; Sutherland-begonia (A); uqamamawene (Z)
(named after P.C. Sutherland, 1822-1900, surveyor-general of Natal, keen plant collector)

Succulent herb, up to 500mm tall. In colonies, in forest, often on mossy rocks and trees, up to 1900m. E Cape to Zim. LEAVES 160-250×100-150mm, **base very oblique**, margins irregularly lobed, sharply toothed, stalks 30-150mm. FLOWERS up to 35mm across, **orange** or **brick-red** (Dec-Mar). FRUIT 3-winged. GENERAL: Used in traditional medicine and as a protective charm. A popular container and garden plant.

ERICACEAE - Erica / Heath Family and genus description (see pg 212)

Erica cerinthoides Red Hairy Heath; Rooihaartjie (A); momonyane, morita-nkoe, semomonyane (SS) (cerinthoides - resembles honeywort, Cerinthe)

Usually tufted, 300-500mm tall, rarely a slender shrub, up to 900mm tall. In crevices of Cave Sandstone sheets, cliffs, on rocky slopes, up to 2300m. SW Cape to Mpum. LEAVES needlelike, in clusters of 4-6, 5-16mm long. FLOWERS **large, 25-35mm long**, white tipped red or red, sepals densely glandular hairy (Nov-Dec). GENERAL: Flowers sucked for nectar by children. A popular garden plant, grown since the 1700s.

Erica oatesii (named after Frank Oates, 1840-1875, naturalist and traveller who came to SA in 1873)

Spreading shrublet up to 400mm or up to 1.2m tall. On streambanks, grassy slopes, 1460-2000m. E Cape to Mpum. STEMS spreading, hairy. LEAVES 3-4 in whorls, narrow, 6-9mm long, recurved or suberect, margins rolled under, tipped with long, gland-tipped hairs. FLOWERS 10-13×7mm, scarlet, pink, white tipped pink, lobes short, hairless, calyx shorter than flower, in few flowered terminal clusters (Nov-Jun).

BORAGINACEAE - Forget-me-not or Borage Family Herbs, shrubs or trees; flowers often in 1-sided inflorescences, curled like a shepherd's crook. Includes herbs borage and comfrey. Widely distributed, ±131 genera, ±2500 species, 17 genera in SAfr (4 exotic). *Cynoglossum* (kyon - dog; glossa - tongue) Fruit covered in small hooked spines. Temp, subtrop. ±75 species, ±8 in SAfr, ±6 in this region.

Cynoglossum hispidum [= C. enerve] Hound's tongue; Ossetongblaar (A); bohomenyana (SS) (hispidum - shaggy)

Erect herb, up to 600mm tall. In moist grassland, up to 1800m. W Cape to Mpum. Plant covered with short rough hairs. LEAVES mostly clustered at base, ±40×12mm. INFLORESCENCE **loosely branched**; FLOWERS tiny, **red-purple**, bell-shaped, **drooping** (Jan-Feb). NUTLETS rounded, up to 12mm diam, **on drooping stalks up to 20mm long**, covered with small hooked spines. GENERAL: Used in traditional medicine.

LABIATAE / LAMIACEAE - Sage/Mint Family (see pg 86) *Leonotis* - Wild Dagga (leon - lion; ous, otis - ear, refers to hair-fringed upper lip) Coarse herbs, shrubs; flowers in dense, many flowered compact clusters around square stems, bracts, calyx teeth spine-tipped. Common name refers to the leaves which are reported to be narcotic when smoked. Afr, ±12 species, ±4 in SAfr, including 1 pantrop weed, 4 in this region.

Leonotis dubia Rooidagga (A); bolila-ba-linonyana (SS); umfincafincane (X) (dubia - uncertain)

Slender, much branched, **soft-wooded shrub**, up to 2m tall. On margins of scrub and forest, up to 1980m. S Cape to CAfr. LEAVES **thin, stalks long, slender**, 30-90mm long, margins coarsely toothed. FLOWERS orange-red, **in small, crowded clusters amongst leaves near stem tips** (Feb-Mar). GENERAL: Used as a tonic and to treat nervous conditions.

Martin von Fintel   *Lal Greene*

Hermannia cristata

Tony Abbott

Hermannia woodii

John Grimshaw

Cynoglossum hispidum

Martin von Fintel

Begonia sutherlandia

Martin von Fintel

Leonotis dubia

Hilliard & Burtt

Erica cerinthoides

Martin von Fintel

Erica cerinthoides

Sheila Peacock

Erica oatesii

41

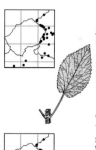

Leonotis intermedia [= *L. dysophylla*] **Broad-leaved Leonotis/Minaret-flower; Klipdagga (A); joala-ba-li-nonyana, moseneke (SS); fincane, isihlungu sedobo, muncwane (X); imunyane, utshwala-bezinyoni obuncane (Z)** (*intermedia* - intermediate between *L. leonorus* and *L. nepetifolia*)

Robust, perennial shrub, 1-2m tall. On rocky hillsides, up to 1800m. Cape to Tanz. Stems branching from **brittle woody base**, green stems velvety. LEAVES 30-90 ×10-50mm, velvety, silvery to yellowish beneath, margins toothed, **stalks short, 10-50mm long**. FLOWERS in compact clusters ±65mm diam, flowers 32-44mm long, **dull orange** (Jan-Jun). GENERAL: Flowers full of nectar, sucked by children, birds, visited by bees, wasps. Used in traditional medicine. A hardy garden plant. **Similar species: *Leonotis leonurus*** **Leonotis, Wild Dagga, Narrow-leaved Minaret flower; Wildedagga, Duiwelstabak (A); imvovo, utywala-bengcungcu (X); umfincafincane (X,Z); umcwili, imunyane, utshwala-bezinyoni (Z)** (*leonurus* - lion coloured) Up to 2(3)m tall. In tall grassland, up to 2000m. E Cape to Mpum. LEAVES **narrow**, 50-100×10-20mm. FLOWERS ±50mm long, **bright orange** (creamy white) (Feb-Sep). GENERAL: Used in traditional medicine for a wide variety of ailments including coughs, dysentery and as a charm to keep snakes away. Frost resistant garden plant, first grown in the 1600s.

SCROPHULARIACEAE - Snapdragon Family (see pg 218) *Phygelius* (meaning of name not clear) Shrubs; leaves opposite; flowers tubular, dull red or pink, in branched inflorescences; fruit a capsule. Endemic, 2 species.

Phygelius aequalis **River Bells; Foksia, Rivierklokkie (A); mafifi-matšo, metsi-matšo (SS)** (*aequalis* - similar in size, equal)

Herbaceous shrub, up to 2m tall. On rocky **streambanks**, 1200-2200m. E Cape to Mpum. Woody at base, stems 4-angled. LEAVES 75-100×40mm, dark green above, paler beneath, margins toothed, stalks ±20mm long. INFLORESCENCE tall, branched; FLOWERS fleshy, ±40mm long, dusky pink to red, **lobes yellow and red inside, stalks short, 2-8 mm** (Oct-Nov). GENERAL: Visited by sunbirds. Used in traditional medicine and as a charm against hail damage to crops. A hardy garden plant, needing damp soil. **Similar species: *Phygelius capensis*** **Southern Phygelius; khama, mafifi-matšo, metsi-matšo (SS)** On steep moist slopes, stream gullies, 2000-2900m. E Cape, Les. FLOWERS **scarlet, tube curved, mouth oblique, stalks long, 12-25mm** (Oct-Apr). GENERAL: Used in traditional medicine and as a charm against lightning.

Jamesbrittenia (named after James Britten, 1846-1924, Keeper of Botany at British Museum of Natural History and editor of Journal of Botany) **Stamens hidden** inside corolla tube. Differs from *Sutera* which has stamens protruding. Mostly Afr, 83 species, 74 in S Afr, ± 8 in this region.

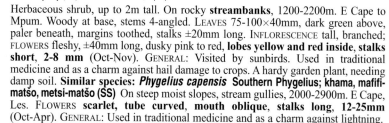

Jamesbrittenia aurantiaca [= *Sutera aurantiaca*] **Cape Saffron; Geelblommetjie, Saffraan-bossie (A); phiri-ea-hlaha-e-nyenyane (SS)** (*aurantiaca* - orange coloured)

Small, bushy, aromatic herb, 60-300mm tall. In sandy or stony, usually **damp** or marshy places, 1370-1900m. Woody, much branched at base, prostrate or erect, branchlets slender, wiry, leafy throughout, glandular hairy. LEAVES 5-30×5-16mm, **finely dissected**, in tufts, covered in short hairs beneath, **glistening glands above**, shortly stalked. FLOWERS solitary, in leaf axils, 6-14mm wide, purple, magenta, bright orange, red or salmon-pink, yellow in throat, stalks ±7-25mm long (Oct-Mar).

Jamesbrittenia breviflora [= *Sutera breviflora*] (*breviflora* - short flowers)

Sprawling, tufted herb, up to 300mm tall. In grassland, rocky places, 1370-3000m. EMR endemic. **Stems and leaves sticky hairy.** LEAVES aromatic, opposite, alternate to clustered above, 10-35×8-35mm, oval, margins ± shallowly toothed, tapering to short stalk. FLOWERS solitary in leaf axils, 2-lipped, **large**, ±12×20mm wide, **bright brick-red** to rose-pink, centre yellow, **tube very short**, 3.5-6mm, **stalks long**, up to 35mm long (Oct-Apr). GENERAL: Hybridises with *J. pristisepala*.

Glumicalyx (*gluma* - husk or glume (of grass), *calyx*) Perennial herbs or shrublets; leaves opposite or alternate; flower tube cylindric or ± bell-shaped, petals 5, 2-lipped, in nodding inflorescences, ± elongated and erect in fruit; fruit a capsule. SAfr, 6 species. Genus is an EMR endemic.

Glumicalyx flanaganii (named after Henry Flanagan, Eastern Cape naturalist and plant collector, one of the first people to collect plants in the high N Drakensberg)

Bushy herb, 150-600mm tall. In damp rocky places, at foot of cliffs, in stream gullies, 1900-3350m. EMR endemic. Stems softly hairy, closely leafy. LEAVES 15-37 ×5-16mm, thick, **finely hairy**, **margins coarsely toothed**. INFLORESCENCE ±30mm long; FLOWERS 6-8mm diam, lobes oblong to roundish, bright orange inside, buff to brownish outside, tube up to 17mm long, **stamens all exserted** (Oct-Mar).

Leonotis leonurus

Neil Crouch

Leonotis intermedia

Martin von Fintel

Phygelius capensis

David McDonald

Glumicalyx flanaganii

David McDonald

Glumicalyx flanaganii

Mike Hirst

Jamesbrittenia aurantiaca

Darrel Plowes

Phygelius aequalis

Neil Crouch

Jamesbrittenia breviflora

Clinton Carbutt

43

Glumicalyx goseloides [= *Zaluzianskya goseloides*] (*goseloides* - looks like the genus *Gosela*)

Perennial herb, up to 450mm tall. On boulder beds, damp rocky grass slopes, up to 2800m. EMR endemic. LEAVES 20-65×4-15mm, thick, margins entire to toothed, ± stalkless. INFLORESCENCE nodding, 30-60mm; FLOWERS 7-9mm diam, nearly regular, **lobes roundish**, orange to orange-red inside, creamy outside, **tube 20-29mm long, 2 stamens hidden** (Nov-Jan). GENERAL: Hybridises with *G. nutans*.

Glumicalyx lesuticus

100-350mm tall. In gritty, rocky places, 2550-3180m. Les endemic. BASAL LEAVES ± hairless, 25×4mm, tapering to broad, flat, stalklike base, leathery, stem leaves 9-15×1.5-4mm, margins toothed. INFLORESCENCE very short, ±20mm diam, lobes orange above, creamy or yellowish below, **tube very short**, 7-11.5mm (Dec-Feb).

Glumicalyx nutans [= *Glumicalyx alpestris*] khoathi, lebohlollo, theleli (SS)

Perennial herb, up to 450mm tall. On rocky grass slopes, bare gritty places, around rock sheets, 1800-3350m. EMR endemic. LEAVES 12-30×4-11mm, **serrated in upper part**, thick, hairy only on margins, grading rapidly into bracts. INFLORESCENCE 20-30×7-8mm, lobes narrow, oblong, **strongly reflexed when fully open**, orange to deep brick-red inside, buff outside (tinged violet), **tube short**, 12-16mm long (Oct-Mar).

Striga (*striga* - harsh, refers to the hairs on stems and leaves) Parasitic herbs; leaves opposite or alternate, sometimes reduced; flowers solitary in axils of bracts. Afr, Asia, Austr, ±40 species, ±7 in SAfr, ±4 in this region.

Striga elegans Large Witchweed; Grootrooiblom; Kopseerblommetjie (A); lethibela, mohohlong, seona (SS); umnaka (X); isona (Z) (*elegans* - graceful)

Small erect herb, up to 300mm tall. In grassland, up to 1800m. Widespread. Stems simple or slightly branched, plant roughly hairy. LEAVES ±20×3mm. FLOWERS large, ±20mm, pink or red, upper and lower lips ± same size (Dec-Mar). GENERAL: Parasitic on grasses. Used in traditional medicine and as a protective charm.

Harveya (named after Dr William Harvey, 1811-1866, chief author of early volumes of Flora Capensis, Prof of botany in Dublin, Ireland) Parasitic herbs; leaves reduced to scales. Mostly Afr, ±40 species, ±25 in SAfr, ±4 in this region.

Harveya scarlatina moshoa-feela (SS)

Dwarf parasitic herb, up to 150mm tall. In scrub, on rocky streambanks, in rock crevices, 1800-2200m. E Cape to Limpopo Prov. LEAVES scalelike, flat against stem. FLOWERS ±30mm diam, **petals small, round**, scarlet, yellow in throat, **tube narrowly funnel-shaped**, 40-50×8-10mm (Dec-Jan).

Hyobanche Parasitic herbs; flowers in thick dense spikes, small oblique, tube cylindrical. S Afr, ± 7 species, 1 in this region.

Hyobanche rubra Broomrape; khehle, moshoa-feela (SS) (*rubber* - red)

Parasitic herb, up to 120mm tall. In stony places, up to 2750m. EMR endemic. Stem mostly buried. INFLORESCENCE a thick, dense, flat topped spike; FLOWERS ±60×6mm, pale to dark salmon-pink, almost red, tube hairy (Oct-Dec).

CUCURBITACEAE - Cucumber/Pumpkin Family Stems with spirally coiled tendrils; male and female flowers separate; stigma 2-3-lobed, fleshy; fruits usually fleshy. Important food plants. Cosmop, ±120 genera, ±735 species, ±18 genera in SAfr. **Zehneria** (named after J. Zehner, botanical artist) Scrambling herbs; tendrils simple; fruits small, berrylike. Trop, ±30 species, 3 in SAfr, 1 in this region.

Zehneria scabra leraka-mposhane, lerakane, monyaka (SS); itanga, simbene, ukalimela (X) (*scabra* - rough, scabrid)

Perennial trailing herb, stems up to 3m long. On damp grassy slopes, up to 2725m. Widespread. LEAVES 30-80×25-60mm, with **rough white dots**, margins sharply toothed. FLOWERS small, ±4mm, white, male in clusters (8-20) on long stems, female solitary, on separate plants (Jan-Feb). FRUIT ±12×8mm. GENERAL: Edible.

Coccinia (*coccinus* - scarlet; *kokkos* - berry, refers to red fruit) Herbaceous creepers. Mainly Afr, ±30 species, ±7 in SAfr, ±3 in this region.

Coccinia hirtella foma, leraka-la-balimo, monyaku (SS) (*hirtella* – rather hairy)

Trailing herb, stems up to 3m long. Among rocks, at edge of scrub, up to 2300m. E Cape to KZN/Mpum. Stems **densely to thinly white hairy**. LEAVES 40-100 ×30-90mm, soft, thinly hairy. FLOWERS solitary, orange-yellow, ±23mm, faintly scented (Oct-Mar). FRUIT ±80×40mm. GENERAL: Leaves cooked as spinach.

COMPOSITAE also called **ASTERACEAE - Daisy Family** (see pg 222) *Helichrysum* (*helios* - sun; *chrysos* - gold) (see pg 146)

Helichrysum appendiculatum Sheeps' Ears Everlasting; Skaapoorbossie (A); senkoto-ana (SS); ibode, indlebeyemvu (Z) (*appendiculatum* - appendage, refers to upper stem leaves) (see pg 104)

Martin von Fintel

Glumicalyx goseloides

Martin von Fintel

Glumicalyx goseloides

David McDonald

Glumicalyx lesuticus

Glumicalyx nutans

Peter Linder

Lal Greene

Helichrysum appendiculatum

Godfrey Symons

Zehneria scabra

Darrel Plowes

Striga elegans

Lal Greene

Helichrysum appendiculatum

Martin von Fintel

Coccinea hirtella

David McDonald

Harveya scarlatina

Hilliard & Burtt

Hyobanche rubra

45

MONOCOTYLEDONS Single seed-leaf, parallel veins; flower parts in threes or multiples of three.

POTAMOGETONACEAE - Pondweed Family Perennial, leafy, aquatic herbs, forming submerged masses in pools and slow moving water. Cosmop, 2 genera, ±90 species, only 1 genus in S Afr, *Potamogeton* (*potomos* - river; *geiton* - neighbour), 7 species in SAfr, 3 in this region.

Potamogeton pusillus Narrow-leaved Pondweed; Smalblaarfonteingras (A); boele, joang-ba-metsi-bo-boholo, ntlo-ea-hlapi-e-kholo (SS) (*pusillus* - very small, weak)

Submerged aquatic, in pools, slow moving water, up to 2400m. Fairly common in SAfr, widespread in N Hemisp. LEAVES submerged, 20-40×1-2mm, blunt-tipped, margins wavy, toothed; **stipular sheath tubular.** INFLORESCENCE 25-70mm, held above the water; FLOWERS pinkish white (Oct-May). FRUIT a small beaked drupe.

APONOGETONACEAE - Waterblommetjie Family Aquatic herbs. Family with 1 genus. *Aponogeton* (*apon* - water; *geiton* - neighbour). Old World, ±43 species, 6 in SAfr, 2 in this region.

Aponogeton junceus Aponogeton; Wateruintjie (A); lijo-tsa-lihohoana (SS) (*junceus* - rushlike)

Aquatic herb, partly submerged or rooted in mud on water's edge. In ponds, marshes, 1800-3000m. Widespread in SAfr. ERECT LEAVES needlelike to spoon-shaped. FLOATING LEAVES oblong, ±170×45mm. INFLORESCENCE 20-40mm long; FLOWERS tiny, white (Nov-Feb). GENERAL: Leaves, flowers, tubers eaten by people and stock.

Aponogeton ranunculiflorus Sehlabathebe Waterlily, Crown Jewels of Sehlabathebe, Rockpool Lily (*ranunculiflorus* - inflorescence resembles N Hemisp *Ranunculus aquatilis*, the White Water-buttercup)

Aquatic herb, in rock pools and tarns, in water 0.2-3.0m deep. Sehlabathebe and environs, about 2600m. LEAVES **submerged**, in tufts, quill-like, rooted on floor of pools. INFLORESCENCE like a **single, white, cup-shaped flower** ±25mm diam, floating on the surface, attached by a long threadlike stalk to submerged plant (Jan).

CYPERACEAE - Sedge family (see pg 248) **Ascolepis** (*askos* - bladder) Cosmop, ± 20 species, 2 in SAfr, 1 in this region.

Ascolepis capensis

Tufted perennial, 150-300mm tall. In marshy ground, up to 2250m. E Cape to Ethiopia. LEAVES grey-green, narrow, rolled when dry. FLOWERHEADS **compact, shiny white,** ±15mm diam, bracts ±50mm long. GENERAL: Suitable for damp areas of the garden.

Bulbostylis (*bolbos* - a bulb; *stylos* - a style, bulbous base of styles) Warm to temp regions. ±100 species, ±15 in SAfr, ±3 in this region.

Bulbostylis oritrephes lejabutle-le-letšoana (SS)

Densely tufted, 70-300mm tall. In stony grassland, up to 2200m. KZN to NW Prov. **Stem bases bulbous,** arranged in neat horizontal rows, stems and leaves very fine, hairlike. LEAVES dark green. INFLORESCENCE a terminal cluster of 1-5 blackish spikelets. GENERAL: Conspicuous in early spring in dry grassland.

ARACEAE - Arum Lily Family Popular ornamentals. The 'petal' is a modified leaf called a spathe. Tiny male and female flowers are carried on the central 'column' or spadix. Mostly Trop, ±105 genera, ±3300 species, 6 genera in SAfr, 1 in this region. *Zantedeschia* (named after F. Zantedeschi, 1773-1846, Italian physician, botanist) First introduced to horticulture in the 1600s. Endemic to SAfr, 8 species, 2 in this region.

Zantedeschia albomaculata Arrow-leaved Arum, Spotted-leaved Arum; Kleinvarkoor, Witvlekvarkoor (A); mohalalitoe, mothebe (SS); intebe (Z) (*albomaculata* - white-spotted)

Deciduous, up to 750mm tall. In marshy ground, on moist, rocky mountain slopes, up to 2400m. E Cape to CAfr. LEAVES arrow-shaped, with or without white spots. FLOWER **spathe cylindrical** (narrow-mouthed) ±170mm long, white, cream to pale yellow, with or without deep purple blotch at base inside (Nov-Dec). FRUIT **green, stems bends towards ground.** GENERAL: Produces a yellow-green dye. Used in traditional medicine. Popular garden plant. **Similar species: *Zantedeschia aethiopica***

White Arum Lily; Varklelie, Witvarkoor (A); mohalalitoe, mothebe (SS); intebe (X,Z); ihlukwe (Z) (*aethiopica* - from SAfr) **Evergreen** (deciduous). Often massed, in marshy places up to 2250m. W Cape to Mpum. **Spathe large, white, funnel-shaped** (wide mouthed) (Aug-Jan). FRUIT **orange tipped green when ripe, stems erect.** GENERAL: Tubers eaten by porcupines, fruit by birds. Used in traditional medicine. Popular garden plant

ERIOCAULACEAE - Pipewort Family Mostly S America, 10 genera, ±1200 species, 2 genera in SAfr. *Eriocaulon* (*erion* - wool; *caulus* - stem, refers to woolly hairs on rhizome) Tufted herbs. Warm regions, 250-400 species, ±12 in SAfr, 4 in this region.

Eriocaulon dregei var. *sonderianum* Water Pom-pom, Pipewort; nyokoana-ea-likhoho, sekolana (SS) (named after Johann Drège, German botanical collector who travelled widely in SA from 1826-1834)

Dainty tufted herb, up to 150mm tall. In marshy places up to 3000m. LEAVES short, soft, grasslike, in basal rosette. FLOWERHEADS compact, hard, black, 5-10mm diam, FLOWERS white, tiny (Aug-Apr). GENERAL: Size varies according to altitude.

Potamogeton pusillus   John Grimshaw   *Aponogeton junceus*   Godfrey Symons   *Bulbostylis oritrephes*   Athol Moralee

Aponogeton ranunculiflorus   Neil Crouch

Aponogeton ranunculiflorus   Lou Zonneveld

Zantedeschia albomaculata   Ken Farnsworth

Eriocaulon dregei   David McDonald   *Ascolepis capensis*   Pam Cooke

Zantedeschia aethiopica   Nolly Zaloumis   *Zantedeschia aethiopica*   Lorraine van Hooff   *Zantedeschia albomaculata*   David McDonald

47

COLCHICACEAE (see pg 22). *Androcymbium* (*andros* - male; *kymbion* - cup) About 40 species, mostly SAfr, ±28 species, 2 in this region.

Androcymbium striatum [= *A. melanthoides* var. *striatum*] Pyjama Flower; Patrysblom (A); khara, khukhoana-e-nyenyane (SS) (*striatum* - striped)

Erect, 150-220mm tall. In damp ground among stones and boulders, gravel patches, about 1800-3000m. E Cape to Trop Afr. **'Stem' formed by leaf-bases.** LEAVES ±300mm long, slender, keeled. FLOWERHEADS hidden within **large, white, petal-like bracts,** suffused and **striped with green** or light violet; FLOWERS small, each tepal partly enfolding a stamen (Dec-Jan). GENERAL: Used in traditional medicine.

Wurmbea (named after F. von Wurm, a Dutch merchant in Java) Afr, Austr, ±38 species, 18 in SAfr, 5 in this region.

Wurmbea elatior Pepper-and-salt Flower; Sout-en-peper-blommetjie (A); khahlana-ea-loti (SS) (*elatior* - tall)

Up to **400mm tall.** In marshes, on streambanks, 1200-3000m. W Cape to Lesotho. LEAVES 2-3, ±45×37mm, partly sheathing stem. FLOWERS white with **shiny deep reddish purple or black patch** (scale) **in the middle of each tepal,** musky described as similar to horse dung, naphthalene, vanilla or a sewage farm (Jan-May).

ANTHERICACEAE Mainly Old World tropics, ±29 genera, ±500 species, 2 genera in SAfr. *Chlorophytum* (*chloros* - green; *phyton* - plant) Mainly trop. Most Afr species of the genus *Anthericum* have been placed in *Chlorophytum*. Afr, Asia, ±165 species, ±36 in SAfr, ±5 in this region.

Chlorophytum cooperi [= *Anthericum cooperi*] Cooper's Anthericum (named after Thomas Cooper, 1815-1913, plant collector)

Slender, erect, perennial, up to 400mm tall. In grassland, often among rocks, up to 2300m. E Cape to Moz. LEAVES **arranged in a fan,** 50-300×3-10mm, **usually folded.** INFLORESCENCE **often with 1-2 short branches;** FLOWERS ±25mm diam, mostly in pairs, glistening white with dark keel, closing at noon (Oct-Dec). GENERAL: Good garden plant. **Similar species:** *Chlorophytum acutum* [= *Anthericum acutum*] Up to 750mm tall. In grassland, often among rocks, up to 2450m. EMR endemic. LEAVES **flat, tapering gradually to a long point.** INFLORESCENCE **unbranched** (Nov-Jan).

Chlorophytum krookianum Giant Chlorophytum (named after P. Krook, c. 1895, a plant collector)

Robust, **up to 2m tall.** In damp places near streams and on forest margins, up to 1800m. LEAVES **broad,** ±1360×80mm, flat or folded. INFLORESCENCE erect, **much branched,** stem stout; FLOWERS white, ±30m diam, tepals with green vein and tip (Nov-Apr). GENERAL: Largest species of this genus in SAfr. Excellent garden plant.

ERIOSPERMACEAE Afr, 1 genus. *Eriospermum* (*erion* - wool; *sperma*) About 100 species, mostly in W Cape, 4 in this region.

Eriospermum cooperi [= *E. natalense, E. sprengerianum*] White Fluffy-seed; Kapokblommetjie (A); khongoana-tsa-ngoana, khukhu-e-kholo, lekoto-la-litšoene, tsebe-ea-khomo (SS) (named after Thomas Cooper, 1815-1913, plant collector)

Up to 800mm tall. In rocky grassland, up to 2250m. E Cape to Zim. LEAVES 1-2, erect, blade ±90×45mm, **produced after flowers** or from different growing point. INFLORESCENCE slender, base of stem with sheathing bract tipped with small blade; FLOWER outer tepals reddish brown or green, inner tepals white, copious nectar from base of filaments (Nov-Jan). SEEDS covered in **woolly white hairs.**

Eriospermum ornithogaloides khongoana-tsa-ngoana, khongoana-tšingoana (SS); incameshela (Z) (*ornithogaloides* - resembles the genus *Ornithogalum*)

100-250mm tall. In colonies, on edges of rock sheets and on sparsely grassed stony places, up to 2400m. E Cape to FS. LEAF solitary, **flat on ground,** 35×25mm, **heart-shaped,** margins red, **fringed with hairs.** INFLORESCENCE few-flowered, separate from leaves; FLOWERS ±10mm diam, **outer tepals spreading, inner erect,** white, midvein blue-green (Oct-Dec). GENERAL: Used to treat earache, barrenness in women.

Androcymbium striatum

Wurmbea elatior

Chlorophytum cooperi

Chlorophytum krookianum

Eriospermum cooperi

Eriospermum cooperi

Eriospermum ornithogaloides

Chlorophytum krookianum

49

ASPHODELACEAE Europe, Asia, Afr, centred in SAfr, particularly *Kniphofia* and *Aloe*, 15 genera, ±780 species, 10 genera in SAfr, 3 in this region. *Trachyandra* (*trachys* - rough; *andros* - male) Afr, ±50 species, 49 in SAfr, ±3 in this region.

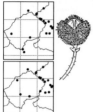

Trachyandra asperata Wilde Knoffel (A); leloelenyana-la-lilomo, motoropo (SS); unjwazi (Z) (*asperata* - rough, with points or hairs)

In clumps, 450-1000mm tall. On cliffs, boulder beds and rocky grass slopes, up to 2750m. LEAVES 1-2 mm broad, **leaf base thin, papery.** INFLORESCENCE **slender, branched;** FLOWERS 15-20mm diam, tepals white with **fine reddish line** (Jan-Feb). CAPSULE ±5mm diam, sparsely or densely hairy. GENERAL: **Very variable,** with a number of subspecies. Acrid smell when touched. **Similar species: *Trachyandra saltii*** (named after Henry Salt, 1780-1827, British traveller) Up to 500mm tall, in grassland. INFLORESCENCE **unbranched, lax and spreading.** *Trachyandra smalliana* (named after Bill Small, formerly forest officer in the Drakensberg, and his wife Alta, in acknowledgement of their assistance to Olive Hilliard and Bill Burtt during their extensive plant collecting in the Southern Natal Drakensberg) In clumps, up to 600mm tall. In damp ground in valley bottoms and on slopes below cliffs 1900-**2500m.** EMR endemic. LEAVES cylindrical, in tufts **held together by a network of fibres at base.** INFLORESCENCE dense; FLOWERS **pure white,** ±10 mm diam (Nov).

Kniphofia - **Red-hot Pokers** (named after J.H. Kniphof, 1704-1763, prof. of medicine art Erfurt University) Mostly Afr, ±70 species, 47 in SAfr, ±15 in this region. Species hybridise readily in the wild, making positive identification difficult at times.

Kniphofia breviflora leloele (SS) (*breviflora* - short flowers)

Slender, **solitary,** up to 800mm tall. On damp grassy slopes, up to 2400m. LEAVES narrow, grasslike, **2-6mm wide,** margins smooth. INFLORESCENCE ±80x24mm; FLOWERS **7-11mm long,** erect to spreading, **whitish yellow,** sometimes dull brownish red (Oct-Mar).

ALLIACEAE - **Onion Family** Subcosmop, ±30 genera, ±720 species, 3 genera in SAfr (2 naturalised), 1 in this region. *Tulbaghia* (named after Ryk Tulbagh, Governor of the Cape, 1751-71, who sent specimens to Linnaeus) Flowers with a corona or fleshy ring at mouth of tube. Some plants have an onion or garlic smell. Afr, mostly SAfr, ±20 species, 5 in this region.

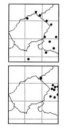

Tulbaghia leucantha Mountain Wild Garlic; sefothafotha (SS) (*leucantha* - bearing white flowers)

150-250mm tall. On damp grassy cliffs and steep rocky places, up to 2500m. E Cape to Zim. LEAVES 50-150×3-6mm. INFLORESCENCE small; FLOWERS 4-8, white, tepal lobes recurved, fleshy ring or corona orange or crimson (Oct-Dec). GENERAL: Used as a culinary herb (garlic smell disappears after cooking). Used to strengthen tobacco and as a protective charm. **Similar species: *Tulbaghia natalensis* Sweet Wild Garlic; iswele lezinyoka (Z)** Sometimes massed, in marshy ground, damp places on rock platforms and cliffs, up to 1800m. KZN endemic. FLOWERS palest pink or white tinged purple, fleshy ring green to yellowish orange (Sep-Dec). GENERAL: Used as a culinary herb. Cultivated to keep snakes away. (see pg 180)

HYACINTHACEAE Afr, Eurasia, N America, ±46 genera, ±900 species, 27 genera in SAfr. Popular ornamentals. *Albuca* (*albus* - white or *albicans* - becoming white) Flowers with 3 inner tepals erect and touching, outer tepals spreading. Afr, Arabia, ±80 species, ±60 in SAfr, ±9 in this region.

Albuca fastigiata var. floribunda Large Spreading White Albuca; umaphipha-intelezi (Z) (*fastigiata* - parallel, erect branches)

Up to 900mm tall. **Hanging from crevices and ledges of damp sandstone cliffs, 1800-2400m.** LEAVES up to 1000×20(30)mm or much smaller, **narrow throughout,** bright green with a silvery band down the middle. INFLORESCENCE **flattish,** FLOWERS **held erect,** ±20mm long, white with broad green stripe beneath tepals, unpleasant scent (Jan-Feb). GENERAL: Used as a protective charm. Easily grown in gardens.

Albuca pachychlamys Soldier-in-the-box; mototse, nkonkophiri-e-kholo (SS)

Up to 250mm tall. In grassland, often rocky, up to 2400m. Widespread. **Brush of dark bristles tops the bulb.** LEAVES narrow, 3mm or less wide. FLOWERS 10-15mm long, tepals white striped green (Sep-Dec). **Similar species: *Albuca humilis*** (*humilis* - small, dwarfish) 30-250mm tall. On edges and seams of rock sheets, gravel and silt patches and rocky grassland, up to 2800m. EMR endemic. LEAVES 1-2, **cylindrical,** usually longer than flowering stem. FLOWERS white, outer tepals striped green, inner tepals tipped yellow (Nov-Jan). *Albuca polyphylla* (*polyphylla* - many leaves) In crevices of rock sheets and gravel and silt patches on rock sheets, seasonally waterlogged, 1980-2865m. EMR endemic. FLOWERS without **yellow on inner tepals.** *Albuca setosa* Widespread. LEAVES ±300×20mm, dark green, produced **after** flowers. FLOWERS ±25mm. (Aug-Jan)

Lal Greene

Trachyandra saltii

Martin von Fintel

Tulbaghia leucantha

Martin von Fintel

Trachyandra saltii

Van Wyk & Malan

Trachyandra asperata

David McDonald

Albuca pachychlamys

Rob Scott-Shaw

Kniphofia breviflora

Pam Cooke

Kniphofia breviflora

David McDonald

Albuca fastigiata

51

Urginea (from Beni Urgen, a tribe living in Algeria where the type specimen was found) Afr, Medit, India, ±100 species, ±24 in SAfr, ±6 in this region.

Urginea capitata [= *Drimia depressa*] **Bergslangkop, Jeukui (A); moretele (SS)** *(capitata - headlike)*

50-150mm tall. In colonies, in short rocky grassland, on rock sheets or in crevices, up to 2400m. E Cape to Limpopo Prov. LEAVES ±150×6mm, often produced after flowers. INFLORESCENCE **compact** (Aug-Oct). GENERAL: Toxic to sheep and cattle. Used as a powerful good luck charm by diviners.

Urginea macrocentra [= *Drimia macrocentra*] **Poison Snake-head; Natalse slangkop (A); injoba (X,Z); isiklenama, ujobo (Z)** *(macrocentra - large spurs)*

Up to 1.5m tall, in colonies. In damp or marshy ground, in gullies and near streams, up to 2700m. KZN endemic. LEAF **solitary**, ±600mm, **cylindrical**, dark green, separate from and usually after the flowering stem. INFLORESCENCE **dense**, (resembling a snake head), **stem robust**; FLOWERS white, lower bracts with tails 30-40mm long, which fall early (Oct-Dec). GENERAL: Poisonous to stock. Used in traditional medicine to treat worms.

Urginea tenella **Dainty Urginea; khoho-ea-lefika (SS)** *(tenella - dainty)*

Small, slender, 50-150mm, in colonies. In shallow soil on sheet rock or cliffs, 1800-3000m. EMR endemic. LEAVES threadlike, produced after the flowers. INFLORESCENCE few-flowered; FLOWERS pinkish white, 3-4 mm, **stalks 10-15mm long, spreading** (Oct-Dec). **Similar species:** *Urginea calcarata* [= *Urginia modesta*] 100-300mm tall; scattered on grassy slopes, up to 2000m; EMR endemic; INFLORESCENCE elongate, **stalks 2-8mm long**, ±erect (Sep-Dec) *Urginea saniensis* Tiny, **20-30mm tall**. In soil and rock crevices, **on summit plateau**. EMR endemic. LEAVES 20-60×**1-1.5mm, roundish**. FLOWERS **1-4**, tepals white inside, chocolate-brown outside (Nov).

Galtonia (named after British scientist Sir Francis Galton, 1822-1911, who travelled widely in SA) Genus endemic to SAfr, 4 species, 3 in this region.

Galtonia candicans **Common Berg Lily; Berglelie (A)** *(candicans - pure white)*

Up to 1.5m tall, in colonies. In damp or marshy ground, in scrubby vegetation, 1350-2100m. E Cape to E FS, KZN. LEAVES erect, green with slight bloom, margins folding inwards, tips blunt. INFLORESCENCE large, stem robust; FLOWERS ±45mm long, tepals hardly spreading, **pure white**, tube pale green (Jan-Mar). GENERAL: Cultivated in Britain since 1862. Excellent garden plant, frost resistant.

Galtonia regalis **Royal Berg Lily** *(regalis - royal, referring to Royal Natal National Park where the type specimen was collected in the Tugela gorge)*

500-800mm tall. In colonies, on wet cliffs, up to 2800m. EMR endemic. LEAVES **lax, spreading**, bright green. FLOWER tube greenish cream, tepals creamy-white (Jan-Feb).

Galtonia viridiflora **Green Berg Lily**

300-900mm tall. On cliffs and steep rocky slopes, drier areas above escarpment. Mainly Lesotho. LEAVES **erect**, glaucous. FLOWERS **pale green** (Jan-Feb). (see pg 248)

Sani Pass -
Cave Sandstone
(foreground) with basalt
cliffs against the skyline

Martin von Fintel

Urginea capitata   Cameron McMaster

Galtonia candicans   Martin von Fintel

Urginea tenella   Anne Rennie

Urginea macrocentra   Lal Greene

Galtonia candicans   Lal Greene

Galtonia viridiflora   David McDonald

Galtonia regalis   Rodney Moffett

Galtonia regalis   Rodney Moffett

53

Drimia (*drymis* - acrid or pungent, some species are poisonous) Bulb with very loose scales, usually above ground. SAfr, ±13 species, 2 in this region.

Drimia elata [= *D. alta, D. robusta*] Satin Squill; Brandui, Jeukbol (A); undongana-zibomvana, isiklenama, umqumba (Z) (*elata* - tall)

250-400(900)mm tall. Often in clumps, in rocky grassland, rock pavements, up to 2100m. S Cape to Bots. BULB large, with **overlapping reddish scales**. LEAVES erect, up to 440×25-55mm, produced after flowers. INFLORESCENCE tall, slender; FLOWERS ±10mm long, **tepal lobes rolled back**, whitish to purplish brown or greenish (Sep-Nov). GENERAL: Poisonous to stock. Used in traditional medicine and as a protective charm. Attractive garden plant. **Similar species: *Drimia sphaerocephala* Round-head Drimia; Snotuintjie (A); hlare-sa-noko (SS)** (*sphaer* - a ball or sphere; *cephal* - a head) 150-500mm tall. In grassland, up to 2000m. E Cape to Mpum. LEAVES follow the flowers, ±115×6mm, margins with fine long hairs. INFLORESCENCE **round, dense**, up to 80mm diam; FLOWER tube very short, tepal lobes folded back, white, pink, mauve, greyish (Nov-Jan). GENERAL: Used in traditional medicine to treat external tumours.

Litanthus SAfr, monotypic genus.

Litanthus pusillus khoho-ea-lefika, khoho-ea-mafika (SS)

Tiny, 10-50mm tall. **Massed on top of mossy boulders**, in rock crevices, up to 1800m. Widespread but not commonly noticed in SAfr. LEAVES few, threadlike. FLOWERS 1-2, white, 4-5mm long, flowering stem threadlike (Nov-Mar). GENERAL: Used in traditional medicine, mixed with certain mosses, to cure headaches.

Scilla (*squilla* - the sea squill) Bulbous herbs. Afr, Europe, Asia, ±40 species, 6 in SAfr.

Scilla nervosa [= *Scilla rigidifolia, Schizocarpha nervosa,*] White Scilla; Sandlelie (A); magaqana (X); seboka (SS); ingcino, ingcolo, umgcinywana, imbizankulu, ingema (Z) (*nervosa* - veined, nerved, refers to leaves)

150-300mm tall, forming small clumps. In grassland, up to 2000m. E Cape to Tanz. BULB **topped with fibres**. LEAVES stiff, erect, sometimes twisted, ±300×**5-30mm**, **veins conspicuous**, margins thickened. INFLORESCENCE compact at first; FLOWERS **small, white**, with emerald green spot at base of tepals, stalks lengthening as the capsules develop (Oct-Jan). GENERAL: Used in traditional medicine. Hardy garden plant.

Eucomis (*eucomis* - beautiful hair or topknot) S Afr, ±10 species, ±4 in this region.

Eucomis bicolor Bontpynappelblom (A); khapumpu-ea-thaba (SS); umbola (Z) (*bicolor* - two-coloured)

Up to 1m tall, in clumps. In damp grassy gullies, on streambanks, in montane forest, massed below basalt cliffs, up to 2800m. E Cape to KZN/Mpum. LEAVES ±600×100mm, often **spotted purple at base**, margins wavy, purplish red. INFLORESCENCE ±300×75mm, terminal bracts large, floppy, margins purple; FLOWERS densely packed, **drooping**, tepals white, green or mauve, edged purple, stamens purple, unpleasant scent (Jan-Feb). CAPSULE inflated. GENERAL: Used in traditional medicine to treat colic. Interesting garden plant. (see pg 21)

Eucomis humilis Dwarf Pineapple Flower, Lowly Pineapple Flower; Beskeie berg-lelie (A) (*humilis* - lowly, modest)

Up to 250(400)mm. In rocky stream gullies, wet rock overhangs, in grassland below cliffs, up to 2900m. EMR endemic. LEAVES ±400×70 mm, keeled, margins wavy tinged purple, spotted purple below. INFLORESCENCE 80-220mm, with dense tuft of **small bracts** edged purple, stem spotted purple; FLOWERS greenish white tinged or edged purple, stamens purple, unpleasant scent (Dec-Feb). (see pg 250)

Ornithogalum (*ornis* - a bird; *gala* - milk, Greek name for bulbous plant with white flowers) Some species are poisonous to livestock. Afr, Europe, Asia, America, ±200 species, ±70 in SAfr, ±5 in this region.

Ornithogalum juncifolium [= *O. leptophyllum*] Grass-leaved Chincherinchee; lijo-tsa-noko (SS); indlolothi encane (Z) (*juncifolium* - leaves like rushes)

50-300mm tall. In damp grassy places, on cliffs, boulders, in grass and sedge tussocks or crevices of rock pavements, up to 2300m. SE Cape to Mpum. LEAVES hairlike, 2-3mm wide, old leaves **persisting as dark brown fibres at base**. INFLORESCENCE narrow, 20-80mm long; FLOWERS 5-10mm diam, tepals white with green stripe (Sep-Dec). GENERAL: Used as protective charm against storms and evil.

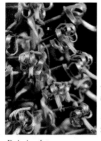

Drimia elata

Martin von Fintel

Litanthus pusillus

Tony Abbott

Drimia elata

Martin von Fintel

Martin von Fintel

Litanthus pusillus

Tony Abbott

Ornithogalum juncifolium

Tony Abbott

Martin von Fintel

Drimia sphaerocephala

Scilla nervosa

Lal Greene

Eucomis bicolor

David McDonald

Eucomis humilis

John Grimshaw

55

Ornithogalum graminifolium metsana-a-manyenyane, nko-ea-ntja (SS) (*graminifoium* - grasslike)

Very variable with two forms in this region: 1. **150-450mm tall**. On moist grassy slopes or cliffs, up to 2400m. LEAVES **2-3, erect**, 3-6 mm broad; INFLORESCENCE **many-flowered**; FLOWERS ±10 mm long, **tepals striped green** (Dec-Feb). 2. **Dwarf form, 25-100mm tall**. In colonies in damp more or less bare earth under Cave Sandstone overhangs, up to 2400m. LEAVES **spreading**. FLOWERS few, white, ±6 mm long (Dec-Apr). SIMILAR SPECIES: *Ornithogalum sephtonii* (named after Paul Sephton of Pitlochrie, Barkly East) In marshy ground ±2400m. EMR endemic. **Only the flowers, and tips of leaves, appear above the ground**; FLOWERS 1-3, white, ±10 mm long (Dec).

Ornithogalum paludosum (*paludosum* - swampy)

100-600mm tall. In moist grassland, up to 3200m. E Cape to Mpum. **No black fibres at base**. LEAVES 10-20mm tall, later leaves narrow. FLOWERS **pure white** (Nov-Feb). **Similar species:** *Ornithogalum diphyllum* 30-70mm tall. In colonies in seepage areas on Cave Sandstone pavements in mud and gravel, 1800-2200m. EMR endemic. LEAVES 2-3, narrow, as tall as flowering stem. INFLORESCENCE congested; FLOWERS 2-10, ±7mm long, white (Dec).

Massonia (named after Francis Masson, 1741-1805, gardener, traveller, plant collector who travelled and collected extensively in the Cape between 1772 and 1795) Small bulbous herbs. SAfr endemic, ± 8 species.

Massonia echinata (*echinata* - prickly, like a hedgehog)

Diminutive, leaves flat on the ground. In damp silt and gravel patches over rock sheets or short damp turf, summit plateau, 2700-3000m. LEAVES 2, ±20×10mm, dull green above, purple below, more or less **covered in soft prickles**. FLOWERS clustered in a small head, white, 10mm long (Dec-Feb).

ASPARAGACEAE - Asparagus Family Subshrubs or climbers. Leaves reduced to scales. Afr, Asia, Europe, 1 genus, ±120 species, ±81 in SAfr, ±5 in this region. *Asparagus* (*aspharagos* - after the name given to the edible *asparagus*).

Asparagus cooperi lehonyeli, lelala-tau-le-leholo, leunyeli, molala-tau-o-moholo (SS) (named after Thomas Cooper, 1815-1913, English plant collector who visited SA)

Scrambling shrublet. Forms spiny tangles at foot of cliffs and on steep rocky slopes, up to 2400m. W Cape to Zim. STEMS erect below, with short sharp spines, twining above. 'LEAVES' **threadlike**, ±10mm long, in tufts, developing after flowers. FLOWERS white with green midrib, ±5mm diam, scent strong, sweet (Oct-Dec). FRUIT ±5mm diam, red. GENERAL: New shoots eaten. Used in traditional medicine to treat kidney and stomach complaints, chest infections, nausea, colic and as a protective charm. Used in the traditional initiation of boys.

Asparagus microraphis [= *Protasparagus microraphis*] lehonyeli, lelala-tau, leunyeli, mankoe, molala-tau (SS) (*microraphis* - small needles)

Evergreen, tangled shrub, up to 1m tall. At foot of cliffs and on steep rocky slopes, up to 2400m. E Cape to KZN/Mpum. LEAVES **small, 2-5 mm long, cylindrical**, in dense clusters. FLOWERS white, in profusion (Oct-Dec). GENERAL: Used in traditional initiation of girls and as a treatment for venereal diseases.

Asparagus ramosissimus [= *Myrsiphyllum ramosissimum*] khopa, sesilatsane (SS); ibutha (Z) (*ramosissimus* - much branched)

Soft herbaceous scrambler, up to 2m. In scrub, on forest margins, up to 2200m. In montane areas, S Cape to Mpum. STEMS green, angled, branches spreading. 'LEAVES' in threes, ±12×1 mm, **flat above, keeled below**. FLOWERS solitary, white, ±8mm diam, hanging, tepals spreading (Nov-Mar). FRUIT red, ±10m diam. GENERAL: Roots sometimes eaten. Used in traditional medicine to treat colic and as a protective charm against snakes.

Tony Abbott

Ornithogalum paludosum

Massonia echinata

David McDonald

Massonia echinata

David McDonald

Asparagus cooperi

Lal Greene

Ornithogalum graminifolium

Neil Crouch

Asparagus microraphis

Tony Abbott

Asparagus ramosissimus

Olaf Wirminghaus

Asparagus microraphis

Rosemary Williams

Asparagus ramosissimus

Olaf Wirminghaus

57

AMARYLLIDACEAE Bulbous herbs. Popular horticultural subjects. Trop and warm regions, ±60 genera, over 800 species, 18 genera in SAfr, 6 in this region. **Haemanthus** (*haima* - blood; *anthos* - flower) Few fleshy leaves, **no stem.** SAfr endemic, 22 species, 1 in this region.

Haemanthus humilis subsp. hirsutus [= *H. hirsutus*] Rabbit's Ears; Bobbejaanoor, Velskoenblaar (A); sekitla, tsebe-ea-phofu (SS) (*humilis* - low growing)

Deciduous, up to 300mm tall. In crevices of rocky cliffs or boulders, in rocky grassland, 1525-2350m. E Cape to Mpum. LEAVES 2, 150-300×55-130mm, hairy. INFLORESCENCE 50-120mm diam, bracts red or pink; FLOWERS white to pale pink, **stamens protrude well above tepals** (Nov-Dec). FRUIT pinkish orange to red, oval, ±15×10mm, with a fruity smell when ripe. GENERAL: Used in traditional medicine to treat stomach complaints, wounds and asthma, and as a protective charm. Grown from seed. (see pg 180)

Nerine (*nerine* - a sea nymph, daughter of sea gods Nereus and Doris) SAfr endemic, ±22 species, 4 in this region. Popular garden plants around the world, with many horticultural hybrids.

Nerine pancratioides White Nerine (*pancratioides* - resembling *Pancratium*, the Spider Lily)

Up to 700mm tall. In moist rocky ground, 1380-1800m. KZN endemic. LEAVES up to 300mm long, bright green, narrow, round at base, flattened towards tip. INFLORESCENCE crowded, stem robust; FLOWERS **white, funnel-shaped,** tepals ±24×5mm, stalks softly hairy (Mar-Apr). GENERAL: Flowers sporadically. Eaten by livestock.

Apodolirion (*apod* - without a foot; *lirion* - white lily) SAfr endemic, ±6 species, 1 in this region.

Apodolirion buchananii icukudwane, indwa (Z) (named after Rev John Buchanan, 1821-1903, Presbyterian clergyman in Natal who collected plant specimens)

Up to 60mm tall. Scattered in grassland, blooms after fires in spring, widespread. BULB deeply buried. LEAVES 1-2, grasslike, blunt-tipped, produced after the flowers. FLOWERS **solitary,** white to pink, 25-35mm, **tube, 50-100mm, acting as a stem,** the ovary in the underground portion, sweetly scented, (Aug-Sep). CAPSULE just reaches the surface of the soil, the thin wall breaking open to release the seeds. GENERAL: Used in traditional medicine to treat stomach complaints.

HYPOXIDACEAE - Star-flower Family S Hemisp, 9 genera, ±130 species, 6 genera in SAfr, 4 in this region. **Hypoxis** (*hyp* - beneath; *oxys* - sharp pointed) Mostly Afr, ±90 species, ±45 in SAfr, ±16 in this region. Research into the medical properties of *Hypoxis* is ongoing.

Hypoxis parvula (*parvula* - very small)

Delicate, up to 150mm tall. In large colonies, in moist grassland, 1200-2500m. LEAVES 25-70×5-15mm, hairy. FLOWERS **solitary,** 10-20mm diam, white or yellow, STALKS 50-150mm long (Sep-Mar). GENERAL: **Var. parvula,** widespread on mountain slopes, 1800-2500m; **flowers yellow.** Var. *albiflora*, in short grass amongst rock sheets, 1200-2000m; **flowers white.** The two colour forms rarely grow together. Hybrids with *Rhodohypoxis* species are not uncommon.

Rhodohypoxis (*rhodo* - rose, red; genus *Hypoxis*) Anthers hidden by inner 3 tepals. SAfr endemic, 6 species, 4 of them confined to the Drakensberg and Lesotho plateau.

Rhodohypoxis baurii Red or White Star; Rooisterretjie (A) (named after Rev Leopold Baur, 1825-1889, pharmacist, missionary and plant collector who came to the Cape in 1847)

Up to 150mm tall. Forms colourful carpets in grassland, rocky places, up to 2900m. LEAVES 25-110×5mm, **dull green,** with **sparse long hairs, midrib grooved to the tip.** FLOWERS 1-2, 20-40mm wide, white, pink or red, tube short with long spreading hairs, also on midrib of outer tepals, lobes spreading flat, faintly scented (Oct-Jan). FRUITING STEM **holds capsule erect with the cap falling off,** seeds scattered by wind or animal movements. GENERAL: Cultivated since the 1920s, popular in Europe and Japan (with a number of cultivars), hardy, requiring well drained soil. Var. *platypetala* (see pg 184), in short **dry** rocky grassland (often on shallow stony soils over rock sheets) up to 2100m. FLOWERS **mostly white,** occasionally pale pink. Hybridises with *R. milloides* and *Hypoxis parvula*.

Saniella (named after the top of Sani Pass) Genus with 2 species, 1 confined to EMR, the other to the Hantam mountains.

Saniella verna [*verna* - spring plant]

Diminutive, up to 80mm tall, often in large colonies. In short, wet turf, above 2700m. EMR endemic. LEAVES 3-6, 40-80×2-4mm, fleshy, deeply channelled. FLOWERS solitary, white, ±30-40mm wide, tube flushed yellow inside, ovary hidden underground (Nov).

David McDonald

Rhodohypoxis baurii

David McDonald

Haemanthus humilis

Haemanthus humilis

Rod Saunders

Lal Greene

Rhodohypoxis baurii subsp. *platypetala*

Lal Greene

Apodolirion buchananii

Pam Cooke

Nerine pancratioides

Nerine pancratioides

Pam Cooke

Hypoxis parvula

David McDonald

Hilliard & Burtt

Saniella verna

59

VELLOZIACEAE - Black-stick Lily or Bobbejaanstert Family (see pg 184) *Talbotia* (named after H. Fox Talbot, in 1867, pioneer photographer, who introduced the plant to cultivation in Britain) Ovary smooth, hairless. Monotypic genus, SAfr endemic.

Talbotia elegans [= *Vellozia elegans*, *V. talbotii*] (*elegans* - elegant, graceful)

Up to 300mm. Forms mats on damp, shady rock faces near streams, up to 1675m. KZN to Mpum. STEMS **long, fibrous, creeping**. LEAVES crowded at tips, 80-120mm, grasslike, sharply keeled, margins rough. FLOWERS solitary, white to pale violet, ±35mm wide, on very slender stems (Dec-Mar). GENERAL: Good container plant.

DIOSCOREACEAE - Yam Family (named after Dioscorides, 1st century AD Greek herbalist) Climbers with tuberous or thick woody rootstock. Male and female flowers on separate plants. Cosmop, in warm regions, 5 genera, ±600 species, SAfr 1 genus, ±16 species, 3 in this region.

Dioscorea retusa [= *D. tysonii*] [*retusa* - blunt]

Slender twiner, up to 3m. On forest margins or in well lit parts of forest, up to 1900m. E Cape to Mpum. STEMS downy. LEAVES with **3-5 leaflets**, 15-100×8-50mm, **margins wavy**, leaf stalk 24-75mm long. INFLORESCENCE: male, up to 75mm long, female, 20-160mm long; FLOWERS dull yellow to pale cream, scented (Dec-Jan).

IRIDACEAE - Iris Family (see pg 122). *Moraea* End of style branches petal-like. (see pg 122)

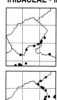

Moraea albicuspa (*albi* - white, *cuspa* - sharp points, refers to the inner tepals)

Up to 600mm tall. On damp grassy slopes, among rocks , 1800-2525m. EMR endemic. LEAVES longer than flowering stem. FLOWERS **large**, white to cream with yellow nectar guides, outer tepals ±30mm long, **inner tepals short**, 7-8mm, **abruptly narrowed to a sharp point**; spathes brown-tipped, ±70 mm (Jan-Mar).

Moraea brevistyla (*brevistyla* - short style)

Up to 350(600)mm tall. In grassland, often near streams, damp areas, up to 2400m. E Cape to Mpum. LEAF **solitary**, 4mm wide. FLOWERING stem branched, all flowers to one side; FLOWERS **small**, outer tepals ±20mm, **spreading horizontally**, white to pale lilac-blue above, grey to purple beneath, **inner tepals, claws and nectar guides yellow with brown spots**, inner tepals deeply divided into 3 narrow lobes (Nov-Mar).

Moraea modesta (*modesta* - modest, refers to its small size)

Up to 200mm tall. In **dry mountain grassland**, up to 3200m. E Cape to Mpum. FLOWERS white to pale blue-mauve, inner tepals short, dark purple (Sep-Dec).

Dietes (*dietes* - two relatives, drawing attention to the position of this genus between *Moraea* and *Iris*) Afr, 5 species, one in this region.

Dietes iridioides (incorrectly called *D. vegeta*) **Small White Dietes, Small Wild Iris; Wilde-iris (A); indawo yehlathi (Z)**

Up to 600mm tall. In large colonies, on forest floor, up to 1950m. Cape to Ethiopia. **Plantlets develop on the flowering stems which bend over with the weight of the fruiting capsules**. LEAVES soft, dark green, **in a fan**, ±40×15-25mm. FLOWERS ±60mm diam, white with yellow nectar guides, claws dotted orange, style branches blue or bluish white, close by midday except on overcast days (Dec-Mar). GENERAL: Used in traditional medicine. Hardy shade garden plant.

Hesperantha (*hesperos* - evening; *anthos* - flower, but only one night-flowering species, *H. tysonii*, is found in this region). (see pg 186)

Hesperantha tysonii **Evening Flower; Aandblom, Bontrokkie (A); khahlana, nala-la-nonyana (SS)** (named after William Tyson, 1851-1920, teacher and plant collector)

Slender, erect, 300-800mm tall. In colonies, in damp or marshy places, along streams, up to 3300m. E Cape to Mpum. LEAVES 100-300×1-2mm, soft. FLOWERS produced **on one side of stem**, ±30mm wide, **silvery white to pale cream** inside, 3 outer tepals tinged or speckled dull red, **tube strongly curved** so that the flower faces downwards, **opening at dusk**, with a **sharp sweet scent** (Oct-Dec). GENERAL: Corms sometimes eaten by children. Easily overlooked unless one goes out at night.

Gladiolus (*gladiolus* - small sword, refers to leaf shape). (see pg.124)

Gladiolus papilio **Butterfly Gladiolus; ibutha, igulusha (Z)** (*papilio* - like a butterfly)

500-750mm high, in colonies. In marshy ground, up to 2400m. E Cape to Limpopo Prov. LEAVES in basal fan, ±500×20mm, firm. FLOWERS **nodding**, 30-50mm long, **tube strongly recurved**, pale creamy yellow, green (pale mauve), with large purplish mauve blotches on lower halves, with or without yellow flare (Dec-Jan). GENERAL: Pollinated by the golden-haired bee *Amegilla capensis*. A hardy garden plant. Grown in the UK since 1866.

60

Talbotia elegans

Pam Cooke

Dioscorea retusa

Tony Abbott

Hesperantha tysonii

Lal Greene

Talbotia elegans

Lal Greene

Moraea brevistyla

Lal Greene

Moraea modesta

Neil Crouch

Moraea albicuspa

Hilliard & Burtt

Moraea brevistyla

Tony Abbott

Dietes iridioides

Martin von Fintel

Gladiolus papilio

Lal Greene

Gladiolus papilio

Rod Saunders

61

Gladiolus woodii (named after John Medley Wood, 1827-1915, botanist and founding curator of Natal Herbarium)
Up to 600mm tall. In rocky grassland, up to 2000m. KZN to Limpopo Prov. LEAVES
2-3, closely sheathing the stem, long leaves only produced by non-flowering plants.
FLOWER **upper tepals larger than lower tepals**, 17-27mm long, **conspicuously
clawed**, colour variable, dark maroon, red-brown, pale blue or yellowish, lower tepal
lobes yellow, feathered red (Oct-Dec).

ORCHIDACEAE - Orchid Family A very large family with highly specialized flowers. Cosmop, ±800 genera, ±20 000 species, 52 genera in
SAfr. *Holothrix* (*holos* - whole or entire; *thrix* - hair, meaning hairy all over) Terrestrial herbs, **2 leaves flat on ground**, flowering stem leafless
and bractless, flowers white to yellowish green, petals lobed. Afr, ±55 species, 23 in SAfr, mainly in the Cape, ±4 in this region.

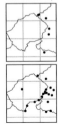

Holothrix orthoceras (*orthoceras* - straight, refers to spur)
60-280mm tall. Frequent, on mossy rocks in forest, on forest margins, up to 1900m.
E Cape to Zim, Malawi. LEAVES dark green **with silvery veins**. FLOWERS white, lip
conspicuous, **shortly 5 lobed**, purple veined; STEM softly hairy (Feb-Apr).

Holothrix scopularia [= *H. multisecta*] (*scopulinus* - bearing small brushes, or *scopulosus* - rocky)
Slender to robust, 110-340mm tall. In rocky grassland and rocky outcrops,
1525-2800m. E Cape to Mpum. **Plant covered in conspicuous spreading hairs**.
LEAVES often withered at time of flowering. INFLORESCENCE **dense, flowers all
arranged on one side**, STEM conspicuously hairy; FLOWERS small, white to dull
yellow or pink, **lip deeply divided into 5-11 slender lobes** (Oct-Feb). (see pg 124)

Huttonaea (named after Caroline Hutton who collected with her husband who was an officer during the frontier wars and later a Cape civil
servant) Petals and lip fringed, petals erect, clawed at base, looking like "shaggy dogs ears"! Genus endemic to SAfr, 5 species, more or less
confined to the Drakensberg mountain range.

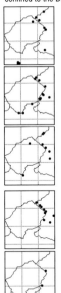

Huttonaea fimbriata (*fimbriata* - fringed)
Slender, 170-300mm tall. Locally common in deep shade of forest floor,
1400-1900m. E Cape, KZN. LEAVES 2, ±80×50mm, **lower leaf larger with a stalk
40-60mm long** (the leaves of all other species have no stalk). INFLORESCENCE
30-100mm long; FLOWERS small, ±10mm wide, sepals and petals white (Jan-Mar).

Huttonaea grandiflora (*grandiflora* - flowers large)
90-250mm tall. On steep damp rocky grassy banks in drainage lines, rarely on forest
floor, (1800)2300-2800m. EMR endemic. LEAVES without a stalk, lower leaf large,
20-60×15-40mm, upper sheathlike. INFLORESCENCE short, 30-50mm long; FLOWERS
white, **large, 20-30mm long**, speckled purplish red on upper petal, **fringes long, up
to 12mm, petal claws completely fused**, blades curving forwards (Feb-Mar).
Similar species: ***Huttonaea oreophila*** (*or* - mountain; *phyll* - leaf) In damp rocky grassland,
1500-2200m. FLOWERS **smaller**, 10-18mm long, **fringes short, 2-4mm**, petal claws
fused at base (Feb-Mar).

Huttonaea pulchra (*pulchra* - beautiful)
150-400mm tall. **On forest floor**, on damp rocks, 1400-1800m. E Cape, KZN and
Graskop in Mpum. LOWER LEAF **long**, up to 120×70mm sheathing stem.
INFLORESCENCE loose, 60-100mm long; FLOWERS **small, ±15mm long, sepals and lip
pale green**, petals white to pale mauve, spoon-shaped, **claws free** (Jan-Mar). **Similar
species:** ***Huttonaea woodii*** (named after John Medley Wood, 1827-1915, botanist, founding curator of Natal
Herbarium)   In marshy **grassland**, 1300-2100m. LOWER LEAF **short**, 40-60mm.
INFLORESCENCE dense, 50-70×20mm; FLOWERS small, ±10mm long, sepals and lip
white to pale green, **petals heavily marked with purple** (Jan-Feb).

On the road to Injasuti,
northern Drakensberg

Lorraine van Hooff

62

Holothrix orthoceras

Pam Cooke

Hubert Kurzweil

Huttonaea grandiflora

Martin von Fintel

Huttonaea oreophila

Tessa Hedge

Holothrix scopularia

David McDonald

Huttonaea fimbriata

Martin von Fintel

Huttonaea woodii

Oskar & Hilde Kurze

Huttonaea pulchra

Lal Greene

Huttonaea fimbriata

Martin von Fintel

Gladiolus woodii

Martin von Fintel

Huttonaea pulchra

Lal Greene

63

Habenaria (*habena* - strap or thong; *aria* - possessing, refers to the long spur) Terrestrial herbs, flowers mostly green and white; median sepal joined with whole or upper lobes of petals forming a hood, lip lobed, spur long. Trop, subtrop, ±800 species, 35 in SAfr, ±12 in this region.

Habenaria dives Death Orchid; lekoesha, ´mametsana (SS); inhluthi yotshani (Z)
(*dives* - rich)

Slender to robust, 170-600mm tall. In grassland, up to 2600m. E Cape to Mpum. LEAVES up to 240×20mm, stiff, with prominent veins. INFLORESCENCE loose to dense, ±300mm long; FLOWERS **small, white** with green-veined sepals, **lip 3-lobed, midlobe longer than side lobes**, spur short, 8-15mm long, tapered from a wide mouth (Jan-Feb). GENERAL: Ground and dried tubers used as an evil charm.

Habenaria falcicornis uklamkleshe (Z) (*falcicornis* - sickle-shaped)

Robust, 220-800mm tall. In marshy grassland, up to 2900m. W Cape to Zim. LEAVES 80-180mm long. INFLORESCENCE looser than *H. dives*; FLOWERS white, **spur longer, 20-40mm** (Jan-Mar). GENERAL: subsp. *falcicornis* with smaller flowers than subsp. *caffra*, differing mostly in flower size and petal shape.

Habenaria epipactidea [= *H. foliosa*] ´mametsana (SS); umabelebuca omkhulu, uklamkleshe, unokleshe (Z) (*epipactidea* - similar to *Epipactus*, a genus of orchid)

Robust, up to 400mm tall. In damp grassland, up to 2400m. Widespread, E Cape to trop E Afr. LEAVES ±100×20mm, clasping stem, overlapping, ribbed, grading into bracts. INFLORESCENCE dense, ±120mm; FLOWERS creamy green, **petals rounded, lip creamy white, protruding forwards, undivided**, ±15mm long with **tiny hairlike processes at base, spur long, 20-30(65)mm**, slender with **thickened tip** (Jan-Feb). GENERAL: Pollinated by hawkmoths. Used in traditional medicine as an emetic. Also used as a protective charm against lightning. **Similar species:** *Habenaria anguiceps* (*anguis* - a snake; *ceps* - head) In grassland up to 2500m. E Cape to Mpum. LEAVES ±45×12mm, grading into bracts. INFLORESCENCE dense; FLOWERS green, **petals pointed**, yellowish green, **lip undivided, spur short**, ±8 **mm long**, strongly inflated (Nov-Feb).

Neobolusia (*neo* - new; *bolusia* - honouring Harry Bolus, 1834-1911, amateur collector who became a towering figure in SA botany) Slender herbs with 1-2 large, long, narrow basal leaves, few smaller stem leaves; inflorescence erect. In montane grassland, SAfr and CAfr, 3 species, 1 in this region.

Neobolusia tysonii ´mametsana-a-manyenyane (named after William Tyson, 1851-1920, teacher, collector)

Up to 500mm tall. In moist or marshy grassland, 1200-2350m. E Cape to Limpopo Prov. LEAVES ±155×20mm at base, stem leaves sheathing, grading into bracts. INFLORESCENCE loose, ±150mm long; FLOWERS 15-20×6mm, sepals spreading, brownish green, lip white with pink marking, **widest towards tip** (Jan-Mar).

Dracomonticola - Drakensberg and Lesotho, 1 species. Leaf solitary, inflorescence slightly nodding.

Dracomonticola virginea [= *Neobolusia virginea*] (*virgineus* - maidenly, pertaining to a virgin)

Up to 250mm tall. In damp and partially shaded rock faces, usually over basalt, 1500-3100m. EMR endemic. LEAF **solitary, oval**, ±40×20mm. INFLORESCENCE dense, ±50mm long; FLOWERS ±15×10mm, sepals white, petals small, ±4×2mm, pale pink with dark pink margins; lip ±6×4mm, margin entire (Oct-Jan).

Upper Loteni valley
below 'Redi Peak'
and 'The Hawk',
southern Drakensberg

David McDonald

64

Habenaria dives

Martin von Fintel

Habenaria falcicornis

Peter Linder

Habenaria epipactidea

Martin von Fintel

Habenaria dives

Pam Cooke

Habenaria falcicornis

Peter Linder

Neobolusia tysonii

Clinton Carbutt

Dracomonticola virginea

Peter Linder

Tony Abbott

Neobolusia tysonii

Martin von Fintel

65

Schizochilus (*schizo* - split, deeply divided; *cheilos* - lip) Terrestrial herb with few narrow leaves near base of stem, **inflorescence dense, usually nodding** or drooping over at tip. S and CAfr, ±11 species, restricted to montane and subalpine grasslands, 8 in SAfr, 4 in this region.

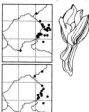

Schizochilus flexuosus (*flexuosus* - winding, bending)

Slender, 50-250mm tall. Locally common in grassland or on damp sheet rock, damp cliffs, 1500-2500m. E Cape, KZN, a few sites in Mpum. LEAVES mostly in basal cluster, slender, ±50×8mm. INFLORESCENCE a dense head, 20-40mm long, **curved**; FLOWERS 5mm diam, **white with yellow lip**, spur longer, 3-4mm (Jan-Feb).

Schizochilus angustifolius (*angustus* - narrow, small; *folium* - leaf)

In stony grassland, **only at high altitudes, 2100-3000m**. EMR endemic. LEAVES 30-60mm long, in basal cluster. INFLORESCENCE dense, **cylindrical**; FLOWERS small, 2-3mm diam, white with yellow lip, spur tiny, 1mm (Jan-Feb).

Satyrium (*Satyros* - refers to the 2-horned satyr, half man, half goat - the two spurs somewhat resemble a satyr's horns) Ovary not twisted, lip forms a hood, 2 conspicuous spurs or 2 pouches. Used in traditional medicine, mixed with other medicines to help with illnesses that are difficult to cure. Afr, Madag, India, China, ±88 species, 37 in SAfr, ±10 in this region.

Satyrium cristatum lekholela-la-bana-ba-seng, ´mametsana (SS) (*cristatum* - tassel-like tips)

Slender, 140-400mm tall. In moist or marshy grassland up to 2400m. E Cape to Limpopo Prov. LEAVES 2(3) spreading near the ground, 20-160×50mm. INFLORESCENCE a dense, slender spike; FLOWERS greenish to creamy white, blotched and streaked dark red, sepals 6-10mm long, spurs 3-12mm long (Jan-Feb). GENERAL: Var. *cristatum*, hood entrance 3-6mm tall, spurs short, 3-7mm long. Var. *longilabiatum*, less common, hood entrance 5-7mm tall, spurs 7-12mm.

Satyrium ligulatum (*ligulatum* - little tongue)

Stout or slender,150-400mm tall. In moist grassland, on streambanks, up to 2400m. W Cape, E Cape, E FS. LEAVES large, 1-3, near base, 30-140mm long. INFLORESCENCE a slender spike; FLOWERS yellowish green to creamy white tinged dull red, **tips of the segments dry out and turn brown** a few hours after opening, sepals 5-10mm long, spur 5-10mm long (Dec-Jan). GENERAL: Pollinated by moths *Agrotis segetum* at night and by butterflies *Acraea horta*, *Vanessa cardui* during the day.

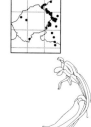

Satyrium longicauda Blushing Bride Satyrium; Langstert-trewwa (A); lekeosha (SS)
(*longicauda* - long tailed)

Slender, 300-450mm tall, in small groups or large colonies. LEAVES usually flat on the ground, **on a separate shoot from the flowering stem**. INFLORESCENCE a crowded slender spike, up to 200mm long; FLOWERS white or red, veins and tips of sepals and petals often darker, sweetly scented (Dec-Mar). GENERAL: Used as protective and love charms. Var. *longicauda* (*longicauda* - long tail) In moist uplands up to 2100m. W Cape to Trop Afr. FLOWERS large, side sepals 5-11mm long, spurs 22-46mm long (Dec-Feb). Var. *jacottetianum* (named after Mlle H Jacottet who, with her brother Rev E Jacottet, collected plants in the high mountains of Lesotho between 1905-14) In wet or dry rocky grassland, up to 3000m. E Cape to Mpum. FLOWERS **smaller, pink to red**, side sepals 4-7mm long, **spurs 15-26mm long** (Jan-Mar). (see pg 192)

Satyrium trinerve [= *S. atherstonei*] (*trinerve* - 3-veined from base of leaf)

Slender, 350-450mm tall. In moist grassland, 1800-3000m. Widespread, E Cape to Trop Afr and Madag. LEAVES 1-3, sheathing at base, 60-250mm, nearly erect, slightly pleated. INFLORESCENCE compact, crowded, 70-150mm long, **bracts conspicuous**, green with broad white margins, **almost horizontally spreading**; FLOWERS white with pale yellow front sepal, spurs short, 1-5mm long (Dec-Jan).

Disa (origin unclear, possibly from *dis* - double, referring to the two large wings in the style or *dis* - rich or opulent, referring to the red of the spectacular *Disa uniflora* the first species of the genus described) Median sepal hooded, prolonged into a spur or pouch. **The direction in which the spur points is useful in identification in the field**. Afr, Madag, Reunion, ±162 species, 131 in SAfr, ±29 in this region.

Disa cephalotes subsp. *cephalotes* (*cephalotes* - a head)

Slender, 150-300mm tall. In small groups, in dry or damp grassland, 1500-2500m. E Cape, FS, KZN. LEAVES up to 200mm long, **hard, narrow**, clustered towards base. INFLORESCENCE **dense, compact, roundish**; FLOWERS white with purplish red spots on the hood, spur 3-6mm long, nearly horizontal (Jan-Feb). GENERAL: This plant looks remarkably similar to *Brownleea galpinii* (see pg 68). Subsp. *frigida* looks very different (see pg 192).

Satyrium cristatum

Schizochilus flexuosus

Disa cephalotes subsp. *cephalotes*

Satyrium longicauda

Satyrium trinerve

Schizochilus angustifolius

Satyrium longicauda

Satyrium trinerve

Satyrium ligulatum

Martin von Fintel

Darrel Plowes

David McDonald

Tom de Waal

Martin von Fintel

Oskar & Hilde Kurze

Neil Crouch

Lal Greene

Ted Oliver

67

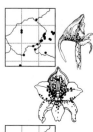

Disa crassicornis ´mametsana (SS) [= D. jacottetiae] (*crassus* - thick; *cornis* - horn, refers to spur)

Robust, up to 500mm (up to 1m at lower altitudes). Occasional, on damp grassy slopes, up to 2200m. E Cape, Les, KZN. LEAVES sometimes on a separate shoot, stem leaves sheathing. INFLORESCENCE large (5-25 flowers), up to 300mm long, bracts papery, reddish brown; FLOWERS **large**, ±50mm diam, thick textured, creamy white to pink mottled purple or pink, **spur 30-40mm long, curving out then down, tip slender, greenish**, strong, sweet scent (Nov-Feb). GENERAL: Flower shape and size varies according to altitude. Cultivated in Europe since the 1800s but difficult to maintain. Populations reduced by farming operations. (see pg 194)

Disa nivea (*niveus* - snow, white)

200-400mm tall. Occasional on moist grassy slopes and on rock ledges, 2250-2500m. EMR endemic. LEAVES rigid, erect, up to 250mm long, overlapping. INFLORESCENCE loose, 50-150mm long; FLOWERS creamy white with dark red blotches at tips of sepals and lip, spur speckled dark red, **horizontal, tip curved down, 25-40mm** (Jan-Feb).

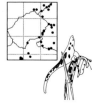

Disa oreophila (*oreophila* - mountain loving)

100-350mm tall. LEAVES **narrow**, ±200×1-3mm. INFLORESCENCE loose, 40-150mm long; FLOWERS white or pink, lightly or heavily spotted purple, **spur almost horizontal** (Dec-Feb). Subsp. *oreophila*, **usually curved or hanging** from damp crevices and grassy ledges of Cave Sandstone cliffs, 1200-2100m. E Cape to Mpum. FLOWERS **small**, sepals 4-6mm, spur 5-10mm (Dec-Feb, mostly Jan). Subsp. *erecta*, **erect**, in shallow soil over rock pavements and damp grassy slopes, 2100-2700m. EMR endemic. FLOWERS **larger**, sepals 6-10mm, spur 10-25mm (Jan-Feb).(see pg 194)

Disa tysonii (named after William Tyson, 1851-1932, teacher and collector)

Robust, 200-600mm tall. In damp grassland, 1800-3000m. E Cape, Les, KZN (W Cape). LEAVES overlapping, narrow, pointed, up to 100mm long. INFLORESCENCE thick, dense; FLOWERS dull greenish cream veined green, lip yellow, hood and spur sometimes tinged pink, **spur club-shaped, 4-6mm, pointing upwards** (Dec-Jan).

Brownleea (named after Rev John Brownlee, early Scottish missionary who collected the type species of the genus, *B coerulea*, in E Cape) Median/odd sepal joins with two lateral petals to form trumpet-shaped hood which tapers gradually into curved spur, lip insignificant. Afr, 7 species, 5 in S Afr, all found in this region.

Brownleea galpinii (named after Ernest Galpin, 1858-1941, banker and renowned amateur botanist)

Slender, 150-500mm tall. On moist grass slopes or in scrub, 1800-3000m. KZN to Zim. LEAVES 2 (4), on stem, 60-200×5-15mm, folded, prominently ribbed, lower leaf larger. INFLORESCENCE **dense, roundish, often one-sided**, ±45×30mm; FLOWERS ±5mm diam, **white to cream**, side sepals 8-10mm long, spotted blue-purple, spur slender, straight, up to 6mm (Feb-Mar). GENERAL: Subsp. *major*, more common in this region, EMR endemic. Lateral sepals 8-10mm long, **petal margins crenulate, fanlike**, lip 1.7-2.5mm long. Subsp. *galpinii*, smaller, less common in this region. Lateral sepals 6-7mm long, upper margin of petals only slightly crenulate, lip erect, less than 1.5mm.

Brownleea parviflora ´mametsana (SS) (*parviflora* - small flowers)

Slender, 200-600mm tall. In moist rocky mountain grassland or *Protea* savannah, 1800-2300m. E Cape to E Afr. LEAVES, 80-200×8-16mm, on stem. INFLORESCENCE dense, **slender, cylindrical spike**, 40-120mm long; FLOWERS small, ±4mm wide, white, sometimes tinged pale mauve, green or brown, **petals oblong to square**, spur pointed downward, short, 3-5mm long (Feb-Apr).

Disperis - **Granny Bonnet Orchids** (*dis* - double; *pera* - pouch, refers to pouches on side sepals) Petals joined to median sepal to form **a helmet-shaped hood**, side sepals each have a noticeable spur or pouch. Afr, India, New Guinea, ±84 species, ±26 in SAfr, 13 in this region.

Disperis fanniniae **Granny Bonnet; Moederkappie (A)** (named after Marianne Roberts, 1845-1938, who pressed and painted plants collected by her brother G.F. Fannin)

Slender to stout, 150-450mm tall. In leaf litter **on forest floor** or on mossy rocks in forest, up to 2100. E Cape to Limpopo Prov. LEAVES 3-4, spreading, clasping, 20-80×10-30mm, dark green above, often purple beneath. FLOWERS **1-8, large, white**, flushed pink or green, speckled green or purple along inner rim of hood, **hood very deep**, 12-20mm long, broad, rounded, **side sepals ±14mm**, finely pointed, spreading downwards, **bracts leaflike** (Jan-Mar). GENERAL: Also in pine and wattle plantations. Cultivated successfully. Pollinated by oil-collecting bees *Rediviva colorata*.

68

Disa nivea

Martin von Fintel

Brownleea parviflora

Martin von Fintel

Brownleea galpinii

Martin von Fintel

Brownleea galpinii

Tony Abbott

Disperis fanniniae

Tessa Hedge

Disa tysonii

John Grimshaw

Disa oreophila

H J Venter

Disa crassicornis

Mike Hirst

Disa oreophila subsp. *oreophila*

H J Venter

69

Disperis lindleyana Granny Bonnet; Moederkappie (A) (named after John Lindley, renowned for his pioneering work on orchids)
150-400mm tall. Frequent, **on forest floor**, also in pine and wattle plantations, up to 1950m. W Cape to Zim. LEAF **heart-shaped, solitary, half way up stem**, dark green, glossy above, ±purplish beneath, 30-60×20-40mm. FLOWERS 1-3(5), white or cream (pinkish), often spotted deep pink, side sepals ±9mm long, spreading, bracts leaflike, scent strong, soapy (Nov-Jan). GENERAL: The plant spreads by suckering.

Disperis thorncroftii (named after G. Thorncroft, 1857-1934, b England, d. Barberton, merchant and plant collector)
150-250mm tall. In leaf litter **on forest floor**, up to 1950m. S Cape to Mpum. LEAVES 2, oval, 15-45×6-33mm, stem-clasping, purple beneath. FLOWERS **1-3, small, white** or pale pink, **heavily spotted green under the broad, shallow hood**, side sepals 7-8mm, spreading, spurs curved, pointing backwards (Dec-Feb). GENERAL: Probably pollinated by oil-collecting bees, *Rediviva* sp.

Disperis wealii (named after James Weale, b. 1838, graduated in law, amateur naturalist, interested in pollination by insects, particularly in orchids and corresponded with Charles Darwin on this subject)
Slender, 50-250mm tall. In damp or marshy grassland, along streams, up to 2500m. E Cape to Limpopo Prov. LEAVES 2-4, clasping,12-20mm. FLOWERS 1-6, white, barred or spotted green under margins of the hood, hood rounded, bell-shaped, 10-12mm deep, side sepals 9-12mm long, spreading, with long, sharply pointed tips (Jan-Mar). GENERAL: Pollinated by oil-collecting bees, *Rediviva* sp.

Pterygodium (*pterygoides*- winglike, refers to side petals) Flowers with median sepal and petal joined to form a very shallow hood, lip with short or tall appendage, no spur. Mainly SW Cape (1 in Tanz), 18 species, 4 in this region.

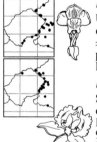

Pterygodium cooperi (named after Thomas Cooper, 1815-1913, plant collector and grower who came to SA in 1859)
Up to 290mm tall. On forest floor or, at higher altitudes, below big rocks and cliffs or on steep wet grass slopes, 1500-2800m. E Cape, Les, KZN. LEAVES 2-4, basal one large, ±160×50mm. INFLORESCENCE up to 100 mm long; FLOWERS ±20×15mm, white flushed pink with age, with a band of dark speckling within the hood, lip white, 3-5mm, side lobes fleshy, appendage 4-5mm tall, standing erect, sharply scented (Jan-Mar).

Pterygodium hastatum ´mametsana-a-manyenyane (SS) (*hasta* - spear-shaped)
Slender, 150-300mm tall. In damp grassland, often among rocks, sometimes on cliffs or in scrub, up to 3000m. E Cape to Mpum. LEAVES 2-4, basal, up to 210×60mm. INFLORESCENCE up to 80mm long; FLOWERS ±20×15mm, pale green to white, hood 9-13mm, sometimes spotted purple inside, **margins of petals tightly wavy, crisped**, lip 4-5mm rounded, crisped, appendage erect, 6-8mm, tip 3-toothed (Jan-Feb).

Pterygodium leucanthum (*leucanthum* - white flowers)
Slender, 150-400mm tall. On damp grassy mountain slopes, 1500-2500m. EMR endemic. LEAVES up to 5, lower ones ±170×35mm. INFLORESCENCE up to 160mm long; FLOWERS ±18×12mm, greenish cream, petals rounded, **lip appendage ±6mm tall, erect, pale green with 2 dark green lobes curving forward at tips**, sharply scented (Jan-Mar).

Polystachya (*poly* - many; *stachys* - ear of corn, meaning ear of corn or spike) Usually epiphytic, base of stem swollen to form a pseudobulb, **lip uppermost**. Pantrop, mostly Afr, ±200 species, 11 in S Afr, 1 in this region.

Polystachya ottoniana amabelejongosi, iphamba lehlathi (Z) (named after Friedrich Otton, Garden Director of Schoneberg, Germany, in the 1800s)
Epiphyte, 40-150mm high, forming small mats. On rocks and tree trunks in forest patches or tree clumps, up to 1800m. S Cape to Limpopo Prov. PSEUDOBULBS **short, fat, vertically flattened**, ±25×15mm, often **forming long chains**. LEAVES 2-3, hard, up to 60×10mm, tips blunt, notched. INFLORESCENCE slender, erect, shorter than leaves; FLOWERS 1-6, white to pinkish or yellow, ±10mm long, **lip 3-lobed, curled, with yellow mid stripe**, pink streak in side sepals, delicately scented (Sep-Dec). GENERAL: Used in traditional medicine. Seeds used as snuff. Very variable.

Eulophia (*eu* - well; *lophos* - crest, refers to the crested lip) Terrestrial herbs. Lip ridged on upper surface. Old and New World, most common in Afr, 42 in SAfr, 9 in this region.

Eulophia ovalis lekholela-la-Matabele, lekoesha, ´mametsana (SS); ihamba lesigodi, iphamba (Z) (*ovalis* - broadly elliptic, oval) (see pg 126)

Eulophia ovalis

Eulophia ovalis

Disperis lindleyana

Polystachya ottoniana

Pterygodium hastatum

Disperis thorncroftii

Pterygodium cooperi

Pterygodium leucanthum

Disperis wealii

71

DICOTYLEDONS Two seed leaves, net veins, flower parts in fours, fives or multiples of these.

SANTALACEAE - Sandalwood Family (see pg 128) *Thesium* (a Greek word) (see pg 128)

Thesium costatum bohoho, marakalle, marakalle-a-manyenyane, sebitsane, sebitsoane (SS) (*costatus* - having lines or riblike ridged stems)

Small, tufted herb, up to 150(300)mm tall. In short rocky grassland, up to 2400m. E Cape to Mpum. LEAVES ±10mm long, narrow with pointed tips, lower leaves spreading, upper close to stem. FLOWERS ±2mm diam, **white, on conspicuous stalks**, flowering stems often topped by long leafy sterile shoots (Oct-Dec).

Thesium imbricatum (*imbricatum* - overlapping)

Dwarf shrublet, up to 120mm tall. On rock sheets, cliffs, very rocky ground on ridges, 1200-2650m. Cape to KZN/Mpum. Old stems rough with leaf bases. LEAVES **needle-shaped**, 4-10×1mm, tips often recurved. FLOWERS clustered at branch tips, lobes white, densely fringed (Oct-Jan).

MESEMBRYANTHEMACEAE - Vygie Family (*Mesembryanthemum* (midday or noon-flowering, refers to the flowers which usually open only in full sunlight) Succulent herbs or shrublets. Flowers brightly coloured, petals many, free, stamens numerous, free. Fruit a many-seeded capsule. Mainly SAfr, ±22 genera with ±1680 species, 122 in SAfr. *Delosperma* (*delos* - conspicuous; *sperma* - seed) (see pg 128)

Delosperma hirtum mabone (SS) (*hirtus* - rough)

Low growing herb, 50-80mm tall. STEMS spreading, flowering branchlets erect, densely leafy, internodes invisible. LEAVES broadest at base, ±50×7mm, **concave to flat above**, keeled, covered with tiny bristle-tipped bumps, margins fringed with almost rigid bristles. FLOWERS ±30mm diam, white or magenta, white at base, stalks 5-30mm (summer).

CARYOPHYLLACEAE - Carnation or Pink Family (see pg 200)*Cerastium* (*keras* - horn, refers to the horned capsules) Annual or perennial herbs. Leaves opposite. Flowers in terminal loose inflorescences, petals notched. Cosmop, ±100 species, 5 in S Afr. (see pg 200)

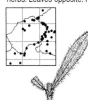

Cerastium arabidis Snow Flower; qoqobala-sa-loti (SS) (*arabidis* – like *Arabis* (Cruciferae)

Loosely tufted herb, up to 300mm tall. In damp grassy places, boulder beds, on summit plateau in wet gravel patches, grass tussocks in marshes, 1675-3000m. E Cape to Mpum. Stem covered in short glandular hairs. LEAVES 10-30×3-10mm, **margins with long hairs**. FLOWERS showy, ±20mm diam, white, **petals deeply notched**, 10-15mm long, sepals ±8mm long, glandular (Nov-Jan). **Additional species:** *Cerastium* sp. **Densely tufted** herb. Forms **small, leafy mats** in wet gravelly places, 2400-3000m. FLOWERS crowded at tips of simple branches, petals ± equal to sepals.

Silene (named after the Greek god Silen, friend of Bacchus) Annual or perennial herbs or shrubs. Leaves opposite. Flowers with inflated tubular calyx. Mostly N Hemisp, ±700 species, 19 in SAfr, 3 in this region (3 naturalised).

Silene undulata [= *S. capensis*] Gunpowder Plant, Large-flowered Campion; Wildetabak (A); lithotoana, molokoloko (SS) (*undulata* - wavy, refers to margins of leaves)

Robust, perennial herb, up to 1m tall. On steep stony damp slopes below cliffs, often in rough growth near overhangs, 1550-2880m. SW Cape to Zim. LEAVES in basal rosette, ±130×30mm, stem leaves ±80×20mm. **Flowering stem leafy, from side of rosette**, ribbed, shortly hairy, sticky or not. FLOWERS 20-40mm diam, **white to pale pink**, petals 2-lobed, calyx ±35mm, **dark ribbed**, scented, **opening in late afternoon or in dull light** (Dec-Mar). GENERAL: Used in traditional medicine. **Similar species:** *Silene bellidioides* ugwayelaso, ugwayintombi, umjuju (Z) Sparsely branched herb, up to 600mm tall. In open grassland, *Leucosidea* scrub, 1800-2500m. LEAVES **mostly in basal rosette**, 80-110×10-20mm. **Flowering stem from centre of rosette**. FLOWERS **open in daylight**, 30mm diam, white to pale pink (Jan-Feb).

Dianthus - **Carnations and Pinks** (*dios* - divine; *anthos* - flower, refers to the scent of some species) (see pg 200)

Dianthus basuticus subsp. *basuticus* Lesotho Dianthus (see pg 200)

RANUNCULACEAE (see pg 128) *Anemone* (*nahamea* - Greek god Adonis who was killed on Mt Olympus, his blood causing red *A. coronaria* plants to spring up) Cluster of leaves at base of flower stalk. No petals, sepals petal-like. Cosmop, ±120 species, 4 in Afr, 3 in SAfr, 2 in this region.

Anemone fanninii Giant Wild Anemone; Grootanemoon (A); umanzamnyama (Z) (after
G.F. Fannin,1832-65, farmer and plant collector who settled at the Dargle. His sister, Marianne pressed his specimens)

Robust perennial herb, flowering stem up to 1m tall. In moist depressions, on slopes, near streams, in marshes, up to 2000m. LEAVES **very large**, 250-350mm diam, **only partly developed at flowering**, 5-7-lobed, thick, velvety above, margins with red-tipped teeth, stalks long, ±700×6mm. FLOWERS 70-90mm diam, creamy white tinged pink, scented (Aug-Dec). GENERAL: Used in traditional medicine. Not easily cultivated.

Thesium costatum

Martin von Fintel

Thesium imbricatum

Hilliard & Burtt

Delosperma hirtum

Godfrey Symons

Cerastium arabidis

Peter Linder

Cerastium sp.

David McDonald

Dianthus basuticus

David McDonald

Silene undulata

Lal Greene

Silene bellidioides

Peter Linder

Anemone fanninii

Hilliard & Burtt

Silene undulata

Rodney Moffett

Clematis (*klema* - refers to the twisting growth) Mostly woody climbers or scrambling shrubs. Leaves opposite, compound, stalk and stem capable of twining. Petal-like sepals sometimes present, styles often persistent, feathery. Mostly temp, ±230 species, 4 in SAfr, 1 in this region.

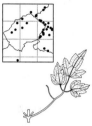

Clematis brachiata Traveller's Joy; Klimop, Lemoenbloeisels (A); morarana-oamafehlo (SS); ityolo (X); ihlonzo leziduli, inhlabanhlanzi, umdlandlathi (Z) (*brachiata* - branches spreading, at right angles)

Vigorous perennial climber. Over scrub, near streams, in boulder beds, up to 2200m. Widespread in SAfr and Trop Afr. LEAVES with 3-7 leaflets, up to 70×40mm, leaf stalks twining. INFLORESCENCES much branched; FLOWERS 20-30mm diam, white, fragrantly scented (Feb-Mar). FRUITS in masses, **persistent styles covered in silvery white hairs.** GENERAL: Used as sticks to stir porridge. Used in traditional medicine to treat skin complaints, abdominal disorders, intestinal worms, head colds, syphilis, as a snakebite remedy and as a protective charm. Lovely garden plant, easily grown from seed or cuttings.

BRASSICACEAE (CRUCIFERAE) - Cabbage or Mustard Family Annual, biennial or perennial herbs and shrubs. Many species are of economic importance such as cabbage, cauliflower, broccoli and ornamentals such as candytuft and wallflowers. Cosmop, ±390 genera, ±3000 species, ±34 genera in SAfr (20 exotic). *Heliophila* (*helios* - sun; *philein* - to love) Annual or perennial herbs or shrubs, rarely climbing. Flowers with 4 petals. Endemic to SAfr, ±75 species, 5 in this region. Mostly in winter rainfall areas.

Heliophila alpina

Prostrate, **low growing** perennial herb, 100-150mm tall. In marshy grassland around wet silt patches **on summit plateau,** 2800-3400m. EMR endemic. **Stems unbranched, mostly reclining,** young parts finely hairy, later hairless. LEAVES 5-10mm long, feathery, **5-7-lobed,** held close to stem. FLOWERS 1-5, at stem tips, petals brownish or greenish white inside, purplish outside (Oct-Dec). FRUIT 10-15×3-4mm.

CRASSULACEAE - Crassula Family Herbs or soft shrubs, usually succulent. Leaves often joined round the stem, or in basal rosette. Cosmop, centres in SAfr and C America, ±33 genera, ±1500 species, 6 genera in SAfr (1 exotic). *Crassula* (*crassus* - thick, refers to fleshy leaves) Delicate annual or perennial herbs or soft-wooded to succulent shrubs, also aquatics. Flowers small, (4)5 petals, stamens and sepals. Attracts butterflies including Tailed Blackeye *Leptomyrina hirundo* and Cape Blackeye *Gonatomyrna lara*. Mostly SAfr, ±300 species, ±150 in SAfr, about 15 in this region.

Crassula brachypetala [= *C. pellucida* subsp. *brachypetala*] (*brachypetala* - short petals)

Loosely branched herb, stems reclining or suberect. In damp shady places around rocks and on cliffs, up to 2200m. STEMS often rooting near base. LEAVES up to 20×15mm, **base stalklike.** FLOWERS starry, in small terminal heads, petals white, 4-6mm long (Jan-Mar).

Crassula dependens [= *C. harveyi*] lengoako, serelilenyana, setšosa (SS) (*dependens* - hanging down)

Well branched perennial herb, up to 200mm tall. Forms small mats on margins and in crevices of damp rock sheets or cliffs, up to 3000m. Widespread, Karoo to Mpum. LEAVES 5-15×1-3mm, **spreading at right angles to the stem, sharp-tipped.** INFLORESCENCE small, terminal; FLOWERS white (Dec-Mar). GENERAL: Used as a protective charm against lightning.

Crassula natans Watergras (A); mohata-metsi-o-monyenyane (SS) (*natans* - swimming, with floating leaves)

Reclining or floating aquatic herb, rooted in mud or gravel, long, unbranched stems trailing in the water, tips floating. In pools or slow flowing streams, 2400-2865m. SW Cape to Mpum. LEAVES 3-7×1-2mm. FLOWERS **1-2 in upper leaf axils,** white or pinkish (Dec-Feb). GENERAL: Used as a lucky charm. **Similar species:** *Crassula inanis* (*inanis* - empty) LEAVES 5-10×2-3mm (much smaller under water), **broader towards base.** FLOWERS **usually more than 3 in each leaf axil,** white (Nov-Mar).

Crassula natalensis bohobe-ba-setsomi, bohohoana (SS)

100-450mm tall. In damp and rocky places on grass slopes, on streambanks, up to 2250m. LEAVES **in basal rosette,** up to 100×30mm, **leaf sheaths 1-3(6)mm long.** FLOWERS small, **petals recurved, 2-3mm long,** tips without a distinct appendage, **white** or pink (Mar-Apr). GENERAL: Used in traditional medicine to treat sore throats and eyes.

Clematis brachiata

Ken Farnsworth

Heliophila alpina

Hilliard & Burtt

Crassula brachypetala

Pam Cooke

Simon Milliken

Clematis brachiata - fruit

Neil Crouch

Crassula dependens

Peter Linder

Neil Crouch

Crassula natans

Crassula natalensis

Crassula nudicaulis bohobe-ba-balisana, sekopo, selatsi, serelilenyana (SS) (*nudus* - naked; *caulis* - stem)

Succulent perennial, flowering stem up to 400mm tall. In rock crevices, on cliffs, up to 1800m. SW Cape to KZN. Stems slightly woody, ± branched. LEAVES **in basal cluster or rosette**, 50-80×6-15mm, green to yellowish brown, spreading, flat above, rounded beneath, narrowing to pointed tip. INFLORESCENCE elongate, stem leafless, flowers in groups, petals cream, 4-6mm long, tubular (Feb).

Crassula papillosa serelilenyane (SS) (papillosa - refers to 'bumpy' seed coat)

Densely branching and rooting herb. **Forms dense mats or cushions**, up to 200mm diam. On dripping cliffs and rock faces at edge of runnels, 2100-2925m. Cape to EMR. LEAVES 1.5-4×0.5-3mm, **tips rounded**. FLOWERS solitary, in leaf axils, 2-3 mm long, white (Dec-Apr). **Similar species: Crassula gemmifera** Tiny succulent herb. **Forms dense mats** in muddy or gritty places bordering streams and pools or in muddy patches over rock sheets, sometimes inundated, 1800-2800m. EMR endemic. Masses of threadlike stems. LEAVES 2×0.25mm. FLOWERS in masses, tiny, 1.5-3mm long, white-pink (Nov-Feb). GENERAL: Heavily grazed.

Crassula peploides [= C. galpinii] serelilenyana, setšosa-se-sefubelu (SS) (*peploides* - like a *Peplis*, Lythraceae)

Prostrate perennial herb. On seasonally wet gravel and silt patches over basalt sheets, sometimes inundated, 2300-2800m. E Cape to Limpopo Prov. LEAVES 5-15×2-3mm, green or red. FLOWERS starry, towards tips of branchlets, petals ±4mm long, white at tips, stamens red (Jan-Apr). GENERAL: Heavily grazed. A lotion made from the roots is used to bathe feverish or tired people.

Crassula sarcocaulis subsp. **rupicola** serelilenyane (SS); umadinsane (Z) (*sarkos* - flesh; *caulis* - stem; *rupicola* - favours rocks)

Succulent shrublet up to 600mm tall. In damp and partly shaded rock outcrops, rock falls and low cliffs, up to 2745m. **Branches up to 50mm diam, with peeling bark.** LEAVES **needlelike**, 8-15× 1-1.5mm. FLOWERS white, ±5mm long, white, cup-shaped, in small, round, terminal heads, unpleasantly scented (Nov-Mar). GENERAL: Used in traditional medicine as an emetic.

Crassula setulosa serelilienyana (SS) (*setulosa* - resembling fine bristles)

Perennial herb, flowering stems 30-150mm tall. Var. *setulosa*: Small mats of leaf rosettes, stems 60-150mm tall. On damp cliffs and rocks, up to 2440m. E Cape to Limpopo Prov. LEAVES 12-30×4-12mm, recurved, close set, hairy at least on margins. Flowering stems **leafy**. FLOWERS in small terminal clusters, petals white, ±4m long, **with distinct appendage**, recurved, pink in bud (Jan-Apr). Var. *rubra* [= var. *curta*] Small mats of leaf rosettes, stems 30-100mm tall. On damp cliffs, crevices and edges of rock sheets, under rock outcrops, overhangs and boulders, up to 3000m. E Cape to EMR. LEAVES up to 12×4mm, spreading in cup-shaped rosettes. Flowering stems leafless. FLOWER **petals with no distinct appendage, recurved** (Jan-Apr). GENERAL: Mixed with tobacco to improve it. Used as a charm for a child born after the death of an older child.

Crassula umbraticola (*umbraticola* - liking shade)

Dainty succulent herb, stems unbranched, 25-150mm high. On damp shady rock faces and on floor and walls of damp overhangs, 1400-2475m. EMR endemic. LEAVES in 2-4 pairs near top of stem, **blade 5-35mm wide, ± round, margins scalloped, narrowed to stalk up to 10mm long**. FLOWERS starry, white, in open inflorescence, petals up to 4mm long, **sharply pointed** (Dec-Feb).

ROSACEAE - Rose Family (see pg 130) **Rubus** (*ruber* - red, also the old Latin name for the plant) Prickly, mostly scrambling shrubs. Leaves simple or 3-5 foliolate. Fruits edible. Mostly N Hemisp, ±250 species, ±17 in SAfr, many of them introduced invasive plants, ±4 species in this region.

★Rubus cuneifolius American Bramble; Amerikanse Braam (A)

Erect to scrambling thorny shrub up to 2m tall. Invades grasslands, forest margins, up to 2000m. Introduced, from America. LEAVES paler beneath, 3 leaflets. FLOWERS **very large, white** (Nov-Dec). FRUITS black. GENERAL: Tasty fruits. A declared weed.

Crassula peploides   *Darren Webster*

Crassula papillosa   *Peter Linder*

Crassula umbraticola   *Martin von Fintel*

Rubus cuneifolius   *Neil Crouch*   *Pam Cooke*

Crassula nudicaulis   *Tony Abbott*

Crassula setulosa   *Lal Greene*

Crassula sarcocaulis subsp. *rupicola*   *Tony Abbott*

Crassula setulosa   *Martin von Fintel*

77

GERANIACEAE - Geranium Family (see pg 206, 236) *Geranium* (*geranos* - a crane) Annual or perennial herbs, shrubs. Flowers symmetrical, solitary. Attracts butterflies. Mainly temp, ±300 species, 31 in SAfr, ±11 in this region.

Geranium wakkerstroomianum White Geranium (from the Wakkerstroom area)

Straggling herb, stems up to 1m long. Often forming loose clumps, in damp sheltered places around rocks, on forest margins, in marshes, 1200-2500m. E Cape to Limpopo Prov. Covered with long, spreading hairs. LEAVES 25-60mm diam, 5-lobed, **lobes shallowly lobed**, lower leaf stalks ±300mm long. FLOWERS white, veined pink or red, petals **narrow, deeply notched**, ±7-17×2.5-5.5mm, stalks up to 65mm long (Oct-Mar). GENERAL: Often mistaken for *G. schlechteri* which has **pink petals**. (see pg 206)

Monsonia (named after Lady Anne Monson, 1714-76, known for her botanical knowledge) Glandular herbs. Flowers symmetrical, petals 5, stamens in 5 groups with 3 in each, 1 longer than others; ovary 5-lobed. Fruit beaked. Afr, SW Asia, ±40 species, ±20 in SAfr, ±5 in this region.

Monsonia attenuata malengoana (SS) (*attenuata* - narrowing to a point)

Slender, tufted, densely leafy perennial herb, 100-500mm tall. In grassland, on rocky mountainsides, up to 2285m. KZN to Limpopo Prov. Covered in long, glandular, **whitish hairs**. LEAVES alternate, **long, narrow**, 25-75×3-10mm, **folded upwards**, margins sharply, finely toothed, stalks slender, ±30mm long, often with a bend at base of blade. FLOWERS greyish white to creamy yellow, petals 20-30×9-20mm, margins wavy, tips square, toothed, strongly blue-grey **net-veined beneath** (Dec-Mar).

Pelargonium (*pelargos* - stork's beak, refers to fruit) (see pg 38)

Pelargonium bowkeri Carrot-leaved Pelargonium, Cat's Tail Pelargonium, Frilled Pelargonium; khoara (SS) (named after Henry Bowker, 1822-1900, naturalist and Cape colonial official)

Deciduous herb, flowering stem up to 350mm tall. In rocky grassland, below Cave Sandstone cliffs, up to 2200m. E Cape to KZN/Mpum. LEAVES 150-300×25-50mm, **finely dissected, feathery**, downy to shaggy hairy, stalks 60-130mm, **juvenile leaves simple**. FLOWER **petals fringed**, ±29×25mm, yellowish or creamy pink with purplish veins (Aug-Sep). GENERAL: Leaves eaten by children. Used in traditional medicine.

RHAMNACEAE - Buffalo-thorn Family Trees, shrubs, climbers, often spiny. Cosmop, trop regions, ±58 genera, ±900 species, 9 genera in SAfr. *Phylica* (probably a mis-spelling by Linnaeus, from phyllikos - leafy) Attracts butterflies. Afr, Madag, ±188 species in SAfr, 2 in this region.

Phylica thodei (named after Justus Thode, 1859-1932, pioneer plant collector in the Drakensberg)

Much branched, rigid small shrub, 200-600(900)mm tall. On Cave Sandstone sheets, on rock outcrops, 1800-2700m. EMR endemic. **Branchlets densely covered with spreading, silky hairs.** LEAVES crowded, 7-9mm long, spreading, margins rolled under, rough above, ± hairless, stalk ±1mm long. FLOWERS small, ±4mm long, in small terminal clusters, **sepals densely covered with woolly white hairs on outer surface** (Aug-May). FRUIT ±4mm diam, wrinkled, **dark red-brown**, hairy.

TILIACEAE - Jute/ Linden Family Often with fibrous bark, star-shaped hairs. Cosmop, 48 genera, 725 species, SAfr, 4 genera. *Sparrmannia* (named after Andrew Sparrman, 1748-1820, botanist, physician, ship's surgeon, pupil of Linnaeus) Afr, ±7 species, 2 in SAfr, 1 in this region.

Sparrmannia ricinocarpa Sparrmannia Bush; senkuruti (SS); isibundane (Z) (*ricinocarpa* - seed like the castor oil plant, *Ricinus*)

Coarse shrubby herb, up to 2m tall. On forest margins, in moist depressions, up to 1900m. E Cape to Ethiopia. LEAVES 3-7-lobed, 30-130×15-100mm, lobes tapering to pointed tip, margins toothed, roughly or softly hairy, stalks ±80mm long. FLOWERS creamy white, ±20mm diam (Dec-Mar). FRUIT ±20mm diam, **covered with long rigid bristles**, ±10mm long. GENERAL: Bark produces good fibre. Leaves eaten as spinach.

THYMELAEACEAE - Fibre-bark / Gonna Family (see pg 136) *Gnidia* (named after the Greek city, Knidos) (see pg 136)

Gnidia propinqua [= *Basutica propinqua*] (*propinqua* - 'close to', closely allied to *G. aberrans*) (see pg 136)

ONAGRACEAE - Evening Primrose Family Flowers with 4 petals, style 4-lobed. Cosmop, ±17 genera, ±674 species, 4 genera in SAfr (2 introduced & naturalised). *Epilobium* (*epi* - upon; *lobos* - pod, the ovary appears to be inferior and is elongated, looking like a fat stalk) Calyx lobes 4, tube prolonged above ovary. Fruit a capsule, seeds with tuft of hairs. Cosmop, except trop, ±185 species, 4 in SAfr, all in this region.

Epilobium salignum noha, noha-ea-loti (SS) (*salignum* - like the willow, refers to leaves)

Erect perennial herb, 0.2-1.6m tall. In marshy places, up to 2300m. Widespread. LEAVES ±20-80×3-20mm, held close to stems, finely hairy, margins faintly toothed, **tapering to both ends**. FLOWERS ±20mm diam, nodding at first, later erect, **white turning pink after pollination, stigma entire** (Jan-May). CAPSULE 30-70mm long, stalk 8-45mm. **Similar species:** *Epilobium capense* noha (SS) Up to 2650m. Stiffly hairy. LEAVES **broad at base, conspicuously veined**, margins coarsely toothed. FLOWERS ± erect, white, **stigma 4-lobed** (Dec-Feb). CAPSULE stalk 10-60mm long.

Geranium wakkerstroomianum

Lorraine van Hooff

Pelargonium bowkeri

Lal Greene

Monsonia attenuata

Martin von Fintel

Phylica thodei

Rob Scott-Shaw

Phylica thodei

Rodney Moffett

Gnidia propinqua

David McDonald

Sparrmannia ricinocarpa

Lal Greene

Epilobium capense

Lal Greene

Epilobium salignum

Jo Arkel

79

UMBELLIFERAE (APIACEAE) - **Carrot Family** Mostly herbs, a few small trees, usually aromatic; stems often with pith or hollow internodes. Leaves usually much divided, stalks sheathing at base. Flowers in flat-topped inflorescences; fruit carpels dry, often ribbed, winged, hairy or prickly. Economically important as food plants eg carrots, parsnips, celery, parsley and herbs aniseed, dill, chervil, fennel. Cosmop, ±453 genera, ±3750 species, 36 genera in SAfr. *Alepidea* (*a* - without; *lepis* - a scale) Perennial herbs; leaf margins bristle-tipped; flowerheads looking somewhat daisylike, with many tiny flowers surrounded by conspicuous petal-like bracts. Afr, ±28 species, mostly SAfr, ±14 in this region.

Alepidea amatymbica Giant Alepidea, Larger Tinsel Flowers; Kalmoes, Slangwortel (A); lesoko, lesooku (SS); iqwili (X); ikhathazo (X,Z) *(amatymbica* - after the amaThembu people)

Robust herb, up to 2m tall. In coarse growth, near streams, in damp gullies, up to 2600m. Cape to Zim. Stems strongly grooved, leafy throughout. LEAVES large, basal, ±250×90 m, stalks up to 250mm long, stem clasping, **not in rosette**, margins prominently toothed, each tooth ending in a bristle, stem leaves stalkless. INFLORESCENCE branched; FLOWERHEADS ±15mm diam, bracts 5, large, **unequal**, pale greenish-white (Jan-Mar). GENERAL: Used in traditional medicine to treat, for example, colds, coughs (the root is sucked for relief) and to wash divining bones.

Alepidea natalensis [= *A. baurii*]

Herb, flowering stem 100-200(550)mm tall. Common in short damp rocky grassland, on cliff ledges, up to 2400m. E Cape to KZN. **Flowering stems bare in upper parts**. LEAVES spreading flat, **in basal rosette**, 20-50×12-25mm, dark green, leathery, **margins toothed, with bristles**, stalks 15-25mm long, stem leaves few, distant. INFLORESCENCE branched; FLOWERHEADS ±15mm diam, bracts 5, equal, white, **tinged pinkish red** with age (Dec-Apr).

Alepidea pusilla (*pusilla* - very small, weak)

Dwarf herb, flowering stems 100-150mm tall. In marshy turf, 2100-3300m. EMR endemic. LEAVES in basal rosette, 8-15×4-7mm, **thick, stalks 20-40mm long**, margins bluntly toothed, **usually without bristles**. FLOWERHEADS white, 5 larger bracts oval, with prominent net veins, **tips rounded** (Jan-Feb).

Alepidea thodei lesokoana (SS) (named after Justus Thode, 1859-1932, pioneer plant collector in the Drakensberg)

Herb, flowering stems 200-300mm tall. In damp turf, at foot of cliffs, on steep slopes, 2400-3000m. EMR endemic. LEAVES mostly basal, with long marginal teeth, **bent backwards, stalks long**. FLOWERHEADS **large, showy**, ±30mm diam, bracts 10-15, irregular, **white, centre dark blue-black** (Jan-Apr).

Alepidea woodii [= *A. tysonii*] (after John Medley Wood, 1827-1915, botanist, founding curator of Natal Herbarium)

Slender herb, 250-600mm tall. On streambanks, steep damp grass slopes, 1800-2400m. KZN endemic. LEAVES papery, mostly in basal rosette, 70-100×1.5-40mm, margins with **fine even teeth at right angles to margins**, stalks long. FLOWERHEAD bracts greenish white above (Jan-Feb).

Conium (*koneion* - plant, and the poison derived from it 'Hemlock') Stout, erect herbs with parsniplike root. Leaves carrotlike, deeply divided, dissected, leaflets well spaced. Asia, Europe, Afr, ±6 species in SAfr, 1 introduced, 2 in this region.

Conium fontanum (*fontanum* - of the springs)

Biennial herb, 1-2m tall. Var. *fontanum* Stout biennial, **plants not particularly aromatic**. Often in big stands, in seepage lines, on marshy streambanks and damp ground at the foot of cliffs, always in open places, 1500-2400m. LEAVES in rosette in first year, stem leaves up to 300mm long, **ultimate leaf lobes broad and blunt**, stalks up to half the total leaf length. INFLORESCENCE branching; FLOWERS in round clusters, petals roundish, white, bracts white tinged green, bracteoles narrow, free to base (Nov-Jan). var. *alticola* (*alticola* - loving the heights) Coarse biennial herb, 0.2-1m tall; **strong unpleasant smell**. In damp places at the foot of basalt cliffs or wet ground on summit plateau, **2800-3200m**. LEAF **lobes narrow, sharply pointed**. FLOWERS (Dec-Mar).

Pimpinella (medieval name for anise, *P. anisum*) Herbs. Flowers in compound umbels. Cosmop, ±150 species, 7 in SAfr, 2 in this region.

Pimpinella caffra mohopu, sehoetjana (SS) (*caffra* - from Kaffraria, old name for E Cape)

Slender perennial herb, stems up to 450mm tall. In damp grassland, up to 2400m. Widespread. STEMS round, wiry, softly hairy. LEAVES few, entire, mostly basal, often missing when in flower, ±15-50mm long, thick, hairy, margins coarsely toothed, **stalks long, slender**, 50-190mm, **stem leaves finely divided**. INFLORESCENCE with 4-12 rays, finely hairy, stems sparingly branched; FLOWERS **white**, in rounded clusters (Feb-Mar). FRUIT flattish, black with greenish ribs when ripe. GENERAL: Used in traditional medicine to treat intestinal worms, and as a protective charm.

Alepidea amatymbica   *Hilliard & Burtt*   *Alepidea natalensis*   *Lal Greene*   *Alepidea woodii*   *Neil Crouch*

Alepidea amatymbica   *Hilliard & Burtt*   *Alepidea natalensis*   *Godfrey Symons*   *Alepidea woodii*   *Neil Crouch*

Alepidea thodei   *Hilliard & Burtt*

Alepidea pusilla   *David McDonald*

Alepidea thodei   *David McDonald*   *Pimpinella caffra*   *Lal Greene*   *Conium fontanum*   *David McDonald*

81

ERICACEAE - Erica / Heath Family Large or small shrubs, often on acid soils. Leaves usually small, firm, in whorls. Flowers with 4-5 petals, ±united into tube. Cultivated as ornamentals, Rhododendrons, Azaleas, Heather (*Erica*) and for fruits Blueberries and Cranberries. Cosmop, ±107 genera, ±3400 species, 20 genera in SAfr. *Erica* (*ereiko* - to rend, refers to the reputed ability of some species to break down gallstones) Leaves in whorls or 3-4, margins recurved. Flowers in terminal inflorescences or clustered in upper leaf axils. Hardy, attractive garden plants and cut-flowers. Mainly Afr, Europe, ±650 species, 600 in SAfr, mainly in SW Cape, ±30 in this region. **Sterile specimens can be mistaken for *Passerina* which has stringy bark, and *Cliffortia* which has alternate leaves, never in whorls of 3 or 4, and conspicuous stipules.**

Erica albospicata (*albo* - white, *spicata* - spike)

Shrublet 150-250mm tall. On steep grassy slopes (rarely on cliffs), up to 2700m. EMR endemic. STERMS simple, **in tufts**. LEAVES 4-9×0.75mm, **blunt-tipped**, 3-4 in congested clusters. FLOWERS white, densely clustered in leaf axils, forming terminal spikes, lobes ±4.5mm long, recurved, calyx lobes 4, ±4.5×1.7mm, white, margins glandular (Nov-Dec). GENERAL: Occasionally found growing as a small well-branched shrub with shorter leaves, ±3mm long, and flowers terminal on short side branchlets.

Erica caffrorum Mountain Heath; Bergboomheide (A)

Sprawling or prostrate shrub over rocks or a small tree, up to 2m tall. Very common, on rocky streamsides, boulder beds, cliffs, rock outcrops, bare patches on slopes, 1500-2300m. Main stem up to 150mm diam at base. LEAVES **in whorls of 4**, very small, 4-7×1mm, stiff, densely covering stems, **shiny bright green**. FLOWERS tiny but showy, white, ±5mm long, **calyx large, conspicuous, pink** (Oct-Mar). **Similar species: Similar species:** *Erica evansii* [= *Philippia evansii*] (named after Maurice Evans, 1854-1920, businessman, politician and pioneer plant collector in the Drakensberg) Shrub 1-2.4m tall. Common along rocky streams, on boulder beds, on steep moist slopes, below Cave Sandstone cliffs, on forest margins, 1800-2300m. KZN to Zim. Twigs **sticky to touch**. LEAVES 1.5-2mm, light green. FLOWERS tiny, white, soon turning brown (Oct-Dec). GENERAL: Browsed by game.

Erica drakensbergensis Drakensberg Erica; Drakensbergheide (A); chalebeke-e-kholo (SS)

Erect shrub, 300-600(900)mm tall. Much branched, forming a spreading shrub or almost treelike. In small colonies, on rocky, grassy, north facing slopes, frequently immediately above Cave Sandstone cliffs, usually in moist places, 1200-2000m. E Cape to Mpum. Stems woody, twisted, bark rough dark grey, flaking, upper branches slender, wiry, new growth softly hairy. LEAVES needlelike, 3-4×1mm long, erect, overlapping. FLOWERS small, bell-shaped, **white**, 3-4.5mm long, in clusters, **brown style prominently protrudes** (Mar-Jul). GENERAL: Lovely in bloom, the pure white flowers show up against the bright green leaves.

Erica flanaganii (named after Henry Flanagan, E Cape naturalist and plant collector, one of the first people to collect plants in the high N Drakensberg)

Stout, rigid, erect, branched shrub, 600-900mm tall. Up to 2430m. EMR endemic. Branches densely leafy, softly hairy. LEAVES erect, crowded, in 4s, 8-10mm long. FLOWERS in 4s, white, 8mm long, softly hairy (Dec).

Erica frigida khoarai (SS) (*frigida* - refers to its liking for high altitudes)

Small, dense shrublet, up to 500mm tall or in mats. Frequent on cliffs and very steep slopes, 1900-3300m. Branches slender, straggling, hairy. LEAVES ± recurved, covered in long hairs, spreading at right angles to stem. FLOWERS **sticky**, often **white**, sometimes **pink** (red) (Nov-Feb).

Erica thodei (named after Justus Thode, 1859-1932, pioneer plant collector in the Drakensberg)

Dwarf, spreading shrublet up to 300mm tall. Forms dense mats and cushions, on damp rock sheets, cliffs and steep rocky slopes, 1900-3300m. EMR endemic. Branches rigid, softly hairy, leafy above, covered with scars. LEAVES in 3s, ±4mm long including stalk, spreading, overlapping, thick, keeled, hairless, shiny. FLOWERS ±4mm long, bell-shaped, **white**, pink, sepals sometimes reddish (Dec-Apr).

Erica caffrorum

Erica caffrorum

Neil Crouch

Erica albospicata

Neil Crouch

Erica thodei

Darrel Plowes

Erica drakensbergensis

J C Nel

Erica drakensbergensis

Hilliard & Burtt

Erica flanaganii

Peter Linder

Erica flanaganii

Peter Linder

Erica frigida

David McDonald

83

PRIMULACEAE - Primrose or Primula Family Mostly N temp, ±22 genera, ±825 species, 3 genera in SAfr. *Anagallis* (*anagelao* - Greek name for Pimpernel plant) Flowers on long stalks. Capsule within persistent calyx. Mainly W Europe, Afr ±30 species, 4 in SAfr, 1 in this region.

Anagallis huttonii **White Pimpernel** (named after Caroline Hutton who collected in the 1800s with her husband, an army officer)

Creeping herb, stems up to 600mm long. In wet places, in slow moving water, up to 2600m. Stems rarely branched, 4-angled. LEAVES ±30mm diam, opposite, spreading, narrowing to short stalks. FLOWERS ±8mm, **white** or pale pink (Nov-Feb). FRUIT a dry capsule, splitting open like a lid, seeds winged.

BUDDLEJACEAE - Buddleja Family Cultivated for ornamentals such as *Buddleja*. Trop to temp, 8 genera, ±120 species, 3 genera in SAfr, ±1 species. *Gomphostigma* (*gomphos* - a club, refers to club-shaped stigma) Silvery hairy shrublets. Afr, 2 species, both in SAfr, 1 in this region.

Gomphostigma virgatum **River Stars; Besembossie, Otterbossie (A); koete-le-boima, moema-thata, moluku (SS); isepha kanonkala, umsola (X)** (*virgatum* - willowy twigs)

Silvery slender shrub, 1-2m tall. In rocky streambeds, often in fast flowing water, 1370-2250m. E Cape to Zim. LEAVES opposite, 10-60×2-5mm, covered in silvery hairs (or hairless), stalkless, with **connecting ridge**. INFLORESCENCES terminal; FLOWERS **white**, ±12mm diam, anthers with purple margins, scented (Dec-Mar). GENERAL: Used in traditional medicine. A popular garden plant.

GENTIANACEAE - Gentian Family (see pg 140) *Sebaea* (see pg 140)

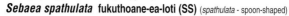

Sebaea spathulata **fukuthoane-ea-loti (SS)** (*spathulata* - spoon-shaped)

Perennial herb, up to 600mm tall. On damp, grassy slopes, in shade of shrubs and boulder, on streambanks, 1950-3200m. EMR endemic. LEAVES in basal rosette, size variable, up to 140×20mm, fleshy, stem leaves smaller. INFLORESCENCE compact; FLOWERS **white**, 10-15mm diam, tube ±10mm, **anthers with conspicuous dark apical glands, sweetly scented** (Oct-Dec).

Sebaea thodeana **marama-a-baroetsana-a-mamasoeu (SS)** (named after Justus Thode, 1859-1932, pioneer plant collector in the Drakensberg)

Low growing herb, flowering stems up to 150mm tall. Forms small mats, in marshy turf on the summit or on damp cliffs, 2100-3000m. EMR endemic. LEAVES up to 40×15mm, crowded towards base. INFLORESCENCE with 1 to several few flowered clusters; FLOWERS white or yellow, tube short, 6-7mm long, petal lobes ±7×4mm, **tips rounded, apical anther gland conspicuous dark red-brown or black** (Nov-Dec).

ASCLEPIADACEAE - Milkweed Family (see pg 140) *Schizoglossum* (*schizo* - cut or split; *glossa* - tongue, refers to the corona lobe which is often split into 2 or more parts) Perennial geophytic herbs. Stems annual from small carrotlike tuber, erect, usually solitary, with milky latex. Flowers lobed to base, corona lobes scalelike and with appendages, often complex, pollinia pendulous, attached at their sides to the translators, with clear apex. Ffruit spindle-shaped, tip beaked, covered with long usually recurved bristles. Afr, ±80 species, 27 in SAfr, ±9 in this region.

Schizoglossum elingue **White or Purple Schizoglossum** (*e* - lacking; *lingua* - tongue, refers to the simple appendage-free corona lobes)

Erect herb, 100-280mm tall. EMR endemic. Stems usually unbranched. LEAVES 35-45×7-15mm, ± lobed at base. FLOWERS in small clusters, **lobes flat, erect, 8-10**×4mm, corona white, 4-5mm, **simple**, no appendages on inner face, **anther appendages inconspicuous** (Nov-Jan). GENERAL: Subsp. *elingue*, in rocky grassland, 1980-2750m; FLOWERS **white**. Subsp. *purpureum*, in damp grassy valley bottoms, 1800-2000m; FLOWERS **pink to purple**.

Schizoglossum hilliardiae **Hilliard's Schizoglosum** (named after Olive Hilliard who has collected widely and published much work on SAfr flora)

Erect herb, 90-350mm tall. On grassy slopes, 1800-2670m. EMR endemic. Stems, if branched, then from base. LEAVES 27-46×6-26mm. FLOWERS in small clusters, lobes 5.5-7.5×3mm, flat, hairless outside, **white striped brown inside**, corona ± equal to the style tip, anther appendages **dull purple**, inconspicuous (Dec-Feb).

Fanninia (named after George Fannin, 1832-1865, botanical collector who farmed in the Dargle, KZN) Small geophytic herbs. Inflorescence terminal on long stalks; flowers large, lobes free to base, hairy, corona lobes simple; pollinia pendulous. Single species genus, SA endemic.

Fanninia caloglossa **Fannin's Beauty** (*calos* - beautiful; *glossa* - tongue)

Small, delicate herb, 100-250mm tall. In grassland, up to 2100m. E Cape, KZN. Stems usually unbranched, covered in white hairs. LEAVES 25-60×4-25mm, hairy. FLOWERS (1)4-6, corolla lobes whitish to pink, 11-14.5×4.5-7mm, **with long white hairs outside**, especially at incurved tips, hairless inside, corona lobes conspicuous, reddish purple (Nov-Jan). FRUIT not known. GENERAL: Pollinated by beetles.

84

Gomphostigma virgatum

Lal Greene

Schizoglossum hilliardiae

Martin von Fintel

Anagallis huttonii

Lal Greene

Fanninia caloglossa

Rodney Moffett

Schizoglossum elingue

Rosemary Williams

Sebaea thodeana

Martin von Fintel

Sebaea spathulata

Martin von Fintel

Sebaea spathulata

Neil Crouch

85

Asclepias (named after the Greek doctor *Aesculapius* who was immortalised in ancient mythology as a god of medicine) (see pg 216, 268)

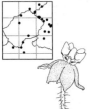

Asclepias multicaulis Doily Cartwheel; Melkbossie (A); lekhoaphela, lenkiling (SS); isikhonde, isiphofu (Z) (*multi* - many; *caulis* - stems)

Compact, prostrate herb, stems 100-200mm long. In sparse grassland, in well drained soils, 1200-2200m. E Cape to Mpum. STEMS **much forked, radiating from central point.** LEAVES held **flat on the ground,** 6-22×3-8mm, harshly hairy, veins prominent below. INFLORESCENCES solitary, erect, stems 13-60mm long; FLOWERS **all held at the same level,** 4×3mm, corona lobes square, compressed sideways, scent sickly sweet (Oct-Dec). GENERAL: Eaten raw or cooked. Sotho name means 'he who draws his legs together when sitting on the ground', refers to crowded, forking stems.

Riocreuxia (named after French botanical artist Alfred Riocreux, 1820-1912) Perennial herbs, usually twining. Leaves heart-shaped. Inflorescences much branched, corolla and corona similar to *Ceropegia*, pollinia clear at tips. Afr, 10 species, 8 in SAfr, 1 in this region.

Riocreuxia torulosa [= *R. torulosa* var. *tomentosa*] Candle-vine; Kandelaarblom (A); morarana-oamoru (SS); ugwapha, unquntane, ushuqu, ushuwa (Z) (*torulosus* - cylindrical with bulges at intervals)

Tangled vine, up to 5m. On forest margins, up to 1800m. E Cape to Limpopo Prov. LEAVES **heart-shaped,** 30-130×17-95mm, stalks 12-65mm. INFLORESCENCES 1-3 at nodes; FLOWERS creamy white, pale yellow, speckled purple, **tubular, with slightly inflated base,** 12-18mm long, **corolla lobes joined at tips to form a cage,** honey scented (Oct-Apr). FRUITS long, thin, paired, 75-180×3mm, tapering to slender beak.

BORAGINACEAE - Forget-me-not or Borage Family Herbs, shrubs or trees. Flowers often in 1-sided inflorescences, curled like a shepherd's crook. Ornamental, including herbs borage and comfrey. Widely distributed, ±131 genera, ±2500 species, 17 genera in SAfr (4 exotic). *Cynoglossum* (*kyon* - dog; *glossa* - tongue) Fruit covered in small hooked spines. Temp, subtrop. ±75 species, ±8 in SAfr, 6 in this region.

Cynoglossum spelaeum [= *C. basuticum*] bohomenyana, motlempe, motle-pere (SS)

Perennial, well branched, leafy herb, up to 1m tall. Sprawling among rocks at mouth of Cave Sandstone overhangs, along base of cliffs, 1700-2300m. EMR endemic. LEAVES large, up to 400×50mm, **softly hairy,** in **persistent central rosette,** stem leaves smaller. INFLORESCENCE large, branching; FLOWERS **white,** 4-5mm long, stalks short, **up to 20mm long in fruit** (Jan-Mar). NUTLETS ±5×4mm, more or less pearshaped, hooked spines mainly on lower surface, hairs with bulbous baseon upper.

Afrotysonia (African *Tysonia*) Tall herbs. Basal leaves very large. Petal lobes reflexed, anthers exserted. Afr 3 species, 2 in SAfr 1 in this region.

Afrotysonia glochidiata [= *Tysonia glochidiata*] (*gloch* - projecting point; refers to nutlets)

Erect herb, up to 1.5m tall. In moist areas, up to 2000m. EMR endemic. LEAVES **basal, large, elegant,** 140-230×65-130mm, **rough, grey-green,** stalks 260-300mm. INFLORESCENCE widely branched, 100-260mm; FLOWERS 4-6.5mm, white or creamy, tube flushed mauvish (Dec-Mar). NUTLETS ±9×10mm, covered in small bristles.

Lithospermum (*lithos* - stone; *sperma* - seed) Perennial herbs. Leaves rough hairy. Mostly temp areas, ±45 species, ±9 in SAfr, 2 in this region.

Lithospermum afromontanum (*afromontanum* - from African mountains)

Straggling, leafy, perennial herb, up to 2m tall. In scrub on margins of forest, up to 1980m. EMR endemic. LEAVES 30-55×5-12mm, scabrid, paler beneath. INFLORESCENCE small, loose; FLOWERS dull pale yellow to white, tube short, 4-7mm, petals rounded (Dec-Jan). NUTLETS roundish, whitish, shiny.

Lithospermum papillosum (*papillosum* - warty or soft protruberances)

Tufted perennial herb, up to 400mm tall. In grassland, 1525-2500m. S Cape to EMR. Stems slender, slightly branched. LEAVES closely spaced, up to 25×8mm, bristly hairy, stalkless. FLOWERS ±4mm, **white to blue,** hidden among densely leafy tips of shoots (Oct-Jan). NUTLETS smooth, shiny.

LABIATAE / LAMIACEAE - Sage/Mint Family Aromatic herbs or shrublets. Stems usually 4-angled. Leaves opposite, each pair at right angles to the next. Flowers 2-lipped. Economically valuable for aromatic essential oils, herbs and ornamentals such as Salvia. Cosmop, ±252 genera, ±6700 species, ±37 genera in SAfr. *Stachys* (Greek for spike, originally an ear of wheat) Flowers in clusters, usually hairy, tube narrow, upper lip erect or arched, sometimes notched, lower lip longer, 3-lobed, spreading. Cosmop, ±300 species, ±42 species in SAfr, ±10 in this region.

Stachys aethiopica African Stachys, Wild Sage; Katpisbossie (A); bokhatha, bolao-balitaola, likhobe-tsa-balisana (SS) (*aethiopica* - from Africa)

Aromatic, perennial herb, up to 600mm tall. In grassland, up to 2300m. W Cape to Swaz. LEAVES 8-35×6-15mm, margins toothed, **stalks short, ±10mm long.** INFLORESCENCE lengthening with age, **flowers in clusters of 3-6, fairly close set, lowest in axils of leaflike bracts,** ±13mm long, white, calyx shaggy hairy, lobes pointed (Oct-May). GENERAL: Visited by honey-bees. Used in traditional medicine. Attractive groundcover.

Asclepias multicaulis

Ashley Nicholas

Asclepias multicaulis

Wally Menne

Cynoglossum spelaeum

Peter Linder

Afrotysonia glochidiata

David McDonald

Riocreuxia torulosa

Martin von Fintel

Lithospermum afromontanum

Tony Abbott

Afrotysonia glochidiata

Rosemary Williams

Lithospermum afromontanum

Tony Abbott

Stachys aethiopica

Wally Menne

Lithospermum papillosum

Lal Greene

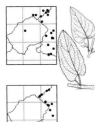

Stachys grandifolia (grandis - large, folia - leaves)

Straggling, much branched, perennial herb, 0.3-1m tall. On forest margins, along mountain streams, up to 2100m. E Cape to Mpum. Stems softly hairy. LEAVES 35-80×28-65mm, thinly, softly hairy above, ± grey velvety beneath, margins finely toothed, **stalks 15-45mm long.** INFLORESCENCE usually unbranched, flower clusters widely spaced; FLOWERS white with mauve spots on lower lip, tube 7-11mm long straight, calyx softly hairy (Dec-Apr). GENERAL: Flowers visited by bees and other insects. **Similar species:** *Stachys kuntzei* (named after Carl Kuntz, 1843-1907) **Upper leaves stalkless.** INFLORESCENCE covered in glandular hairs, flower clusters ± closely spaced, **bracts broad, leaflike at base,** reduced upwards; FLOWERS 7-9mm long, white to pink, **calyx lobes spine-tipped,** densely glandular hairy.

Pycnostachys (pyknos - dense; stachys - a spike) Perennial herbs or soft shrubs. Flowers in dense terminal spikes, lower lip large, boat-shaped, calyx with 5 rigid lobes. Afr, Madag, ±37 species, 3 in SAfr, 1 in this region.

Pycnostachys reticulata — Slender Pycnostachys, Blue Soldier; uhlalwane, umvuthuza (Z) (reticulata - network, refers to veins)

Erect, perennial herb, 0.2-1.2m. **In marshy places,** up to 1980m. E Cape to Tanz. Stems sparsely branched, softly woody below, downy throughout. LEAVES 40-110 ×8-30mm, margins toothed, stalks very short. INFLORESCENCE dense, ±50×20mm; FLOWERS pale to deep blue or mauve, 8-18mm long, calyx purplish red, with 5 spikelike lobes (Mar-Apr). GENERAL: Used as a mouthwash. Grown from seed.

Plectranthus (plektron - a spur; anthos - flower, refers to base of flower tube) Herbs or shrubs, often fleshy. Flower clusters in spikelike inflorescences. Attract butterflies. Afr, Arabia, India, Austr, ±300 species, ±45 in SAfr, mostly endemic to the area east of the Drakensberg plateau.

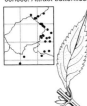

Plectranthus calycinus [= Rabdosiella calycina] Upland Fly Bush; Spoorblom (A) (calycinus - in the form of a calyx)

Coarse herb or soft shrub, up to 1.5m tall. In grassland, rocky places, up to 1950m. E Cape to Limpopo Prov. Stems annual, hairy. LEAVES 40-100×20-45mm, leathery, rough to hairless above, hairless to densely velvety beneath with orange gland dots, margins toothed, stalk very short. INFLORESCENCE **dense, branched, leafy,** 100-300mm long; FLOWERS creamy with lip tipped purple, 8-11mm long, hairy (Feb-Apr). GENERAL: Strongly scented. Attractive hardy garden plant.

Plectranthus grallatus Tuberous Spur-flower; Knolspoorsalie (A); umnyama-wempunzi (Z) (grallatus - stems rodlike, stilted)

Soft wooded shrub, 0.4-1.5m tall. On damp forest floor, in shelter of big rocks, along streamsides, 1340-2000m. E Cape to Mpum. Stems annual, brittle, fleshy. LEAVES 50-160×35-140mm, smooth or rough, **reddish brown gland dots beneath,** margins irregularly toothed with small teeth between, stalks 20-100mm long. INFLORESCENCE branched; FLOWERS 9-13mm, **white** flushed pink, a few spots on upper lip (Nov Feb).

Becium (ancient name for sage) Slightly woody herbs. Attracts Blues butterflies. Mainly Afr, Arabia, India, ±33 species, ±4 in SAfr, 1 in this region.

Becium obovatum [= B. grandiflorum] Cat's Whiskers; Katsnor (a); idada, iziba, ufukuzela, umathanjane (Z) (obovatum - egg-shaped, attached at the narrow end)

Herb, up to 300mm tall. In grassland, up to 1675m. E Cape to Bots. LEAVES 15-40 ×5-20mm, margins entire or with few shallow teeth. FLOWERS 10-17mm, white to pale mauve, **upper lip frilly** with violet lines, stamens protruding, calyx enlarging to 10mm in fruit (Sep-Feb). GENERAL: Used in traditional medicine and as a hair restorer.

SOLANACEAE - Tomato/Potato/Tobacco Family Herbs, shrubs, rarely climbers, trees, often spiny. Petals united. Fruit a berry. Economically important for food plants such as the potato, tomato, for tobacco, drugs and ornamentals. Subcosmop, ±90 genera, ±2600 species, 9 genera in SAfr, 5 of them exotic. *Solanum* (Latin name for'Nightshade') Flowers in clusters. Trop, ±1400, ±25 in SAfr, ±15 introduced weeds.

Solanum retroflexum Sobosobo Berry; Nastergal (A); limomonyane, lintšontšo, mofukuthoane (SS); umsobo wesinja (X); ugqumugqumu, umsobosobo (Z) (retroflexum - turned back, refers to petals)

Slender bushy herb, up to 700mm tall. In damp, partly shaded places, on cliffs, rock outcrops, up to 2000m. Widespread. LEAVES ±50×20mm, margins coarsely toothed or shallowly lobed. FLOWERS ±16mm diam, white, **petals, calyx lobes reflexed** (Jan-Feb). FRUIT black, ±8mm diam. GENERAL: Browsed by bushbuck. Fruits eaten by people and animals, considered poisonous when green. A delicious preserve is made from the fruits. Leaves used as a pot herb or relish. Used in traditional medicine.

Plectranthus grallatus   *Stachys grandifolia*   *Stachys kuntzei*

Plectranthus calycina   *Plectranthus calycina*   *Stachys kuntzei*

Becium obovatum

Pycnostachys reticulata   *Solanum retroflexum*

89

SCROPHULARIACEAE - Snapdragon Family Annual or perennial herbs, shrubs, some parasitic. Flowers often 2-lipped, sometimes with pouches or spurs. Famous for the drug plants Digitalis (foxgloves) and ornamentals such as snapdragons, veronicas. Cosmop, especially temp and trop mountains, ±290 genera, ±4500 species, 80 genera in SAfr. *Nemesia* (*Nemesion*, name used by Dioscorides for a similar plant) Flower tube short **with single spur**, with or without bosses in mouth of spur (seen as inverted bumps on underside of tube), upper lip 4-lobed, lower entire or slightly notched; fruit flattened, halves boat-shaped, seeds winged. SAfr endemic genus, ±65 species, 60 in SAfr, ±6 in this region.

Nemesia silvatica White Forest-Nemesia (*silvatica* - from forest)

Bushy herb, up to 1m tall. In rocky places **in forest, on forest margins**, up to 1950m. E Cape to KZN. LEAVES 20-70×10-35mm, margins toothed, stalks 5-20mm long. INFLORESCENCE leafy, branched, **becoming long and slender in fruit**; FLOWERS large, ±20mm, **white**, 2 bosses inside mouth tinged yellow, **spur 6-9mm long** (Oct-Apr).

Diclis (*diclis* - double folding, a reference to bilobed spur) Annual or perennial herbs. Leaves opposite. Flowers in axils, tube short, spur 2-lobed. Fruit a capsule. Afr, Madag, ±10 species, ±4 in SAfr, 2 in this region.

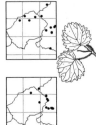

Diclis reptans Dwarf Snapdragon; koenana, leanya-poli, ponye (SS); isinama (Z) (*reptans* - creeping and rooting)

Sprawling, mat forming herb, stems up to 200mm long. **In damp, shady places, among rocks**, up to 2000m. S Cape to Limpopo Prov. Stems reddish, hairy, **tips erect**. LEAVES ±30×35mm, **margins deeply, sharply toothed**, stalks long, ±25mm. FLOWERS solitary in leaf axils, stalks long, white with violet spots, palate yellow, spur slender, violet, calyx lobes pointed, **upper lobe narrow** (Oct-Feb). GENERAL: Edible. Used in traditional medicine to treat distemper in dogs. **Similar species: *Diclis rotundifolia* koenana, leanya-poli, ponye (SS)**(*rotundifolia* - round leaves) **Completely prostrate herb. On bare ground in grassland**, up to 3200m. E Cape to NW. LEAVES less toothed. FLOWER spur shorter and broader, calyx **upper lobe oval** (Sep-Mar).

Manulea (*manus* - a hand, refers to 5 spreading corolla lobes) Annual or perennial herbs; rarely shrubby. Leaves mostly clustered at base. Flowers in clusters in long inflorescences. Fruit a capsule. Afr. Mostly S Afr, ±74 species, ±6 in this region.

Manulea florifera (*florifera* - bearing many flowers)

Perennial herb, up to 1m tall. On damp, open grassy slopes, 1500-2100m. EMR endemic. Stems hairy, **unbranched below the inflorescence**. LEAVES mostly basal, 80-200×13-25mm, margins obscurely toothed or entire, upper leaves smaller, more distant. INFLORESCENCE **large, branched**, up to 200mm long; FLOWERS small, **in congested clusters**, white (tube yellow at base) or mauve (tube purplish) (Dec-Mar).

Jamesbrittenia (named after James Britten, 1846-1924, Keeper of Botany at British Museum of Natural History, editor of Journal of Botany) **Stamens hidden** inside corolla tube. Differs from *Sutera* which has stamens protruding. Mostly Afr, 83 species, 74 in S Afr, ±8 in this region.

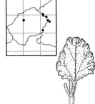

Jamesbrittenia dentatisepala [= *Sutera dentatisepala*] (*dentatus* - toothed; *sepala* - sepals)

Perennial **dwarf shrublet**, stems 150-260mm long, reclining or erect. In gritty patches in stream gullies, 1980-3000m. EMR endemic. LEAVES opposite, 8-22 ×6-15mm, grey-green, abruptly narrowed to a stalk, margins with rounded or pointed teeth, shallow lobes, glandular hairy. FLOWERS solitary in upper leaf axils on short stalks, 10-15mm wide, **white with conspicuous orange-brown markings** in centre (Jul-Dec-Jan). GENERAL: Leaves have a foetid smell when crushed. Flowers have an orange centre, a feature shared with *Zaluzianskya ovata* which, with *Z. chrysops* is found in the same area which suggests a common pollinator.

Jamesbrittenia lesutica (*lesutica* - named after Lesotho)

Rigid, much branched, rounded shrublet, up to 1m tall. EMR endemic. On rocky ledges and slopes, at about 2400m. Stems slender, erect, leafy, covered in large glistening glands. LEAVES 10-15×4-7mm, deeply lobed into 4-7 pairs of lobes, tapering to a broad stalk. FLOWERS solitary in upper leaf axils, **white**, ±15mm wide, **wedge-shaped, deeply notched, tube long**, ±20mm (Dec-Mar).

Sutera (after Johan Suter, 1766-1827, Swiss botanist, physician, prof of Greek & Philosophy) **Stamens protrude**. SAfr, ±47 species, ±4 in this region.

Sutera floribunda Kerriebos (A); boluma (SS); usikisiki lwehlathi (Z) (*floribunda* - flowering abundantly)

Much branched, aromatic, perennial herb, stems up to 1m long. On grassy slopes in shelter of rocks, along rocky steambanks, in boulder beds, up to 2600m. E Cape to Zim. Stems softly hairy. LEAVES 10-40×10-30mm, margins toothed, **narrowing abruptly to short stalks**. INFLORESCENCE **large, leafy, branching, branchlets opposite**; FLOWERS in profusion, ±12mm wide, white, pollen yellow, **stalks slender**, ±10mm (Jan-May). GENERAL: Used in traditional medicine. Grown from cuttings.

Nemesia silvatica

Martin von Fintel

Nemesia silvatica

Martin von Fintel

Diclis reptans

Wally Menne

Manulea florifera

Martin von Fintel

Manulea florifera

Lal Greene

Jamesbrittenia lesutica

Martin von Fintel

Diclis rotundifolia

Lal Greene

Jamesbrittenia dentatisepala

Rod Saunders

Jamesbrittenia lesutica

Mike Hirst

Sutera floribunda

Martin von Fintel

91

Glekia (name derived from the initials of G.L.E. Krebs who first sent the plant to Europe) - Monotypic genus, EMR endemic.

Glekia krebsiana

Twiggy shrublet, 230-600mm tall. Forms cushions on bare cliffs and rocky mountain sides, 1200-2150m. EMR endemic. LEAVES 6-36×2.5x14mm, thick, glandular, margins finely toothed, gradually narrowed to a very short stalk. INFLORESCENCE terminal, flowers forming crowded clusters 20-40mm long; FLOWERS 6-14mm wide, tube 7-13mm long, white inside with an orange patch at base of lip, **heavily bearded around mouth**, each petal with a blue-purple patch outside, fading brown (May-Oct).

Zaluzianskya (named after Adam Zalusiansky von Zaluzian, 1558-1613, physician and botanist from Prague) Annual or perennial herbs. Flowers in leaf axils or terminal inflorescences; flower tube elongate, cylindric with 5 lobes, regular or 2-lipped, usually white above, red below in this region. Fruit a capsule. Afr, ±55 species, 53 in SAfr, ±13 in this region.

Zaluzianskya chrysops (chrysops - golden eye)

Small herb, stems 35-150mm long. In damp bare areas, boulder beds, gravelly places, exposed scree slopes, 1980-3000m. EMR endemic. Stems solitary to branching, **hairs coarse, white, spreading downwards.** LEAVES **in crowded basal rosette,** 10-40×5-15mm, thinly hairy. FLOWERS ±15mm diam, in **few flowered spike,** white with **bright orange 'eye',** dark red outside, tube 30-43mm long, opens at dusk (Oct-Dec).

Zaluzianskya crocea (crocea - saffron-coloured)

Annual herb, stems 30-120mm long, erect at first, then reclining. In damp gravelly patches around bare rock sheets, 1920-2600m. EMR endemic. Stems leafy, simple or sparingly branched, coarsely hairy. LEAVES 7-25×3-10mm, tips pointed, upper margins with 2-3 pairs teeth, thinly hairy. FLOWERS 6-8mm diam, in dense terminal spikes, **white fading to pinkish mauve,** 'star' around mouth **yellow,** fading to orange red, lobes coppery orange below, tube 18-32mm long, **open in sunshine** (Dec-Apr).

Zaluzianskya microsiphon Short-tubed Drumsticks; Kortbuis-Zaluzianskya (A); malithungthung (SS) (microsiphon - small tube)

Perennial herb, up to 400mm tall. In rocky grassland, 1525-2745m. Stems 1-3, with shaggy white hairs. LEAVES **in basal rosette,** 35-90×8-20mm, stem leaves overlapping, 20-65mm long, margins entire to faintly toothed, ± hairy on margins and midrib. INFLORESCENCE **dense, long;** COROLLA LIMB **held vertically, 2 lobes up, 3 down,** tube 20-40mm long, lobes deeply notched, white inside, pinkish red outside, **open in full sun** (Dec-Apr). GENERAL: Flower size variable, tube short in some areas.

Zaluzianskya oreophila (oreophila - mountain-loving)

Annual herb, 100-250mm tall. In damp, rough grassland, silty loam, 2285-3200m. EMR endemic. Stems with **white hairs, leafy.** LEAVES 15-40×2-5mm margins coarsely toothed, thinly hairy beneath. INFLORESCENCE elongating; COROLLA LIMB held vertically, lobes 4-5mm long, white, hairless inside, red, glandular hairy outside, mouth with circlet of hairs, tube 17-30mm long, opens at dusk (Dec-Jan).

Zaluzianskya ovata [= Z. montana] lebohlollo, letaabe, theleli, theleli-ea-loti (SS) (ovata - egg-shaped)

Aromatic, twiggy, **leafy shrublet, stems well branched,** up to 450mm long. **In damp shady places,** on bare silty or gravelly patches (at very high altitudes), 1950-3230m in this region. Cape mountains to KZN. Stems with **spreading white hairs.** LEAVES 15-60×4-35mm, base wedge-shaped, margins irregularly toothed or lobed. INFLORESCENCE **compact, few flowered;** COROLLA LIMB held horizontally, ±22mm diam, white inside, pinkish red outside, sometimes with brilliant round orange 'eye', tube 30-58mm long, opening at dusk (Oct-Jan). **Similar species:** *Zaluzianskya distans* (distans - far apart) Tufted herb, **stems leafy, mostly unbranched.** Under scrub, boulders, 1765-2200m. LEAVES 20-60×9-30mm. INFLORESCENCE **elongating;** FLOWERS **widely spaced,** sometimes with pale yellow 'eye' (Dec-Mar).

Zaluzianskya pulvinata (pulvinus - little cushion, refers to the cushions of leaf rosettes)

Cushion forming perennial herb, up to 30-100(150-300)mm tall. On bare stony places, around rock sheets or rock outcrops, 1550-3000m. E Cape to Mpum. LEAVES **in small rosettes,** 10-25×1-5mm, **thick,** variable. INFLORESCENCE crowded; COROLLA LIMB **held horizontally,** ±16mm diam, lobes deeply notched, white inside, red outside, tube 30-50mm long, opens at dusk, in dull light, sweetly scented (Oct-Jan).

Glekia krebsiana

Mike Hirst

Zaluzianskya chrysops

Hilliard & Burtt

Zaluzianskya crocea

Hilliard & Burtt

Zaluzianskya ovata

Hilliard & Burtt

Zaluzianskya pulvinata

Peter Linder

Zaluzianskya pulvinata

Peter Linder

Zaluzianskya microsiphon

David McDonald

Zaluzianskya microsiphon

Tom De Waal

Zaluzianskya oreophila

Mike Hirst

93

Zaluzianskya turritella (turritella - a tower, refers to the habit of the plant)

Diminutive annual herb, 25-100mm tall. In basalt gravel and silt, 2940-3300m. EMR endemic. Stems simple or with 2-6 branches from base, with **spreading glandular hairs**, closely leafy. LEAVES 8-20×5-15mm, **thick, fleshy**, aromatic, dark green above, purple beneath. FLOWERS in short crowded spike, **bracts mostly larger than leaves, increasing in size upwards**; COROLLA LIMB held horizontally, white inside, mouth bearded, dark red outside, tube 21-27mm long, opening at dusk (Jan).

Glumicalyx (gluma - husk or glume (of grass), calyx) see pg (42)

Glumicalyx montanus

Small, tufted perennial herb, 150-300mm tall. Gritty or gravelly places on rock sheets or in boulder beds of streams, 2350-3200m. EMR endemic. Stems finely hairy, leafy. LEAVES 5-20 x 2-8mm, **leathery**, margins toothd. INFLORESCENCE, **small, roundish**, up to 15mm diam; FLOWERS 4-5mm diam, lobes oblong, **creamy to pale yellow, tube short, 4-6mm long**, stamens all exserted (Dec-Mar).

Limosella (limosus - muddy; ella - diminutive) Marsh or aquatic herbs, usually creeping, rooting at nodes. Leaves usually in rosette. Flowers among leaves. Cosmop, ±11 species, ±8 in SAfr, 4 in this region.

Limosella inflata (inflata - refers to the inflated leaf bases)

Aquatic herb. Locally common in rock pools, in water up to 1m deep, in marshes, rooted in mud, above 2200m. LEAVES 5-40×2.5-15mm, floating, **leaf base appears fleshy but is inflated**, attached to long, threadlike stalks. FLOWERS floating, white, ±11m diam, **calyx lobes much longer than the flower tube, stalks long, threadlike** (Nov-Mar). GENERAL: Found in pools with *Aponogeton ranunculiflorus*.

Limosella longiflora bolibana, joang-ba-metsi, tšika-metsi (SS) (longiflora - long flowers)

Tiny aquatic herb, up to 50mm tall. In dense colonies, in mud and shallow water, 1800-3000m. KZN to Mpum. LEAVES needle-shaped, 25-50mm, erect to spreading. FLOWERS ±7mm diam, very pale blue to pink, **calyx strongly 5-veined**, erect, lobes pointed, stalks slender, erect in flower, bending in fruit (Sep-Nov). **Similar species:** *Limosella maior* Herb, 25-150mm tall. Muddy margins of streams, pools, in beds of streamlets through marshes, 1800-2400m. LEAVES 7-15mm broad, narrowed to long stalk. FLOWERS ±8mm diam, bluish white, stalks up to 45 mm long (Sep-Mar).

Limosella vesiculosa (vesicula - bladder refers to the 'blisters' that develop on the calyx tube)

Forms extensive mats. Periodically inundated, in marshy turf and muddy places along streams or around tarns, 1980-3000m. EMR endemic. Leafy stolons, rooting at nodes, producing new plants. LEAVES **roundish**, 2-6×1.5-5.5mm, stalks ±15mm long. FLOWERS ±8mm wide, white, **calyx tube becomes wrinkled from bladdery swellings**, scented (Nov-Mar).

Lindernia [= *Ilysanthes*] (after F.B. von Lindern, botanist and author from Strasburg) Warm areas, ±80 species, ±7 in SAfr, 1 in this region.

Lindernia conferta [= *Ilysanthes conferta*] (conferta - crowded, refers to leaf rosettes)

Aquatic herb, 100-200mm, lower parts submerged, rooting. In shallow, rocky mountain pools, 1800-2150m. KZN to Mpum. LEAVES 4-16×1-6mm, shiny, minutely dotted, **fleshy**, crowded at top of stems **in floating rosettes**. FLOWERS in leaf axils, ±8mm diam, white blotched purple on lower lip and throat (Dec-Feb).

Hebenstretia (named after Johann Hebenstreit, 1720-91, prof of medicine at Leipzig and St Petersburg) Annual or perennial herbs or shrubs. Flowers in dense slender inflorescences, tube slender, with 4 short lobes. Afr, ±25 species, mainly W and SW Cape, ±6 in this region.

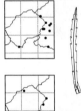

Hebenstretia dura Eastern Shrubby Slugwort; tšitoane, tšitoare-ea-setlolo (SS) (durus - hard)

Tufted perennial herb, up to 800mm tall. In damp, often rocky grassland, up to 2450m. E Cape to Limpopo Prov. Stems simple, hairy or not. LEAVES crowded, 8-30×1-5mm, margins toothed. INFLORESCENCE slender, elongated, ±150mm long; FLOWERS ±20mm long, white or pale yellow, with yellow, orange or scarlet blotch at base of lower lip (Nov-Feb). GENERAL: Mixed with fat to make a perfumed ointment. **Similar species:** *Hebenstretia cooperi* [= *H. basutica*] **tšitoane (SS)** (named after Thomas Cooper, 1815-1913, English plant collector and cultivator who came to the SA in 1859) **Soft wooded shrub**, up to 1.5m tall. In boulder beds, rocky streamsides, rock outcrops and cliffs, 1675-2550m. EMR endemic. LEAVES serrate. INFLORESCENCE up to 120mm long; FLOWERS white with orange or red blotch at base of upper lip (Oct-Mar). GENERAL: Mixed with fat to make a superior perfumed ointment.

Limosella inflata   *Lindernia conferta*   *Zaluzianskya turritella*

Martin von Fintel   Hilliard & Burtt   Mike Hirst

Limosella longiflora

Trevor Coleman

Limosella longiflora   *Hebenstretia cooperi*   *Hebenstretia dura*

David McDonald   Neil Crouch   Clinton Carbutt

Limosella vesiculosa

Peter Linder

Glumicalyx montanus   *Hebenstretia dura*

Hilliard & Burtt   David McDonald

95

Selago (an ancient name, used by Linnaeus) Leaves alternate or in clusters. Flowers small, in dense, round or broad, branching, sometimes irregular inflorescences. Attracts butterflies of the *Lepidochrysops* genus. Afr, ±190 species, mostly SAfr, ±10 in this region.

Selago immersa (*immersa* - immersed)

Erect or sprawling, forming bushy clumps, 300-600mm tall. In rough grassland in valley bottoms, on boulder beds, (1500)1800-2440m. EMR endemic. Stems bare below, branching and closely leafy above, softly hairy. PRIMARY LEAVES **in clusters, 4-10×1-4mm**, narrowed to a broad stalklike base, **margins with 1-4 pairs sharp teeth** in upper part. INFLORESCENCE large, leafy, side branches up to 150mm long; FLOWERS up to 6mm wide, **pure white** (Oct-Jan).

Selago melliodora (*melliodora* - smelling of honey)

Bushy perennial herb, 0.2-0.5(1)m tall. On steep scrubby mountain slopes, basalt scree slopes, 2400-2800m. EMR endemic. Young parts **covered in soft long hairs.** LEAVES clustered, 5-12×1-2mm, tips **bluntish**, base slightly narrowed, margins entire, ± rolled under, **softly hairy.** INFLORESCENCES narrow, pyramidal, flowers 3-4mm wide, in small rounded heads, white flushed mauve, honey scented (Jan-Mar).

Selago monticola (*monticola* - mountain loving)

Perennial herb, 0.3-1m tall. On grassy slopes, in valleys near streams, 1400-2100m. EMR endemic. **Stems few, erect, simple to sparingly branched below,** closely leafy, downy. LEAVES 7-20(35)×1-3(10)mm, narrowed at base, margins thickened, entire, toothed on larger leaves, hairy above. INFLORESCENCE loose, flower clusters **±10mm diam** (elongating in fruit to 30-50mm); FLOWERS ±5mm diam, white (throughout year).

Selago trinervia [= *S. racemosa, S. tysonii*] (*trinervia* - 3-veined)

Perennial herb, 150-750mm tall. In damp grassy places, steep rocky slopes, foot of Cave Sandstone cliffs, up to 2200m. KZN. LEAVES **usually solitary**, not clustered, 10-55×1-8mm, **flat, leathery**, margins entire or with few very small teeth, 3-veined, hairy on margins, midrib below. INFLORESCENCE congested, ± loosely branched, up to 100mm in fruit; FLOWERS white, tube sometimes purplish, bracts leafy (Oct-May).

Harveya (named after Dr William Harvey, 1811-1866, chief author of early volumes of *Flora Capensis*, Prof of botany in Dublin, Ireland) Parasitic herbs. Leaves reduced to scales. Mostly Afr, ±40 species, ±25 in SAfr, ±4 in this region.

Harveya speciosa Tall White Ink-flower; Inkblom (A); mokunye, seona (SS); isinama (X); umshelezana omhlophe (Z) (*speciosa* - beautiful)

Showy parasitic herb, up to 700mm tall. In long grass or amongst shrubs, on streambanks, up to 2000m. E Cape to Mpum. LEAVES slightly fleshy, scalelike, ±30mm. FLOWERS **large, ±70mm wide and long,** creamy white, yellow in throat, scented (Oct-Apr). GENERAL: Turns blue-black when bruised. Used in traditional medicine. Parasitic on grasses and plants of the family Compositae (Asteraceae).

GESNERIACEAE - African Violet Family Flowers ±2-lipped, 5-lobed. Economically important for ornamentals such as Gloxinia, African violet. Trop, subtrop, ±139 genera, ±2900 species, 1 genus in SAfr. *Streptocarpus* (*streptos* - twisted; *karpos* - fruit) Some plants die after flowering (monocarpic); leaves continuously growing from base. Fruit a capsule with spirally twisted valves. Afr, ±125 species, ±45 in SAfr, 4 in this region.

Streptocarpus pentherianus (named after Arnold Penther, 1865-1931, who collected in SA and Zim)

Perennial herb, up to 150mm tall. On mossy rocks in forest, shady moist places on Cave Sandstone cliffs, up to 2000m. KZN to Mpum. LEAVES **1-3**, ±120×80mm, ± reddish beneath, sparsely hairy, margins scalloped. INFLORESCENCE with ±12 small flowers, ±18mm, white, tube tinged violet, **narrow, strongly curved, mouth like a keyhole,** pale yellow (Nov-Mar). CAPSULES **short,** 9-20×2mm, **deflexed.**

Streptocarpus pusillus (*pusillus* - weak, small)

Small herb, up to 120mm tall. On damp rock overhangs, in moist shady places on cliffs, 1650-2600m. E CAPE to KZN/MPUM. LEAVES 1(3), ±220×160mm. FLOWERS small, ±18mm, white, sticky glandular outside, **tube cylindrical, mouth round** (Nov-Apr). CAPSULE 15-25×2mm. GENERAL: Plant dies after flowering.

ACANTHACEAE - Acanthus Family (see pg 240) *Adhatoda* (a Malabar name) Old World genus, many species, 2 in SAfr, 1 in this region.

Adhatoda andromeda Adhatoda; Valsmoeraskruid (A); umusa omncane (Z)

Perennial herb, 60-400mm tall, in colonies. In rocky grassland, up to 1950m. Rootstock woody. Stems annual. LEAVES 7-40×2-15mm. FLOWERS ±20mm wide, white with red markings, bracts narrow, 25-30mm (Sep-Feb). GENERAL: Used in traditional medicine to treat nausea.

Selago melliodora

Mike Hirst

Selago monticola

Trevor Coleman

Lal Greene

Selago trinervia

Tony Abbott

Streptocarpus pusillus

Hilliard & Burtt

Adhatoda andromeda

Lorraine van Hooff

Godfrey Symons

Streptocarpus pentherianus

Martin von Fintel

Selago immersa

Martin von Fintel

Harveya speciosa

97

RUBIACEAE - Gardenia Family Leaves opposite or whorled, stipules between leaf stalks. Petals united into a tube; fruit crowned with persistent calyx. Economically important for crops such as coffee, quinine and ornamentals such as *Gardenia*, *Ixora*. Cosmop, ±630 genera, ±10 200 species, 61 genera in SAfr. *Kohautia* (after Francisci Kohaut, plant collector) Herbs. Old World trop, ±60 species, ±15 in SAfr, 1 in this region.

Kohautia amatymbica [= *Oldenlandia amatymbica*] Tremble Tops; lehlokoana, ´mangoakoane, morokolo-poli (SS); ikhubalo elimnyama, labantwana (X); umfana-ozacile, umqanda, umhungulo (Z) (*amatymbica* - named after the amaThembu people)

Slender perennial herb, up to 600mm tall. In grassland, up to 2500m. Cape to Zim. LEAVES ±45×2mm, widely spaced. FLOWERS ±12mm diam, white, cream to brownish above, green to purplish or brown beneath, tube long, ±20mm, open in late afternoon, sometimes sweetly scented (Oct-Dec). GENERAL: Conspicuous in recently burnt veld. Used in traditional medicine and as a protective charm.

VALERIANACEAE - Valerian Family Flowers irregular or spurred. Fruits crowned with persistent calyx. Cosmop (N Temp), ±15 genera, ±400 species, 2 genera in SAfr. *Valeriana* (perhaps from *valeo* - be well) Flowers small, oblique or 2-lipped. Mainly N Temp, ±200 species, 1 in SAfr.

Valeriana capensis Cape Valerian; Wildebalderjan (A); motetele (SS)

Foetid perennial herb, up to 1m tall. S Cape to EAfr. LEAVES mainly basal, mostly compound, ±200mm long, margins irregularly toothed. INFLORESCENCE a crowded cluster; FLOWERS ±6mm diam, white to mauve (Oct-Jan). GENERAL: Leaves used in traditional medicine. Var. *capensis*, unbranched, up to 1.5m tall, in damp ground near streams, up to 2200m. LEAVES compound. INFLORESCENCE branching towards top of stem; FLOWERS fragrant. Var. *lanceolata*, slender, often in clumps, up to 750mm tall; on grassy slopes, in stabilized boulder beds, up to 2750m. BASAL LEAVES entire or with 1-2 lobes. INFLORESCENCE branched. Var. *nana*, 70-300mm tall, in short wet grassland, 2050-3000m. EMR endemic. LEAVES entire.

DIPSACACEAE - *Scabiosa* Family Flowers 2-lipped, clustered in dense heads surrounded by a whorl of small bracts (involucre), those on outer edge have longer lobes, calyx papery. Popular ornamentals. Mostly Medit, also Afr, Asia, ±11 genera, 350-400 species, 2 genera in SAfr. *Cephalaria* (*kephale* - head) **Calyx without bristles,** flowers ± regular, 4(5)-lobed. Europe, Asia, Afr, ±60 species, ±15 in SAfr, 3 in this region.

Cephalaria galpiniana subsp. *simplicior* ˇtsoene (SS) (named after Ernest Galpin, 1858-1941, great SA naturalist and collector; *simplex* - simple)

Herb up to 300mm tall. Forms mats at high altitudes, 2000-2750m. EMR endemic. LEAVES basal, mostly lobed, **lobes small, narrow, margins entire or toothed**, stem leaves few. FLOWERING HEAD large, pale cream, ±30mm diam (Nov-Mar).

Cephalaria natalensis

Robust herb, up to 1(2)m tall. Forms dense stands on streambanks, forest margins, up to 2590m. EMR endemic. Stems hollow. LEAVES **large, compound**, 150-180mm long, **leaflet margins jagged**, hairy beneath, stalks 20-170mm long. FLOWERHEADS ±25mm diam, white, **bracts black-tipped** (Dec-Apr).

Cephalaria oblongifolia tšoene (SS) (*oblongifolia* - oblong leaves)

Erect herb, up to 1m tall. In marshy ground, grassland, up to 2100m. E Cape to KZN/Mpum. LEAVES **in basal rosettes**, ±600×40mm, leathery, **margins entire**, stalks slender, ±300mm long, lower stem leaves slender, ± lobed, entire or toothed. FLOWERHEADS ±20mm diam, white, silky outside, bracts pointed, silky (Nov-Mar).

Scabiosa (*scabiosus* - rough, scurfy) Leaves opposite, often in basal rosette, entire, toothed, lobed or divided. Flowerheads surrounded at base by 1-2 rows of bracts, **calyx lobes with long bristles**, flowers with 5 unequal lobes. Europe, Afr, Asia, ±100 species, 9 in SAfr, 2 in this region.

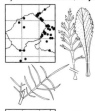

Scabiosa columbaria Wild Scabious; Bitterbos, Meerjarige skurfkruid (A); ´mamokhale, moholungoane, selomi, tlhako-ea-pitsi, (SS); ilelemimoya, isilawu esikhulu, iyeza lamehlo, makgha (X); ibheka, ubucubele, udoloqina, uxhaphozi (Z) (*columbaria* - dove-coloured)

Herb up to 750mm tall. In grassland, on basalt outcrops, up to 3200m. Cape to Europe. LEAVES **in basal rosette**, 40-180×40mm, margins entire to deeply lobed, stem leaves smaller. FLOWERHEADS 10-25mm diam, **stems solid, branched**, 120-300mm long; FLOWERS white (pink), **calyx with 5 long, purplish red, bristlelike lobes** (Oct-Feb). GENERAL: Grazed by stock. Used in traditional medicine. Lovely garden plant.

Scabiosa drakensbergensis Drakensberg Scabious

Large, sprawling, leafy perennial herb, up to 1.5m tall. In rocky places, on margins of scrub, 1500-2000m. EMR endemic. **Stems hollow below**, densely softly hairy. LEAVES **deeply divided**, stalkless; LEAFLETS ±80×45mm, margins coarsely toothed, upper segments narrow. FLOWERHEADS 25-30mm diam, stalks up to 300mm long, FLOWERS white, ±7mm, bracts softly hairy, longer than marginal flowers (Oct-Apr).

Cephalaria oblongifolia

Valeriana capensis

Valeriana capensis

Lal Greene

Lal Greene

Lal Greene

Scabiosa columbaria

Lal Greene

Scabiosa columbaria

Scabiosa columbaria

Kauhautia amatymbica

Martin von Fintel

Cephalaria natalensis

Martin von Fintel

Lal Greene

Cephalaria galpiniana var. *simplicior*

Hilliard & Burtt

Scabiosa drakensbergensis

Martin von Fintel

Scabiosa drakensbergensis

Martin von Fintel

CUCURBITACEAE - Cucumber/Pumpkin Family (see pg 44) *Zehneria* (named after J. Zehner, botanical artist) (see pg 44)

Zehneria scabra (*scabra* - rough, scabrid) (see pg 44)

CAMPANULACEAE - Bell Flower/Canterbury Bell Family (see pg 240) *Wahlenbergia* (see pg 240)

Wahlenbergia pulvillus-gigantis (*pulvillus* - cushion; *gigantos* - a giant, refers to Giants Castle where the type specimen was collected)

Herb **forming dense green cushions** up to 150mm diam × 60mm deep, flowering stems up to 120mm tall. In damp partially shaded crevices of cliff faces, 2100-2700m. EMR endemic. LEAVES congested, ±9×2mm. FLOWERS 1-5, white, tube ±15mm long, veined pale purple, stems very slender, threadlike, up to 80mm long (Dec-Jan).

LOBELIACEAE - Lobelia Family Herbs, often with milky sap. Flowers often 2-lipped, inverted on the stalks. Includes well known ornamentals. Cosmop, ±30 genera, ±1000 species, 5 genera in SAfr. *Cyphia* (*kyphos* - twiner) Erect or twining. Afr, ±60 species, ±35 in SAfr, ±7 in this region.

Cyphia elata lekoto, lenkoto (SS); ibutha lentaba, egela, igonsi (Z) (*elata* - tall)

Stiffly erect perennial herb, 100-450mm tall. In rocky grassland, crevices of Cave Sandstone platforms, up to 2745m. E Cape to Mpum. STEMS simple, leafy. LEAVES overlapping below, ±100×60mm, margins with small teeth, base clasping stem. INFLORESCENCE dense, ±100×20mm; FLOWERS ±9mm long, creamy white with mauve markings (Jan-Feb). GENERAL: Root edible. Used in traditional medicine.

Cyphia natalensis

Perennial, twining herb, over bushes. On forest margins, in scrubby stream gullies, 1400-2000m. KZN endemic. LEAVES ±35×10mm, margins toothed, stalk short, slender. FLOWERS in clusters leaf axils, white tinged purple (Jan-Feb).

Lobelia (named after Matthias de L'Obel, 1538-1616, Flemish nobleman, botanist, physician to King James I) Herbs or shrublets. Flowers 5-lobed, regular or 2-lipped. Fruit a capsule. Trop and subtrop, mostly American, ±300 species, ±70 in SAfr, ±5 in this region.

Lobelia vanreenensis (named after Van Reenen's pass)

Delicate, perennial herb, forming clumps, 250-400mm tall. In damp partially shaded places on cliffs, under rock outcrops, sometimes in forest, 1500-2350m. LEAVES 20-40×12-26mm, irregularly, bluntly lobed, **terminal lobe long narrow**, stalks 20-50mm long. FLOWERS 8-10mm long, whitish (pale blue), yellow on palate (Jan-Apr). GENERAL: Similar growth form to *L. preslii* with which it can be found growing.

COMPOSITAE (refers to the composite nature of the flowerheads), also called ASTERACEAE **- Daisy Family** (see pg 144) **Aster** (*astron* - a star, refers to the radiate head of flowers) Perennial herbs, soft shrublets. Flowerheads on long stems; tips of ray florets 3-toothed; pappus bristles rough, easily detached. Mainly N Hemisp, ±250 species, ±16 in SAfr, ±7 in this region.

Aster bakerianus phoa (SS); noxgxekana, umthekisana (X); udlatshana, umaqhunsula, umhlungwana (Z) (after J G Baker, 1834-1920, botanist, keeper of the herbarium at Royal Botanic Gardens, Kew)

Perennial herb, 300-450mm tall. Locally common in open grassland, near streams, up to 2000m. S Cape to Tanz. **Stems roughly hairy throughout**, simple or forking from near base. LEAVES up to 80×20mm, margins more or less toothed, base half clasping. INFLORESCENCE branched; FLOWERHEADS: ±30mm diam, deep pink to whitish, bract margins tinged purplish, with **long spreading hairs at least on midline** (Aug-Dec). GENERAL: Used in traditional medicine to treat a wide variety of complaints: coughs, urinary and eye infections, headaches, sores, internal parasites, syphilis, snakebite, psychiatric disturbances and as protective charms. Slow growing, from seed. (see pg 222)

Aster pleiocephalus (*pleiocephalus* - many heads)

Erect herb, up to 500mm tall. In grassland, on forest margins, rocky outcrops, up to 2000m. Mostly KZN. STEMS **roughly hairy**. LEAVES up to 80(100)×10mm, **margins usually toothed, roughly hairy on both surfaces**, stalkless. FLOWERHEADS up to 25mm diam, in **open branched inflorescences, ray florets white**, disc florets yellow (Sep-Dec).

Felicia (named after Herr Felix, d 1846, German official at Regensburg) Herbs with hairy fruits. Afr ±80 species, mainly SAfr, ±11 in this region.

Felicia linearis (*linearis* - pertaining to a line, refers to long, narrow leaves)

Perennial herb up to 150mm tall, in tufts, forming small mats. In damp grassland, at edge of wet rock sheets, 1800-3350m. LEAVES glossy, erect, up to 80×1.5mm, **hairless**, in basal rosettes. FLOWERHEADS up to 20mm diam, rays mauve, pink, soon curving back, disc yellow, one flower from each rosette of leaves, young heads nodding (Feb-Apr).

Zehneria scabra   Tony Abbott

Zehneria scabra   Hilliard & Burtt

Wahlenbergia pulvillus-gigantis   Hilliard & Burtt

Cyphia elata   Martin von Fintel

Cyphia natalensis   Hilliard & Burtt

Lobelia vanreenensis   Martin von Fintel

Aster bakerianus   Martin von Fintel

Aster pleiocephalus   Tom De Waal

Felicia linearis   Lal Greene

101

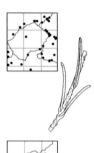

Felicia muricata [= *Aster muricatus*] Bloublommetjie, Blouheuning Karooblommetjie, Kapokblommetjie (A); koelehane, ˊmamileng, mohantšoane, mokhoto, mosala-tsela (SS) (*muricata* – pointed)

Low growing, well branched bushy herb, up to 200(500)mm tall. On poor stony grassland or disturbed places, roadsides, not common in this region, up to 2450m. Widespread in SAfr. **Twigs rough with sparse, stiff hairs**. LEAVES up to 15×1mm. FLOWERHEADS up to 15mm diam, solitary at tips of branchlets, white, pink, blue or mauve, fold under at night, opening fully in sunlight (Aug-May). GENERAL: Grazed by sheep and goats. Sometimes a weed, dominant on overgrazed areas. Used in traditional medicine to relieve headaches and as a douche for cows ill after calving.

Felicia petiolata [= *Aster petiolatus*] khotolia-ea-thaba, morarana (SS) (*petiolata* - stalked, refers to the comparatively long leaf stalks)

Straggling herb forming large tangled masses. At foot of damp shady cliffs, in *Leucosidea* scrub, 1800-2250m. NE Cape to EMR. Stems very long, reclining or pendulous, slender, hairy, leafy throughout. LEAVES thinly hairy, alternate, **up to 25×15mm, stalks up to 10mm** long, very slender. FLOWERHEADS up to 30mm diam, rays pink to whitish, disc yellow (Oct-Feb). GENERAL: Used to ensure a good harvest.

Denekia (after a Dutch botanist friend of Thunberg who described the genus) Perennial herb. SAfr to Zim, Angola, 1 species.

Denekia capensis toane-mohlaka (SS)

Perennial herb, 150-700mm tall. In marshy ground, up to 2600m. Widespread. Plant size and shape highly variable depending on growing conditions. Stems simple. LEAVES 10-200×2-25mm, stem-clasping or tapering into a stalk, softly hairy above, **white felted below** (sometimes hairless), margins toothed or entire. FLOWERHEADS small, ±3mm diam in tight clusters, flowers white or bluish, with characteristic delicate **1-2 pappus bristles**. (see pg 222)

Gnaphalium (*gnaphaleon* - a downy plant) Small annual or perennial woolly herbs. Worldwide, number of species uncertain, 3 in this region.

Gnaphalium limicola (*limicola* - dweller in mud)

Creeping, branching perennial herb, **forming close, spreading mats**. In muddy streambeds and ditches, on bare, marshy ground, 2400-2500m. EMR endemic. **Stems grey felted**, closely leafy. LEAVES 5-15×1-3mm, **spathulate**, silvery grey felted. FLOWERHEADS ±4×4mm, in small clusters, **stalks conspicuous, ±25mm long** (Oct-Mar).

Troglophytum Annual or perennial woolly herbs. SAfr, 6 species, 1 in this region.

Troglophytum capillaceum subsp. *diffusum* [= *Helichrysum capillaceum* var. *diffusum*] mosuoane-oa-lehaha (SS)

Much branched, loosely spreading herb, often forming big mats. In damp, partially shaded places on cliffs, under Cave Sandstone overhangs, 1800-2450m. Widespread in mountains of SAfr. Young parts grey cobwebby. LEAVES 3-20×3-20mm, stalks up to 10mm long, **thinly grey-woolly**. FLOWERHEADS small, ±3×2mm, in clusters, **bracts cobwebby, silvery white**, sweetly honey scented (Jan-Jul).

Helichrysum (see pg 146) Mainly Afr, ±600 species, ±244 in SAfr, ±55 in this region. **Page layout groups similar species.**

Helichrysum natalitium imphepho (Z)

Robust perennial herb, up to 1m tall. **In moist streamlines, damp rough grassland**, 1800-2100m. KZN endemic. Thinly greyish white woolly or cobwebby, very leafy. LEAVES up to 200×20mm, tapering at both ends, **running down stem in long narrow wings**, glandular above. INFLORESCENCE widely branched; FLOWERHEADS ±3×1mm, in clusters up to 20mm diam, matted together at base with whitish wool, **bracts creamy white** (Jan-Apr). GENERAL: Burnt to invoke the goodwill of ancestors.

Helichrysum rugulosum motlosa-ngoaka, motoantoanyane, pulumo-tšeou, toane (SS) (*rugulose* - wrinkled, refers to tips of bracts)

Tufted perennial herb, 100-300mm tall. In stony grassland, up to 2500m. S Cape to Limpopo Prov. LEAVES 15-25×2-5mm, margins ± rolled under, upper surface thinly cobweb felted, white felted beneath, hairs often stringy. INFLORESCENCES compact, flat topped; FLOWERHEADS ±5×4mm, bell-shaped, **bract tips crisped, purplish or pink to creamy** (Dec-Mar). GENERAL: Used in traditional medicine to fumigate huts when children are ill and as an ingredient in protective charms.

Felicia muricata

Denekia capensis

Felicia petiolata

Helichrysum natalitium

Gnaphalium limicola

Troglophytum capillaceum

Helichrysum rugulosum

103

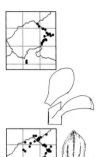

Helichrysum confertum (confertum - crowded)

Compact dwarf shrub, in cushions up to 1m diam. On cliff faces, 1800-3000m. EMR endemic. Old branches bare, gnarled. LEAVES in 'rosettes', **10-20×6-10mm**, narrowing to short, stalklike base, tips rounded, **greyish above**, white-woolly-felted beneath. INFLORESCENCE **held close to the plant, flowering stems closely leafy**. FLOWERHEADS very variable in size, ±8-16×5-8mm, larger heads solitary or a few, smaller heads in clusters, outer bracts pale golden brown or pinkish, bases webbed with wool, inner milky white, flowers yellow tinged red (**Jul-Sep**). GENERAL: Winter to spring flowering.

Helichrysum sutherlandii molepelle, ntlo-ea-mokhoabane, senkotoana (SS) (named after

P.C. Sutherland, 1822-1900, medical doctor, became government geologist then Surveyor General in Natal; corresponded with William Hooker at Kew and sent parcels of plants and seeds)

Well branched shrublet, up to 400mm tall. In clumps, hanging from Cave Sandstone cliffs, rock outcrops and earth cliffs above streams, 1500-3000m. LEAVES up to 25×12mm, thinly grey-woolly to hairless above, white-felted beneath. INFLORESCENCES **much branched, 20-120mm wide, held well away from plant**; FLOWERHEADS small, 4-5×5-7mm, outer bracts pale brownish, webbed together with wool, inner bracts milky-white (**Feb-Jul**). GENERAL: Summer/winter flowering. Similar to *H. confertum* which usually flowers much earlier. **A compact, small-leaved form with short flowering stems is found mostly above 2600m.** Used in traditional medicine as a dried powder, applied to cuts in the skin of a sick person.

Helichrysum krebsianum (named after Ludwig Krebs, 1820-1828, Cape Naturalist to the King of Prussia)

Perennial herb, flowering stem up to 600mm tall, solitary, thinly white-cottony. In open grassland, up to 2100m. E Cape to KZN. LEAVES clustered at base, up to 200×50mm, including stalk 70-100mm long, **blade strongly 3-veined**, harshly hairy above, thinly woolly beneath, stalks thin, wiry. INFLORESCENCE **spreading**, flat-toppped; FLOWERHEADS **roundish**, ±5×5mm, **bracts with rounded tips**, creamy white (pale yellow) (Oct-Feb).

Helichrysum mundtii phefo-ea-liliba (SS) (named after Johannes Mundt, 1791-1831, Prussian

pharmacist, botanist, land surveyor who worked in SA)

Robust perennial herb, up to 1.5m tall, flowering stems leafy, woody at base, thinly white-felted in upper parts. Forms dense stands, in marshy places, up to 2100m. Cape to Angola, Tanz. BASAL LEAVES up to 600×60mm, **finely net-veined, surface wrinkled, hairless above, white-felted, 3-veined beneath**, lower half tapering into long, narrowly winged stalks, stem leaves narrow, running onto and **winging the stem**. INFLORESCENCES **large, much branched**; FLOWERHEADS ±4×3.5mm, in small clusters, bracts creamy white (Feb-Apr). GENERAL: Used in traditional medicine to treat chest complaints.

Helichrysum albo-brunneum (albo - white; brunneum - dark brown)

Perennial herb with several leaf rosettes, flowering stems decumbent then erect, 150-300mm tall, loosely greyish white-woolly, closely leafy. On damp stony or rocky slopes, in grass tufts along streams, in marshes on the summit, 2200-3300m. E Cape to KZN/Mpum. BASAL LEAVES 30-80×10-35mm, **densely greyish white-woolly**. FLOWERHEADS broadly bell-shaped, large ones solitary at stem tip, small ones in crowded inflorescence of 5-15 heads, outer **bracts glossy white, tipped dark or light brown**, flowers yellow (Dec-Feb).

Helichrysum appendiculatum Sheeps' Ears Everlasting; Skaapoorbossie (A);

senkotoana (SS); ibode, indlebeyemvu (Z) (appendiculatum - with an appendage, refers to upper leaves)

Perennial herb, flowering stems up to 550mm tall, grey-woolly. In grassland, up to 2100m. SW Cape to Mpum. BASAL LEAVES spreading, up to 80×20mm, tip tapering, base broad, clasping, **upper stem leaves often tipped with a small coloured bract**. INFLORESCENCE compact to spreading; FLOWERHEADS 7–15mm long, **bracts dull** creamy white or yellowish often suffused **pink to red or purplish**, tips shortly to long-pointed and then sometimes recurved (Jan-Mar). GENERAL: White underside of leaves stripped to make fringes and body ornaments. (see pg 44)

Helichrysum confertum

Neil Crouch

Helichrysum sutherlandii

John Grimshaw

Helichrysum sutherlandii

Martin von Fintel

David McDonald

Helichrysum albo-brunneum

Helichrysum krebsianum

Godfrey Symons

Helichrysum appendiculatum

Lal Greene

Helichrysum mundtii

Anne Rennie

105

Helichrysum chionosphaerum Tiny Snowball Everlasting; Sewejaartjie (A); molepelle, senkotoana (SS) (*chio* - snow, white; *sphaer* - ball, refers to round white flowerheads)
Mat-forming perennial herb, flowering stems up to 150mm tall. Forms **carpets up to 1m across** in rocky grassland, on cliffs, rock sheets, big boulders, up to 2450m. NE Cape to Zim. Stems well branched, prostrate, young parts leafy. LEAVES 10-100×1-3(5)mm, upper surface green, lower sometimes silky-felted, **wool usually confined to the 3 veins and margins**. FLOWERHEADS **7-12 long**, 12-25mm across spreading bracts, **solitary or in clusters of up to 4, bracts glossy white**, sometimes yellowish, equal to yellow florets (Sep-May). GENERAL: Leaf length and woolliness variable. Plants on rock sheets have much shorter leaves than plants in grassland.

Helichrysum swynnertonii (named after C.F.M. Swynnerton, 1877-1938, a plant collector in Rhodesia (Zimbabwe) where the original specimen was collected)
In spreading clumps or mats. On stony mountain slopes, 1800-2300m. E Cape to Kenya. Flowering stems leafy below, **grey-felted**. LEAVES up to 80×**10mm**, ± erect, both surfaces covered in loosely woven, grey, **stringy woolly hairs**, bases webbed to stem by stringy woolly hairs. FLOWERHEADS **solitary**, **±13-18mm long, bracts pointed**, in ±10 series, glossy white, equal to florets (Oct-Dec).

Helichrysum grandibracteatum (*grand* - large; *bracteatus* - bracts)
Tufted perennial herb, flowering stems up to 200mm tall. Scattered in poor stony grassland, 1800-2450m. E Cape to KZN. BASAL LEAVES rosetted, up to 120×4mm, (stem leaves much smaller), tips pointed, **green, hairless above, silvery silky-woolly felted below, striped by strongly raised parallel veins**. FLOWERHEADS 8-10mm long, 18-20mm across spreading bracts, **several in terminal cluster**, bracts in ±12 series, much longer than the flowers, **dull** white, flowers yellow (Sep-Nov).

Helichrysum sessilioides (*sessilioides* - resembling *H. sessile*)
Compact, smoothly rounded, cushion-forming dwarf shrub, from 50mm to 1m across. Growing against cliff faces, on steep rocky mountainsides, on dolerite or basalt, 2000-3200m. EMR endemic. **Old stems woody, gnarled**. LEAVES 4-15×1-5mm, blunt-tipped, closely overlapping, appearing as rosettes from above, **green with silvery tissue paperlike covering**, white-felted below. FLOWERHEADS **stalkless, solitary, large**, 20-30mm across the spreading bracts, outer bracts pale brown, pink or red, inner tinged white or pink (Jul-Dec). **General:** Formerly confused with *Helichrysum sessile* which has narrow leaves covered in thick white silky hairs. (see pg 224)

Helichrysum hyphocephalum (*hyphocephalum* - webbed head)
Mat-forming perennial herb, flowering stems up to 60mm long. **Hanging over Cave Sandstone cliffs, big boulders**, 1830-2350m. EMR endemic. Branches slender, prostrate, old ones bare to leafy, **new shoots silvery silky**. LEAVES up to 20×4mm, slightly **sickle-shaped**, with **silvery** grey, silky tissue paper covering. FLOWERHEADS ±5mm long, **up to 10 in a tight terminal headlike cluster**, webbed together at base in silvery tissue paperlike covering, bracts in ±4 series, hardly overlapping, **outer bracts large**, up to 6×3mm, **spoon-shaped**, **milky white**, inner much shorter, narrower, looking like petals of a flower (Dec-Feb).

Helichrysum glaciale (*glaciale* - frozen, refers to pretty 'icecream' colouring of the flowerheads)
Rounded dwarf shrublet, up to 200mm tall and 300mm wide. In cracks and ledges on face of basalt and dolerite cliffs, 2500-2900m. EMR endemic. Main stem very short, gnarled, woody, branches slender. LEAVES **roundish**, ±5×5mm, closely overlapping, **thick, greyish white woolly**. FLOWERHEADS 10-13mm long, 20mm across spreading bracts, solitary on leafy flowering stems, bracts in ±11 series, **loosely overlapping**, outer bracts palest brown, inner bracts, white, **tinged crimson at base** (Nov-Jan).

Helichrysum album (*album* - white, refers to flowerhead)
Perennial herb, flowering stems up to 150mm tall, from side of new leaf rosettes. Small colonies on steep slopes, basalt cliffs, 2000-3300m. EMR endemic. BASAL LEAVES in 1 or several rosettes, 35-60×25mm, tips rounded, **thickly, loosely, greyish white woolly**. FLOWERHEADS solitary, ±20mm long across spreading (radiating) bracts, bracts glossy white, red at base inside (Jan-Mar).

Martin von Fintel

Helichrysum chionosphaerum

Darrel Plowes

Helichrysum swynnertonii

Lal Greene

Helichrysum chionosphaerum

Mike Hirst

Helichrysum album

Mike Hirst

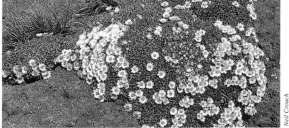

Neil Crouch

Helichrysum sessilioides

Helichrysum glaciale

Hilliard & Burtt

Helichrysum hyphocephalum

Godfrey Symons

Helichrysum grandibracteatum

107

Helichrysum argentissimum (*argentissimum* - very silvery)

Perennial herb with many leaf rosettes forming **thick mats up to 1m wide**, flowering stems terminal, up to 150(400)mm tall. On stony grassy slopes or sandstone cliffs, up to 2400m. E Cape to KZN. BASAL LEAVES 30-50(120)×3-4(6)mm, **silvery grey silky woolly**, tips pointed. FLOWERHEADS solitary, ±20mm long across spreading bracts, **glossy white**, inner with a red or pink blotch at base (Sep-Jan). GENERAL: Can be mistaken for *H. lingulatum* which is found in the Underberg area southward to the Cape Drak. Much resembles *H. argentissimum* but easily distinguished by its **differently shaped leaves clad in wool**.

Helichrysum bellum (*bellus* - neat, charming)

Perennial herb with **1 or 2 leaf rosettes**, flowering stems terminal, up to 150(300)mm tall. On stony turf on steep slopes and on summit plateau, 2400-3300m. EMR endemic. BASAL LEAVES up to 50(150)×15-20mm, **thin, soft, with long glandular hairs, margins white woolly when young**. FLOWERHEADS solitary, ±15mm long, 30mm across spreading (radiating) bracts, **bracts snow-white** (Jan-Mar).

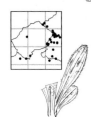

Helichrysum ecklonis [= *H. calocephalum, H. lamprocephalum, H. scapiforme*] Ecklon's Everlasting; toane-balingoana-e-kholo, toane-ea-loti (SS); umthi wechanti (X) (named after Christian Ecklon, 1795-1868, apothecary, traveller and plant collector)

Tufted perennial herb, flowering stems up to 500mm tall. In large colonies, on grassy slopes, up to 2750m. E Cape to Mpum. BASAL LEAVES rosetted, up to 100(200)×20mm, upper surface loosely woolly cobwebby, sometimes hairless and then **3-5 veins are visible, upper surface margins and lower surface downy woolly**. FLOWERHEADS **large, solitary**, 25-30mm long, 50-60mm across spreading bracts, bracts in ±10 series, loosely overlapping, much longer than the flowers, **glossy white to deep pink** (Sep-Dec). GENERAL: Used in traditional medicine. (see pg 224)

Helichrysum lingulatum (*lingulate* - tongue-shaped, refers to the leaves) (see pg 224)

Helichrysum marginatum mankhama-khama, senkotoana, toane-balingoana-e-tšoeu (SS) (*marginis* - edge or border, referring to the white leaf margins)

Mat-forming dwarf shrub, **flowering stems terminal to rosettes**, woolly, up to 150m tall. On cliff faces, rock sheets, steep stony mountain slopes, 2440-3300m. EMR endemic. Main stems prostrate, branching, thick and woody with age, with many crowded leaf rosettes. LEAVES up to 40×10mm, **leathery, green with white woolly margins**. FLOWERHEADS solitary, ±15-20mm, 30-40mm across spreading bracts, **bracts dull white**, inner with red blotch near base (Dec-Feb).

Helichrysum monticola (*monticola* - mountain loving)

Perennial herb, flowering stem **terminal to leaf rosette**, up to 300mm tall. In small clumps, on stony grass slopes, 1500-2700m. E Cape to Mpum. BASAL LEAVES in flattish rosette, **hairless to cobwebby above**, up to 90×15mm. FLOWERHEADS solitary or in small inflorescence, **bracts glossy white**, inner tinged pink or red at base (Dec-Feb). GENERAL: Easily confused with *H. adenocarpum* (see pg 224) but the position of the flowering stem easily distinguishes them.

Helichrysum confertifolium (*confertifolium* - crowded leaves)

Mat-forming perennial herb, sometimes over 1m across, composed of many crowded leaf rosettes, flowering stems closely leafy, up to ±100mm tall. In rocky grassland, over rock sheets, up to 2750m. E Cape to Limpopo Prov. Rootstock stout, woody, branches prostrate, rooting. LEAVES 10-40×2-3mm, **enveloped in silvery white 'felt'**. FLOWERHEADS solitary ±25mm across spreading bracts, bracts **glossy white**, mostly rich brown to reddish brown outside in upper part (Nov-Jul).

Helichrysum milfordiae (named after Mrs Helen Milford who first collected the plant)

Pretty, **silvery**, mat-forming subshrub, flowering stems terminal, up to 120mm tall. On rocks or growing from cracks in cliff faces, 2985-3500m. EMR endemic. Old stems woody, gnarled, young stems very slender, creeping, with **many congested leaf rosettes**. LEAVES up to 14×9mm, **tips rounded, silvery silky woolly**. FLOWERHEADS ±15mm long, 30mm across spreading bracts, **bracts glossy white**, mostly **tipped red or dark brown** (Dec-Feb).

Helichrysum argentissimum

Helichrysum bellum

Helichrysum ecklonis

Martin von Fintel

David McDonald

Pam Cooke

Helichrysum lingulatum

Helichrysum marginatum

Helichrysum monticola

Neil Crouch

Darrel Plowes

David McDonald

Helichrysum milfordiae

David McDonald

Helichrysum confertifolium

Helichrysum milfordiae

Tom de Waal

Mike Hirst

109

Helichrysum tenax var. *pallidum* (see pg 156)

Stoebe (*stoibe* - a stuffing) Shrubs. Leaves often ericoid, twisted, sometimes clustered. Afr, ±25 species, 20 in SAfr, 1 in the summer rainfall area.

Stoebe vulgaris Zigzag Bush; Bankrotbos (A); sehalahala (SS) (*vulgaris* - common)

Spreading, intricately branched shrub, up to 2m tall. On rocky slopes, Cave Sandstone platforms, up to 2200m. E Cape to Zim. Branches slender, wiry, densely leafy, young parts woolly. LEAVES tiny, ericoid, 2-4×0.5mm, blue-grey, cobwebby beneath. FLOWERHEADS tiny, yellow-brown, clustered on short side shoots, forming a spreading inflorescence (Sep-Oct). GENERAL: The small white woolly galls are frequently mistaken for flowers. Weedy at times.

Metalasia (*meta* - change; *lasia* - hairy, woolly) Shrubs. 52 species, 47 endemic to W Cape, 1 in this region.

Metalasia densa [the plants in this region were mistakenly referred to as *M. muricata*] Drakensbergse steekbos, Blombos (A); lehlohlo, sehalahala-se-seputsoa, tee (SS) (*densa* - dense or compact)

Stiff, compact, low and cushionlike, up to 1m wide, or a much branched shrub, up to 2m tall. On rocky slopes and ridges, dominant on eroded places, up to 2550m. LEAVES small, 6-10mm long, clustered, in tufts in axils of leaves, usually twisted, sharp-tipped, white-woolly above. FLOWERHEADS up to 7×2mm, in compact terminal clusters 20-40mm wide, bracts hard, brownish, white-woolly, inner tips white, flowers purple-tipped (Jul-Oct), sweetly scented. GENERAL: Browsed by sheep. Leaves and twigs brewed as a tea. Used for fuel. Also used, with other plants, as a fumigant during illness or after a death.

Athrixia (*a* - without; *thrix* - hair) Erect perennial herbs or shrubs. Afr, Madag, ±14 species, 9 in SAfr, ±5 in this region.

Athrixia angustissima phefshoane-e-nyenyane (SS) (*angustissima* - very narrow)

Straggling perennial herb, up to 350mm tall. In moist grassland, up to 2600m. EMR endemic. Stems slender, wiry, leafy. LEAVES in rosettes, ±200×100mm, tips rounded; STEM LEAVES slender, spreading, ±50×1-3mm, smooth above, white-felted below. FLOWERHEADS ±25mm diam, solitary, ray florets white, disc florets yellow, bracts with pointed, recurved tips, cobwebby (Dec-Feb). GENERAL: Summer flowering. Leaves used for a tea. Used in traditional medicine to bathe aching feet.

Athrixia fontana sepinare, shoeshoe-e-nyenyane (SS) (*fontana* - spring)

Erect perennial herb, up to 200(400)mm tall. In marshes, on streambanks, on moist grassy slopes, more rarely on cliffs, 1500-3000m. Mountains from S Cape (Somerset East) to KZN. Flowering stems stiff, thinly white felted. LEAVES very variable in shape and hairiness. In grassland: up to 80×20mm, long and broadly rounded, very hairy above. In marshy ground: up to 180×10mm, longer and thinner, hairless above. On cliffs: up to 55×40mm, ± oval, hairy above. STEM LEAVES reduced to bracts above. FLOWERHEADS solitary, up to 25mm diam, rays white often tinged pink, disc yellow, bracts very long, slender, tips recurved, cobwebby (Dec-Apr). GENERAL: The differences in the leaf shape and hairiness are so extreme that one could mistake them for different species.

Athrixia pinifolia (*pinifolia* - leaves like a pine)

Shrub up to 1m tall. On damp rock cliffs, along rocky streambanks, 1500-2150m. EMR endemic. Branches bare below, leaves crowded towards tips. LEAVES needlelike, up to 30×2mm, rigid, tips pointed, roughly hairy on the margins. FLOWERHEADS solitary, on slender softly hairy stalks up to 60mm long, rays white, ± tinged pink or purplish below, disc yellow, bracts thin, dry (scarious) (Jul-Feb).

Printzia - Shrubs. SAfr endemic, 6 species, 4 in this region.

Printzia nutans (*nutans* - nodding)

Perennial herb, up to 2m tall. In colonies, on grassy mountain slopes, at foot of moist cliffs, around bare rocks, 2000-2650m. EMR endemic. LEAVES up to 200×60mm, narrowing to eared base, margins coarsely toothed, roughly hairy, clammy, gland-dotted below, aromatic. FLOWERHEADS nodding, dull creamy yellow, ±15×25mm with a few short rays, bracts hairy, stalks up to 100mm long (Feb-Mar).

Helichrysum tenax var. *pallidum*

Metalasia densa

Hilliard & Burtt

Martin von Fintel

Athrixia angustissima

Martin von Fintel

Stoebe vulgaris

Neil Crouch

Athrixia pinifolia

Lal Greene

Printzia nutans

Peter Linder

Printzia nutans

Peter Linder

Athrixia fontana

David McDonald

Athrixia pinifolia

Neil Crouch

111

Callilepis *(kallos* - beauty; *lepis* - scale) Perennial herbs. Flowerheads large, solitary. SAfr endemic, 5 species, 1 in this region.

Callilepis laureola Callilepis; Wildemargriet (A); amafuthomhlaba, ihlamvu, impila (Z)
(*laureola* - smaller Laurel)

Perennial herb, up to 600mm tall. In grassland, up to 1800m. E Cape to Moz. LEAVES up to 65×20mm, 3-veined. FLOWERHEADS solitary, **large**, ±60mm diam, ray florets **white, disc florets purplish black** (Aug-Nov, after fires). GENERAL: Tubers highly poisonous yet used in traditional medicine. Responsible for many deaths.

Eumorphia (*eumorphia* - good form) Shrubs or shrublets. 6 species, endemic to SAfr mountains, 2 in this region.

Eumorphia prostrata (*prostrata* - prostrate)

Low, spreading, aromatic shrub up to 600mm tall, or prostrate or hanging down cliff faces, 1900-2730m. EMR endemic. LEAVES opposite, up to 10×1.5mm, often 2- to 3-forked at the tips, in clusters from leafy dwarf shoots in axils, **silvery, silky, hairs lying flat**. FLOWERHEADS solitary, terminal, ±20mm wide, rays white tinged pink at base, disc yellow, **bracts without oil glands** or very inconspicuous ones (Jan-Apr).

Eumorphia sericea lirullello (SS) (*sericea* - silk)

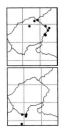

Much branched dwarf shrub, up to 500mm tall. In rough mountain grassland or in dwarf shrub communities, often near streams, 2800-3170m. EMR endemic. Branches grey silky woolly, bare below, rough with leaf scars, twigs leafy. LEAVES grey **silky woolly, hairs fluffed up from leaf surface**, long and narrow or 3-lobed, ±8×1.5mm, in clusters from dwarf shoots in axils. FLOWERHEADS ±25mm diam, terminal, on short stalks, **bracts with large, orange oil glands** on the inner face, rays usually white (rose-pink), disc yellow (Dec-Jul). GENERAL: Used as for fuel. **subsp.** *sericea*, shrub **appears grey** from the dense hair cover. KZN Drak. **subsp.** *robustior*, shrub more robust, ±1m tall, **appears to be green**, with thinner hair cover. E Cape Drak.

Artemisia (honouring Artemis, Greek goddess of the chase) Aromatic herbs, subshrubs. Mainly N Temp, ± 400 species, 3 in SAfr, 1 in this region.

★*Artemisia afra* Wormwood; Wilde als (A); lengana (SS); umhlonyane (Z) (*afra* - from Africa)

Grey, aromatic, shrubby perennial, up to 2m tall. In rank growth in gullies, on forest margins, up to 2425m. Widespread. LEAVES up to 80×40mm, finely divided, segments up to 10×2mm, entire or toothed, dark green above, grey-white hairy beneath. INFLORESCENCE many flowered, leafy, nodding at stem tip; FLOWERHEADS 3-4mm diam, creamy yellow (Feb-May). GENERAL: Used in traditional medicine.

Achillea (after Achilles, hero of Homer's Iliad) Perennial herbs. Leaves usually compound. About 115 species, 1 naturalised as a weed in SAfr.

★*Achillea millefolium* Common Yarrow; Duisendblaarachillea (A) (*mille* - thousand; *folium* -leaf)

Aromatic herb, up to 500mm tall. In colonies, in grassland, on roadsides. Introduced weed (N America). LEAVES up to 150mm long, segments narrow. INFLORESCENCES flat; FLOWERHEADS white, ±5×3mm, rays few, short, broad (Nov-May).

Senecio (*senex* - old man, refers to whitish hairs of pappus) (see pg 162)

Senecio subrubriflorus mahoaneng, mahoanyana (SS) (*subrubriflorus* - nearly red flowers)

Tufted herb, up to 600mm tall. On rocky mountain slopes, 1100-2355m. KZN to Mpum. Plant **leafy, sticky hairy**, aromatic. BASAL LEAVES up to 200×40mm, **deeply, narrowly lobed**, with long stalklike base, margins toothed or lobed. FLOWERHEADS ±10×5mm, pale mauve, white (Jan-Apr). GENERAL: Used in traditional medicine.

Dimorphotheca (*di* - two or twice; *morph* - shape; *theka* - a fruit, refers to two kinds of fruit found in the same fruiting head) (see pg 226)

Dimorphotheca caulescens [= *Osteospermum caulescens*] Bietou (A); bohlahlo, mohlahlo, phela (SS) (*caulescens* - stem)

Tufted perennial herb, up to 300mm tall. In moist rocky grassland, gullies, on Cave Sandstone cliffs, up to 2500m. E Cape to Mpum. BASAL LEAVES up to 150×20mm, margins entire, wavy, narrowed to stalklike base. FLOWERHEADS solitary, ±40mm diam, ray florets **creamy white above**, bluish beneath, disc florets whitish (Nov-Feb).

Eumorphia prostrata

David McDonald

Eumorphia prostrata

David McDonald

Callilepis laureola

Wally Menne

★ *Artemisia afra*

Rosemary Williams

Senecio subrubriflorus

Pam Cooke

Dimorphotheca caulescens

Martin von Fintel

Eumorphia sericia subsp. *robustior*

Hilliard & Burtt

Eumorphia sericia

David McDonald

★ *Achillea millefolium*

Martin von Fintel

113

Hirpicium (*hirpex* - a harrow) Annual or perennial herbs. SAfr, ±12 species, 1 in this region.

Hirpicium armerioides   Skynloodkruid (A); shoeshoe, shoeshoe-ea-loti (flowerhead), tsikitlane, tsikitlane-ea-loti (whole plant) (SS) (*armerioides* - resembles the genus *Armeria*)

Mat-forming perennial herb, up to 250mm high. On poor, stony ground, rock sheets, up to 3200m. E Cape to Mpum. LEAVES in basal rosette, up to 100×4mm, ± lobed, bristly above, often with long white hairs, white-felted beneath. FLOWERHEADS 25-50mm diam, ray florets **white above, yellow to purplish black beneath** (Sep-Apr).

Berkheya (after Dutch botanist Jan le Francq van Berkhey, 1724-1812) (see pg 176)

Berkheya cirsiifolia   mohata-o-mosoeu, ntšoantsane-e-kholo, tšehlo-ea-thaba (SS)

Stout perennial herb, up to 1.5m tall. In colonies on moist grassy slopes, streambanks, 1800-3000m. EMR endemic. Stems softly hairy. BASAL LEAVES up to 300×80mm, up to 6 lobes each side, glandular above, white-felted beneath, margins deeply, sharply toothed, **upper leaves broad at base, clasping, running onto stem in spiny wings**. FLOWERHEADS up to 80mm diam, **ray florets white or yellow,** disc florets yellow, **bracts leaflike, up to 10mm broad, tips with spines 5-10mm long** (Jan-Mar).

Berkheya draco

Stiff bushy shrub, up to 1m tall. In small colonies, in gullies in grassland, in boulder beds of streams. EMR endemic. Stems very leafy, becoming leafless with age below. LEAVES rigid, clasping, up to 90mm long, **compound, lobes up to 14×4mm, widely spaced, spine-tipped,** green above, white-felted below. FLOWERHEADS 50-90mm diam, **rays white** or tinged mauve, **disc mauve,** bracts narrow, up to 3mm wide (Nov-Jan).

Berkheya leucaugeta (*leucaugeta* - white-rayed)

Robust perennial herb, 1-1.5m tall. In marshy depressions on hillsides, in scrub, 1800-2160m. EMR endemic. Stem simple below, branching into a big spreading inflorescence. At flowering, only the stems leafy. LEAVES up to 400×135mm, **base narrowed and running down stems in narrow wings, margins shallowly lobed, lobes rounded, spines short,** 2.5-4mm long. FLOWERHEADS up to 80mm across, many, rays white, disc florets yellow, bracts broad, up to 25×8mm, spiny (Feb).

Dicoma (*di* - two; *kome* - tuft of hairs) Woody perennials. Floral bracts sharp, pointed. Afr, Socotra, India, 35 species, 19 in SAfr, 1 in this region.

Dicoma anomala   Aambeibos, Gryshout, Koorsbossie, Maagbossie, Swartstorm (A); hloenya (SS); inyongana (X); isihlabamakhondlwane, umuna (Z)

Reclining perennial herb, stems 50-600mm long, leafy throughout. In poor stony grassland, crevices of rock sheets, up to 2075m. Widespread. LEAVES **narrow,** up to 90×2-10mm, green above, white-felted beneath. FLOWERHEADS 15-30mm diam, purplish pink or whitish, **bracts narrow, sharply pointed,** branches curve upwards (Jan-May). GENERAL: Used to make a tea and to treat a wide variety of ailments.

Gerbera (named after Traugott Gerber, died 1743, German naturalist) Perennial herbs, often with woolly crown. Leaves in rosette. The Barberton Daisy, *G. jamesonii*, is a well-known ornamental with many cultivars and hybrids. About 30 species, mostly SAfr, ±4 in this region.

Gerbera ambigua   Botterblom, Griekwateebossie (A); moarubetso, moku-betso, tsebe-ea-pela (SS); ucabazane, uhlambihloshane, ulimi-lwenkomo (Z) (*ambigua* - doubtful)

Perennial herb, flowering stems up to 350mm high. In moist or rocky grassland, up to 2500m. Widespread. LEAVES very variable, 50-80×25-35mm, thinly hairy above, **white felted** to thinly hairy **beneath,** stalks often 20-30mm long. FLOWERHEADS 30-50mm diam, ray florets white above, pink or coppery beneath (Sep-Feb). **Pappus white.** GENERAL: A form with leaves green below was described as *G. viridifolia.*

Gerbera parva (*parva* - small)

Perennial herb, flowering stems up to 200mm high. In colonies, on damp cliff faces, in gullies, 1900-2650m. EMR endemic. BASAL LEAVES up to 30mm diam, **shiny dark green above,** base heart-shaped, margins sharply toothed, **stalks slender,** up to 150mm long. FLOWERHEADS up to 25mm wide, rays white, tinged pink below (Oct-Dec).

Gerbera piloselloides   Swartteebossie (A); moarubetso, mothuntšetso, tsebe-ea-pela (SS); ubulawu, umqwashu (X); indlebeyempithi, uhlango olumpofu, umoya-wezwe (Z)

Perennial herb, up to 300mm tall. In grassland, up to 2900m. Cape to China. LEAVES **in flattish rosette** up to 90×60mm. FLOWERHEADS 15-25mm diam, **ray florets** white, pink or yellow, stem **swollen beneath flowerhead** (Jul-Feb).

114

Rod Saunders

Lal Greene

Hirpicium armerioides

Gerbera piloselloides

Tony Abbott

Martin von Fintel

Simon Milliken

Gerbera parva

Gerbera ambigua

Berkheya draco

Hilliard & Burtt

Mike Hirst

Berkheya cirsiifolia

Berkheya cirsiifolia

Hilliard & Burtt

Tony Abbott

Berkheya leucaugeta

Dicoma anomala

115

MONOCOTYLEDONS   Single seed-leaf, parallel veins; flower parts in threes or multiples of three.

CYPERACEAE - Sedge family (see pg 248). *Cyperus* (*cyperus* - sedge) Cosmop, ±650 species, ±70 in SAfr, 6 in this region.

Cyperus sphaerocephalus [= *C. flavissimus, C. obtusiflorus* var. *sphaerocephalus, C. obtusiflorus* var. *flavissimus*] Yellow Sedge; Geelbiesie (A); lejabutle-le-lesehla, monakalali-oa-litšoene (SS) (*sphaerocephalus* - round head)

Perennial, up to 450mm tall. In rocky grassland, up to 2000m. E Cape to Trop Afr. LEAVES stiff, tough, grey-green. SPIKELETS conspicuous **bright golden yellow**, ±30mm diam (spring). GENERAL: Flowerheads plaited into necklets worn by girls in Les.

XYRIDACEAE (*xyron* – plant with sharp leaves) Perennial marsh herbs. 1 genus in SAfr. *Xyris* Trop, ±240 species, 7 in NE SA, 2 in this region.

Xyris capensis Common Xyris; hloho-tsa-makaka, kaka-hlothoana (SS); udoyi oluncane (Z)

Grasslike perennial, 30-300mm tall. In marshy places, up to 2400m. W Cape to Trop Afr. LEAVES erect, 50-150×4 mm, tapering to hard points, **arranged in a fan**. INFLORESCENCE compact, shiny brown, **bract margins entire, flowering stem round**, wiry, usually twice as long as leaves; FLOWERS delicate, yellow, 3-5 open at a time (Nov-Feb). GENERAL: Stems used for making beer strainers. **Similar species: *Xyris gerrardii*** (named after William Gerrard who collected widely in SA in the early 1800s) Up to 300mm tall. In marshy areas, up to 2100m. KZN to Zim. LEAVES soft, thin. Bract **margins white, ragged**.

COMMELINACEAE - Commelina Family Trop, ±40 genera, ±650 species, 7 genera in SAfr, 2 in this region. *Commelina* (named by Linnaeus after the three Commelin brothers. Johann and Caspar were well known botanists but the third brother died before achieving anything in the botanical world. Refers to the 2 large and 1 insignificant tepals in the *Commelina* flowers) Trop, ±170 species, 16 in SAfr, 2 in this region.

Commelina africana Yellow Commelina; Geeleendagsblom (A); khopo, khotsoana, tabola-lefalo (SS); lekzotswana (X); idangabane (Z)

Perennial herb, prostrate, spreading. In grassland, up to 2400m. SA to Trop Afr. Size very variable. LEAVES flat or folded, smooth or hairy. FLOWERS yellow, usually closing before midday (Nov-Feb). GENERAL: Used in traditional medicine to treat a wide variety of ailments. Useful to speed up decomposition of compost and as a foliar feed.

ASPHODELACEAE (see pg 50). *Bulbine* (*bulbine* - bulbous plant) Hairy stamens. Superficially resembles *Bulbinella* flowers which have non-hairy stamens and are only found in the Cape. Afr, Austr, ±50 species, ±46 in SAfr, ±4 in this region.

Bulbine abyssinica Bushy Bulbine; Geelkatstert, Wildekopieva (A); moetsa-mollo (SS); intelezi (X); ibhucu (Z) (*abyssinica* - Abyssinia, now Ethiopia)

Tufted herb, up to 700mm. Very variable. In rocky grassland, in shallow soil on cliffs, up to 2400m. Widespread. LEAVES in basal rosette, fleshy, cylindrical, ±3mm broad, **lower margins winged white, base pinkish**. INFLORESCENCE large, densely crowded; FLOWERS ±14mm diam, yellow, stamens feathery, **stalks held straight after flowers or fruits fall** (Dec-Jan). CAPSULES round, held upright. GENERAL: Used in traditional medicine, excellent for a range of skin complaints. Hardy, attractive garden plant. **Similar species:** *Bulbine favosa* (*favosa* – like a honeycomb) In crevices of cliffs, around rock sheets, up to 2250m, S EMR. **Dainty, not clumped**. FLOWERS pale yellow (Nov-Jan).

Bulbine narcissifolia Strap-leaved Bulbine; Wildekopieva (A); khomo-ea-balsaa, serelelile (SS) (*narcissifolia* – leaves like *Narcissus*)

Up to 300mm tall. Solitary or in colonies, on poor soils, in grassland. Widespread. LEAVES in a fan, ±300×12-20mm, **flat, hard**, grey-green, sometimes twisted. INFLORESCENCE short, dense, 25-35mm diam (Nov-Apr). GENERAL: Used in traditional medicine to induce pregnancy in barren women and barren cows.

Kniphofia - **Red-hot Pokers** (named after J.H. Kniphof, 1704-1763, prof. of medicine at Erfurt University) (see pg 22)

Kniphofia fibrosa Yellow Berg Poker (*fibrosa* - fibre)

Up to 600mm tall, solitary. On damp grassy slopes up to 2000m. S EMR southwards. LEAVES grasslike, 3-4mm wide, keeled, forming fibres at base, margins finely toothed, smooth near base. INFLORESCENCE 25-70×25-30mm; BUDS and FLOWERS pale yellow, 12-20mm long (Jan-Mar).

Kniphofia ichopensis Ixopo Red-hot Poker; Ixopovuurpyl (A); umathunga, icacane (Z)

(*ichopensis* - named after Ixopo where the plant was first discovered)

Robust, up to 900mm tall, solitary or in small groups. Frequent in vleis and moist grassland, 1450-2600m. LEAVES few, 500-800×5-10mm. INFLORESCENCE 100-300×60-70mm, **bracts long, narrow, pointed**; BUDS dull yellow, tinged red; FLOWERS 30-42mm long, **cream, yellow-green to salmon-pink** (Nov-Apr).

Cyperus sphaerocephalus

Tony Abbott

Commelina africana

Neil Crouch

Xyris capensis

Lal Greene

Bulbine narcissifolia

David McDonald

Xyris gerrardii

Lal Greene

Bulbine abyssinica

David McDonald

Kniphofia fibrosa

Cameron McMaster

Kniphofia ichopensis

Martin von Fintel

Kniphofia ichopensis

Rob Scott-Shaw

117

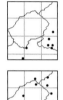

Kniphofia parviflora [= *K. modesta*] ihlinzanyoka (Z) *(parviflora - small flowers)*

Up to 800mm tall, solitary. In grassland, marshy places, up to 2000m. E Cape to KZN. LEAVES slender, **forming fibres at base**, margins smooth. INFLORESCENCE **one-sided**, tall, slender, up to 750×7mm; BUDS greenish brown to maroon, FLOWERS **small**, about 10×2mm, creamy yellow to greenish, scented (Jan-Mar).

Kniphofia porphyrantha Dwarf Red-hot Poker; Hoëveldvuurpyl (A); leloele (SS); icacane, umathunga (Z) *(porphyrantha - purple flowers, but no Kniphofia is purple)*

Up to 600mm tall, in big clumps. In damp or marshy grassland, 1500-2300m. KZN, FS, Gaut, Mpum. LEAVES soft, **yellow-green**, often with waxy bloom, **6-15mm broad, margins smooth**. INFLORESCENCE **bi-coloured**, dense, ±80×50mm; BUDS spreading, orange-red tipped yellow; FLOWERS 30-40mm long, lemon yellow (Dec-Feb). GENERAL: Used in traditional medicine to treat female ailments.

HYACINTHACEAE Afr, Eurasia, N America, ±46 genera, ±900 species, 27 genera in SAfr. Popular for ornamentals. *Albuca* (*albus* - white or *albicans* - becoming white) Flowers with 3 inner tepals erect and touching, outer tepals spreading. Afr, Arabia, ±80 species, ±60 in SAfr, ±9 in this region.

Albuca shawii Small Yellow Albuca; Lanternblom (A) *(named after John Shaw, 1837-1890)*

150-400mm. On cliffs, in rocky grassland, up to 2400m. E Cape to Limpopo Prov. LEAVES covered with **short sticky hairs**. FLOWERS few, ±15mm, yellow, **nodding**, scented (Sep-Feb). GENERAL: Liquorice smell when crushed. **Similar species: Albuca rupestris** (*rupestris* -growing among rocks) Edges and crevices of rock sheets, rocky cliffs, up to 2450m. EMR endemic. FLOWERS **larger**, ±24 mm, yellow, **held erect**, pleasant scent (Nov-Dec).

AMARYLLIDACEAE Bulbous herbs. Popular horticultural subjects. Trop and warm regions, ±60 genera, over 800 species, 18 genera in SAfr, 6 in this region. *Cyrtanthus* (*kyrtos* - curved; *anthos* - flower, referring to the frequently curved flower tube) Afr, mainly SAfr, ±50 species, 9 in this region.

Cyrtanthus attenuatus *(attenuatus - slender)*

Robust, up to 500mm tall. On streambanks, in rocky grassland, above 2450m, on the summit plateau. EMR endemic. LEAVES 3-4, ±400×5-10mm, **narrowing gradually to both ends**, produced with leaves. FLOWERING STEM hollow; FLOWERS slender, **dull yellowish green, lobes roundish**, 6-7×5mm (Sep-Dec).

Cyrtanthus breviflorus Yellow Fire-lily; Geelvuurlelie, Wildekrokus (A); lematlana-la-loti, moroloane, moroloane-o-moholo (SS); uvelabahleka (Z) *(breviflorus – short flowers)*

75-300mm tall. In marshy, grassy places, up to 3000m. E Cape to Kenya. LEAVES strap-shaped, 60-250×1-14mm. FLOWERS 1-10(20), bright yellow, **tube short**, 5-10mm, lobes 20-25mm, scented (Aug-Nov). GENERAL: The plants can vary greatly in stature depending on habitat, the wetter it is at flowering, the taller the plants. Bulb edible. Used in traditional medicine to treat intestinal worms and as protective and love charms. Good garden plant, from seed.

Cyrtanthus flanaganii Flanagan's Cyrtanthus, Yellow Dobo Lily; Geeldobolelie (A)

(named after Henry Flanagan, 1861-1919, citrus farmer, plant collector, gardener who bequeathed his collections to the nation)

Up to 200mm tall. In damp turf, on wet cliffs, 2000-3300m, withstands frost and snow. EMR endemic. LEAVES ±200×20mm, **blunt-tipped**, produced with the flowers. FLOWERS **bright** yellow, **tube long, narrow**, 40-55mm, **lobes oblong**, ±15×9mm, sweetly scented (Nov-Dec).

Cyrtanthus stenanthus Long-tubed Cyrtanthus; lepontoana, moroloanyane-oa-litšoene (SS); impingizana encane ebomvu (Z) *(stenanthus - narrow anthers)*

Up to 400mm. In damp grassland, stony places, up to 2800m. E Cape to Mpum. LEAVES ±300×2-5mm. INFLORESCENCE erect to nodding; FLOWERS **turned to one side**, dull red, orange or yellow, ±45mm long, **very slender**, slightly contracted at throat, lobes spreading, ±3mm, **paler than the tube**, sweetly scented (Oct-Mar). GENERAL: Bulb is eaten. Used as a protective charm against lightning.

Albuca rupestris

Tony Abbott

David McDonald

Albuca shawii

David McDonald

Kniphofia parviflora

Kniphofia porphyrantha

David McDonald

Auriol Batten

Albuca shawii

Peter Linder

Cyrtanthus attenuatus

Cameron McMaster

Cyrtanthus breviflora

Martin von Fintel

Cyrtanthus flanaganii

Martin von Fintel

Cyrtanthus stenanthus

119

HYPOXIDACEAE - Star-flower Family S Hemisp, 9 genera, ±130 species, 6 genera in SAfr, 4 in this region. *Hypoxis* (*hyp* - beneath; *oxys* - sharp pointed) Mostly Afr, ±90 species, ±45 in SAfr, ±16 in this region. The genus is under revision. Research into the medicinal properties of *Hypoxis* is ongoing.

Hypoxis argentea Small Yellow Star-flower; leihlo-khoma le leholo, lesikitlane, moli (SS); ixalanxa (X); inonwe (X,Z); isinana (Z) (*argentea* - silvery)
Up to 400mm. In grassland, on rocky outcrops. LEAVES narrow, **V-shape**d, 50-500 ×1-7mm, 2 prominent ribs, densely covered in silky **yellowish hairs**. INFLORESCENCE slender, branched, much shorter than leaves; FLOWERS small, in pairs, ±20mm diam (Aug-Apr). GENERAL: Rootstock eaten, also used to treat cracked teats of cows and wounds on horses. Attractive garden ground cover. **Similar species: *Hypoxis filiformis*** Grass Star-flower; moli-letsane (SS); izinongwe (Z) (*filiformis* - threadlike) Small, slender, erect, grasslike plant. In marshy grassland up to 2400m. LEAVES **threadlike**, 80-200×1-3mm, rigid, **U-shaped** in cross section, with fine hairs on margins. FLOWERING STEM as long as leaves, silky hairy towards tip; FLOWERS 12-25mm diam, often with 4 tepals (Oct-Dec).

Hypoxis iridifolia [= *H. nitida*] moli-boea (SS); inkomfe (Z) (*iridifolia* - iris-like leaves)
Up to 600mm tall. In dry rocky grassland, up to 2000m. LEAVES **narrow**, 70-600 ×3-20mm, erect to arching, twisted with age, **shiny, hairless**, thick, leathery, folded, **margins and keel edged with a line of dense white hairs**. FLOWERING STEMS almost as long as leaves; FLOWERS ±50mm diam, (Oct-Dec). **Similar species: *Hypoxis galpinii*** (named after Ernest Galpin, 1858-1941, SA naturalist and 'prince' of plant collectors) In grassland, up to 1900m. LEAVES **broader**, ±500×15-45mm, erect, **almost hairless**, ribbed with raised vein on either side of keel, dry leaves dark red-brown. FLOWERS 20-35mm diam (Sep-Feb).

Hypoxis ludwigii (named after C.F.H. von Ludwig, 1784-1847, German pharmacist, businessman, patron of natural sciences and plant collector who settled in the Cape in 1805)
In damp or marshy grassland and streamsides, (coast) 2100-2450m. E Cape to KZN. LEAVES **long, narrow**, 300-450×6-8mm, leathery, margins and keel bristly. Flowering stem long, weak, loosely hairy; FLOWERS yellow, ±35mm diam, 4-12 in a **flat-topped cluster** (Nov-Feb).

Hypoxis multiceps moli-motsane, morethetlo (SS); inkomfe (Z) (*multiceps* - bearing many heads)
Low growing at flowering. In grassland, up to 2000m. LEAVES **produced after the flowers**, in 3 ranks, ±300×55mm, arching, flat, ribbed, **hairs dense, rough, yellowish**. INFLORESCENCE **appears before leaves, stem short, thick**, flat, hairy; FLOWERS in opposite pairs, large, yellow, 20-40mm diam (Jun-Nov). GENERAL: Leaves continue to grow when flowering is over. Used as a protective charm against lightning. **Similar species: *Hypoxis costata*** moli-kharatsa (SS) (*costata* - with lines or riblike ridges) Up to 150mm tall. On stony, grassy slopes, 2050-2400m. LEAVES **produced with flowers**, broad, ±180×40mm, rigid, sickle-shaped, **conspicuously ribbed**, densely hairy or hairless, thickened submarginal veins. FLOWERING STEMS **as long as leaves**, FLOWERS large (Oct-Jan).

Hypoxis rigidula Silver-leaved Star-flower; moli-tieane (SS); inkomfe (Z) (*rigidula* - stiff)
Up to 900mm tall. In small to large groups. On grassy slopes, up to 2300m. Widespread in SAfr. Variable (two varieties). LEAVES **erect**, ±900×3-15mm, **flat, strongly ribbed, covered in white hairs, forming a stem at base**. FLOWERS 3-11, large, ±40mm diam, yellow (Nov-Mar). GENERAL: Plants eaten by baboons. Leaves used to make strong lasting rope. Used in traditional medicine. An attractive garden plant. **Similar species: *Hypoxis acuminata*** moli-motsanyane, thoto-linyenyane (SS) (*acuminata* - long pointed) Up to 300mm tall, in large communities. In damp grassland, up to 1980m. LEAVES **narrow**, erect, in **spreading tuft**, short stem at base, 150-300×2-5mm, **V-shaped** in cross-section, ribbed, with long dense hairs above, sparse beneath. FLOWERS 2-6, smaller, 20-35mm diam (Oct-Jan).

Hypoxis argentea

Martin von Fintel

Hypoxis costata

Neil Crouch

Hypoxis acuminata

Pam Cooke

Hypoxis filiformis

Tony Abbott

Hypoxis multiceps

Martin Kunhardt

Hypoxis iridifolia

Yashica Singh

Hypoxis rigidula

Lal Greene

Hypoxis ludwigii

Hilliard & Burtt

121

IRIDACEAE - Iris Family Temp regions, ±70 genera, ±1800 species, ±32 genera in SAfr, ±12 in this region. ***Romulea*** (*romulus* - named after founder and first king of Rome) S Europe and Afr, ±88 species, ±77 in S Afr, centred in the winter rainfall area, 3 in this region.

Romulea macowanii Macowan's Romulea; khukhu (SS) (named after P MacOwan, 1830-1909, plant collector, appointed government botanist in the Cape, eminent scientist)

A lovely, crocuslike flower, 200-400mm tall. In large colonies, in wet turf, 2250-2900m. E Cape to KZN. LEAVES **slender**, 150-400× ±1mm. FLOWERS **golden yellow becoming orange at base**, tepals 10-35mm long, 3 outer tepals brownish purple outside (Jan-Mar). GENERAL: Two varieties found in this region: Var. *alticola* [= *R. longituba* var. *alticola*] FLOWERS **large**, tepals 15-35mm long, tube 35-65mm long. Var. *oreophila:* FLOWERS **small**, tepals 10-25mm long, tube short, 13-27mm long; bracts white in lower half. **Similar species:** *Romulea luteoflora* var. *sanisensis* In marshy turf at Sani Top, 2900m. EMR endemic. FLOWERS **small**, tepals ±15mm long, **yellow**, three outer tepals lined purple-brown outside (Nov).

Moraea (Linnaeus altered the original spelling from *Morea* to *Moraea* to associate the name with his father-in-law, J Moraeus, a physician in Sweden) End of style branches petal-like. Afr, Madag, Austr. ±200 species, ±180 in SAfr, mostly SW Cape, 15 in this region.

Moraea alticola teele-e-kholo (SS) (*alticola* - from high altitudes)

Robust, up to 1m tall. **In large clumps**, in stream gullies, marshy grassland on the summit, sometimes in spectacular, large colonies, 2400-2900m. EMR endemic. **Base of leaf and flowering stem encircled with a pale network of fibres** (cataphylls). LEAF **solitary**, 15-30mm wide, flat, margins thickened. FLOWERS **large**, ±90mm wide, **pale yellow** with darker yellow nectar guides on the outer tepals (Nov-Jan). GENERAL: Leaves used to make rope. These high altitude plants were previously incorrectly named *M. spathulata*, until the plant was described in 1973. **Similar species:** *Moraea spathulata* ihlamvu elincane, indlolothi, ingqunda (Z) (*spathulata* - spatula-like, refers to shape of inner tepals) **Solitary** or in small clumps, in moist grassland. S Cape to Zim. Fibres at base brown, not netted. LEAF long, **narrow, ±15mm wide**, twisted. FLOWERS **bright yellow** (Nov-Dec). GENERAL: Popular, hardy, garden plant, flowers last 3 days.

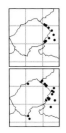

Moraea carnea (*carnea* – flesh-coloured)

Up to 500mm tall. On damp grassy slopes, along streams, 2200-2700m. EMR endemic. LEAF solitary, 3-6mm wide, channelled. FLOWERS **cream, veined and flushed purple to pale red-brown,** style crests **usually dark reddish brown.** (Nov-Dec).

Moraea huttonii Large Golden Vlei Moraea; teale-ea-noka (SS) (named in honour of Henry Hutton, amateur botanist who collected in E Cape in the mid 1800s)

Up to 1m tall. **In large clumps, in or close to mountain streams and rivers**, often among rocks, up to 2400m. E Cape to KZN/Mpum. Cataphyll fibres at base dark brown, not netted. LEAF usually longer than stem, 5-25mm wide, margins incurved. FLOWERS large, **bright yellow** with large, deep yellow nectar guides on outer tepals and **dark brown to purple blotch on each style crest**, sweetly scented (Sep-Oct). GENERAL: A lovely garden plant.

Moraea trifida (*trifida* - refers to 3-lobed inner tepals)

Up to 550mm tall, **solitary**. In moist grassland, on seepages, up to 2400m. E Cape to Mpum. LEAF solitary, **stiff, hard**, usually shorter than flowering stem. FLOWERS small, ±20mm long, creamy yellow spotted brown to green, **outer tepals reflexed, inner tepals** ±15mm, erect, **trilobed**, yellow and green (Oct-Feb).

Moraea unibracteata (*unibracteata* - single bract, refers to solitary sheathing bract on flowering stem)

Up to 350mm tall, solitary. In moist grassland, up to 2200m. KZN endemic. LEAF solitary, stiffly erect, **usually longer than flowering stem, clasping in lower half.** FLOWERING STEM erect, bract leaf sheathing, overlapping spathes; FLOWERS large, outer tepals 30-45mm long, **pale yellow** veined green, nectar guides deep yellow (Oct-Nov).

Homeria (after the Greek poet Homer or *omereo* - meet together, refers to filaments united around the style) Mainly SW Cape, ±32 species, 1 in this region.

Homeria pallida Geeltulp (A); teele (SS); indlolothi, ingqunde (Z) (*pallida* - somewhat pale)

Slender, erect, up to 500mm tall. Often in large colonies, in damp places, 1370-1525m. Widespread in S Afr. LEAF soft, bluish-green, ribbed, trailing, longer than the flowering stem. FLOWERS small, yellow with greenish brown speckles at base, sweetly scented (Sep-Dec). GENERAL: Very poisonous to cattle. Indicates over grazing.

Romulea macowanii

Cameron McMaster

Homeria pallida

Martin von Fintel

Moraea carnea

Pam Cooke

Moraea trifida

Lal Greene

Moraea huttonii

Neil Crouch

Moraea huttonii

Martin von Fintel

Moraea trifida

Neil Crouch

Moraea alticola

Martin von Fintel

Moraea alticola

Cynthia Giddy

Moraea unibracteata

Lal Greene

Moraea unibracteata

Lal Greene

123

Tritonia (*triton* - a weathercock, refers to the variable direction of the stamens of the different species) SAfr to Tanz, 28 species, mostly in coastal areas of S Cape, 2 in this region.

Tritonia lineata Pencilled Tritonia, Yellow Tritonia; Bergkatjietee (A); khahla-e-nyenyane, khetleleli (SS); isidwi esimpofu (Z) (*lineata* - marked with lines)

Up to 300mm tall. In grassland, up to 2400m. SE Cape to Mpum. LEAVES 150-300 ×7-10mm, midvein prominent. FLOWERS cream to pale yellow with dark veins (Sep-Dec). GENERAL: Used in traditional medicine to treat stomach complaints in babies and heal infections in the navel of a newborn child. Suitable for gardens.

Gladiolus (*gladiolus* - small sword, refers to leaf shape) Hybrids created since the early 1800s have produced the cut-flowers and garden plants popular worldwide. Known as *itembu* (X) 'fruits of the earth' corms are dug up and eaten in rural areas. Afr, S Europe and Middle East, ±260 species, ±165 species in SAfr, ±14 in this region.

Gladiolus longicollis Honey-flower; Aandblom (A); khahla-e-nyenyane, khukhu-rupa (SS); umbejo (Z) (*longicollis* - long-necked, refers to the elongate flower tube)

Solitary, up to 500mm high. Scattered in rocky grassland, up to 2900(3300)m. Widespread, W Cape to Limpopo Prov. LEAF **solitary**, sheathing stem, ±5mm wide. FLOWERS 50-80mm wide, cream to pale yellow with reddish brown to purple speckles and dark lines, **tube long, narrow, 50-60(120)mm**, open in late afternoon and have a strong, sweet scent in the evening (Oct-Dec). GENERAL: Pollinated by hawkmoths. Corms eaten by game birds and small mammals.

Gladiolus pubigerus [= *G. pugioniformis*] (*pubigerus* - bearing hairs, refers to the downy hairs on the lowest leaf or catophyll of the flowering stem and the leaves of non-flowering plants)

200-400mm high. In moist grassland, 1450-2500m. E Cape to Mpum. LEAF solitary, partly sheathing the lower half of the flowering stem, hairy, up to 50(100)mm long, second leaf shorter, hairless and sheathing. FLOWERS 20-30mm long, **tepals nearly equal, sharply pointed**, pale greenish yellow, fading to light brown, stongly scented in the mornings (Oct-Jan). GENERAL: Inconspicuous in green grassland.

ORCHIDACEAE - Orchid Family A very large family with highly specialized flowers. Cosmop, ±800 genera, ±20000 species, 52 genera in SAfr. *Holothrix* (*holos* - whole or entire; *thrix* - hair, meaning hairy all over) Terrestrial herbs. **2 leaves flat on ground**. Flowering stem leafless and bractless, flowers white to yellowish green, petals lobed. Afr. ±55 species, 23 in SAfr, mainly in the Cape, ±4 in this region.

Holothrix incurva (*incurva* – curved inwards, refers to spur)

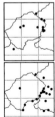

70-170mm tall. Frequent in damp crevices and ledges in cliffs, 1500-2900m. EMR endemic. LEAF margins fringed with hairs. FLOWERS **yellowish** green to yellow, sepals very hairy, **lip deeply divided into 5 slender lobes**; STEM softly hairy (Dec-Apr).

Holothrix scopularia [= *H. multisecta*] (*scopulinus* - bearing small brushes; or *scopulosus* - rocky)

Slender to robust, 110-340mm tall. In rocky grassland and rocky outcrops, 1525-2800m. E Cape to Mpum. **Plant covered in conspicuous spreading hairs**. LEAVES often withered at time of flowering. INFLORESCENCE **dense, flowers all arranged on one side**; STEM conspicuously hairy; FLOWERS small, white to dull yellow or pink, **lip deeply divided into 5-11 slender lobes** (Oct-Feb). (see pg 62)

Holothrix thodei (named after Hans Justus Thode, 1859-1932, pioneer plant collector in the Drakensberg)

100-250mm tall. In moist rocky grassland or rock crevices, 1500-2600m. Mountains from E Cape to Mpum. LEAVES densely hairy, withered at time of flowering. FLOWERS yellowish to brownish green, **lip short, 3-lobed, middle lobe much longer**; STEM with **long, downward pointing hairs** (Jan-Mar).

Schizochilus (*schizo* - split, deeply divided; *cheilos* - lip) Terrestrial herb with few narrow leaves near base of stem. **Inflorescence dense, usually nodding** or drooping over at tip. S and CAfr, ±11 species, restricted to montane and subalpine grasslands, 8 in SAfr, 4 in this region.

Schizochilus zeyheri (named after Carl Ludwig Zeyher, 1799-1858, botanical collector in the Cape in 1822)

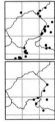

Slender, 150-600mm. In marshy mountain grassland, up to 1950m. E Cape to Limpopo Prov. LEAVES narrow, 40-140×3-10mm, **mostly sheathing lower half of stem**. INFLORESCENCE loose, up to 100mm long; FLOWERS **large, 4-6mm diam, bright yellow**, sepals ±11mm, lip deeply 3-lobed, **spur straight, 2-6mm** (Nov-Mar). GENERAL: Very variable size and growth form. **Similar species: *Schizochilus bulbinella*** (*bulbinella* – small bulb or small *Bulbine*) Slender, up to 250mm tall. Frequent, in shallow soil over rock, 1500-2500m. EMR endemic. LEAVES **in basal cluster**. INFLORESCENCE dense, 20-40mm long; FLOWERS **small**, ±3mm diam, yellow, sepals ±3.5mm (Jan-Feb).

Cynthia Giddy

Gladiolus longicollis

Martin von Fintel

Tritonia lineata

Mike Hirst

Gladiolus longicollis

Martin von Fintel

Gladiolus pubigerus

Peter Linder

Holothrix incurva

Martin von Fintel

Holothrix scopularia

H J Venter

Holothrix thodei

Anne Rennie

Gladiolus pubigerus

Clinton Carbutt

Schizochilus zeyheri

Martin von Fintel

Schizochilus bulbinella

Neil Crouch

Schizochilus bulbinella

125

Liparis (*liparos* - shiny oily, refers to leaves) Usually terrestrial, with or without pseudobulbs. Throughout warm and temperate regions, most common in Trop Asia, ±250 species, 4 in S Afr, 1 in this region.

Liparis bowkeri (named after Mary Barber, nee Bowker, 1818-1899, an ardent student of nature, writer, painter, who came to SA in 1820 with her family)

Terrestrial or epiphytic, 100-200mm tall. In small crowded colonies, occasional in leaf litter on forest floor or on mossy rocks and tree trunks, up to 1800m. E Cape to Trop Afr. PSEUDOBULBS **soft, green**, 20-70mm tall, **in closely packed groups**. LEAVES 2-3, basal, blade broad, soft, **veins prominent**, 45-120×25-70mm. INFLORESCENCE loose; FLOWERS **translucent yellowish green** fading brown, side sepals oblong, flat, ±12mm long, **petals long, slender, hanging down**, 8-12×1mm (Dec-Mar). GENERAL: Used traditionally as a good luck or love charm.

Eulophia (*eu* - well; *lophos* - crest, refers to the crested lip) Terrestrial herbs. **Lip ridged on upper surface.** Old and New World, most common in Afr, 42 in S Afr, 9 in this region.

Eulophia leontoglossa **Lion's Tongue or Lion's Tooth Orchid; Leeutong (A); lekholela, lekoesha, loetsana (SS); iphamba (Z)** (*leontoglossa* - tongue like a lion's)

60-300mm tall. In stony grassland, up to 1980m. E Cape to Mpum. LEAVES stiffly erect, up to 300×9mm, partly to fully grown at flowering. INFLORESCENCE **nodding**; FLOWERS white to lemon-yellow or pink tinged green, sepals and petals 8-16mm long, slightly spreading, lip crests yellow to brown (Sep-Dec). GENERAL: Used as a protective charm against lightning.

Eulophia calanthoides (*calanthos* - bearing beautiful flowers, resembling *Calanthe*)

Slender, 300-600mm tall, sometimes in small scattered colonies. In damp coarse vegetation on forest margins, up to 2200m. E Cape to Mpum. LEAVES thin-textured, fully developed at flowering, up to 700×60mm. INFLORESCENCE crowded at first, becoming longer and looser as flowers open; FLOWERS **large**, sepals and petals, 26-30mm long, spreading, sepals purplish brown, green inside, petals and lip very pale yellow, main veins speckled blue, crest bright yellow, spur ±5mm long (Dec-Jan).

Eulophia ovalis **lekholela-la-Matabele, lekoesha, ´mametsana (SS); ihamba lesigodi, iphamba (Z)** (*ovalis* - broadly elliptic, oval)

Robust, 150-400mm tall. In damp grassland, up to 2000m. E Cape to Limpopo Prov (subsp. *ovalis*). LEAVES **leathery**, fully developed at flowering. INFLORESCENCE loosely spreading; FLOWERS **'flattish'**, sepals brownish to maroon outside, 14-26mm long, petals white tinged yellow or lilac flushed maroon outside, the veins inside speckled blue, lip the same colour as petals, **spur cylindrical**, 2.5-5.6mm long, lip crest fleshy outgrowths extend **just over halfway up the midline** (Dec-Jan). GENERAL: Infusion from tubers used by young men when courting and to treat infertility. Subsp. *ovalis* occurs in this region.(see pg 70) Subsp. *bainesii* with a short, flattened **spur**, is found further north, SA to Trop Afr.

Eulophia parviflora [= *E. olivieriana*] **imfeyamasele (Z)** (*parviflora* - with small flowers)

Stout, 200-500mm tall. On rocky north-facing grass slopes, up to 1500m. E Cape to Limpopo Prov. LEAVES **leathery**, up to 250×16mm, partly developed at flowering. INFLORESCENCE crowded, elongate; FLOWER **sepals and petals blunt**, 7-20mm long, sepals dull brownish green outside, rich orange-brown inside, petals pale yellow, veins brownish red inside, lip side lobes purplish brown, midlobe yellow with broad fleshy ridges, pleasant scent (Oct-Dec). GENERAL: Used in traditional medicine.

Eulophia welwitschii [= *E. zeyheri*] **umlunge (Z)** (named after Friedrich Welwitsch, 1806-1872, botanist in Namibia)

Slender, up to 900mm tall. In grassland or marshy areas, up to 1500m. Widespread, E Cape to Trop Afr. LEAVES **stiff, erect, pleated**, up to 23mm wide. INFLORESCENCE short, dense; FLOWERS **large, sepals and petals not spreading**, pale creamy lemon to bright yellow, 25(46)×12mm, lip with reddish purple on side lobes, spur slender (Nov-Feb). GENERAL: Infusion of tubers used by young men when courting.

Liparis bowkeri

Eulophia calanthoides

Eulophia calanthoides

Eulophia leontoglossa

Eulophia ovalis

Eulophia parviflora

Eulophia welwitschii

Eulophia welwitschii

127

DICOTYLEDONS Two seed leaves, net veins, flower parts in fours, fives or multiples of these.

SANTALACEAE - Sandalwood Family Usually parasitic on roots of other plants. Flowers small, petals absent. Fruit a nut. Trop, subtrop, ±34 genera, ±540 species, 6 genera in SAfr. *Thesium* (a Greek word) Old World, ±325 species, ±180 in SAfr. Genus not well understood in SAfr.

Thesium pallidum [= *T. floribundum*] umahesaka-obomvu (Z) (*pallidum* - pale)

Rounded clumps, up to 500mm tall. In grassland, often rocky, up to 2450m. E Cape to Mpum. Stems erect, angular. LEAVES narrow, up to 30mm long. FLOWERS small, creamy white or greenish, in small clusters terminating in very short side shoots (Nov-Mar). FRUIT oval, **shiny**. GENERAL: Widely used in traditional medicine.

MESEMBRYANTHEMACEAE - Vygie Family (see pg 200) *Delosperma* (*delos* - conspicuous; *sperma* - seed) Succulent perennials. Leaves soft, glistening or hairy; fruit without covering membranes. Popular garden plants. Afr, ±163 species, mostly SAfr, ±8 in this region.

Delosperma nubigenum mabone, motabo (SS) (*nubigena* - living in clouds)

In big mats on moist cliffs. 2500-3200m. EMR endemic. Stems roundish, much branched. LEAVES **small**, erect, tips pointed, narrowing to base, covered with small bumps. FLOWERS ±20mm diam, **yellow**, stalks short (Dec-Jan). GENERAL: A beautiful sight in full flower. Much cultivated in Britain and the USA.

RANUNCULACEAE - Buttercup Family Leaf bases forming a sheath. Flowers with sepals commonly petal-like, petals equal to, or larger than sepals, or absent. Includes ornamentals *Anemone*, *Delphinium* and *Ranunculus*. Mostly N Hemisp, ±60 genera, ±1750 species, 7 genera in SAfr. *Ranunculus* (dimunitivie of *rana* - a frog, because the plants are found in marshy areas) Cosmop, ±250 species, 7 in SAfr, 4 in this region.

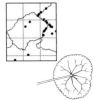

Ranunculus baurii [= *R. cooperi*] Large-leaved Ranunculus; qojoana (SS) (named after Rev. Leopold Baur, born 1825, Germany, died 1889 in Queenstown, pharmacist, missionary, botanist)

Herb, 0.15-1.2m tall. Often in tall, dense stands in moist grassland, wet ground near streams and waterfalls, on forest margins or, small plants forming mats in standing water on the summit, 1400-3000m. E Cape to Mpum. Stature very variable. LEAVES 8-300mm diam, ± round, **white veined**, margins red, with blunt teeth, stalks up to 300mm long, **often attached to centre of blade**. INFLORESCENCE branched in large plants, flowers solitary in small plants; FLOWERS 20-30mm diam, glossy yellow (Oct-Jan).

Ranunculus meyeri Bog Buttercup; bolila-ba-linku-ba-metsi, hlapi-ea-metsi-e-nyenyane (SS) (named after E. Meyer, the well known botanist who was responsible for naming many of Drège's collections)

Dwarf, mat forming herb, with trailing, rooting stems. In marshy turf or in shallow running water, 1500-3000m. Cape to Zim. LEAVES fleshy, **4-20mm diam**, **roundish, base deeply heart-shaped**, stalks ±75mm long. FLOWERS solitary, 10-15mm diam, **petals few, long, narrow**, glossy yellow, stalks ±75mm long (Oct-Feb).

Ranunculus multifidus Common Buttercup; Botterblom, Kankerblaar (A); hlapi (SS); ishashakazane, isijojokazana, uxhaphozi (Z) (*multifidus* - divided into segments)

Perennial, erect herb, mostly 150-300mm tall. In damp ground near streams and marshes up to 2900m. On the summit, up to 70mm high. Widespread. **Hairy or not**. LEAVES bright green, **2-3 pairs leaflets, deeply divided, margins deeply toothed**. INFLORESCENCE branched, **stems hollow**, or flowers solitary in small plants; FLOWERS 15-20mm diam, petals 5, glossy yellow (Oct-Dec). GENERAL: Used in traditional medicine to treat a wide variety of ailments. Garden plant for damp areas.

CRASSULACEAE - Crassula Family Herbs or soft shrubs, usually succulent. Leaves often joined round the stem, or in basal rosette. Cosmop, centres in SAfr and C America, ±33 genera, ±1500 species, 6 genera in SAfr (1 exotic). *Kalanchoe* (from the Chinese for one of these species) Succulent herbs or small shrubs; 4 petals, tube round or angled. Cosmop, ±200 species, 14 in SAfr, 1 in this region.

Kalanchoe thyrsiflora White Lady; Geelplakkie, Meelplakkie, Voëlbrandewyn (A); serelile (SS); utywala bentaka (X); utshwala benyoni (Z) (*thyrsiflora* - elongated inflorescence)

Robust succulent, up to 1.5m tall, **covered in silvery bloom**. On cliffs, rock outcrops, up to 2000m. NE Cape to Mpum. LEAVES in basal tuft, 80-120×30-70mm, flat, grey-green, tinged red. FLOWERS in **crowded, tightly packed** inflorescence, petal lobes yellow, sweetly scented (May-Jun). GENERAL: Flowering stem arises in second year, dying down after flowering. Used in traditional medicine. A popular garden plant.

Crassula (*crassus* – thick, refers to fleshy leaves) (see pg 74)

Crassula vaginata Yellow Crassula; erekisi-e-nyane, rete-la-thotha (SS); umakhule-fingqana, umdumbukane (Z) (*vaginata* - sheathed)

150-500mm tall. On damp grass slopes, up to 2400m. Basal LEAVES withered at flowering, stem leaves up to 100×15(30)mm, **lower leaf sheaths (5)8-15mm long**. FLOWERS **yellow**, scented (Sep-May). GENERAL: Ground roots used in sour milk as famine food by the Zulu. Used in traditional medicine. Easily grown from seed.

Ranunculus multifidus   David McDonald

Ranunculus meyeri   Lal Greene

Thesium pallidum   Tony Abbott

Delosperma nubigenum   Mike Hirst

Ranunculus multifidus   Martin von Fintel

Ranunculus baurii   Rob Scott-shaw

Delosperma nubigenum   Peter Linder

Ranunculus baurii   David McDonald

Kalanchoe thyrsiflora   Martin von Fintel

Crassula vaginata   Cameron McMaster

129

ROSACEAE - Rose Family Trees, shrubs or herbs, often prickly. Leaves with pair of stipules at base of leaf stalk. Petals 5, numerous stamens. Fruits often edible. Economically valuable for deciduous fruits such as the apple, pear, cherry, plum, peach, blackberry, raspberry, strawberry and ornamental trees and shrubs such as the rose. Mostly N Hemisp in cooler areas, ±107 genera, ±3000 species, 18 genera in SAfr. *Geum* (said to be from the scented root) Roots astringent, some species pleasantly aromatic. Temp regions, ±71 species, 1 in SAfr.

Geum capense hlapi-ea-loti, qojoana-ea-Lesotho, thejane (SS)

Softly hairy perennial herb, flowering stems 300-600mm tall. In small colonies, in damp places on turf slopes, stepped crags and gullies, 2000-3000m. E Cape to KZN. LEAVES in basal rosettes, ±75×50mm, thick, dark green, deeply lobed, margins toothed, stem leaves small. INFLORESCENCE branched, few flowered; FLOWERS ±35mm diam, yellow (Oct-Dec).

LEGUMINOSAE (FABACEAE) **- Pea or Legume Family** Second largest flowering plant family. Leaves usually bipinnately compound. Fruit usually a pod. Three subfamilies, Mimosoideae: flowers tiny, in dense heads or spikes (eg *Acacia*). Caesalpinioideae: flowers large, petals irregular, never in 'butterfly' pattern (eg *Cassia*). Papilionoideae, the largest subfamily: petals in typical 'butterfly' pattern. Economically important for food, fodder, dyes, oils and ornamentals. Cosmop, ±650 genera, ±18000 species, ±149 genera in SAfr. *Lotononis* (a combination of two generic names, *Lotus* and *Ononis*) Herbs or shrublets; leaves digitately 3(5) foliolate. Mostly Afr, ±144 species in SAfr, ±20 in this region.

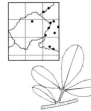

Lotononis eriantha Russet Lotononis; lefehloane, molomo-monate, phehloane (SS)
(*eriantha* - woolly flowers)

Perennial shrublet, up to 300mm tall. In grassland, up to 2400m. E Cape to Limpopo Prov. Stems **much branched**, curved upwards from base. LEAFLETS ±12×3mm, **narrow**, tip with short point, stalks very short, stipules as long as leaflets, hairs spreading. INFLORESCENCES terminal, **few flowers** surrounded by leaves; FLOWERS ±8mm, yellow turning reddish brown, **densely hairy** (Sep-Mar). GENERAL: Used traditionally as a charm. **Similar species:** *Lotononis procumbens* (*procumbens* - prostrate) Prostrate herb. INFLORESCENCE terminal, crowded; FLOWERS **hairless** (Nov-Jan).

Lotononis laxa [= *L. woodii*] 'musa-pelo-oa-matlapa-o-monyenyane (SS) (*laxa* - wide, loose)

Well branched perennial herb, forming small mats. On bare stony ground and rock sheets, 1200-1800m. E Cape to Mpum. STEMS **prostrate**. LEAVES silvery. FLOWERS solitary at stem tips, ±10 mm long, yellow (Dec-Feb).

Lotononis pulchra (*pulchra* - beautiful)

Semi-prostrate herb. In rocky grassland, up to 2300m. KZN to Limpopo Prov. LEAFLETS ±18×6mm, stalks ±5mm long. INFLORESCENCE ±35mm diam; FLOWERS **hairless** (Dec-Jan).

Dichilus (*di* - two; *cheilos* - lip, refers to the calyx which is distinctly 2-lipped) Slender undershrubs or herbs; stipules inconspicuous; strongly reflexed standard and wings, calyx 2-lipped. SAfr, 5 species, 2 in this region.

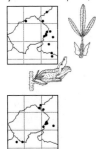

Dichilus reflexus (*reflexus* - turned back)

Perennial shrublet. In rocky streambeds, on moist slopes, up to 2700m. E Cape to Zim. FLOWER **standard hairless, calyx long** (more than half the length of the keel), **lobes long, pointed**. GENERAL: Plants in this region were formerly referred to as *D. lebeckioides*. **Similar species:** *Dichilus strictus* lesita-tlali (SS) (*strictus* - erect or upright) Perennial shrublet, up to 600mm (1m) tall. In moist grassland, on rocky streambeds, rock outcrops, up to 2400m. E Cape to Mpum. Stems unbranched, leafy, stiffly hairy. LEAFLETS **slender**, 7-15×1.5-3mm, usually folded, hairless above, densely hairy on margins and beneath. FLOWERS yellow, ±10mm long, up to 4 at ends of branchlets, **standard hairy at the tip, calyx short, lobes short, sharp** (Nov-Jan).

Melolobium (*melos* - a joint; *lobos* - pod) Shrubs or shrublets, often spiny, sticky; leaves 3 foliolate; flowers in terminal inflorescences, small, yellow. SAfr ±20 species, 6 in this region.

Melolobium alpinum motšoehla, 'musa-pelo-o-moholo-oa-thaba (SS) (*alpinum* - alpine)

Sticky, tufted, erect herb, up to 300mm tall. On grassy slopes, in valleys, 1200-2300m. E Cape to KZN/Mpum. Stems leafy, **usually unbranched**. LEAFLETS **narrow**, hairless or slightly hairy, stipules shorter than stalks. INFLORESCENCE terminal, slender, leafless, ±100mm long; FLOWERS yellow, red with age (Nov-Jan). PODS curved, **constricted between seeds**. GENERAL: Used as a sedative. **Similar species:** *Melolobium obcordatum* lethokho, linaoana-tsa-thaba, seakha (SS) (*obcordatum* - refers to the leaf shape) **Much branched** herb, up to 450mm, forming mats or low cushions. In boulder beds, on streamside cliffs, at foot of Cave Sandstone cliffs, up to 2450m. E Cape to EMR. **Covered in stalked glands and soft hairs**. LEAFLETS **heart-shaped, tips sharply notched**. FLOWERS in loose spikes, ±75 mm long.

Geum capense

Peter Linder

Lotononis pulchra

Lal Greene

Lotononis laxa

Mike Hirst

Lotononis eriantha

David McDonald

Lotononis eriantha

Martin von Fintel

Dichilus strictus

Braam van Wyk

Dichilus reflexus

Martin von Fintel

Dichilus reflexus

Clinton Carbutt

Melolobium alpinum

Tony Abott

131

Argyrolobium (*argyros* - silver; *lobos* - pod) Herbs or shrublets; leaves 3 foliolate, often with silky silvery hairs; flowers usually in many flowered inflorescenes. S Europe to India, mostly Afr, ±70 species, ±50 in SAfr, ±18 in this region.

Argyrolobium harveyanum tsoetla-e-kholo (SS) (named after William Harvey, 1811-66, a great botanist, who spent time in SA between 1835 and 1842. He wrote the major part of the first 3 volumes of Flora Capensis)

Very slender, erect perennial herb, up to 650mm tall. On rocky grass slopes, up to 2600m. E Cape to Zim. **Stems unbranched, softly downy.** LEAFLETS ±30×3mm, almost stalkless, 1-2 (often missing), stalks ±18mm long, stipules small. FLOWERS 1-2, small, ±10mm, almost stalkless, opposite leaves, plain yellow, among upper leaves (Sep-Dec). GENERAL: Grazed by stock. **Similar species:** *Argyrolobium tuberosum* Little Russet Pea; lebesa, lekolomache, tsoetsoetlela, tsoetla-e-nyenyane (SS); uvemvane olubomvu (Z) (*tuberosum* - resembling tubers) **Stems branch above, hairs flat against stem.** LEAFLET stalks 8-20mm long. FLOWERS **yellow inside, red-brown outside** (Dec-Feb). GENERAL: Tubers sucked by children for sweetish taste. Leaves eaten as spinach.

Argyrolobium marginatum (*marginatum* - edge or border)

Perennial herb, softly silvery hairy, stems much branched, ± prostrate. In grassland, up to 2000(2400)m. LEAFLETS 12-30×10-15mm, stipules ±10×3mm, stalks up to 10mm long, covered in soft silky hairs, margins golden. FLOWERS 10-15mm long, yellow, turning orange or brownish with age, in small clusters on stems longer than leaves (Nov-Feb). GENERAL: Grazed.

Argyrolobium robustum [formerly referred to as *A. speciosum* which is not found in this region] Liquorice Bean; Soethoutbossie (A); umuzimuka (Z) (*robustum* - large, refers to leaves)

Stout perennial shrublet, 300-600mm. In wooded grassland, up to 1600m. E Cape to Mpum. Stems sparsely branched LEAVES large, **grey-green, slightly fleshy;** LEAFLETS 50-170×20-80mm, stalks 15-40mm long, stipules leafy, ±25×10mm. INFLORESCENCE, **100-150 mm long,** stem up to100 mm; standard petals roundish, ±13mm, yellow with reddish veins (Sep-Jan). PODS ±60-85×4mm. GENERAL: Used in traditional medicine.

Argyrolobium stipulaceum (*stipulaceum* - with prominent stipules)

Perennial herb, up to 150mm tall. On grassy slopes, up to 2400m. E Cape to KZN. Stems tufted, mostly unbranched. Plant thickly **covered with silvery silky hairs.** LEAFLETS up to 25×8mm, stalks 2-5mm, **stipules large, leaflike,** up to 25×12m. INFLORESCENCE small; FLOWERS ±15mm, yellow turning orange-brown, silky behind, calyx silky, upper lip 2-lobed, lower 3-lobed (Sep-Jan). PODS inflated, ±30mm.

Argyrolobium tomentosum Velvety Yellow Bush Pea; umadlozana, umlomomnandi (Z) (*tomentosum* - densely covered with short hairs)

Erect, loosely branched, slender, straggling herb, 0.6-1m tall. Locally common, on forest margins, disturbed areas, up to 1800m. LEAFLETS 25-35×18-24mm, **thin, pale green, sparsely hairy,** stalks 25-35mm long, stipules small. INFLORESCENCES **on long stems** in leaf axils; FLOWERS ±15mm, bright yellow (Jan-Mar). PODS 60-100×5-8mm, flattened. GENERAL: Used by diviners (*sangomas*) to sharpen their divining powers.

Rhynchosia (*rhynchos* - beak, refers to style) Prostrate, creeping or scrambling herbs or shrublets; leaves 3 foliolate, usually with resinous dots; flowers mostly yellow. Attracts butterflies. Trop, subtrop, ±200 species, ±70 in SAfr, ±8 in this region.

Rhynchosia adenodes monya-mali (SS); ungazini (Z) (*adenodes* - with glandular knots)

Erect or spreading creeper, up to 400mm. In grassland. E Cape to Limpopo Prov. Stems ±1m long, downy. LEAFLETS ±15mm, firm, with **tiny red gland dots beneath,** stalks ±25mm long. INFLORESCENCE on slender stem ±50mm long; FLOWERS yellow, striped brown (Sep-Jun). GENERAL: Browsed by stock. Used traditionally to treat dysentery in calves.

Rhynchosia cooperi (named after Thomas Cooper, 1815-1913, English plant collector and cultivator who came to live SA in 1859, son-in-law of John Medley-Wood)

Trailing herb, stems up to 1m long, mostly prostrate. In moist grassland, on streambanks, up to 1800m. Stems hairless. LEAVES **held erect,** stalks ±40mm long; LEAFLETS ±25×22mm, **oval to roundish,** hard, veins conspicuous beneath, terminal leaflet on short stalklet. INFLORESCENCES **erect,** ±180mm long, flowers in short dense clusters on long stem; FLOWERS conspicuous, orange-yellow, 14-18mm (Feb-Mar).

Argyrolobium robustum

Pam Cooke

Argyrolobium marginatum

Lal Greene

Rhynchosia adenodes

Geoff Nichols

Argyrolobium harveyanum

Argyrolobium stipulaceum

Trevor Coleman

Lal Greene

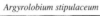

Argyrolobium stipulaceum

Lal Greene

Rhynchosia cooperi

Martin von Fintel

Argyrolobium tomentosum

Martin von Fintel

133

Rhynchosia harmsiana (named after Herman Harms, 1870-1942, German botanist)
Vigorous, prostrate, twining herb. In streamside scrub and in drainage lines, up to 2050m. Many slender stems, with reddish brown hairs. TERMINAL LEAFLETS 20-30 ×15-25mm, stalks downy. INFLORESCENCES loose, in leaf axils, stems 50-100mm long; FLOWERS 5-7, 10-15mm, yellow, standard with purple-brown lines, calyx bell-like, 8-10mm, lobes longer than tube (Nov-Feb). PODS ±20mm, roughly hairy.

Rhynchosia totta Yellow Carpet Bean; sebalibetloa (SS); ingqungqumbe, isikhonde (Z) *(totta - meaning not known)*
Slender, twining creeper, often on grass stalks. In grass on slopes below cliffs, up to 2500m. E Cape to Ethiopia, Arabia. **Stems very slender**, hairless or slightly downy. LEAFLETS ±35×5-10mm, hairless when mature, veins prominent, leaf stalks ±30mm long. FLOWERS 1-4 on slender stems, 6-12mm, bright yellow, aging reddish (Dec-May). PODS ±15×5mm, hairy. GENERAL: Sweet tubers eaten raw or roasted.

Eriosema *(erion - wool; sema - sign, refers to woolly standard)* Herbs or shrubs; usually 3 foliolate, terminal leaflet stalked, with resinous dots. Inflorescence on stems twice as long as flower cluster. Attracts butterflies. Warm regions, Afr, ±130 species, ±36 in SAfr, ±4 in this region.

Eriosema kraussianum Pale Yellow Eriosema (named after Christian Krauss, 1812-90, German scientist, traveller, collector)
Erect tufted herb, 150-200mm tall. In colonies in stony grassland, up to 2000m. Rootstock woody. **Stems covered in silvery silky hairs**. LEAVES green or ± silvery, on short stalks, leaflets ±30×6-8mm, stipules brown. INFLORESCENCES ±40mm long, stems ±50mm long; FLOWERS ±8mm, pale yellow (Sep-Nov). PODS ±15×8mm, hairy.

LINACEAE - Flax family Stipules often glandlike. Petals twisted. Cosmop, ±15 genera, ±300 species, 2 genera in SAfr. *Linum* *(lionon - flax)* Herbs or undershrubs. Economically important for Flax, linen, linseed oil. Cosmop, ±230 species, ±5 in SAfr, 1 in this region.

Linum thunbergii Wild Flax; Wildevlas (A); bohlokoana (SS); ithalelimpofu (Z) (named after Carl Thunberg, 1743-1828, pupil of Linnaeus, who collected at the Cape en route to Japan)
Tufted perennial herb, up to 400mm tall. In moist grassland, up to 2300m. Widespread. Stems slender, branching above. LEAVES narrow, ±10mm long, **tips sharply pointed**, stalkless, **stipules brown, glandlike**. FLOWERS ±15mm diam, yellow, buds reddish, sweetly scented (Nov-Mar). GENERAL: Used in traditional medicine.

EUPHORBIACEAE - Rubber or Euphorbia Family (see pg 256) *Euphorbia* (see pg 256)

Euphorbia clavarioides Lion's Spoor; Melkpol, Vingerpol (A); sehloko (SS); isantilele, isihlekehleke (Z) *(clavarioides - Clavaria-like, resembles this fungus)*
Rounded, cushionlike succulent, ±300mm tall by 600mm wide. On steep rocky slopes, rock sheets, up to 2750m. E Cape to Limpopo Prov. Stems 10-20mm diam, olive green to brownish, rounded at tips, closely massed. FLOWERS with 3-5 bright yellow bracts (Oct-Jan). GENERAL: Used to prepare bird lime. Children eat the dried sap as 'chewing gum'. Fruit eaten by baboons. Used in traditional medicine.

MALVACEAE - Hibiscus Family Flowers often with epicalyx (leafy whorl below calyx); stamens partly united into tube around style, branched above. Economically important for cotton, okra and ornamentals. Cosmop, ±90 genera, ±2000 species, 22 genera in SAfr (7 exotic). *Hibiscus* *(ibiskos - old Greek name for the Marsh Mallow plant)* Herbs, shrubs, rarely trees, often with star-shaped hairs; flowers showy, epicalyx of 5-20 bracts, usually as long as sepals. Attracts butterflies including. Cosmop, trop, subtrop, ±300 species, ±50 in SAfr, ±5 in this region.

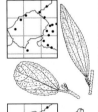

Hibiscus aethiopicus Common Dwarf Wild Hibiscus; lereletsane-le-leholo, motaung, naletsana, sefala-bohoho (SS); ibunda elimpofu, ihlalanyosi elimhlophe, uvemvane (Z) *(aethiopicus - from Africa)*
Low growing, tufted herb, stems erect, 140-350mm tall, or prostrate. In grassland, on steep slopes, up to 1800m. Cape to Zim. STEMS **covered in rough hairs**. LEAVES 10-80×6-40mm, **tips blunt**, 3-5 veins from rounded base, hairy to hairless, stalks 5-15mm. FLOWERS ±50mm diam, **creamy** yellow, aging pink, epicalyx bracts 9-7, short (Nov-Jan). GENERAL: Very variable. Used in traditional medicine.

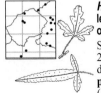

Hibiscus trionum Bladder Hibiscus; Terblansbossie (A); lefefane, lereletsane, lereletsane-le-leholo, motaung, naletsana (SS); iyeza lentshulube (X); uvemvane olukhulu (Z) *(trionum - name of a malvaceus plant)*
Straggly annual herb. In scrub, grassland, up to 2450m. Widespread. LEAVES 20-60mm diam, stalks 10-40mm long. FLOWERS 25-40mm diam, creamy yellow with deep red centre, epicalyx bracts 12, calyx ±25mm long, **conspicuously green to purple-veined**, lobes united almost to tip, **becomes inflated and papery in fruit** (Jan-Mar). GENERAL: Very variable. Used in traditional medicine.

Rhynchosia harmsiana

Rhynchosia totta var *totta*   *Linum thunbergii*

Eriosema kraussianum

Euphorbia clavarioides

Euphorbia clavarioides

Hibiscus trionum

Hibiscus aethiopicus

135

STERCULIACEAE - Cocoa-Sterculia Family Star-shaped hairs usually present. Petals usually twisted in bud. Fruit dry, splitting into carpels when ripe. Economically important for cocoa from the S American tree *Theobroma cacao* and for ornamentals. Cosmop, ±72 genera, ±1500 species, 7 genera in SAfr. *Hermannia* (named after Paul Herman, 1646-1695, professor of botany in Leiden, one of the first collectors to visit the Cape) Stipules often leaflike; calyx papery. Attracts butterflies. Afr, Arabia, Austr, S America, ±180 species, ±162 in SAfr, ±10 in this region.

Hermannia gerrardii Gerrard's Yellow Hermannia; Bitterblaar (A) (named after W.T. Gerrard, English naturalist and traveller who collected in Natal in 1860)

Coarse **prostrate herb**, stems long. On steep grass slopes, rock outcrops, 1200-2250m. KZN. Stems simple or branched, roughly hairy. LEAVES up to 120×75mm, hairy, margins toothed, stalks up to 20mm long. INFLORESCENCE branched, hidden amongst large leaves; FLOWERS pale yellow, calyx lobes pointed (Mar-May).

Hermannia malvifolia (*malva* - mallow; *folia* - leaves, refers to the soft leaves, similar to the mallow plant *Malva rotundifolia*)

Prostrate or scrambling herb, forming tangled clumps, stems wiry, 300-60mm long. In moist scrub in valleys, at foot of Cave Sandstone cliffs, 1800-2400m. EMR endemic. LEAVES 10-30×10-35mm, margins toothed, stalks up to 10mm long. FLOWERS solitary, pendulous, ±8mm long, pale yellow (Oct-Feb).

GUTTIFERAE/CLUSIACEAE Mainly trop, ±40 genera, ±1000 species, 2 genera in SAfr. *Hypericum* (Latin for St John's Wort) Sometimes placed in the family HYPERICACEAE. Leaves, flowers with clear or black gland dots. Includes ornamentals and noxious weeds, some species used for medicinal and magical purposes since earliest times. St John's Wort is used in the treatment of depression. Temp, ±400 species, ±10 in SAfr, 4 in this region. *Hypericum patulum*, a small introduced shrub (China, Japan), invades roadsides, forest margins, up to 1980m in EMR.

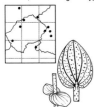

Hypericum aethiopicum subsp. *sonderi* Small Hypericum; Vlieëpisbossie (A); bohohoana, ho-ila, leilane-bohohoana, leilane-la-bale, tabane (SS); isimayisane, isimonyo, isivumelwane, unsukumbili (Z) (*aethiopicum* - from Africa; *sonderi* - named after Otto Sonder, 1812-81, German apothecary and botanist who helped Harvey write the first three volumes of *Flora Capensis*)

Tufted perennial herb, 100-30mm tall. On steep rocky slopes, up to 2400m. E Cape to Trop Afr. Stems erect, **cylindrical**, mostly unbranched. LEAVES in opposite pairs, stalkless, 8-20×34-15mm, heart-shaped at base, margins ± with black dots. FLOWERS ±25mm diam, yellow tinged reddish, sepals reddish brown, black-dotted (Sep-Feb). GENERAL: Conspicuous after fires. Used in traditional medicine. Delicate garden plant.

Hypericum lalandii Spindly Hypericum, Laland's St John's Wort; Laland-se-Sint Janskruid (A); bohlokoana, bohlokoanyana (SS) (named after Pierre Delalande, 1787-1823, French naturalist)

Erect herb, 40-500mm tall. In marshy or damp grassland, up to 2100m. SW Cape to Sudan. Very variable in size and shape. **Stems slender, 4-angled.** LEAVES 8-20 ×35 mm, held erect, margins recurved, stalkless, without gland dots. FLOWERS 20-30mm diam, solitary or few in terminal clusters, yellow or orange, **no dark dots**, sepals tapering to a fine point, ribbed (Nov-Feb). GENERAL: Used in traditional medicine.

THYMELAEACEAE - Fibre-bark / Gonna Family Perennial herbs, shrubs or small trees. Flowers are peculiar, with a conspicuous, coloured calyx, sepals petal-like, petals small, scalelike or absent. Bark tough, fibrous, stripping off, difficult to break. Cosmop, ±50 genera, ±600 species, 8 genera and 192 species in SAfr. *Gnidia* (named after the Greek city, Knidos) Perennial herbs or shrubs; sepals erect, spreading or reflexed, coloured, petals alternating with calyx lobes or sometimes missing. Mostly Trop and SAfr, ±140 species, ±100 in SAfr, ±13 in this region.

Gnidia aberrans [= *Basutica aberrans*] (*aberrans* - straying from the normal)

Gnarled dwarf shrublet, up to 200mm tall. On steep slopes or on summit plateau, 2100-3200m. EMR endemic. LEAVES up to 6×2mm, **densely silky hairy**. FLOWERS creamy yellow, in axils of leaves, calyx tube **8-10mm long, lobes 4, oblong, tips pointed, petals 4, long and narrow**, 4 stamens, no staminodes (Oct-Feb). **Similar species:** *Gnidia propinqua* [= *Basutica propinqua*] (*propinqua* - 'close to', allied to *G. aberrans*) On rocky turf and rock platforms, 2500-3200m. EMR endemic. LEAVES **hairless**. FLOWERS pale cream, calyx tube short, **±5mm long, lobes blunt**, broader than long (Nov-Dec). (see pg 78)

Gnidia baurii (after Rev Leopold Baur, 1825-1889, pharmacist, missionary, botanical collector in the Cape in 1847)

Tufted perennial, stems up to 150(900)mm long. In grassland, on bare or rocky places, up to 2440m. E Cape to KZN. LEAVES ±15×3mm, tips pointed, **silky beneath**. FLOWERS **in pairs**, in leaf axils, **towards ends of branches**, calyx tube ±10mm, **pale creamy yellow**, silky outside, sepals oval, tips pointed, petals 8, blunt (Oct-Jan). **Similar species:** *Gnidia renniana* (after Anne Rennie, who has collected extensively on Mawahqua Mountain) Dwarf shrublet, 50-150mm tall. On steep slopes or bare sandstone, up to 2100m. EMR endemic. LEAVES 9-16×2.5mm, ± hairless. FLOWERS ±6mm long, **solitary, in all leaf axils** (Oct-Nov).

Hilliard & Burtt

Pam Cooke

Hermannia gerrardii

Hermannia malvifolia

Martin von Fintel

Gnidia aberrans

Darrel Plowes

Neil Crouch

Hypericum aethiopicum

Gnidia aberrans

Braam van Wyk

Tony Abbott

Martin von Fintel

Hypericum lalandii

Gnidia baurii

Gnidia propinqua

137

Gnidia caffra [= *Lasiosiphon caffer*] **Gifbossie (A)** *(caffra - from Kaffraria, old name for E Cape)*

Slender shrublet, up to 500mm tall. In grassland, on rocky outcrops, up to 1600m. E Cape to Limpopo Prov. Sparsely, **softly silvery hairy**. LEAVES narrow, ±30×6mm, tips sharply pointed. INFLORESCENCE loose; FLOWERS shiny lemon-yellow, ±10mm diam, **sepals large**, narrow, petals tiny (Oct-Jan). GENERAL: Conspicuous after fires.

Gnidia capitata [= *Lasiosiphon capitatus*] **Gifbossie, Kerriebossie (A); setele, thopa-e-nyenyane, thopana (SS); isidikili (Z)** *(capitata - head-shaped)*

Tufted shrublet, up to 300mm tall. In rocky grassland, up to 1800m. Widespread. LEAVES **narrow**, ±30×3-6mm, sharply pointed, green to **blue-grey**. INFLORESCENCE surrounded by wider leaves; FLOWERS ±6mm diam, calyx tube 15-25mm, silky hairy, sepals mustard/orange, yellow above, silky beneath, petals small, scalelike (Oct-Dec). GENERAL: Conspicuous after fires. Used in traditional medicine.

Gnidia compacta [= *Arthrosolen compactus*]

Dwarf, gnarled shrublet, forming little mats up to 300mm diam. On stony grass slopes, bare ground or rock platforms, 1800-2600m. EMR endemic. LEAVES crowded. FLOWERS **bright yellow**, calyx tube and lobes **hairy with tuft of hairs at back of the tip of each lobe, roundish, no petals**, stamens not exserted (Oct-Jan).

Gnidia kraussiana [= *Lasiosiphon kraussianum*] **Lesser Yellow-head; Harige gifbossie (A); thobeha, thopa (SS); umfukuzane, umsilawengwe, inhlashane, isidikili, umfuzane (Z)**
(named after Christian Krauss, 1812-90, German scientist, traveller, collector, in SA 1839-40)

Robust shrublet, up to 500mm tall. In grassland, up to 2130m. E Cape to Trop Afr. Plant hairless to densely hairy. LEAVES 15-40×5-20mm. INFLORESCENCES ±40mm diam, **surrounded by ring of overlapping leaves**; FLOWERS ±15mm diam, yellow, calyx tube slender, silky, 10-15mm long, lobes 5-7mm long (Aug-Dec). GENERAL: Conspicuous after fires. Poisonous to stock. Widely used in traditional medicine.

Gnidia polyantha [= *Lasiosiphon polyanthus*] **inhlanhla elempofu (Z)** *(poly - many, anthos - flowers)*

Slender, silvery silky subshrub, 0.4-1.2m tall. On steep rocky, grassy or shrubby slopes, around boulders, rock sheets, up to 2425m. LEAVES crowded on upper stems, 15-30mm long. FLOWERS in crowded heads, calyx tube slender, 12-18mm long, lobes 5-6mm long, bright yellow, **silky outside** (May-Sep).

Struthiola (*struthion* - small bird, refers to seed, like the beak of a sparrow) Ericalike shrubs or shrublets. Flowers stalkless, petals surrounded by stiff hairs, visible in mouth of calyx tube. Endemic to SAfr, ±30 species.

Struthiola anomala (*anomala* - anomalous refers to the lack of encircling bristles in the flower)

Shrublet, up to 400mm tall. In grassland. Ngele Mtn. LEAVES overlapping, ±11×2mm, white hairy when young. FLOWERS ±10mm, in axils, forming long inflorescence, calyx creamy green, tube 7-9mm long, lobes up to 3.8×1mm, **petals reduced to 2 very small fleshy lobes at base of each sepal, no encircling bristles** (Nov-Dec). **Similar species:** *Struthiola angustiloba* In rocky places, 1600-2500m. EMR endemic. **Petals well developed, encircling stiff hairs longer than the petals.**

UMBELLIFERAE (APIACEAE) - Carrot Family (see pg 80) *Bupleurum* (*bupleurum* - ox-rib, refers to strongly veined leaves) Annual or perennial herbs. Leaves ± crowded at base of stem, entire, grasslike. Flowers yellow, in compound umbels. Mainly Europe, Asia, Afr, ±180 species, 1 in SAfr.

Bupleurum mundii **lekhasi (SS)** (named after Johannes Mund, 1791-1831, born in Berlin and died at the Cape, pharmacist, botanical collector and land surveyor)

Slender, erect, tufted, perennial herb, 300-600mm tall. In damp rocky grassland, on slopes or in stabilised boulder beds, 1525-3200m. E Cape to Mpum. LEAVES mostly basal, grasslike, 150-200×2-4mm. INFLORESCENCE very open, main stem leafless, branching low down; FLOWERS bright yellow (Dec-Feb). FRUITS ribbed.

Polemannia (after Peter Poleman, 1780-1839, chemist, who settled in the Cape in 1802) Shrubs, small trees. Leaves 3-foliolate, with **distinct sub-marginal veins.** Mericarps compressed, winged. SAfr, 2 species, both in this region.

Polemannia simplicior (*simplicior* - simple, refers to undivided leaf shape)

Rounded shrub, 0.5-3m tall. On steep, **open**, rocky slopes, up to 2500m. Bark peeling. LEAVES 10-40×5-13mm, stalks 12-30mm long, **leaflets mostly entire.** UMBELS ±40mm diam; FLOWERS yellowish (Jan-Mar). **Similar species:** *Polemannia montana* Slender shrub, small tree, 1(3)m. On rocky stream banks. **Stems canelike.** **Leaflets deeply dissected**, segments drawn out into slender point. Unpleasant scent.

138

Struthiola anomala   Gnidia caffra   Gnidia compacta

Gnidia kraussiana   Gnidia capitata   Gnidia polyantha

Bupleurum mundii   Polemannia simplicior

139

GENTIANACEAE - Gentian Family Herbs, sometimes aquatic. Leaves mostly opposite. 4-5 petal lobes, often twisted in bud, ovary superior. Cultivated as ornamentals. Cosmop, ±78 genera, ±1225 species, 9 genera in SAfr. *Sebaea* (named after Albert Seba, 1665-1736, Dutch naturalist and author. His museum was called 'the wonder of Europe') Herbs. Stems often angled or winged. Anthers often with apical or basal glands, style often with stigmatic swelling. Afr, Madag, India, Austr, New Zealand, ±115 species, ±45 in SAfr, ±18 in this region.

Sebaea marlothii (named after H.W.R. Marloth, 1855-1931, pharmacist and botanist, author of *Flora Capensis*)
Mat-forming herb. In marshy ground, 2560-3000m. EMR endemic. STEMS creeping. LEAVES crowded, ±20×10mm, **fleshy**, narrowed abruptly into stalklike base ±10mm long. FLOWERS **1-5**, terminal, stalkless, yellow, tube 5-9mm long, lobes 5-9×3-5mm, rounded, **apical anther glands very large, dark**, calyx narrowly winged (Nov-Feb).

Sebaea natalensis
Erect, tufted herb, up to 250mm tall. In damp grassland, around rock sheets, up to 2200m. E Cape to Mpum. STEMS simple or branching above. LEAVES roundish, ±13×15mm. INFLORESCENCES congested; FLOWERS ±15mm diam, petals rounded, 4-7.5mm, tube short, 5-7mm, yellow, **anthers tipped with short, small, round gland**, calyx segments conspicuously winged, drying straw-coloured (Feb-Apr).

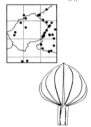

Sebaea sedoides isivumelwane esikhulu, umanqweyana, umsolo (Z) (*sedoides* - resembles *Sedum*, Stone Crop)
Herbs, 200-650mm tall. In damp grassland, marshes, up to 2100m. Cape to Zim. Stems simple or branched. LEAVES ±25mm diam or 15×6mm. INFLORESCENCE **dense**, small or large, **bracts numerous**, erect; FLOWERS **small**, 5-15mm diam, tube **usually longer than petals**, yellow, creamy white, calyx lobes joined at base, keeled (Dec-May). GENERAL: Var. *confertiflora* and var. *schoenlandii* in this region, differing in size and shape of flowers. Used in traditional medicine. **Similar species:** *Sebaea leiostyla* (*leio* - smooth, *styla* - style) Up to 100mm tall. On damp grassy slopes, in stream gullies, in shelter of bushes, up to 2600m. KZN to Trop Afr. FLOWERS ±14mm diam. (see pg 13)

Sebaea thomasii marama-a-baroetsana (SS) (named after H.E.P. Thomas, 1879-1948, British Army officer who served during the Anglo Boer War and collected a few plants in the Orange Free State)
Rounded clumps or mat forming perennial herb. On wet cliffs, rocky stream gullies, partially shaded, 2000-2900m. LEAVES up to 21×14mm, roundish, slightly fleshy, narrowed to stalklike base. FLOWERS in small terminal clusters, yellow, **very showy**, tube up to 20mm long, petal lobes ±10×6mm, tips round to pointed (Aug-Nov).

ASCLEPIADACEAE - Milkweed Family Herbs, shrubs, vines, epiphytes, usually with milky latex. Flowers bisexual, petal lobes 5, free or fused, sometimes with a corona, stamens forming a column with simple to complex fleshy basal corona in 1-2(3) whorls, pollen in wax masses (pollinia), attached in pairs. Fruit with paired follicles, often only 1 develops. (Now included in Apocynaceae in the subfamily Asclepiadoideae.) Cosmop, ±253 genera, ±2000 species, 63 genera in SAfr. *Xysmalobium* (*xysma* - filings or shavings; *lobos* - lobes, refers to the small corona lobes that resemble cut slivers or whittlings - follicle) Stout to delicate perennial geophytic herbs, sometimes ± shrubby, with milky latex. Stems produced annually from tuber, leaf margins rough, venation prominent. Corona lobes reduced to small lobules. Afr, 40 species, 21 in SAfr, ±7 in this region.

Xysmalobium tysonianum Sulphur Cartwheel (named after plant collector William Tyson, 1851-1920
Prostrate or reclining herb, stems up to 230mm long. In rocky mountain grassland, 1200-2600m. LEAVES lance-shaped, 35-53×12-20mm, ± leathery. INFLORESCENCES **solitary, terminal, roundish, stems 50-100 mm long**; FLOWERS **yellowish**, corolla lobes erect, oval, 2.5-35×1.5-2.5mm, tips curved inwards, **corona lobes orange, longer than 'petals'**, sweet smelling (Oct-Feb). FRUIT smooth, spindle-shaped. GENERAL: Leaves described as smelling like 'smelly feet'.

Schizoglossum (*schizo* - cut or split; *glossa* - tongue, refers to the corona lobe which is often split into 2 or more parts) (see pg 266)

Schizoglossum flavum Yellow Schizoglossum (*flavum* - yellow)
Erect, unbranched herb, 150-300mm tall. On grassy slopes, 1460-2300m. EMR endemic. LEAVES 30-70×10-20mm, hairy. FLOWERS in small clusters, **yellow or lime-green**, erect, corolla lobes 7-9×3-4mm, **flat, outer surface hairless, corona simple**, 3-4mm, much longer than style tip, no appendages on inner face, flat, erect (Oct-Feb). FRUIT not yet known.

Schizoglossum montanum lebatheke (SS)
Prostrate herb, forming small mats. On damp stony grassland, around rock sheets, 2100-2835m. EMR endemic. LEAVES oval. FLOWERS greenish yellow, petal tips incurved, corona white (Nov-Jan).

Sebaea sedoides subsp. *sedoides*

Martin von Fintel

Sebaea sedoides subsp. *confertifolium*

Durrel Plowes

Sebaea natalensis

Lal Greene

Sebaea thomasii

John Birks

Schizoglossum montanum

David McDonald

Xysmalobium tysonianum

Wally Menne

Sebaea marlothii

Mike Hirst

Xysmalobium tysonianum

Tony Abbott

Schizoglossum flavum

Martin von Fintel

141

Schizoglossum stenoglossum Simple Schizoglossum (*stenos* - narrow; *glossa* - tongue, refers to narrow corona lobes)
160-510mm tall. In mountain grassland, up to 2700m. KZN to Mpum. LEAVES 45-58 ×5-15mm. FLOWER lobes oblong, 8-9×3mm, flat, hairless, **corona lobes simple**, erect, exceeding style tip (Oct-Jan). GENERAL: Subsp. ***flavum*** Up to 2100m. FLOWER **lobes greenish yellow striped brown**, hairy; corona lobe tips inflexed. Subsp. *latifolium* Up to 2700m. FLOWER **lobes dark maroon or brown**, corona lobe tips relaxed.

Aspidonepsis (*aspido* - Aspidoglossum; *anepsia* - cousin, refers to the relationship with this genus) Erect grasslike geophytic herbs. Stems long, thin, with long internodes, produced annually, milky latex. Leaves long, narrow. Inflorescences few, in upper nodes. Flowers yellow or brown, corona lobes held well above flower lobes, with a central cavity that may or may not contain a central tonguelike appendage. Pollinarium wishbone-shaped. Fruit solitary, erect, spindle-shaped, smooth. SAfr endemic, 5 species, all in mountainous habitats, 4 in this region.

Aspidonepsis cognata Large Suncup [= *Asclepias cognata*] (*cognitus* - now understood, refers to the confusion in identifying it as a species separate from *Aspidonepsis flava* and *A. diploglossa*)
Slender, erect, unbranched herb, 180-550mm tall. Scattered in mountain grasslands, in damp areas, near streams, 1200-2100m. E Cape to KZN. LEAVES long, narrow, 10-68×0.5-6mm, margins rolled under. FLOWERS 1-7, in terminal clusters, large, 7-17mm wide, lobes spreading, 6-10×2.5-6mm, **greenish brown or brownish yellow, ± purple outside, corona lobes large, ±5mm tall, bonnet-shaped, overtopping style tip, central cavity with tonguelike appendage** (Nov-Jan).

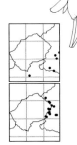

Aspidonepsis flava Small Suncup [= *Asclepias flava*] (*flavus* - pale yellow, refers to the flower colour)
Slender herb, 180-475mm tall. In scattered colonies, in mountain grassland, up to 2000m. E Cape to KZN. Stems 1(3), branched from base. LEAVES 7-80×0.5-7mm. FLOWERS 4-20, small, 5-8mm wide, lobes spreading, ±5×3mm, **pale yellow, corona lobes yellow, small, 1-1.5mm tall, boxing glove-shaped, with reflexed armlike upper appendages, central cavity with** sausage-shaped appendage (Nov-Jan).
Similar species: ***Aspidonepsis diploglossa*** [=*Asclepias diploglossa*] (*diplo* - two; *glossa* - tongue, refers to the the corona lobe which itself has a lobe) In grassland, 1500-2400m. FLOWERS brilliant yellow, larger, 6-13mm wide, corona lobes larger, 4-6mm tall, cup-shaped, central cavity with broad central appendage not exceeding the flower centre (Nov-Jan).

SCROPHULARIACEAE - Snapdragon Family (see pg 218) *Manulea* (*manus* - a hand, refers to 5 spreading corolla lobes) Annual or perennial herbs (shrubby). Leaves mostly clustered at base. Flowers in long inflorescences. Fruit a capsule. Afr, mostly SAfr, ±74 species, ±6 in this region.

Manulea crassifolia fukuthoane, meqilane, nohana-metsana (SS) (*crassifolia* - thick-leaved)
Tall, robust, **perennial** herb, 300-600(1000)mm tall. In damp grassland, 1675-3000m. E Cape to Mpum. LEAVES in **basal rosette**, 60-170×7-30mm, thick, margins entire to finely toothed. INFLORESCENCE **long, narrow**, ± branched, flowering stem ± bare; FLOWERS in dense clusters, dull to deep golden yellow (subsp. *crassifolia*), dull yellow to **mauve** (subsp. *thodeana*), calyx 2-lipped (5 lobes) (Dec-Mar). GENERAL: Subsp. *crassifolia* Mainly in Les, E FS. Subsp. *thodeana* Mainly on the face of Drak.

Manulea platystigma (*platystigma* - stigma compressed, flat)
Dwarf perennial herb, 40-300mm tall. On silt patches over rock sheets, loose scree, **summit plateau**, 2900-3300m. EMR endemic. LEAVES in basal rosette, 15-80 ×4-15mm, thick, **tips blunt**, narrowed into long flat stalklike base, finely glandular hairy. INFLORESCENCE long; FLOWERS 9-12mm wide, **in clusters of 2-3**, dull to bright yellow, sometimes deep red-brown, back of throat yellow-orange, scented (Dec-Feb).

Zaluzianskya (named after Adam Zalusiansky von Zaluzian, 1558-1613, physician and botanist from Prague) (see pg 92)

Zaluzianskya rubrostellata (*rubro* - red, *stellata* - star)
Annual herb, stems erect or reclining, 20-140mm long. In basalt grit, 2350-3300m. EMR endemic. Stems sparingly branched, sparsely hairy. LEAVES 7-20×1.5-6mm, thick. FLOWERS in terminal headlike cluster, corolla limb held horizontally, ±12mm diam, lobes **chocolate-brown below, bright yellow above with slightly raised red star** around the mouth, tube 20-30mm long, opening at dusk (Dec-Mar).

Melasma (*melas* - black, plants turn black on drying) Herbs with rough stems. Calyx inflated in fruit. Trop Afr, Trop America, ±5 species, 1 in SAfr.

Melasma scabrum seona, tika-letša (SS) (*scabrum* - rough)
Hemiparasitic herb, up to 600mm tall. On streambanks, marshy places, up to 2400m. W Cape to Mpum. Rough hairy. LEAVES up to 70×10mm, stalkless, margins, lobed at base. FLOWERS ±30mm diam, pale yellow with deep red centre (sometimes missing), **calyx tube 10-ribbed**, stalks ±60mm long (Jan-Mar). **Calyx inflated in fruit.**

142

Schizoglossum stenoglossum subsp. *flavum*

Aspidonepsis cognata

Aspidonepsis diploglossa

Aspidonepsis flava

Manulea platystigma

Zaluzianskya rubrostellata

Manulea crassifolia

Manulea crassifolia

Melasma scabrum

143

Alectra (*alektor* - a cock) Hemiparasitic herbs. Plants turn black when bruised. Afr, Mdag, Asia, ±40 species, ±17 in SAfr, ±4 in this region.

Alectra basutica [= *Melasma basutica*] **moema-osi, seona (SS)**

Up to 500mm tall. Scattered in grassland, 1650-1980m. EMR endemic. Parasitic on grass. LEAVES ±15×5mm, overlapping, stalkless, blunt-tipped. INFLORESCENCE a long spike, **bracts with a few teeth**; FLOWERS dull yellow veined red, **filaments bearded** (Jan-Mar). **Similar species: *Alectra pumila* seona (SS)** (*pumila* - diminutive, dwarfish) Rough, dwarf herb, 40-80mm tall. E Cape to Bots. FLOWERS (Jan-Feb).

Alectra sessiliflora **Verfblommetjie (A); mokhele, seona (SS)** (*sessiliflora* - stalkless flowers)

Branching herb, up to 250(600)mm tall. In moist grassland, up to 2900m. W Cape to Trop Afr. Parasitic on grass. Stems purple, sparsely hairy. LEAVES ±30×20mm, margins with blunt teeth. INFLORESCENCE terminal, **bracts leaflike with prominent teeth**; FLOWERS ±15mm diam, yellow, **just protruding from short calyx** (Nov-Mar).

LENTIBULARIACEAE - Bladderwort Family Perennial herbs, aquatic or in swamps. Submerged leaves modified into bladderlike pitchers with traps for catching insects. Flowers 2-lipped, spurred or pouched at base. Cosmop, ±3 genera, ±245 species, 2 genera in SAfr. ***Utricularia*** (*utriculus* - little leather bottle, refers to insect trapping bladders on leaves and runners) Cosmop, ±180 species, ±18 in SAfr, 5 in this region.

Utricularia arenaria (*arenarius* - sand)

Tiny, erect, leafless herb, up to 80mm tall. In marshy pools over rock sheets, up to 2400m. E Cape to Ethiopia. FLOWERS pale violet or yellow, with yellow patch on lip (Jan-Mar). **Similar species: *Utricularia prehensilis* Large Yellow Bladderwort; Blaaskuid (A); iphengulula (Z)** Stems twisted around grass stalks, up to 200mm. In marshy places up to 2000m. FLOWERS large, yellow, spur twice as long as lip (Jan-Feb).

RUBIACEAE - Gardenia /Coffee Family Leaves opposite or whorled, stipules between leaf stalks. Petals crowned into a tube. Fruit crowned with persistent calyx. Economically important for cofeee, quinine and ornamentals such as *Gardenia*. Cosmop, ±630 genera, ±10 200 species, 61 genera in SAfr. ***Galium*** (*galion* - 'milk plant' of Dioscorides) Herbs. **Leaves whorled**, stipules leaflike. Cosmop, ±400 species, ±12 in SAfr, 3 in this region.

Galium capense subsp. *garipense* **mabone, lefero, sehorane (SS)** (*gariep* - vernacular name for the Orange River)

Tufted to sprawling herb, stems 200-500mm long. In moist grassland, stream gullies, boulder beds, up to 3000m. E Cape to Mpum. LEAVES in whorls, 10-20×0.5-1mm. INFLORESCENCE widely branching; FLOWERS small, creamy or greenish yellow, sweetly scented (Nov-Mar). FRUITS covered with curled white hairs.

COMPOSITAE (refers to the composite nature of the flowerheads), also called **ASTERACEAE - Daisy Family** The largest family of flowering plants, mostly herbs, sometimes shrubs, rarely trees. Flowers crowded into a dense head (capitulum) made up of few to many small florets clustered on a base (receptacle), surrounded by one or more rows of green or coloured bracts, florets are either tubular or strap-shaped (resembling petals - ray florets). Fruit usually small, dry (rarely fleshy), usually surmounted by a tuft of hairs or scales (the much reduced calyx, pappus). Economically important for crops eg lettuce, sunflowers, chicory, Pyrethrum insecticide and for a large number of ornamentals. Cosmop, ±1535 genera, ±25000 species, ±250 in SAfr. ***Nidorella*** (*nidor* - strong smell) Afr. ±13 species, ±11 in SAfr, ±7 in this region.

Nidorella undulata **mokoteli-o-moholo (SS)** (*undulata* - wavy)

Perennial herb, up to 1m tall. In **damp or marshy grassland**, up to 2450m. S Cape to Zim. BASAL LEAVES up to 300×40mm, in a rosette, often withered at flowering, stem leaves gradually smaller upwards, **all leaves narrowed to a broad, winglike base, mostly hairless**. FLOWERHEADS ±4mm diam, yellow, in many compact clusters, bracts glandular, flowering stems with **glandular soft hairs** (Dec-Jan-Mar).

Chrysocoma (*chrysos* - gold; *kome* - hair) Bushy shrublets. Leaves sometimes ericoid. SAfr, ±18 species, 1 in this region.

Chrysocoma ciliata [= *C. tenuifolia*] **Bittter Bush; Bitterbos (A); sehalahala (SS)** (*ciliata* - hairy)

Bushy, ericoid, sticky shrublet, up to 1m tall. In open rocky places or in scrub, up to 3000m. SW Cape to Mpum. Branches bare below, closely leafy towards tips. LEAVES up to 8mm long. FLOWERHEADS 6×10mm, yellow, **solitary**, at ends of branchlets, very sweetly scented (Sep-May). GENERAL: Blooms profusely. Fuel plant in mountain areas, collected and sold, green or dry. A weed on overgrazed land.

Alectra basutica

David McDonald

Alectra pumila

Darren Webster

Utricularia arenaria

Hilliard & Burtt

Utricularia prehensilis

Lal Greene

Alectra sessiliflora

Lorraine van Hooff

Galium capense subsp. *garipense*

Neil Crouch

Nidorella undulata

Martin von Fintel

Chrysocoma ciliata

David McDonald

Chrysocoma ciliata

Martin von Fintel

Heteromma (*heteromma* - boss-eyed) Coarse herbs. SAfr endemic, 3 species, EMR endemics.

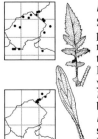

Heteromma decurrens lesitsi, moqhoboqhobo-o-moholo (SS) (*decurrens* - running down)

Stout, erect, large perennial herb, up to 2m tall. In dense stands, on margins of forest patches, in scrub, at foot of damp cliffs, up to 2100m. EMR endemic. **Roughly hairy,** main stem up to 50mm diam. LEAVES up to 200×70mm, **deeply lobed,** irregularly toothed, **narrowed to a stalklike base running down the stem in 2 broad wings.** INFLORESCENCES large, branching; FLOWERHEADS **bell-shaped,** up to 8×8mm, bright yellow, **outer bracts pointed** (Oct-Apr). **Additional species:** *Heteromma simplicifolium* (*simplicifolium* - simple leaves) Distinguished from *H. decurrens* by its simple leaves, basal ones with stalks up to 150mm long. FLOWERHEAD bracts pointed (Dec-Mar). *Heteromma krookii* (named after P. Krook who collected herbarium specimens for A. Penther in 1895) **Stem simple, bare below, well branched above,** leaves there crowded towards the tips. FLOWERHEADS **top-shaped,** easily distinguished by **the blunt bracts** (Sep-Feb).

Helichrysum (*helios* - sun; *chrysos* - gold) Herbs, shrubs, sometimes dwarfed and cushion forming. Usually hairy or woolly. Flowerheads solitary or in compact or spreading inflorescences. Mainly Afr, ±600 species, ±244 in SAfr, ±55 in this region. **Page layout groups similar species.**

Helichrysum callicomum motoantoanyane, pulumo-tšeou (SS) (*callicomum* - beautiful hair)

Tufted perennial herb, up to 400mm tall. On river flats, gravelly banks, overgrazed areas, 1800-2400m. E Cape to Zim. Stems with woody base, tufted, closely greyish white felted, densely leafy. LEAVES up to 25×6mm, blunt-tipped, **closely greyish felted.** INFLORESCENCE 60-80mm diam; FLOWERHEADS cylindric, ±4×1mm, bracts straw-coloured, not spreading (Feb-May). GENERAL: Used as a protective charm.

Helichrysum dasycephalum moqabola, motoantoanyane, senkotoana (SS) (*dasy* - thickly hairy; *cephalum* - head)

Dwarf shrub up to 30mm tall, forming stiff twiggy mats and cushions. On rock sheets, hard bare earth, 1900-2560m. Branches **covered in silvery grey tissue paperlike felt,** densely leafy. LEAVES small, rigid, up to 20×5mm, tips hooked. INFLORESCENCE up to 20mm diam; FLOWERHEADS in tight clusters, usually webbed together with delicate 'tissue paper', bracts silvery with woolly hairs in a thin skin, tips sometimes pale brown, flowers yellow (Feb-Apr).

Helichrysum odoratissimum imphepho (X,Z); phefo-ea-setlolo, tooane (SS) (*odoratissimum* - very sweet smelling)

Much branched, straggling, aromatic perennial herb, up to 600mm tall. In large clumps, on damp grass slopes, particularly around rocks and at the foot of cliffs, up to 2400m. Cape to Zim, Malawi, Moz. Stems thinly greyish white woolly, very leafy. LEAVES very variable, 5-60×1.5-15mm, **broadest above the middle, base clasping, running down the stem in wings,** thinly or thickly greyish white woolly. FLOWERHEADS ±3mm long, **very matted together with wool at the base,** in dense or loose terminal clusters, bracts tightly overlapping, outer pale brown, inner bright yellow, flowers 7-15, yellow (Jan-Jun). GENERAL: An essential ingredient for herbalists, used to invoke a trance. Leaves pleasantly scented, burnt to fumigate a sickroom, treat colds and to invoke the goodwill of the ancestors. **Similar species:** *Helichrysum gymnocomum* imphepho (Z) Up to 700mm tall. In rank growth, near overhangs and rock faces, 1500-3000m. Cape to Les. FLOWERHEADS **usually single-sexed, flowers 4-7** (Feb-Jul). GENERAL: Burnt to invoke the goodwill of ancestors.

Helichrysum krookii leme-la-khomo (SS) (named after P. Krook who collected herbarium specimens for A. Penther in 1895 on a journey from the E Cape to Natal and the Orange Free State)

Perennial herb, up to 400mm tall. In small colonies, in moist grassland, 1500-2800m. LEAVES up to 100×50mm, **mostly clustered in a rosette at base,** glandular-hairy, abruptly narrowed into the broad, clasping base. INFLORESCENCE **20-70mm diam;** FLOWERHEADS 3-4×2-3mm, **felted together with wool,** bracts bright yellow (Jan-Feb).

Helichrysum umbraculigerum (*umbraculigerum* - bearing woolly umbrellas)

Aromatic perennial herb, up to 1m tall. On damp grass slopes, streamlines, up to 2500m, on forest margins at lower altitudes. S Cape to Zim. Young parts thinly grey-woolly, **leafy throughout.** LEAVES **very variable,** 20-80×**3-25 mm,** ± cobwebby or greyish white woolly above, thickly woolly beneath. INFLORESCENCE **'umbrella-like';** FLOWERHEADS 3×1mm, **felted together with wool,** bracts golden yellow (Jan-Apr).

Heteromma decurrens   *Heteromma krookii*   *Helichrysum krookii*

Helichrysum callicomum   *Helichrysum dasycephalum*

Helichrysum odoratissimum   *Helichrysum umbraculigerum*   *H. umbraculigerum*

147

Helichrysum subglomeratum thethebijane, thethebilone (SS) (*subglomeratum* - hemispherical)
Tufted perennial herb, flowering stems 80-600mm long, often reclining at base. Sometimes massed, in short stony grassland up to 3000m. E Cape to Limpopo Prov, Ang. One to several leaf rosettes with several flowering stems to each rosette. LEAVES spreading, in basal rosette, up to 120×15mm or much smaller, tips blunt, with close, **silvery silky felted covering.** INFLORESCENCE 20-40mm across, **matted below with wool**; FLOWERHEADS in small congested clusters, **bracts bright yellow** (Mar-Jun).

Helichrysum albirosulatum (*albirosulatum* - white rosettes)
Prostrate, well branched shrublet, up to 120mm tall. On Cave Sandstone sheets, 1800-2450m. EMR endemic. Main branches bare, up to 10mm diam, silvery white felted, closely leafy throughout. LEAVES in rosettes at branch tips, up to 25×6mm, **spatulate**, covered with silvery white, slightly glossy felt. INFLORESCENCE 10-20mm across; **bracts pale yellow** (Jan-Mar).

Helichrysum glomeratum (*glomeratum* - clustered into a head, referring to inflorescence)
Perennial herb, up to 450mm tall. Often in large colonies, in open grassland, E Cape to Mpum. Stems erect, **densely leafy**. LEAVES ±30×10mm, broad at base, **tapering to a pointed tip**, covered in **silvery silky hairs**, in compact basal rosette, **stem leaves closely overlapping**. INFLORESCENCE flat, 20-50mm across; FLOWERHEADS 3-4 ×1-1.5mm, in congested clusters, **matted with wool at base**, bracts bright yellow (Feb-May). GENERAL: Sage-scented when crushed.

Helichrysum nanum (*nanum* - dwarfish, small)
Mat-forming perennial herb, flowering stem up to 50-120mm tall. In large mats in poor stony grassland or on rock sheets, colonizing eroded areas, 1800-2575m. Main branches slender, rooting, with many erect shoots. LEAVES in close rosettes, **stiff, erect**, up to 35×**1mm**, covered in **silvery silky felt**, tips blunt, **margins strongly rolled under**. INFLORESCENCE flattish, 15-20mm across; FLOWERHEADS 4-5×1.5mm, felted together in small clusters, **outer bracts brownish**, **inner pointed**, bright yellow (Mar-Jun).(see pg 14) **Similar species:** *Helichrysum subfalcatum* (*subfalcatum* - nearly sickle-shaped) Flowering stems 10-200mm tall. On steep stony mountain slopes, in stream gullies, on low broken cliffs, 2140-2800m, often in large colonies. Main stems prostrate, mat-forming, with numerous, congested leaf rosettes, flowering stems terminal. LEAVES 30-60×**2-7mm**, slightly sickle-shaped, tips pointed, with **silvery smooth tissue-paperlike covering** on greenish upper surface, **silvery white beneath**. FLOWERHEADS 4×3mm, closely webbed together, bracts tipped yellow (Jan-Mar).

Helichrysum evansii [= *H. alticolum* var. *montanum*] (named after Maurice Evans, 1854-1920, businessman, politician and pioneer plant collector in the Drakensberg)
Mat-forming perennial herb, flowering stems 20-50mm tall. On cliff faces, rock platforms or stony ground, 1900-3200m. EMR endemic. LEAVES spatulate, covered with greyish white woolly felt, up to 45×15mm, tips rounded. INFLORESCENCE roundish, 10-20mm across; FLOWERHEADS 5-6×3mm, bracts bright yellow, felted together at base with grey wool (Sep-Oct, Feb-Apr).

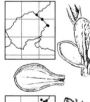

Helichrysum aureonitens Gouesewejaartjie (A); toane-ntja, toane-poli (SS); impepho emhlophe, inkondlwane (Z) (*aureonitens* - shiny gold or lustrous gold)
Silvery grey perennial herb, up to 300mm tall. Often in large in colonies, in damp grassland, up to 2450m. E Cape to Ang, Moz. Stems slender, leafy. LEAVES ±20×3mm, woolly. FLOWERHEADS ±4×3mm, up to 30 in compact clusters at branch tips, bracts yellow to pale brown (Sep-Feb). GENERAL: Used to invoke the goodwill of ancestors and by diviners to induce trances. Used to keep red mites away.

Helichrysum cymosum subsp. *calvum* Yellow-tipped Straw-flower; impepho (Z)
(*cymosum* - refers to the inflorescence; *calvum* - hairless, refers to the lack of pappus)
Thinly woolly, spreading shrublet. In stony grassland, on steep slopes, (1200)1800-3170m. E Cape to KZN/Mpum. LEAVES **small**, narrow, ±10×2-4mm, crowded, 'tissue papery' above, skinlike beneath, tapering to sharp, hairlike tips. INFLORESCENCE compact; FLOWERHEAD bracts transparent, glossy yellow (Dec-Mar). GENERAL: A garden groundcover. Used to invoke the goodwill of ancestors and to induce trances.

Helichrysum albirosulatum

Helichrysum evansii

Helichrysum nanum

Helichrysum subglomeratum

Helichrysum subglomeratum

Helichrysum aureonitens

Helichrysum cymosum

Helichrysum glomeratum

149

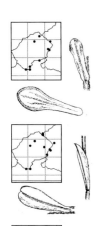

Helichrysum basalticum

Prostrate, perennial herb, flowering stems 40-120(400)mm long. In crevices of basalt rock sheets or bare shallow rocky soil, about 2900m. EMR endemic. **One or several rosettes crowded on the crown** with several lateral flowering stems. ROSETTE LEAVES **broad**, up to 40×15mm, tips blunt, **thickly grey woolly**. INFLORESCENCE a **congested, rounded cluster 15-20mm wide**, at tip of stem, up to 4 clusters per stem; FLOWERHEADS bell-shaped, ±4×4mm, felted together at base, bracts tawny yellow, tipped golden brown, flowers yellow (Feb-Mar).

Helichrysum flanaganii phefo (SS) 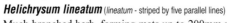(named after H.J. Flanagan, 1861-1919, plant collector of note, who first collected the species on top of Mont-aux-Sources)

Much branched, perennial herb, **forming large thick mats**, flowering stems erect, 40-200mm long. In short damp grassland and on damp rock sheets, 1650-3200m. EMR endemic. LEAVES **narrow**, up to 8(20)×4mm, closely grey-white woolly on both surfaces or without wool (green). INFLORESCENCE a terminal cluster ±18mm wide; FLOWERHEADS bell-shaped, ±3×3m, bracts tawny yellow tipped golden brown (Oct-Dec).

Helichrysum lineatum (lineatum - striped by five parallel lines)

Much branched herb, forming mats up to 200mm wide. In short grassland (growing in tufts), on bare soil on the summit, 2900-3200m. EMR endemic. LEAVES 4-10 ×3-7mm, in basal rosettes, **greyish white woolly-felted**, tips rounded, **leaves webbed to stems**. FLOWERHEADS cylindric, ±5×2mm, many clustered in a **terminal inflorescence surrounded by leaves**, bracts light golden brown, blunt-tipped, **outer ones webbed with wool to surrounding leaves** (Jan-Feb).

Helichrysum hypoleucum 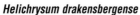(hypoleucum - white below, refers to leaves)

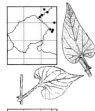

Softly woody scrambling shrub, ±2m. On forest margins, steep grassy slopes, at foot of cliffs, 1200-2000m. EMR endemic. **Branches white-felted.** LEAVES up to 80×50mm, **heart-shaped**, narrowing to pointed tip, green above, **white-felted beneath, 5-veined from base, stalks up to 25mm long**, narrowly winged, clasping. INFLORESCENCES branched, spreading; FLOWERHEADS 2×2mm, in congested clusters, outer bracts woolly, inner glossy, silvery translucent, flowers bright yellow (Feb-Apr). GENERAL: Attractive garden subject in light shade.

Helichrysum drakensbergense

Bushy perennial herb or shrublet, up to 400mm tall. Often in large colonies, locally common, on grassy slopes or in scrub, along streams, 1525-2740m. EMR endemic. Stems often reclining and rooting at base, forking in upper part of erect stems, **grey-woolly**, leafy in lower half. LEAVES up to 90×30mm, **grey-woolly, spatulate**, tapering to base. INFLORESCENCE a **tightly congested flattish cluster 20-25mm across, felted together at base**; FLOWERHEADS ±6×4mm, bracts glossy, straw-coloured, flowers yellow (Nov-Jan).

Helichrysum acutatum Taaisewejaartjie (A); uzangume (Z) 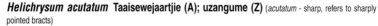(acutatum - sharp, refers to sharply pointed bracts)

Perennial **silvery grey** herb, up to 450mm tall. In rocky grassland, up to 2000m. E Cape to Limpopo Prov. Woody rootstock. LEAVES ±250×50mm, sticky, **lightly cobwebby or thickly grey-woolly, 3-veined**, narrowing to long, winged base. INFLORESCENCE a dense cluster 40-60mm diam; FLOWERHEADS ±5-7×3mm, **bracts closely overlapping**, outer webbed together with wool, **glossy bright yellow** (Sep-Jan). GENERAL: Used in traditional medicine.

Helichrysum oreophilum (oreophilum - mountain loving)

Perennial herb, up to 300mm tall. In short stony grassland, 1550-2450m. KZN to Gauteng, Mpum. LEAVES up to 80×15mm, **thinly grey silky woolly, only main vein visible beneath**. INFLORESCENCE **flat-topped, branched**; FLOWERHEADS ±7×5mm, **bracts loosely overlapping**, cobwebby at base, tapering to **long, narrow, pointed tips, lemon-yellow** (Oct-Feb). GENERAL: Invades overgrazed grassland or eroded areas.

Helichrysum lineatum

David McDonald

Helichrysum basalticum

Anne Rennie

Helichrysum flanaganii

David McDonald

Helichrysum flanaganii

David McDonald

Helichrysum oreophilum

Martin von Fintel

Helichrysum drakensbergense

Hilliard & Burtt

Helichrysum acutatum

Sheila Peacock

Helichrysum hypoleucum

Martin von Fintel

151

Helichrysum montanum toana-ea-loti (SS)

Dwarf shrub, 100-450mm high, **forming thick mats 1m wide or more**. On cliffs and rock outcrops, 1800-2500m. Branches very short, congested, densely leafy. LEAVES up to 25×8mm, appearing rosetted from above, broad, **thickly greyish white woolly, striped with 3-5 parallel veins**. INFLORESCENCES terminal to each rosette of leaves; FLOWERHEADS 5-8×4-5mm, bases woolly, in compact terminal inflorescence, bracts loosely overlapping, bright yellow (**Dec-Apr**).

Helichrysum splendidum Cape Gold; Geelsewejaartjie (A); phefo-ea-loti, toane-moru (SS)

(*splendidum* - shining)

Slender erect shrub, 0.6-1.5m tall. On forest margins, rocky places, stream gullies, mountain tops, 1900-2590m. S Cape to Trop Afr. Old parts of stems rough with leaf scars. LEAVES **narrow**, 10-30×1-2mm, grey-woolly above (rarely smooth or hairless), whitish woolly beneath, margins rolled under, **tipped with a short hard point** (mucro). INFLORESCENCE compact or open, terminating long leafy branches; FLOWERHEADS 5-8×4-5mm, **bracts glossy bright yellow** to orange (**Oct-Feb**). GENERAL: Aromatic or lavender scented. Used in traditional medicine to treat rheumatism. A good fuel plant in the mountains. Useful garden plant, grown from cutting or seed.

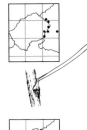

Helichrysum tenuifolium (*tenuis* - narrow; *folium* - leaf)

Rounded shrub, up to 2m tall. In colonies, in boulder beds of streams, among rock outcrops, in fynbos, above 1650m. Endemic, known only from KZN. LEAVES narrow, 7-18×1-1.5mm, tips hooked, with short hard point (mucro), margins rolled under, **upper surface hairless**, white-woolly below. INFLORESCENCE of **compact flattened clusters 10-20mm wide**; FLOWERHEADS ±4-5×4-5mm, bases woolly, bracts glossy, palest brown tipped reddish or orange when young, tips of inner bracts bright yellow (Nov-Dec). GENERAL: Can be confused with *H. trilineatum* which has leaves gland-dotted above. *H. tenuifolium* has closely appressed trichomes (seen with a lens).

Helichrysum trilineatum hukobetsi, phefshoana-ea-loti (SS) (*trilineatum* - leaves marked with 3 parallel lines)

Aromatic, rounded shrublet, 150-600(1200)mm tall. Often in large colonies, on steep mountain slopes, summit plateau on grass slopes or among rock outcrops, in gullies, 1800-3100m. Old branches bare, rough with leaf scars, greyish white woolly, closely leafy. LEAVES 3-25×1-5mm, blunt, tips recurved, with short hard point (mucro), margins rolled under, **blade ribbed with 3 parallel veins, upper surface white woolly on both surfaces or green and minutely gland-dotted above**, white-woolly beneath. INFLORESCENCE of compact clusters terminating all the branchlets; FLOWERHEADS 4-8×4-6mm, woolly at base, in compact clusters, bracts bright yellow (throughout the year). GENERAL: Used for fuel in Les.

Helichrysum witbergense (named after the Witteberg, above Lady Grey)

Spindly or rounded shrub, up to 900mm tall. In large colonies, locally common, on moist grassy mountain slopes or valley bottoms, ±2800m. EMR endemic. Old branches bare, branchlets white-woolly, closely leafy. LEAVES 7-18×1-1.5mm, **broadest at base, narrowed above to a sharp** (acute) **tip, upper surface ± green, sticky**, lower white-woolly, parallel veins conspicuous. INFLORESCENCE a compact cluster, 15-20mm wide, terminating branchlets; FLOWERHEADS ±8×5-6mm, bracts closely overlapping, outer, light brown, inner bright yellow, flowers yellow (Nov-Feb).

Bundles of
*Helichrysum
trilineatum*, ready for
use as fuel in Lesotho

David McDonald

Helichrysum montanum

David McDonald

Helichrysum splendidum

Darrel Plowes

Helichrysum splendidum

Hilliard & Burtt

Helichrysum montanum

David McDonald

Helichrysum witbergense

John Grimshaw

Helichrysum trilineatum

David McDonald

Helichrysum trilineatum

David McDonald

Helichrysum trilineatum

Mike Hirst

Helichrysum tenuifolium

Hilliard & Burtt

153

Helichrysum nudifolium Hottentot's tea; Hottentotstee (A); mohlomela-tsie, mohlomela-tsie-oa-thaba, mohlomela-tsie-oa-thota (SS); icholocholo (X,Z); isidwaba-somkhovu, umagada-emthini (Z) *(nudifolium - hairless leaves)*
Perennial herb, flowering stems up to 1.5m tall, leafy below, nearly leafless above. FLOWERHEADS ±4-5×2.5-3mm, bracts pale yellow (Nov-Mar). Widespread. Variable leaf shape, size, hairiness and inflorescence. Two forms common in this region up to ±2500m. 1. MAIN LEAVES ±20-30mm broad, hairless. INFLORESCENCE **wide-spreading**. Boulder beds of rivers, grassland near streams. 2. MAIN LEAVES ±5-20mm broad, often white-felted below. INFLORESCENCE **contracted, headlike**. GENERAL: Leaves cooked, eaten in some areas. Used in traditional medicine. Grown from seed.

Helichrysum pilosellum [= *H. latifolium*] boleba, boleba-ba-liliba, leboko, papetloane-ea-liliba, papetloane-e-kholo, tsebe-litelele (SS); isicwe (X,Z); umadotsheni, umaphephesa (Z) *(pilosellum - shaggy hairs)*
Perennial herb, up to 450mm tall. In open grassland, up to 2400m. Widespread. LEAVES few, mostly at base, spreading ± flat, ±150(250)×40(60)mm, **dark green, rough above**, white-felted beneath, **main veins 5-9, netted together**. Flowering stem terminal to rosettes, leafy only near base, woolly-felted. INFLORESCENCE a terminal cluster; FLOWERHEADS 5×5mm, bract tips clear (pellucid), crisped, flowers bright yellow (Oct-Mar). GENERAL: Used in traditional medicine.

Helichrysum pallidum [= *H. undatum* var. *agrostiphilum*] boleba, bolebatsi, papetloane-ea-thaba (SS) *(pallidum - rather pale, refers to bracts)*
Robust perennial herb, up to 400(650)mm tall, leafy in lower half. In open grassland, 1800-2700m. E Cape to Mpum. BASAL LEAVES up to 400×120mm including **long stalklike base**, blade roughly hairy, grey-green above, thinly greyish white-felted below, 5-7 veins, midrib, side veins conspicuous, tertiary veins form a conspicuous ladderlike pattern. INFLORESCENCE flat-topped; FLOWERHEADS ±6-7×6-7mm, back of bracts woolly, tips oval, cream to pale yellow (Nov-Feb).

Helichrysum cephaloideum [= *H. adscendens* var. *cephaloideum*] mosuoane-oa-thaba (SS); bhade (Z) *(cephaloideum - headlike)*
Perennial herb with several flowering stems, **loosely grey-woolly, leafy**, up to 400mm tall. **In stony grassland** up to 2600m. E Cape to Zim. ROSETTE LEAVES **often withered at flowering**, ±20-50×10-20mm, tips pointed, **covered in loose grey wool**. STEM LEAVES smaller. INFLORESCENCE **a compact, roundish cluster**, up to 30mm wide, often webbed together at base with wool; FLOWERHEADS 4-5(6)mm long, bell-shaped, glossy bright yellow or deep straw-coloured, bracts spreading (**Nov-May**). **Similar species:** ***Helichrysum auriceps*** *(auriceps - golden heads)* Up to 600mm tall. In grassland, up to 2000m. ROSETTE LEAVES ±65-150×8-16mm, loosely grey-woolly. INFLORESCENCE **a tight ball** up to 45mm across; FLOWERHEADS (6)7-8mm long, congested, glossy bright yellow, bracts spreading (**Feb-Apr**).

Helichrysum pagophilum *(pagophilum - lover of crags)*
Very compact, hard, rounded, cushion-forming dwarf shrub, up to 100mm tall and up to 1m across. On cliff faces, small rock sheets, 2750-3500m. EMR endemic. Main stem woody, bare, gnarled, main branches prostrate, rooting, with many tightly congested densely leafy branchlets. LEAVES closely overlapping, appearing rosetted, **thick, rounded**, ±4-6×4-6mm, **grey-silky woolly**. FLOWERHEADS **cup-shaped, 5-7mm long**, 10-14mm across spreading bracts, stalkless, solitary at tips of branchlets, bracts in ±6 series, loosely overlapping, **glossy lemon-yellow** or whitish (Nov-Jan).

Helichrysum herbaceum [= *H. squamosum*, *H. monocephalum*] Monkey-tail Everlasting; hlohoana-kholoana, tlhako (SS); impepho-yamakhosi (Z) *(herbaceum - herblike, not woody)*
Perennial herb, up to 400mm tall. In short grassland, up to 2600m. Cape to Tanz. BASAL LEAVES rosetted at first, up to 50×20mm, ± hairless above, white-felted below; STEM LEAVES 10-20×1-2mm, overlapping, greyish white to cobwebby above, loosely felted below. FLOWERHEADS up to 20mm long, 28mm across spreading bracts, **bracts often run down stem, outer glossy golden brown, inner lemon-yellow** (Dec-Mar). GENERAL: Burnt to invoke goodwill of ancestors.

Helichrysum nudifolium — *Lorraine van Hooff*

Helichrysum pallidum — *Cameron McMaster*

Helichrysum pilosellum — *Lal Greene*

Helichrysum auriceps — *Martin von Fintel*

Helichrysum herbaceum — *Tom de Waal*

Helichrysum auriceps — *Martin von Fintel*

Helichrysum cephaloideum — *Lal Greene*

Helichrysum herbaceum — *David McDonald*

Helichrysum pagophilum — *John Grimshaw*

Helichrysum pagophilum — *Hilliard & Burtt*

155

Helichrysum aureum leabane, tšoene **(SS)** (*aureum* - golden, refers to bracts)
Very variable leaf size, hairiness and flowerhead size. LEAVES in basal rosette. flowering stems leafy, several from base of rosette. FLOWERHEAD bracts bright yellow. **Var.** *monocephalum* (*monocephalum* - one-headed) Grassland, coast to 3000m. E Cape to Zim. BASAL LEAVES ±30-120×10-20mm, greyish white woolly, sometimes margins only. FLOWERHEADS usually solitary, 17-32mm across spreading bracts, flowering stems 50-300mm **(Jul-Nov)**. *Var. scopulosum* (*scopulosum* - on rocks) Rock faces, boulders, base of cliffs, ±1700-2750m. EMR endemic. Like var. *monocephalum* FLOWERHEADS larger, up to 45mm across, outer bracts brownish, inner yellow **(Jul-Dec)**. **Var.** *serotinum* (*serotinum* - late to flower) Grassland, ±1800-2600m. EMR endemic. Like var. *scopulosum,* flowering stem cobwebby in upper part, not throughout **(Dec-May)**.

Helichrysum cooperi **Geelsewejaartjie (A); bohloko, phefo-ea-thaba, toane-balimo, toane-balingoana (SS); umadotsheni (Z)** (after Thomas Cooper, 1815-1913, English plant collector)
Biennial, flowering stems up to 1.5m tall. In grassland, scrub, margins of forest, to ±2500m. KZN. STEMS stout, leafy, bristly. LEAVES **bright green**, in rosette in first year, ±150(250)×60mm, withered at flowering, **glandular or woolly;** STEM LEAVES ±65-130×20-45mm, **blade running back down stem in wings**, glandular on both surfaces, margins sometimes woolly. INFLORESCENCE large, leafy, wide spreading, **woolly below the heads only**; FLOWERHEADS shallowly cup-shaped, ±10-12mm long, 15-25mm across spreading bracts, bracts glossy bright yellow (Dec-Apr). GENERAL: Used as a fumigant, as a love charm and as part of a traditional remedy for snakebite.

Helichrysum heterolasium (*heterolasium* - 'different wool' refers to different hairiness of basal and stem leaves)
Biennial herb, flowering stems up to 800mm tall. In tall rough grassland on steep slopes, in boulder stream valleys, 2280-2850m, growing socially. EMR endemic. ROSETTE LEAVES **thinly grey-white woolly**, up to 100×350mm, withered and persisting at base of stem in second year; STEM LEAVES **green**, up to 90×25mm. INFLORESCENCE branched, stalks leafy; FLOWERHEADS **large**, ±30-40mm across the spreading bracts, bracts glossy, inner bright yellow, outer pale golden brown (pink) (Jan-Apr).

Helichrysum tenax **Sticky Everlasting; Klewerige reusesewejaartjie (A)** (*tenax* - holding fast))
Conspicuous subshrub, (0.6) up to 1.8m tall, **each branch topped with a rosette of leaves**. On grassy mountain slopes, in boulder beds, in disturbed areas, up to 2150m. E Cape to KZN. **Main stem thick, woody, branching** near ground, **old dry leaves persistent**. LEAVES up to 180(250)×80mm, mostly much smaller, bright green, **sticky**, traces of wool on margins, main veins; STEM LEAVES overlapping, up to 80×20mm, margins wavy. FLOWERING STEMS 300-450mm, **sticky**, white-woolly, from side of leaf rosettes; FLOWERHEADS 25-35mm across spreading bracts, shallowly cup-shaped, loosely white-woolly at base, bracts glossy yellow (Oct-Dec). GENERAL: Insects get stuck on the sticky leaves but plant is not insectivorous. **Var.** *pallidum* Steep rocky places, about 1500m. Ngele Mtn. STEM LEAVES **densely greyish white-woolly**. FLOWERHEAD **bracts creamy white** (Oct-Nov). (see pg 110)

Relhania (after Rev Richard Relhan FRS, 1754-1823) Often sticky. Leaves rigid, ± ending in a stiff point. SAfr endemic, 13 species, 2 in this region.

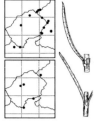

Relhania acerosa [= *Nestlera acerosa*] ´mamenoana, masepa-a-lekhoaba, moholu-oa-lekhoaba, moholu-oa-pela, rapeisi **(SS)** (*acerosa* - sharp)
Gnarled, well branched dwarf shrublet, up to 300mm tall. Often in colonies, on rock sheets, rocky slopes, up to 3000m. EMR endemic. LEAVES crowded towards ends of branches, up to 20×1mm, sharp-tipped, **gland-dotted**, slightly sticky, loosely white-woolly, becoming hairless, 3-5 veins below. FLOWERHEADS solitary, terminal, ±20mm wide, bracts light brown, ray florets yellow (Jul-Nov). **Additional species:** *Relhania dieterlenii* [= *Nestlera dieterlenii*] ´mamenoana, rapeisi **(SS)** (named after Anna Dieterlen, 1859-1965) Large shrub up to 1.6m tall. Lesotho endemic. Leaves softly woolly (Oct-Jan).

Helichrysum aureum var. *monocephalum*

Helichrysum aureum var. *serotinum*

Relhania dieterlenii

Helichrysum heterolasium

Relhania acerosa

Relhania dieterlenii

Helichrysum tenax var. *tenax*

Helichrysum tenax var. *tenax*

Helichrysum cooperi

157

Macowania (named after Peter MacOwan, 1830-1909, Director of Cape Town Botanical Gardens, first prof of botany at SA College) Tall or dwarf shrubs, often intricately branched and glandular. Leaves overlapping. Afr. 12 species, 10 in SAfr, ±7 in this region.

Macowania corymbosa (corymbosa - heads arranged in flat-topped inflorescence)

Erect, spindly, **sticky** shrub, up to 1.5m tall. In shrub communities along streams, on steep slopes, 1525-2590m. EMR endemic. Young branches covered in closely overlapping leaves. LEAVES up to 40×3mm, margins rolled under, thinly woolly below, glandular bristly above and on midrib below. FLOWERHEADS ±25mm diam, crowded terminally, yellow, **bracts edged dark brown, glandular bristly** (Mar-Jul).

Macowania glandulosa (glandulosa - glandular)

Dwarf, much-branched shrub forming low compact cushions up to 450mm tall. In crevices of Cave Sandstone cliffs, rock sheets and large outcrops or fallen boulders, 1830-2400m. EMR endemic. LEAVES up to 20×2.5mm, green above, **covered in gland dots**, margins strongly rolled under, white-woolly below. FLOWERHEADS yellow, **stalkless**, bracts pale brown, sometimes with a purple-brown patch towards the tips, (Sep-Nov).

Macowania hamata (hamata - hooked)

Straggly shrub, up to 1m tall and 1m diam. On steep moist rocky slopes, on cliffs above streams, 1800-2200m, prominent on Sani Pass. EMR endemic. Young branches white woolly, densely leafy. LEAVES **spreading**, ±10-13×1.2mm, glossy green above, **densely white-woolly beneath, tips pointed, strongly hooked, margins rolled under, merging into the pointed tip**. FLOWERHEADS yellow, **stalkless**, bracts straw-coloured to brownish near tips, thinly woolly (Dec-Feb).

Macowania pulvinaris ´mamotasi (SS) (pulvinaris - a cushion)

Dwarf, spreading, aromatic shrub, forming low compact cushions. Conspicuous in ericoid shrub communities, 2000-2950m. EMR endemic. Young stems densely leafy. LEAVES up to 20×1.2mm, green, roughly glandular above, white-woolly below, margins strongly rolled under, midrib strongly raised below, **tips broadly pointed**. FLOWERHEADS yellow, **on short, bare stalks**, bracts straw-coloured, lightly woolly (Dec-Jan).

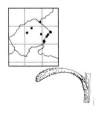

Macowania sororis (sororis - sister, the type collection was made by a nun)

Dwarf, much branched, aromatic shrub, forming low, compact cushions. **On cliffs and rock outcrops, 2133-3000m**. EMR endemic. **Young stems densely leafy.** LEAVES up to 13×2mm, overlapping, shiny, roughly glandular hairy above, **white-woolly below**, at least when young, margins strongly rolled under. FLOWERHEADS yellow, **on short stalks** (Jan-Apr). **Similar species:** *Macowania conferta* (conferta - crowded, dense) Dwarf shrub, forming low compact cushions. On rock outcrops on steep grassy slopes ±1800m. **Ngeli Mtn endemic.** LEAVES dark green, **not woolly below**, ±15×2mm, midrib strongly raised below. FLOWERHEADS **stalkless**, ±20mm diam, rays bright yellow, florets darker (Jan).

Athanasia (everlasting) Shrubs or herbaceous perennials. About 39 species, SAfr endemics, mainly in the Cape, 1 in this region.

Athanasia grandiceps (grandiceps - large head)

Shrub 0.5-1.5m tall with **strong, rather sickly smell**. In rough grass and scrub in boulder strewn valley, locally common but as yet found only in the upper Mlambonya and upper Pholela Valley, 1800-2100m. EMR endemic. Stems ± branched above. LEAVES up to 50mm long, **deeply lobed, lobes up to 15mm long**, base broad, half clasping, hairless or with a few long white-woolly hairs. FLOWERHEADS **large, 15-25mm diam, bright yellow**, solitary, on long, white-woolly leafy stems, 150-250mm long, becoming bare, **hollow and inflated under the flowerheads**, bracts straw-coloured, horny, with hard, raised keel, tips greenish (Nov-Dec).

Macowania corymbosa

Martin von Fintel

Macowania glandulosa

Martin von Fintel

Macowania corymbosa

Hilliard & Burtt

Macowania sororis

Hilliard & Burtt

Macowania hamata

Martin von Fintel

Macowania sororis

David McDonald

Macowania pulvinaris

Mike Hirst

Athanasia grandiceps

Hilliard & Burtt

159

Inulanthera (*inul* - related genus *Inula*; *anthera* - anther) Shrubs or shrublets. SAfr, 10 species, ±7 in this region.

Inulanthera calva [= *Athanasia calva*] (*calva* - bald)

Softly woody shrub, up to 1.5m tall. In forest margin scrub, grassland, up to 1900m. S KZN to Mpum. Stems thinly white-woolly. Leaves ±40×4mm, tufted, hairless to densely hairy, **mostly 3-toothed at tip**, sometimes with a pair of teeth on sides, stipulelike lobes at base. Inflorescence compact, 60-150mm wide; Flowerheads yellow, ±6mm diam (Mar-May). General: Crushed leaves smell like eucalyptus.

Inulanthera thodei [= *Athanasia thodei*] khato, lelingoana, sehalahala-se-seputsoa (SS) (named after Justus Thode, 1859-1932, pioneer plant collector in the Drakensberg)

Much branched, very aromatic shrub, up to 1.2m tall. On basalt, rocky slopes and gullies, sometimes a constituent of fynbos, 2300-3200m. EMR endemic. Old stems bare, rough with leaf scars, young stems woolly, densely leafy. Leaves stalkless, up to 40×2mm, **entire or 2-3-lobed at the tips**, margins rolled under, white-woolly below, loosely woolly above, no leaf tufts in axils. Inflorescence dense, terminal; Flowerheads up to 30, yellow, roundish, ±7mm diam (Mar-Apr). General: Used to fumigate a hut where someone has died. Makes poor quality fuel.

Phymaspermum (*phyma* - swelling; *sperma* - seed) Shrub or shrublets. SAfr, 19 species, 2 in this region.

Phymaspermum acerosum [= *Athanasia acerosa*] Geelblombos (A); isibhaha-segceke, umhlonishwa (Z) (*acerosa* - needle-shaped, like a pine needle)

Well branched shrub up to 1.5m tall. In colonies, in grassland, on forest margins, up to 2000m. Stems woody, **densely leafy**. Leaves variable, 10-45mm long, with large glandlike swelling at base of midrib beneath, 5-7-lobed or simple, lobes 3-30mm long. Inflorescence dense, flat-topped; Flowerheads yellow, **narrowly cylindric**, 5×2-3mm, **bracts narrow, gutter-shaped** (Apr-Jun). General: Invades overgrazed grassland. Used in traditional medicine and as a charm to ward off lightning.

Cotula (*kotule* - a cup, refers to receptacle) Herbs. Leaves usually compound, finely dissected, rarely simple. Stems sometimes swollen beneath flowerheads. Mainly S Hemisp, ±55 species, ±43 in SAfr, ±7 in this region.

Cotula hispida (*hispida* - hairy)

Tufted perennial herb, up to 400mm tall. In moist grassland, along base of cliffs, around rock outcrops, up to 3000m. Stems reclining at base. Leaves ±30×15mm, thinly hairy, lobes narrow, **stalks ±80mm long**, base half-clasping, upper leaves stalkless, becoming smaller, reduced to bracts. Flowerheads solitary, 10-15 mm diam, yellow reddening with age, stalks bare, slightly swollen below flowerheads (Jan-Apr).

Cotula paludosa (*paludosa* - marshy)

Mat-forming herb, flowering stems up to 180mm tall. In yellow carpets in marshy ground on the summit, 2600-2900m. EMR endemic. Leaves in rosettes, up to 100×20mm, including **stalk up to 50mm long**, lobes up to 6×1mm, silky hairy in bud, **otherwise hairless**, stalk flat, base clasping. Flowerheads 10-25mm wide, bright yellow, reddening with age (Jan-Mar).

Cotula radicalis (*radicalis* - rooting)

Tufted perennial herb, up to 150mm tall. Often in small colonies, in damp grassy rocky places, on steep slopes, 2400-3050m. EMR endemic. Flowering stems silvery hairy. Leaves **silvery hairy**, in rosette, narrowly oblong, up to 45×5mm, **comblike**, segments divided into 1-5 lobes, stalk up to 50mm long. Flowerheads bright yellow, flat, ±15-20mm diam, **bracts silvery hairy**, with broad dark margins (Dec-Feb).

Cotula socialis (*socialis* - consorting together ie in large colonies)

Mat-forming perennial herb, flowering stems up to 150mm tall. In large colonies, on steep grassy mountain slopes, 2300-3050m. EMR endemic. Leaves **nearly stalkless**, in rosettes, up to 45×10mm, **lobes reduced in size downwards**, 2.5×0.25-.0.5mm. Flowerheads yellow, 10-17mm diam, reddening with age (Dec-Mar). General: Can be confused with *C. hispida* which has leaves with stalks 30-50mm long and lower lobes hardly reduced in size. **Similar species:** *Cotula membranifolia* (*membrani* - thin parchment; *folia* - leaves) Up to 400mm tall, not in large colonies. On damp earth banks, up to 2450m. EMR endemic. Leaves **with distinct stalk**, rosette leaves less deeply dissected, **lobes broad**, ±6×4mm (Dec-Mar).

Inulanthera calva   *Lorraine van Hooff*

Inulanthera thodei   *David McDonald*

Inulanthera thodei   *David McDonald*

Phymaspermum acerosa   *Lorraine van Hooff*

Cotula radicalis   *Hilliard & Burtt*

Cotula paludosa   *David McDonald*

Cotula hispida   *David McDonald*

Cotula socialis   *David McDonald*

Schistostephium (schizo - cut; stephos - crown, refers to deeply toothed florets) Woody perennials, often aromatic. Afr, *12 species*, 9 in SAfr, 2 in this region.

Schistostephium crataegifolium Golden Flat-flower; Bergkruie (A); kobo-ea-marena, kobo-kholo, leapi, lehakanya (SS) (crataegifolium - leaves like Crataegus)

Tufted, **silky grey**, aromatic, perennial herb, up to 500mm tall. On rough grassy slopes, up to 1950m. E Cape to Mpum. Leaf size and flowerhead size very variable. LEAVES stalkless, up to 45×30mm, sharply and deeply toothed, lobed or cut almost to midrib, **lobes pointed**, bristle-tipped, margins entire or with 1-2 teeth. INFLORESCENCE terminal; FLOWERHEADS 5-10mm diam, bright yellow (Dec-Apr). GENERAL: Used in traditional medicine and as a charm to chase away hail.

Gymnopentzia (gymno - naked, refers to the genus Pentzia but without a pappus) Shrub, monotypic. SAfr endemic.

Gymnopentzia bifurcata [= G. pilifera] sehalahala (SS) (bifurcata - forked, refers to leaves)

Shrub, up to 1.2m tall. In boulder beds, on rocky streambanks and rock outcrops, 1525-3050m. E Cape to Mpum. Branches white-hairy. LEAVES **opposite, simple or 1-3-forked**, 10-40mm long, lobes slender, usually hairless (shaggy). INFLORESCENCE showy, terminal; FLOWERHEADS yellow, roundish, 4-5mm diam (Mar-Jul).

Pentzia (named by Thunberg in 1800 after his student C.J. Pentz) Shrubs, subshrubs or herbs. Afr, ±23 species, 21 in the Cape, 2 in this region.

Pentzia cooperi lebaila, leriane, napjane (SS) (named after Thomas Cooper, 1815-1913)

Well branched aromatic shrub, up to 1.5m tall or dwarfed. In rocky stream gullies, on steep slopes, 2300-3000m, conspicuous in Les. Cape to Gauteng. Stems and leaves hairless, cobwebby at first. LEAVES crowded, up to 15×2mm, entire or 2-3-toothed at tips, gland-dotted, stalkless. INFLORESCENCES crowded, flat-topped; FLOWERHEADS ±4mm diam bright yellow, honey-scented (Feb-Apr). **Similar species:** *Pentzia tortuosa* sehalahala (SS) (tortuosa - tortuous) Rounded, dwarf shrub, intricately branched, aromatic, 150-250mm tall. On rock sheets , constituent of shrub communities, up to 2600m. EMR endemic. Hairless. LEAVES 6-8×3mm. FLOWERHEADS ±4mm diam, stalks ±50mm long (Jan-Apr).

Cineraria (cinerarius – light grey, refers to leaf colour of some species) Herbs or subshrubs. Afr, ±50 species, ±37 in SAfr, in need of revision.

Cineraria aspera Grey Cineraria; moholu-oa-pela (SS) (aspera - rough)

Bushy, **greyish white** woolly annual herb, up to 1m tall and as wide. Colonises poor stony mountain slopes, a weed along roadsides, 1950-2400m. Cape to Mpum. LEAVES up to 100×50mm, long and narrow, compound, lobes irregularly toothed, lower leaves stalked, **roughly hairy on both surfaces**, often **thinly grey-white woolly or cobwebby as well**, especially when young. INFLORESCENCE **compact**, flat-topped; FLOWERHEADS yellow, with 5-8 rays (Apr-Jul). GENERAL: Used in traditiional medicine.

Cineraria dieterlenii khotolia-e-kholo-ea-thaba, moholu-oa-pela (SS) (named after Anna Dieterlen, 1859-1945, missionary, teacher and plant collector in Lesotho from 1877-1919)

Perennial, straggling herb, ±1m tall. In damp shady places, on forest margins, along watercourses, 1500-2560m. KZN endemic. **Stems branched**, thinly hairy. LEAVES up to 60×80mm, **kidney-shaped, deeply lobed, margins coarsely toothed**, softly hairy, cobwebby below, young buds white-woolly, stalks ±50mm long, basal ears large. INFLORESCENCE **open**; FLOWERHEADS ±20mm diam, rays 8, yellow (Jan-May).

Cineraria lyrata khotolia, tlali-tlali (SS) (lyrata - like a lyre or harp)

Annual herb, up to 600mm tall. On disturbed ground, up to 2450m. W Cape to Mpum, uncommon in KZN. STEMS branch near base. LEAVES up to 80×30mm, deeply lobed, lobes mostly in 2-3 pairs, margins toothed, lower leaves with long slender stalks, upper leaves stalkless, broad based, clasping, thinly white-woolly when young. FLOWERHEADS in branched inflorescences, rays 8, yellow (Oct-Mar).

Senecio (senex - old man, refers to whitish hairs of pappus) Herbs, shrubs, rarely trees. Flowerheads solitary or in inflorescences, bracts in a single row, margins interlocking. One of the very large genera of flowering plants, ±2000 species worldwide, ±300 in SAfr, ±80 in this region.

Senecio achilleifolius Slootopdammer (A) (achilleifolius - leaves like those of the genus Achillea)

Shrubby perennial herb up to 600mm tall. In dense mats, in rocky streambeds, in damp hollows over rocks, sometimes trailing in shallow water, up to 3000m. S Cape to Mpum. **Stems long, slender, stiff, prostrate to ascending**, woolly at first. LEAVES up to 40mm long, **deeply, finely lobed**, lobes 2-4(20)mm long, **woolly at first**, hairless later. FLOWERHEADS ±25mm wide, rays yellow, sweetly scented (Jan-Apr).

Schistostephium crataegifolium   *Pentzia cooperi*   *Pentzia cooperi*

Van Wyk & Malan

Mike Hirst

Martin von Fintel

Cineraria dieterlenii   *Gymnopentzia bifurcata*

Mike Hirst

Peter Linder

Cineraria aspera   *Cineraria lyrata*   *Senecio achilleifolius*

Mike Hirst

Martin von Fintel

Hilliard & Burtt

163

Senecio asperulus moferefere, khotolia-ea-thaba, lehlomane-la-thaba, lehlongoana-la-thaba, letapisoana, letapisoana-la-naheng, makhona-tsohle (SS) *(asperulus - rough)*

Perennial herb, up to 600mm tall. In poor stony soil in grassland, on Cave Sandstone rocks, often becoming a weed along roadsides, 1900-2650m. E Cape to FS, Gaut. Rhizome thick, branching, producing many congested leaf rosettes. BASAL LEAVES up to 300×2-10mm, thick, rigid, rough, **margins often rolled under, toothed in broad leaves**, gradually narrowed to a flat stalklike base. INFLORESCENCE on long scaly stalks; FLOWERHEADS solitary or few, bright yellow, bracts 10-12×10-12mm, glandular hairy (Dec-Apr). GENERAL: Mixed with tobacco to make it milder.

Senecio brevilorus *(brevi - short; lorus - strap)*

Perennial herb, forming loosely tufted mats up to 600mm wide, flowering stems up to 800mm tall. Among boulders on edge of rocky streams, 2100-2400m. EMR endemic. BASAL LEAVES up to 75×20mm, shaped like a spatula, stem leaves progressively smaller upwards. FLOWERHEADS solitary or few at stem tip, sometimes nodding, pale yellow, **rays inconspicuous**, bracts 8-10mm long (Mar-Apr).

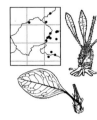

Senecio coronatus Woolly Grassland Senecio; Sybossie (A); lehlomane, lehlongoane, moremoholo, motabo, papetloane-ea-motabo (SS); ikhubalo lesikhova, indlebe yebokwe (X); izonkozonko, ubulibazi (Z) *(coronatus - crowned)*

Perennial herb, 100-400(750)mm tall. In colonies, on rocky soils in grassland, up to 2400m. S Cape to Tanz. **Rootstock silky woolly**. LEAVES leathery, mostly basal, 100-400×50-80mm, **lightly cobwebby** (to hairless), margins finely toothed, tapering to long broad, clasping stalklike base. INFLORESCENCE open, branched, **stems stout, loosely woolly**; FLOWERHEADS ±25mm diam, butter-yellow, bracts thinly woolly (Nov-Jan). GENERAL: Used in traditional medicine. Leaves cooked with maize meal.

Senecio deltoideus undenze (X) *(deltoideus - triangular)*

Much branched, slender, slightly succulent scrambler. On forest margins, in forest, up to 1950m. SW Cape to Kenya. **Stems zigzag**. LEAVES ± **triangular**, 50-80×30-70mm, thin, ivylike, widely spaced, **margins irregularly toothed**, stalks ±30mm long, leaflike ears clasping at base (or absent). INFLORESCENCES widely branched; FLOWERHEADS small, sometimes with **1-4 yellow rays, sweetly honey scented** (Mar-Jun). GENERAL: Used in traditional medicine. Good bee plant. Grown from cuttings. **Similar species:** *Delairea odorata* Cape Ivy [= *Senecio mikanioides*] *(odorata - sweet smelling)* Cape to KZN, Les. **Terminal stems straight**. LEAF **base broad, sharply 3-5-lobed on each side**, stalks ±70mm long. FLOWERHEADS **without rays** (Jan-May). GENERAL: Frost sensitive. Cultivated as a window plant in Europe where it has escaped in places.

Senecio dissimulans *(di - twice; simulans - imitative, similar, refers to its resemblance to S. hypochoerideus)*

Perennial herb, up to 400mm tall. Common on moist grassy slopes, 1800-3000m. EMR endemic. **Covered in sticky hairs**. LEAVES mostly basal, 70-150×3-15mm, narrowing to broad, flat, stalklike base, margins finely to coarsely toothed. FLOWERHEADS solitary or few, yellow, ±30mm diam, with 8-13 rays (Nov-Feb). **Similar species:** *S. hastatus* Leaves thinner, at least the basal ones finely to broadly lobed. *S. hypochoerideus* Leaves broader, 15-30mm wide, hairs not sticky.

Senecio glaberrimus lehlomane (SS) *(glaberrimus - completely without hairs)*

Perennial herb up to 600mm tall. In colonies in grassland, up to 2500m. E Cape to Mpum. Rootstock woody with **woolly crown**, flowering stems tall, leafy. LEAVES **smooth, grey-green**, up to 140×40(100)mm, **base often clasping**, margins thickened, ± rolled under, sometimes running onto stem, main veins prominent. INFLORESCENCE large, loose; FLOWERHEADS bright yellow, 10-23mm diam (Feb-Nov).

Senecio gramineus *(gramineus - grasslike, refers to the narrow leaves)*

Perennial herb, 100-350mm tall. In crevices and around margins of rock sheets and stony ridges, mainly on the summit, 2100-3300m. E Cape to KZN. Flowering stems solitary from each leaf tuft, **grey cottony**, with few leaves, **bare below flowerheads**. LEAVES mostly basal, **narrow, ±50-200×1-2mm**, covered in **grey, felted, silky wool**, **margins strongly rolled under**. FLOWERHEADS often solitary, occasionally few, ±20mm diam, yellow, on long stalks (Nov-Jan).

Senecio gramineus

Senecio brevilorus

Senecio glaberrimus

Senecio deltoideus

Senecio asperulus

Senecio coronatus

Senecio dissimulans

165

Senecio harveianus khotalia (SS) (named after Dr William Harvey, 1811-66, Irish born treasurer general of the Cape Colony, chief author of the early volumes of *Flora Capensis*, later Prof of Botany, Dublin)
Perennial, bushy herb, up to 1.2m tall, stems branching from base. On rocky outctops, bare places on mountains, up to 3000m. E Cape to KZN/Mpum. LEAVES **narrow**, up to 100×10mm. FLOWERHEADS yellow rays, many series of bracts, inner ±6-9mm long (Feb-May).

Senecio haygarthii (named after Walter Haygarth, 1862-1950, who collected in Natal and E Griqualand, botanical artist who had illustrations in *Natal Plants* by Wood & Evans)
Handsome, erect, robust, perennial shrubby herb, up to 1m tall. In colonies, along watercourses, in shrub communities on mountain slopes, 1500-2450m. EMR endemic. Stems many, densely leafy, white felted, unbranched below inflorescence. LEAVES up to 60×25mm, **green, cobwebby when young and hairs not always completely absent with age, white felted beneath, deeply, narrowly lobed**, margins rolled under. INFLORESCENCES **congested, flat**, branched; FLOWERHEADS ±10mm diam, yellow (Sep-Dec). GENERAL: Grown from seed, attractive garden plant.

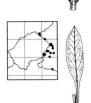

Senecio heliopsis (heliopsis - like the sun)
Perennial herb, up to 1m tall. In colonies, **in well drained grassland**, up to 2400m. E Cape to KZN/Mpum. BASAL LEAVES **broad**, up to 300×**90mm**, slightly fleshy, margins entire to minutely toothed, **narrowing to broad, long, stalklike clasping base, stem leaves reduced to bracts on upper part of stem.** INFLORESCENCE branched, with 3-9 yellow FLOWERHEADS **large, showy, ±30mm** diam (Sep-Dec). Similar species: *Senecio caudatus* (caudatus - tailed) **Perennial herb, 250-700mm tall. In marshy grassland or on hummocks in marshes**, up to 2425m. E Cape to Mpum. LEAVES **narrow**, up to 200×10(20)mm.

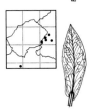

Senecio hygrophilus Blou Vleibossie (A) (hygrophilous - moisture loving)
Perennial herb, up to 1m tall, in colonies, **In damp grassland, valley bottoms**, up to 2450m. E Cape to Mpum. Stems simple, leafy, blue-green. LEAVES mostly 90-160×30-75mm, **broadest in middle or upper half**, margins entire to slightly toothed, slightly fleshy, aging leathery, narrowing to half clasping stalklike base. INFLORESCENCE crowded, flat topped; FLOWERHEADS yellow, ±20mm across, 1-2 ray florets (Nov-Dec). **Similar species:** *Senecio adnatus* (adnatus - adhering) **On drier grassy mountain tops**, up to 2500m. E Cape to Mpum. LEAVES **long, narrow, tapering**, up to 150×20mm, **broadest in lower part** (Nov-Jan). GENERAL: Poisonous to stock.

Senecio inornatus lehlongoana-le-leholo, lehlomane-le-leholo (SS); inkanga, uhlabo (Z) (inornatus - not ornamental)
Perennial herb, up to 1.8m tall. In colonies, on moist grassy slopes, streambanks, up to 3000m. Cape to Tanz. Stems ± woody, simple, leafy. **Leaf size, texture, margins, flowerheads very variable.** BASAL LEAVES **long**, up to 600×50mm, tapering to stalklike base, thin, margins minutely toothed; stem leaves eared and clasping at base, running onto stem thus producing wings. INFLORESCENCE crowded, branched; FLOWERHEADS **small**, yellow, with **±5 ray florets**, short (Jan-Mar). GENERAL: Visited by ants and stingless bees. Used in traditional medicine.

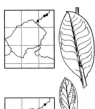

Senecio isatidioides (isatidioides - like *S. isatideus*, see below)
Perennial herb, up to 2.4m tall, in colonies. In dense stands on forest margins and other damp places, 1600-1800m. Stem simple, **leafy throughout, leaves decreasing slightly in size upwards.** LEAVES leathery, up to 200×115mm, **base rounded and stem clasping, shortly winging stem**, margins finely toothed, **side veins ascend sharply then spread at right angles before looping upwards near margin.** INFLORESCENCE flattish, branched; FLOWERHEADS in congested clusters (Oct-Feb). **Similar species:** *Senecio isatideus* Dan's Cabbage; Blou Vleibossie (A); lebato, lehlomane-le-leputsoa, lehlongoane-le-leputsoa (SS) (isatideus - resembles the genus *Isatis*, family Cruciferae/Brassicacae) **In grassland**, up to 1900m. LEAVES **decrease in size upwards, veins sharply ascending.** Flowering (Dec-Jan). GENERAL: Poisonous to stock, particularly in early spring. The new green leaves appear before the grasses.

Senecio harveianus

David McDonald

Senecio inornatus

Rob Scott-Shaw

Senecio inornatus

Peter Linder

Senecio haygarthii

Neil Crouch

Senecio heliopsis

Lal Greene

Senecio isatidioides

Martin von Fintel

Senecio hygrophilus

Olaf Wirminghaus

Senecio isatideus

Martin von Fintel

Senecio isatidioides

Martin von Fintel

167

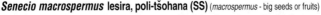

Senecio macrospermus lesira, poli-tšohana **(SS)** (*macrospermus* - big seeds or fruits)
Large, handsome, grey woolly perennial herb, ±1m tall. In large colonies, on steep, damp, mountain slopes, 2200-3000m. **Large clumps** of leaf rosettes, flowering stems stout, leafy. BASAL LEAVES up to 600×80mm, margins wavy, with tiny teeth, tapering to **broad, clasping, stalklike base**. INFLORESCENCE branched; FLOWERHEADS yellow, large, **bracts 15-18 mm long**, rays ±13 (Dec-Mar). GENERAL: Used as a protective charm. The silvery grey colour of the plant is retained under garden conditions.

Senecio napifolius (*napifolius* - leaves like those of a turnip)
Perennial herb, up to 800mm tall. In colonies, in open grassland, moist depressions, up to 2300m. Cape to N EMR. Stems simple, hollow, leafy in lower part, harshly hairy to smooth. LEAVES up to 200×90mm, **deeply lobed**, margins coarsely and sharply toothed, lower leaves tapering to broad, flat, half clasping, stalklike base, upper leaves eared, all harshly glandular hairy on both surfaces. INFLORESCENCE compact, congested; FLOWERHEADS ±25mm diam, yellow (Nov-Jan).

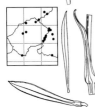

Senecio othonniflorus lehlomane-le-lenyenyane, lehlongoane-le-lenyenyane **(SS)** (*othonniflorus* - flowers like those of *Othonna*)
Perennial herb up to 600mm tall. On damp ground around rock sheets or rock outcrops, on grassy rocky slopes, 1800-2800m. S Cape to Mpum. **Crown woolly**. LEAVES crowded below, stalkless, up to 120×15mm, **± erect, fleshy, grey-green**, long, narrow, tapering to pointed tip, margins ± rolled under. FLOWERHEADS often solitary or few in a spreading inflorescence, bracts about 12, broad, flat, flowers bright yellow, flowering stems erect, smooth (Dec-Feb). GENERAL: Indicator of overgrazed land. Used in traditional medicine.

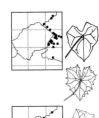

Senecio oxyriifolius False Nasturtium; Kappertjieblaar **(A)**; idumbe, idumbe lasendhle, ihlula **(Z)** (*oxyriifolius* - with leaves like those of *Oxyria* (Polyonaceae), N Europe)
Fleshy, bluish green perennial herb, up to 1m tall. In stony or rocky grassland, up to 2300m. S Cape to Tanz. Leaves clustered near base of plant. Stems bare above. LEAVES **rounded**, up to 90×90mm, shape and margins very variable, margins toothed or sharply angled, **peltate, stalk long, slender, up to 150mm**. FLOWERHEADS loosely arranged, bright yellow (Nov-Jan). GENERAL: Attractive, hardy garden plant, from seed. Used in traditional medicine and to prevent sorcery. **Similar species: *Senecio rhomboideus*** lekoto-la-litšoene, lelutla-la-pula **(SS)** (*rhomboideus* - diamond-shaped, refers to leaves) **Fleshy perennial herb**, up to 1m tall. In grassland, on rocky outcrops, up to 3000m. S Cape to Limpopo Prov. LEAVES up to 200×80mm, **blue-green, tapering to broad, flat, stalklike, half clasping base**, margins widely toothed in upper part, lobed or sharply toothed. FLOWERHEADS few to many, on long stalks, loosely arranged, yellow (Nov-Mar). GENERAL: Used in traditional medicine.

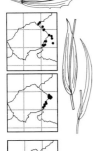

Senecio scitus (*scitus* - known)
Slender, erect herb, up to 600mm tall, in groups. On grass slopes, **up to 2200m**. KZN to Mpum. LEAVES few, leathery, hairless, up to 160×20-40mm, **tapering to narrow, pointed tip**, margins thickened, clasping at base. FLOWERHEADS yellow, with 8-10 rays (Oct-Mar). **Similar species: *Senecio parascitus*** (*para* - related to; *S. scitus*) In grassland, **between 2000-3000m**. EMR endemic. LEAVES mostly crowded on lower part of stem, up to 160×27mm, base clasping, margins slightly thickened, leathery with indistinct side veins. FLOWERHEADS with 7-8 rays, bright yellow (Dec-Feb). GENERAL: *S. glaberrimus* is similar but leaves are shorter and broader and flowerheads smaller, with up to 5 rays. (see pg 164)

Senecio paucicalyculatus (*paucicalyculatus* - few rather than many bracts below the involucre)
Perennial herb, stems up to 1m tall, simple below inflorescence. In marshy grassland in black, peaty, waterlogged soil, 1200-2300m, rarely up to 2800m. Les, FS to Mpum. Flowering stems simple, from centre of each leaf rosette. LEAVES **mostly in basal rosette**, up to 150×50mm, margins finely toothed, narrowing to broad, flat, stalklike clasping base. FLOWERHEADS few to many, loosely arranged, ±40mm diam, yellow (Sep-Jan).

David McDonald

Van Wyk & Malan

Senecio oxyriifolius

Senecio macrospermus

Tony Abbott

Senecio scitus

Braam van Wyk

Tony Abbott

Senecio othonniflorus

Senecio rhomboideus

Tony Abbott

Peter Linder

Lal Greene

Senecio napifolius

Senecio parascitus

Senecio paucicalyculatus

169

Senecio seminiveus khotolia-ea-noka (SS) (*seminiveus* - more or less white, derived from the fleeting white woolliness of the leaves)

Compact, branches erect to prostrate, twiggy, dwarf shrub, in rounded clumps. On damp cliffs, rock sheets, 2100-3200m. EMR endemic. **Stems widely branching,** loosely white-woolly, densely leafy. LEAVES up to 30mm long, closely, finely, deeply lobed, with broad half clasping base, **unfurled leaves densely white-woolly,** mature leaves mostly without wool. FLOWERHEADS large, yellow, with 13 spreading rays, bracts 7-8mm long (Feb-Mar). **Similar species:** *Senecio tanacetopsis* [= *S. tanacetoides*] molepelle, mosuane-oa-matlapa (SS) **Spreading shrub** with long, slender, **reclining or pendulous branches,** hanging down cliffs or spreading over rock sheets, up to 2075m. E Cape to Les, rare in KZN. LEAVES **grey-woolly on both surfaces.** FLOWERHEAD bracts 4-5 mm long (Feb-Mar). GENERAL: Lacks the peculiar white woolly leaf buds, contrasting with the green mature leaves, characteristic of the allied *S. seminiveus.* Leaves used to stop a nose bleed.

Senecio tamoides Canary Creeper; Kanarieklimop (A); ihlozi elikhulu, uqobaqoba (Z) (*tamoides* - resembling *Tamus*)

Showy, semi-succulent climber, to top of canopy. Common in forest patches, up to ±1800m. E Cape to Zim. Mature stems corky. LEAVES up to 80×80mm, ± triangular in outline, **unequally lobed,** stalks ± as long as blade. INFLORESCENCES **crowded, 120-150mm wide;** FLOWERHEADS yellow, ±15mm diam, ±5 ray florets (Apr-Jul), sweetly scented. GENERAL: Visited by butterflies (Pieridae). Used in traditional medicine to treat flatulence and anthrax in cattle. Lovely garden plant that dies back in winter in colder areas.

Senecio thamathuensis (*thamathuensis* - named after Thamathu Cave where the type specimen was collected)

Shrubby perennial herb, up to 1m tall. In damp scrub below cliffs, **conspicuous on rockfalls,** at high altitude, 1950-2400m. EMR endemic. Stems much branched, leafy. LEAVES 30-65mm long, **deeply lobed, lobes ±10-18×1-3mm.** FLOWERHEADS yellow, ±15mm diam, many in large spreading inflorescence (Jan-Feb).

Senecio ulopterus (*pterus* - wing, refers to winged stems)

Perennial herb, up to 600mm tall, sometimes in large stands on disturbed soil. In moist grassland, up to 2400m. BASAL LEAVES up to 120×40mm, ± abruptly narrowing to stalklike base, thinly hairy, margins with rounded or pointed teeth, sometimes withered away at flowering, stem leaves stalkless, half clasping and running onto stem in wings, **wings crisped, wavy.** FLOWERHEADS pale, whitish, 9-11mm long, **nodding when young,** up to 20 in spreading inflorescence (Dec-Jan).

Euryops (*eurys* - large; *ops* - eye, refers to showy flowerheads) Shrubs or shrublets. Leaves alternate, often crowded, shape variable. Flowerheads large to small, on short or long stalks. Afr, 98 species, ± 89 in SAfr, 11 in this region.

Euryops acraeus (*acraeus* - the summit, edge)

Rounded, well branched shrub, up to 1m tall. In rocky places, in cracks in south-facing basalt cliffs, 1800-3300m. EMR endemic. Stems bare below, rough from leaf bases, leafy near tips. LEAVES 10-30×2-4mm, flat, **leathery,** covered with whitish bloom when young, margins flat or rolled inwards, tips bluntly 3-toothed. FLOWERHEADS yellow, ±30mm diam, stalks 10-40mm long, wiry (Dec-Feb). GENERAL: A hardy, handsome shrub, grown in Britain.

Euryops candollei tloatloatloa (SS) (named after Augustin Pyramus de Candolle, 1778-1841, Swiss botanist and principal founder of the natural system of botany)

Dense, **ericoid,** rounded shrub or shrublet, 0.5-1.5m tall to about 1m wide. In montane grassland, on slopes and rocky places, particularly on bare soil and eroded places, 1500-3000m. Mtns near Graaff-Reinet to S Les. Branches often prostrate and rooting at base. LEAVES 2-5×1mm, **closely overlapping, erect, flat against stem,** or ± spreading, **tips sharp, inflexed, often white.** FLOWERHEADS yellow, small, ±15mm wide, stalks 2-25mm long (Nov-Apr). GENERAL: The rounded bushes are an almost solid mass of yellow flowers.

Senecio thamathuensis

Hilliard & Burtt

Senecio seminiveus

Rod Saunders

Euryops acraeus

Clinton Carbutt

Senecio tamoides

Martin von Fintel

Senecio ulopterus

Tony Abbott

Euryops acraeus

Clinton Carbutt

Euryops candollei

Hilliard & Burtt

Euryops candollei

David McDonald

171

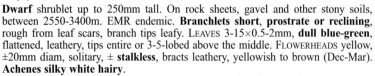

Euryops decumbens (*decumbens* - partly reclining)
Dwarf shrublet up to 250mm tall. On rock sheets, gavel and other stony soils, between 2550-3400m. EMR endemic. **Branchlets short, prostrate or reclining**, rough from leaf scars, branch tips leafy. LEAVES 3-15×0.5-2mm, **dull blue-green**, flattened, leathery, tips entire or 3-5-lobed above the middle. FLOWERHEADS yellow, ±20mm diam, solitary, ± **stalkless**, bracts leathery, yellowish to brown (Dec-Mar). **Achenes silky white hairy**.

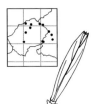

Euryops evansii sehlakoana **(SS)** (named after Maurice Evans, 1854-1920, English businessman, plant collector, who came to Natal in 1875, joint author with John Medley Wood of *Natal Plants* vol. 1)
Spindly shrub, up to 2m tall. In colonies, in scrub along rocky watercourses, montane grassland, 1200-3000m. EMR endemic. Main stems bare, rough with leaf scars, leaves clustered at tips. LEAVES 10-100×2.5-20mm, **grey-green**, leathery, **flat, tips 3-toothed**. FLOWERHEADS ±50mm diam, yellow, 1-5 in terminal clusters (Nov-Apr). GENERAL: Used in traditional medicine to treat headaches. Three subspecies have been described. Subsp. *evansii* The common, most widespread plant: LEAVES 40-100×7-20mm, **widest at or below the middle**. Subsp. *dendroides*: Known only from Maletsunyane Falls, C Les. LEAVES **widest above the middle**. Subsp. *parvus*: Giants Castle and Cathedral Peak only. LEAVES **smaller, narrower**, 10-35×2.5-5mm (Oct-Dec).

Euryops laxus Harpuisbossie **(A)** (*laxus* - loose, limp)
Perennial herb, up to 350mm tall. In open or rocky grassland, up to 2200m. KZN to Mpum. STEMS **annual**, from thick woody rootstock, leafy towards base. LEAVES variable in size and shape, erect or spreading, 10-110mm, entire or with ±4 pairs lobes, soft, flat or thickish to needlelike. FLOWERHEADS ±40mm diam, yellow, **on stalks 50-250mm long**, ray florets widely spaced (Aug-Dec). GENERAL: One of the first plants to shoot up after grass fires.

Euryops montanus sehalahala **(SS)** (*montanus* - of mountains)
Erect, compact, rounded shrub or shrublet, up to 1m tall but often dwarf. In rocky places, including cliff faces, 2000-3300m. EMR endemic. LEAVES 5-20×6-15mm, **green**, 2-4-lobed or entire, tapering to roundish base. FLOWERHEADS up to 30mm wide, stalkless (Oct-Apr). **Achenes not silky hairy**.

Euryops tysonii sehlakoana-se-senyenyane **(SS)** (named after William Tyson, born in Jamaica 1851, died Grahamstown 1920, a teacher and plant collector)
Erect, handsome, much branched shrub, up to 1.5m tall. In colonies, on rocky mountain slopes, boulder beds of streams, 1200-2500m. EMR endemic. Stems leafy towards tips, rough with leaf scars below. LEAVES 10-30×2-8mm, glossy green, flat, leathery, **closely set, often overlapping**, erect to spreading. FLOWERHEADS ±25mm diam, yellow, solitary in upper leaf axils, **forming a crowded terminal cluster**, stalks up to 40mm long, sweetly scented (Sep-May). GENERAL: Attractive garden shrub.

Othonna (*othonna* - a Syrian plant, name used by Pliny) Shrubs, subshrubs or herbs, often semi-succulent. Afr, ±120 species, mainly SAfr.

Othonna burttii (named after B L Burtt, distinguished botanist)
Mat-forming herb. On rock edges and cliff faces on Cave Sandstone, on short stony turf on the summit, 1800-2700m. EMR endemic. Stems up to 200mm long, soon clothed just with remains of leaf bases and leaf remains. LEAVES erect, almost rosetted at branch ends, 20-80×1-8mm, flattened, leathery to semi-succulent, fleshy, blue-green, sometimes with red line along margins. FLOWERING STEMS bare, erect, 80-220mm; FLOWERHEADS ±25mm across spreading yellow rays (Nov-Dec). GENERAL: Grazed by eland.

Euryops decumbens

David McDonald

Euryops montanus

Euryops decumbens

Pam Cooke

Hilliard & Burtt

Euryops montanus

Hilliard & Burtt

Othonna burttii

Hilliard & Burtt

Euryops evansii

Clinton Carbutt

Euryops laxus

Wally Menne

Euryops laxus

Martin von Fintel

Euryops tysonii

Martin von Fintel

Euryops evansii

David McDonald

Euryops tysonii

Clinton Carbutt

173

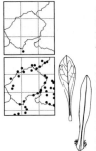

Othonna sp.
Succulent herb forming small cushions. Hardly known. LEAVES 25-30mm long, fleshy, ± cylindrical, 3mm diam, marked with indented veins. FLOWERHEADS yellow, 4-5, stalks 50-75mm long; flowering stems very slender, up to 150mm tall (Jan-Feb).

Othonna natalensis Geelbossie (A); naka, phela (SS); incamu (Z)
Perennial herb, up to 550mm tall. In colonies, in stony grassland, on grassy cliffs, up to 2700m. E Cape to Zim. LEAVES in basal rosettes, erect, up to 150×40mm, **thick, blue-green**, flushed reddish purple at base, tapering to stalklike base, margins entire. FLOWERHEADS solitary, 30-40mm across spreading yellow rays, stalks 50-400mm long, simple or forked (Sep-Dec). GENERAL: Eaten by people and stock when food is scarce. Used as a salad vegetable. Roots rich in oil. Used in traditional medicine to treat nausea and worm infestations in calves.

Osteospermum (*osteon* - bone; *sperma* - seed, refers to hard achenes or fruits) Attracts butterflies. Trop and SAfr, Somalia and SW Arabian Peninsula, ±45 species. Mostly SAfr, ±35 species, 2 in this region.

Osteospermum attenuatum (*attenuatum* - drawn out, refers to tapering leaf bases)
Mat-forming perennial herb, stems up to 400mm long. In moist, open grassland, 1675-2300m. EMR endemic. LEAVES up to 55×10mm, **tapering to stalklike base**, margins toothed. FLOWERHEADS solitary, ±25mm diam, yellow, ray florets purplish red beneath, stalks 30-40mm long (Dec-Feb).

Osteospermum thodei (named after Justus Thode, 1859-1932, pioneer plant collector in the Drakensberg)
Compact, erect, well branched shrub, up to 1.5m tall. On stony grass slopes, rocky ridges and rock platforms, on moist slopes above streams, 1800-2700m. EMR endemic. Young stems, flowering stalks and leaves covered in stalked glands. LEAVES stalkless, up to 45×20mm, tips blunt to pointed, base broad, half-clasping. FLOWERHEADS solitary, 20-30mm diam, yellow, stalks ±30mm long (Nov-Feb).

Chrysanthemoides (*chrysanthemoides* - like a *Chrysanthemum*) Shrubs. Fruit a drupe or berry. Trop to SAfr, 2 species, 1 in this region.

Chrysanthemoides monilifera subsp. canescens Bush-tick Berry; Boetabessie, Bietou (A); monokotsoai-oa-makhoaba, motlempe, ntlo-ea-lekhoaba (SS); ulwamfithi (X); inkhupuyana, itholonja, umtholombe (Z) (*monilifera* - necklace, refers to arrangement of the fruits; *canescent* - grey)
Succulent bushy shrub, up to 2m tall. In rocky places below cliffs, among boulders, 1800-2440m. Mtns of E Cape to Mpum. **White woolly hairs on leaves and stems**. LEAVES 15-75×5-40mm, narrowing to short stalks, thick, leathery, margins coarsely toothed. FLOWERHEADS ±30mm diam, in small, terminal clusters (all year). FRUITS **fleshy, berrylike**, green ripening **purplish black**. GENERAL: Flowers attract bees, ants, beetles and butterflies. Fruits eaten by people and birds. Leaves browsed by antelope. Used in traditional medicine. Hardy windbreak, from seed or cuttings.

Ursinia (possibly named after Johann Ursinus, 1808-1866, author of *Arboretum Biblicum*) Herbs. Mostly SAfr, ±39 species, ±4 in this region.

Ursinia alpina (*alpina* - alpine)
Mat forming, perennial herb, flowering stems up to 250mm long. On edge of rock sheets, cliffs, among rocks, up to 2745m. EMR endemic. LEAVES up to 40mm long, **crowded in tufts, lowermost ± prostrate, lower half stalklike**, lobes fine, up to 5mm long, **tips with a tiny outgrowth**. FLOWERHEADS large, up to 40mm wide, yellow, rays reddish below, stalks with bracts, **pappus of 5 white, petal-like scales** (Dec-Mar). Similar species: *Ursinia montana* **leabo (SS)** Edge of rock sheets, in crevices of sandstone platforms, in short stony turf, 1980-3170m. EMR endemic. LEAVES up to 35(50)mm long, **two thirds being stalk**, lobes up to 7mm long, **thick, roundish blunt**, simple or forked, with coarse white hairs at first. FLOWERHEADS yellow, ±25mm diam, stalk without bracts, **pappus of 5 broad, white petal-like scales** (Nov-Mar).

Ursinia tenuiloba umuthi wezifuba (Z) (*tenuiloba* - drawn out lobes)
Flowering stems up to 150mm long. **In clumps**, in short, rocky grassland, up to 2200m. E Cape to KZN/Mpum. Woody rootstock, **annual stems**. LEAVES up to 50mm long, upper part finely lobed, lower half stalklike, lobes ±10mm long, **narrow, tapering to slender pointed hairlike tips**, white-hairy at first. FLOWERHEADS ±30mm diam, ray florets yellow above, reddish below, **pappus of broad, white petal-like scales** (Aug-Jan). GENERAL: First to bloom after burning. Used in traditional medicine.

Othonna sp.

Osteospermum attenuatum

Hilliard & Burtt

Hilliard & Burtt

Osteospermum thodei

John Grimshaw

Martin von Fintel

Othonna natalensis

Martin von Fintel

Chrysanthemoides monilifera

Ursinia montana

David McDonald

Chrysanthemoides monilifera

Martin von Fintel

Ursinia alpina

Lal Greene

Ursinia tenuiloba

Lal Greene

Arctotis (*arktos* - bear; *otis* - ear, Linnaean flight of fancy) Woolly/glandular herbs. Mostly SAfr, ±64 species, 1 in this region.

Arctotis arctotoides [= *Venidium arctotoides*] **putsoa-pululu (SS); ubushwa (X)**

Mat-forming perennial herb, flowering stems up to 200mm long. On wet, bare ground or scree, marshy places, 1500-2900m. SW Cape to KZN. LEAVES basal, ±100-200×20-80mm, margins deeply lobed or obscurely toothed, **white-felted beneath**, narrowing to stemlike base. FLOWERHEADS 25-40mm diam, yellow, **ray florets often purplish brown beneath**, bracts white woolly (Sep-Mar).

Haplocarpha (*haplo* - one; *karphos* - small dry particle, refers to one ring of pappus scales) Afr, 10 species, 5 in SAfr, 2 in this region.

Haplocarpha nervosa (*nervosa* - vein or nerve)

Perennial herb, **forming extensive mats, in marshy places**, shallow muddy streams, up to 3000m. Montane, SE Cape to Zim. LEAVES in flat rosette, very variable in size and shape, 25-70×10-25mm, narrowing to broad, clasping stalk 10-60mm long, **margins entire, toothed, wavy or lobed, white-felted beneath, green veins conspicuous**. FLOWERHEADS yellow, ± 50mm diam, flowering stems white-cobwebby, very short or up to 80mm long (Sep-Apr). GENERAL: Leaves used as a vegetable.

Haplocarpha scaposa **Tonteldoosbossie (A); khutsana, lengoako, leshala, lisebo, moarubetso, papetloane (SS); isikhali, umkhanzi (X)** (*scaposa* - leafless flowering stems)

Perennial herb, flowering stems up to 300mm tall. In large colonies, in grassland, up to 2450m. Cape to EAfr. LEAVES in basal rosette, up to 150×70mm, margins entire or shallowly toothed, blade green above, **white-felted beneath**. FLOWERHEADS 60-80mm diam, pale yellow, bracts white-cobwebby, flowering stems **stout** (Nov-Apr). GENERAL: Crushed leaves used by women during menstruation. Used by diviners. White felt of leaves once used as tinder for tinder boxes. Attractive garden plant.

Gazania (named after Theodor of Gaza, 15ᵗʰ century translator of botanical works) Perennial herbs. SAfr, ±17 species, 1 in this region.

Gazania krebsiana **Common Gazania; Bruingousblom (A); shoeshoe** (flowerhead), **tsikitlane** (whole plant) **(SS); isapokwe, umkwinti (X); ubendle (X,Z)** (named after G.L.E. Krebs, 1792-1844, German apothecary and plant collector who came to SA in 1817)

Tufted perennial herb, flowering stems 100-130mm long. In short stony grassland, up to 3000m. E. Cape to Trop Afr. LEAVES up to 160×2-5mm, lobed or not, white-felted beneath. FLOWERHEADS solitary, 30-70mm diam, ray florets yellow, **sometimes with dark reddish blotch at base**, a greenish or reddish line below (Aug-Mar). GENERAL: Flowers eaten raw. Felt from back of leaves was rolled into twine to make skirts in Les. Used in traditional medicine. Popular garden plant, in cultivation since 1755.

Berkheya (after Dutch botanist Jan le Francq van Berkhey, 1724-1812) Perennial herbs, shrubs, often thistlelike. Leaves spiny. Flower bracts usually spiny. Afr, ±75, mostly SAfr, ±71 species, ±15 in this region.

Berkheya macrocephala **ntšoantšane, sehohlo-se-seholo (SS)** (*macro* - large; *cephala* - head)

Handsome perennial herb, up to 500mm tall. In small colonies, on grassy hillsides, 1525-2450m. E Cape to KZN. LEAVES mostly basal, in rosette, up to 400×120mm, blade deeply divided into **10-12 lobes each side, ± overlapping**, margins toothed, spiny, stem leaves widely spaced, upper leaves entire, heart-shaped at base. FLOWERHEADS **large, solitary**, golden-yellow to orange, ±100mm diam, bracts up to 8mm wide, tips and margins spiny **(Oct-Nov-Deç). Similar species: *Berkheya multijuga* Doringrige bergdissel (A); mohatollo, ntsoantsane-ea-loti (SS); imboziso emhlophe, ukhakhasi (Z)** (*multi* - many; *juga* - ribbed, refers to many deeply cut lobes) Flowering stems up to 600mm. In dense patches on steep moist grassy slopes below cliffs, on gravelly streambeds, 1850-3200m. EMR endemic. LEAVES up to 400×150mm, lobed nearly to midrib, overlapping, margins coarsely, irregularly toothed, teeth spine-tipped, **up to 15 lobes each side, ± white-woolly to cobwebby below**. FLOWERHEADS up to 8, yellow, 60-100mm, bracts up to 5mm wide, spiny, white-cobwebby beneath, flowering stems from side of leaf rosette **(Dec-Apr)**. GENERAL: Used in traditional medicine.

Berkheya montana **mohatollo, ntšoantšane-ea-loti (SS)** (*montana* - of mountains)

Robust herb, up to 2m tall. In dense stands, on margins of forest and scrub patches, up to 1900m. EMR endemic. Stems covered with slender spines ±7mm long, **leafy throughout**. LEAVES up to 200×100mm, harshly hairy above, cobwebby beneath, margins minutely toothed, bristly. INFLORESCENCE spreading; FLOWERHEADS 30-40mm diam, yellow, bracts ±2.5mm broad, tips and margins spiny (Feb-Mar). GENERAL: Used in traditional medicine and against witchcraft.

Haplocarpha nervosa

Hilliard & Burtt

Arctotis arctotoides

David McDonald

Haplocarpha nervosa

Peter Linder

Arctotis arctotoides

David McDonald

Gazania krebsiana

Darrel Plowes

Haplocarpha scaposa

Cameron McMaster

Berkheya montana

Martin von Fintel

Berkheya macrocephala

Tom de Waal

Berkheya multijuga

Mike Hirst

177

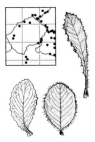

Berkheya rhapontica ntšoantšane, pepetloane-e-meutla (SS); ikhakhasi, iphungula (Z)
Perennial herb, up to 1.2m tall. In small colonies, on grass slopes, grassy stream-banks, often among rocks, 1800-2600m. E Cape to KZN. BASAL LEAVES rosetted, up to 300×100mm, **harshly hairy above**, similar or white-felted beneath, margins entire or wavy lobed to coarsely toothed, **stem leaves run onto stem in broad or narrow spiny wings.** INFLORESCENCE **long and narrow**, stem stout; FLOWERHEADS 20-40mm diam, yellow, bracts ±2mm wide, cobwebby on backs, tips and margins spiny, pappus scales up to 1 mm long, ± **blunt** (Dec-Apr). GENERAL: Used in traditional medicine to treat dry coughs. There are three subspecies and 3 varieties of subsp. *aristosa*. **At high altitude the plants tend to get smaller, have fewer stem leaves and less well developed wings on the stem and fewer flowerheads.**

Berkheya rosulata Rosette Thistle; ntšoantšane (SS) (*rosulata* - leaves form a rosette)
Handsome, **rounded shrub**, up to 1m tall. In crevices of vertical basalt cliffs, 2225-2650m. EMR endemic. Stems branch near tips, **young stems white-felted**, leafy. LEAVES up to 40×15mm, glossy dark green above, white-felted below, **almost rosetted at tips of new shoots**. FLOWERHEADS solitary, **on white-felted stems 150-300mm long**, 50-70mm diam, bracts up to 3mm broad, tips and margins spiny, white-felted beneath (Dec-Feb).

Berkheya setifera Buffalo-tongue Berkheya; Rasperdisseldoring (A); leleleme-la-khomo, ntšoantšane (SS); indlebe-lenkomo (X); ulimi-lwenkomo, ikhakhasi, ulimi-lwenyathi (Z) (*setifera* - bristles)
Perennial herb, up to 1.2m tall. In colonies, in open grassland, up to 2000m. E Cape to Zim. LEAVES basal, up to 400×120mm, **green on both surfaces**, upper surface with **coarse, straw-coloured bristles, harshly hairy beneath**, margins entire to shallowly lobed, almost spiny. FLOWERHEADS few, on long stalks, ±60mm diam, yellow, bracts ±1mm wide, tips and margins spiny (Nov-Jan). GENERAL: Used for brushing hair, as a pot herb (young leaves used as spinach) and in traditional medicine to treat stomach complaints. Also used to repel evil spirits.

Berkheya speciosa subsp. **ovata** Skraaldisseldoring (A); ntšoantšane (SS); uma-phola (Z)
(*speciosa* - beautiful)
Perennial herb, flowering stem solitary, up to 500mm tall. In colonies in moist grassland and in rank growth along streams, ± 1800-2300m. E Cape to KZN above 1525m. LEAVES basal, 50-150×25-50mm, green, harshly hairy or hairless above, **white-felted beneath**, margins very minutely toothed, **stalks 15-45mm**. FLOWERHEADS usually solitary, rarely up to 4, ±70mm diam, yellow, bracts ±2mm wide, tips and margins spiny (Nov-Dec).

Sonchus - Cow Thistles Herbs, sometimes woody at base. Leaves in rosettes or alternate. Flowerheads in irregular branched inflorescences. Europe, Asia, Afr, ±60 species, a few have become cosmopolitan weeds.

Sonchus integrifolius Thistle; leshoabe, sethokojane-se-seholo, naka-la-tholo (SS)
Perennial herb, flowering stems up to 400mm tall. On rocky grass slopes, 1800-2250m. W Cape to Zim. Stems with widely spaced leaves. LEAVES in rosettes, several from a single crown, up to 120×30mm, very variable. FLOWERHEADS solitary or few, yellow or pink (Aug-Jan).

Lactuca (Latin word for lettuce; *lact* - milky, refers to juice from plant when pressed) Herbs, usually hairless. Leaves in rosettes or alternate. Flowerheads usually in branched inflorescences. Temp Eurasia, Afr, ±100 species, ± 6 in SAfr.

Lactuca tysonii leharasoana (SS) (named after William Tyson, 1851-1920, teacher and plant collector)
Perennial herb, ±350mm tall. On grass slopes, in thicket, up to 2400m. E Cape to KZN. ROOTSTOCK slender, creeping. LEAVES basal, ±200×60mm. FLOWERHEADS ±20mm, yellow, a few in branched inflorescences (Sep-Dec).

Berkheya rhapontica

Lal Greene

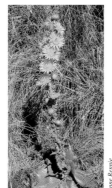

Anne Rennie

Berkheya rhapontica

Jo Arkel

Sonchus integrifolius

Rosemary Williams

Lactuca tysonii

Berkheya setifera

Tony Abbott

Geoff Nichols

Berkheya setifera

David McDonald

Berkheya rosulata

Cameron McMaster

Berkheya speciosa

David McDonald

Berkheya rosulata

MONOCOTYLEDONS Single seed-leaf, parallel veins, flower parts in threes or multiples of three.

COMMELINACEAE - Commelina Family Trop, ±40 genera, ±650 species, 7 genera in SAfr, 2 in this region (see pg 116). *Cyanotis* (*cyanotis* - refers to blue flowers) Warm regions of Europe, Asia, Afr, ±50 species, 7 in SAfr, 1 in this region.

Cyanotis speciosa Doll's Powderpuff; Bloupoeierkwassie (A); khopo, khopa, theepe- balingoana (SS); umagoswana (X); ingonga, inkombo, isosonga, udabulamafu, umakotigoyile (Z) (*udabulamafu* (Z) - cloud breaker, used as a charm to ward off lightning)

150-450mm tall. In damp grassland, up to 2250m. SAfr to Tanz. LEAVES in basal tuft, sheaths purple, leaf blade 170×8mm, long hairs beneath. FLOWERS in tight clusters, pink, mauve, purple or blue, **stamens conspicuously hairy or feathered**, closing at midday (Nov-Jan). GENERAL: Grazed by cattle. Roots used in traditional medicine.

COLCHICACEAE (see pg 22) *Wurmbea* (after F. von Wurm, a Dutch merchant in Java) Afr, Austr, ±38 species, 19 in SAfr, 5 in this region.

Wurmbea kraussii (named after Christian Krauss, 1812-1890, German scientist, traveller and collector)

Up to 100mm tall. In damp places, on grassy slopes, up to 2450m. E Cape to Swaz. **One narrow basal leaf** enclosed with the stem in basal sheath, 1 or more stem leaves. FLOWERS white or pinkish, **patch (or scale) on tepals raised, tips free** (Nov-Dec). **Similar species:** *W. burttii* (named after B. L. Burtt, distinguished botanist) **Tiny, 30-50mm tall**. In wet silt and gravel, 2400-2900m. EMR endemic. **Leaf thick,** roundish. Flowers white, with 2 raised, self coloured patches (Dec-Jan).

ALLIACEAE - Onion Family (see pg 50) *Tulbaghia* (see pg 50)

Tulbaghia natalensis Sweet Wild Garlic; iswele lezinyoka (Z)

HYACINTHACEAE (see pg 50) *Drimiopsis* (resembling *Drimia*) Afr, ±15 species, 5 in SAfr, 1 in this region.

Drimiopsis lachenalioides (*lachenalioides* - resembling *Lachenalia*)

60-150mm tall. In grassland, up to 2100m. E Cape to KZN. LEAVES smooth to hairy, 100-200×25-40mm, with purplish wavy bars on undersurface near base, sometimes purple blotched on upper surface. INFLORESCENCE dense; FLOWERS ±12mm long, **bright pink** (Nov-Dec).

Ledebouria (after Carl Ledebour, 1785-1851, German prof of botany) Genus under revision. Afr, Asia, ±46 species, ±38 in SAfr, ±6 in this region.

Ledebouria cooperi [= *Scilla cooperi*] Cooper's Ledebouria; lepjetlane (SS); icubudwana, icukudwane (Z) (named after Thomas Cooper, 1815-1913, English plant collector and grower)

Up to 200mm tall. On grassy slopes, up to 2100m. E Cape to Limpopo Prov. LEAVES **erect**, 100-200×20mm, widest in upper third, glossy green, with dark spots towards base, **longitudinal purple stripes beneath**. FLOWERS usually **uniformly pink** (Oct-Dec). GENERAL: Used in traditional medicine. Pretty in the garden.

Ledebouria ovatifolia [= *Scilla ovatifolia*] boekhoe (SS); icubudwana, untanganazibomvu (Z) (*ovatifolia* - oval leaves)

Up to 80mm tall, solitary. In stony grassland, up to 1980m. Widespread. LEAVES 50-120×30-60mm, **flat on ground**, glossy with purple spots above, **purplish below**, with threads when torn. INFLORESCENCE lax, very short; FLOWERS pink to purplish green, **tepals recurved** (Sep-Nov). GENERAL: Leaves eaten by porcupine. Leaves formed into twine for binding mats. Planted as a good luck charm.

Lachenalia - Cape Hyacinth In cultivation for over 200 years, with many cultivars and hybrids. About 110 species, 1 in this region.

Lachenalia campanulata (*campanulata* - bell-like)

70-200mm tall. On cliffs, 1980-2400m. A rare find in this region. LEAVES usually 2, ±200mm long, cylindrical, tapering to a point. INFLORESCENCE dense, 25-35 ×12-15mm; FLOWERS bell-shaped, white tinged red (Dec).

AMARYLLIDACEAE Bulbous herbs. Popular horticultural subjects. Trop and warm regions, ±60 genera, over 800 species, 18 genera in SAfr, 6 in this region. *Haemanthus* (*haima* - blood; *anthos* - flower) Few fleshy leaves, **no stem**. SAfr endemic, 22 species, 1 in this region.

Haemanthus humilis subsp. *hirsutus* [= *H. hirsutus*] Rabbit's Ears; Bobbejaanoor, Velskoenblaar (A); sekitla, tsebe ea phofu (SS) (*humilis* - low growing)

Deciduous, up to 300mm tall. In crevices of rocky cliffs or boulders, in rocky grassland, 1525-2350m. E Cape to Mpum. LEAVES **2**, 150-300×55-130mm, hairy. INFLORESCENCE 50-120mm diam, bracts red or pink; FLOWERS white to pale pink, **stamens protrude well above tepals** (Nov-Dec). FRUIT pinkish orange to red, oval, ±15×10mm, with a fruity smell when ripe. GENERAL: Used in traditional medicine to treat stomach complaints, wounds and asthma. Grown from seed. (see pg 58)

Cyanotis speciosa

Martin von Fintel

Tony Abbott

Godfrey Symons

Martin von Fintel

Cyanotis speciosa

Wurmbea kraussii

Drimiopsis lachenalioides

Tony Abbott

Rosemary Williams

Hilliard & Burtt

Ledebouria cooperi

Ledebouria ovatifolia

Lachenalia campanulata

Geoff Nichols

Tulbaghia natalensis

Clinton Carbutt

Martin von Fintel

John Grimshaw

Tulbaghia natalensis

Haemanthus humilis

Haemanthus humilis

181

Nerine (*nerine* - a sea nymph, daughter of sea gods Nereus and Doris) Popular garden plants around the world, with many horticultural hybrids. SAfr endemic, ±22 species, 4 in this region.

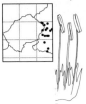

Nerine appendiculata Nerine; umlukulo (Z) (*appendiculata* - having appendages)

Up to 900mm tall, evergreen. In marshy areas, near streams, 1065-1800m. LEAVES ±450×5mm, **deeply channelled**. INFLORESCENCE crowded, 10-20 flowers, flowering stem twisted, bracts reddish; FLOWER tepals 25-30×3-5mm, pale to deep pink, midvein darker, **stamens with conspicuous white appendages at base**, ±10mm (Jan-Apr). GENERAL: A popular garden plant. **Similar species:** *Nerine angustifolia* Ribbon-leaved Nerine; Berglelie (A); lematlana (SS) (*angustifolia* - narrow leaves) In marshy areas. E Cape, E FS, Les to Mpum. LEAVES **flattish**. INFLORESCENCE with **less than 10 flowers**, bracts narrow, folded back, **stalks softly hairy** (Feb-Apr). GENERAL: Used as a protective charm against lightning and illness. A hardy garden plant.

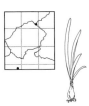

Nerine bowdenii Large Pink Nerine; Grootpienknerina (A) (named after A.C. Bowden, Surveyor General of the Cape who collected *N. bowdenii* in 1903 in the mountains near King Williamstown)

Robust, up to 700mm tall, deciduous. In moist ground around rocks, at base of cliffs, up to 3300m. E Cape to N Drak, but not S Drak. LEAVES 350-730×25mm, **broad, flat**, turning yellow at time of flowering. INFLORESCENCE ±200mm diam; FLOWERS **large**, tepal lobes 50-70×8-12mm, recurved, margins wavy, bright pink (white), with a dark rose line through the centre (Jan-May). GENERAL: Plants smaller in the south. Frost resistant. A popular garden plant, long lasting cut-flowers.

Brunsvigia (honours the House of Brunswick) SAfr endemic, ±20 species, ±4 in this region.

Brunsvigia grandiflora Giant Candelabra Flower; Kandelaarblom (A); isichwe (X); umqhele-wenkunzi (Z) (*grandiflora* - large flowers)

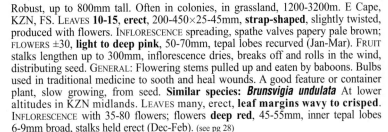

Robust, up to 800mm tall. Often in colonies, in grassland, 1200-3200m. E Cape, KZN, FS. LEAVES **10-15, erect**, 200-450×25-45mm, **strap-shaped**, slightly twisted, produced with flowers. INFLORESCENCE spreading, spathe valves papery pale brown; FLOWERS ±30, **light to deep pink**, 50-70mm, tepal lobes recurved (Jan-Mar). FRUIT stalks lengthen up to 300mm, inflorescence dries, breaks off and rolls in the wind, distributing seed. GENERAL: Flowering stems pulled up and eaten by baboons. Bulbs used in traditional medicine to sooth and heal wounds. A good feature or container plant, slow growing, from seed. **Similar species:** *Brunsvigia undulata* At lower altitudes in KZN midlands. LEAVES many, erect, **leaf margins wavy to crisped**. INFLORESCENCE with 35-80 flowers; flowers **deep red**, 45-55mm, inner tepal lobes 6-9mm broad, stalks held erect (Dec-Feb). (see pg 28)

Brunsvigia natalensis Natal Candelabra Flower; Kandelaarblom (A); umbhola (Z)

Up to 450mm tall. Scattered in grassland, on rocky outcrops, up to 2280m. KZN to Limpopo Prov. LEAVES **2-6, flattish** to semi-erect, 150-250×70-100mm, short, broad, blunt tipped, **rough on upper surface**, produced with flowers. INFLORESCENCE with 30-60 flowers; FLOWERS ±40mm, deep pink (red), stalks 40-120mm (Oct-Dec). FRUIT as for *B. grandiflora*. GENERAL: Habitat reduced due to draining of marshy areas. Zulu name refers to the rotten smell around the bulb. Used in traditional medicine to 'straighten bones of children'.

Brunsvigia radulosa Candelabra Flower; Kandelaarblom, Misryblom (A); lematla (SS) (*radulosa* - rough, rasping)

Up to 800mm tall, solitary. In grassland, up to 2000m. NW Cape to Limpopo Prov. LEAVES 4-6, usually absent at time of flowering, **flattened on the ground**, 250-500×100-200mm, **thick, rough on both surfaces**. FLOWERS pink or red, 45-55mm, shape regular (Nov-Feb). GENERAL: Bulb used to seal leaking clay pots. Used in traditional medicine to induce pregnancy in barren women and for difficult confinement cases. A good feature or container plant.

Nerine bowdenii

David McDonald

Nerine bowdenii

David McDonald

Nerine appendiculata

Hilliard & Burtt

Brunsvigia grandiflora

Rod Saunders

Brunsvigia radulosa

Brunsvigia radulosa

Pam Cooke

David McDonald

Brunsvigia natalensis

Rod Saunders

183

Crinum (*krinon* - lily) Robust, deciduous bulbous plants with large flowers. Pantrop, mainly Afr, ±65 species, ±20 in SAfr, 1 in this region.

Crinum bulbispermum River Lily, Orange/Vaal River Lily; Vleilelie (A); Ielutla, mototse (SS); umnduze (Z) (*bulbispermum* - bulblike seed)

Up to 900mm tall. In colonies in marshy ground, near rivers and streams, up to 1600m. NW Cape to Limpopo Prov. LEAVES **bluish grey-green**, soft, folded upwards, **sheathing at the base, forming a stem ±450mm tall.** FLOWERS drooping, narrow, tube ±110mm, tepal lobes ±100×30mm, white to deep pinkish red with darker keel, faintly scented (Sep-Dec). FRUIT 70mm diam, **tipped with a ring.** GENERAL Used in traditional medicine to treat a wide variety of ailments. Hardy, fast growing garden plant, from seed.

Cyrtanthus (*kyrtos* - curved; *anthos* - flowers, refers to the frequently curved flower tube) Afr, mainly SAfr, ±50 species, 9 in this region.

Cyrtanthus erubescens Killick's Pink Lily/Cyrtanthus (*erubescens* - blushing)

Up to 500mm tall. In cracks of wet rock outcrops and cliffs, scrubby streambanks, 2000-2700m. N EMR endemic. LEAVES 2-4, **strap-shaped**, 200-600×20-60mm, midrib prominent beneath, appearing with flowers. FLOWERS **pink**, 30-40mm long, tube short, 8-10mm, **lobes widely spreading**, erect or suberect (Nov). GENERAL: This lovely plant resembles a pink *Agapanthus*. A sighting of the plant in flower is a great reward for the hiker or climber.

HYPOXIDACEAE - Star-flower Family S Hemisp, 9 genera, ±130 species, 6 genera in SAfr, 4 in this region. *Rhodohypoxis* (*rhodo* - rose, red; genus *Hypoxis*) Anthers hidden by inner 3 tepal lobes. SAfr endemic, 6 species, 4 of them EMR endemics.

Rhodohypoxis baurii Red or White Star; Rooisterretjie (A) (named after Rev Leopold Baur, 1825-1889, pharmacist, missionary and plant collector who came to the Cape in 1847)

Up to 150mm tall. Forms colourful carpets in grassland, rocky places, up to 2900m. LEAVES 25-110×5mm, **dull green**, with **sparse long hairs, midrib grooved to the tip.** FLOWERS 1-2, 20-40mm wide, white, pink or red, tube short with long spreading hairs, also on midrib of outer tepals, lobes spreading flat, faintly scented (Oct-Jan). FRUITING STEM **holds capsule erect with the cap falling off**, seeds scattered by wind or animal movements. GENERAL: Cultivated since the 1920s, popular in Europe and Japan (with a number of cultivars), hardy, requiring well drained soil. Three varieties (see pg 58). **Var. confecta** On **damp** grassy slopes, among outcropping rocks, common on the summit plateau in short damp turf amongst rock sheets, 1900-2900m. E Cape to Mpum mtns. FLOWERS pink or white, with some red (some opening white, turning pink then deep red with age). **Similar species: *Rhodohypoxis milloides* Usually found in marshes**, 1500-2400m. KZN endemic. LEAVES **bright green, hairless, midrib not grooved to tip.** FLOWERS deep pink to deep red (Oct- Jan).

Rhodohypoxis deflexa (*de* - down, *flexus* - bent)

Diminutive. In marshy turf, sometimes forming pure swards, 2600-3200m. EMR endemic. LEAVES **spreading**, up to 65×5mm, held nearly horizontally just above the ground. FLOWERS **small**, 7-13mm wide, light to dark pink, with white sports (Nov-Feb). FRUITING STEM **gradually bends so that the ripe capsules lie on the marshy ground**, splitting into 3 valves. GENERAL: Plants grazed by sheep and goats.

Rhodohypoxis rubella (*rubella* - reddish)

Dainty, grasslike, up to 30mm tall. In myriads, in shallow pools, seasonally flooded silt patches, mostly on the summit, (2000)3050m. EMR endemic. LEAVES 10-45×1-1.5mm, **wiry, only developing fully after flowering.** FLOWERS solitary, **small**, 10-18mm wide, bright pink. Ovary hidden by leaf sheaths, developing below ground (Nov-Dec). **Similar species:** *Rhodohypoxis incompta* Edges of tussocks bordering silt patches, rock sheets, 2300-2900m. EMR endemic. FLOWERS **large**, 16-40mm wide (Nov-Jan).

VELLOZIACEAE - Black-stick Lily Family Fibrous perennials, stems protected by non-inflammable leaf bases. Afr, Madag, S America, 6 genera, ±80 species, 2 genera in SAfr and this region. *Xerophyta* (*xeros* - dry; *phytos* - plant) Afr, Madag, Brazil, ±40 species, ±9 in SAfr, 2 in this region.

Xerophyta viscosa [= *Vellozia viscosa*] Small Black-stick Lily; Bobbejaanstert (A); lefiroane, lethepu (SS) (*viscosa* - sticky)

Up to 600mm tall. Forms large mats or clumps on moist sandstone cliffs and outcrops, 1200-2400m. Cape to Zim. STEMS blackened, rough with **recurved leaf bases.** LEAVES ±180mm long, keel and margins with short stiff hairs. FLOWERS ±80mm wide, lilac to deep mauve/magenta, flowering stems ±390mm long, **speckled with black glands** (Nov-Mar). GENERAL: Leaves plaited into rope.

Godfrey Symons

Crinum bulbispermum

Godfrey Symons

Cyrtanthus erubescens

Simon Milliken

Cyrtanthus erubescens

Darrel Plowes

Rhodohypoxis baurii

Hilliard & Burtt

Rhodohypoxis rubella

Rhodohypoxis milloides

Lal Greene

Xerophyta viscosa

Clinton Carbutt

Hilliard & Burtt

Rhodohypoxis deflexa

Neil Crouch

Xerophyta viscosa

185

IRIDACEAE - Iris Family Temp regions, ±70 genera, ±1800 species, ±32 genera in SA,fr ±12 in this region. *Romulea* (*romulus* - named after the founder and first king of Rome) S Europe and Afr, ±88 species, ±77 in SAfr, centred in the winter rainfall area, 3 in this region.

Romulea thodei [sometimes included in the tropical species *R. campanuloides*] (named after Justus Thode, 1859-1932, pioneer plant collector in the Drakensberg)

50-100(550)mm tall, occasional. In wet silt, gravel or bare soil or in short stony turf, 2100-3000m. EMR endemic. LEAVES slender, 80-550×0.8-2mm. FLOWERS pale to **bright pink inside, becoming yellow or whitish deep inside the tube, 3 outer tepals striped buff and purple outside** (Dec-Feb).

Hesperantha (*hesperos* - evening; *anthos* - flower but only one night flowering species, *H. tysonii*, is found in this region) Sub-Saharan Afr, ±75 species, mostly SAfr, 14 in this region.

Hesperantha baurii subsp. *baurii* khahla-e-nyenyane, khukhu-e-nyenyane, qelo (SS); isidwa (Z) (named after Rev L. Baur, 1825-89, pharmacist, missionary, amateur botanist; arrived in the Cape in 1847)

Slender, erect, 150-750mm tall. Common in moist open grassland, up to 2450m. E Cape to Limpopo Prov. LEAVES 2, basal, straight, **firm**, margins thickened, midrib raised, side veins raised. INFLORESCENCE erect, stem zigzag; FLOWERS ±30mm wide, bright magenta (white) (Jan-Mar). GENERAL: Corms eaten by children. **Similar species:** *Hesperantha grandiflora* (*grandiflora* - large flowers) Erect, 150-700mm. In damp grassy and often shady places in streamlines, on forest margins and cliffs, 1600-3000m. EMR endemic. FLOWERS large, pink, ±50mm wide, **tube 25-40mm long, sharply curved at top so that flower face is held vertically** (Jan-Apr). *Hesperantha scopulosa* (*scopulosa* - rocky) **Pendulous**, flowering stems up to 250mm long. In crevices of wet cliffs, 1500-2200m. EMR endemic. LEAVES limp, flat, 45-370×5-10mm. FLOWERS ±40mm diam, tube 25-40mm long (Feb-Apr).

Hesperantha coccinea [= *Schizostylis coccinea*] Scarlet River Lily; Rooirivierlelie (A); khahlana (SS) (*coccinea* - scarlet)

Up to 600mm tall. In clumps, **on streambanks**, often in water, up to 1830m. E Cape to Limpopo Prov. LEAVES ±400×10mm, midrib distinct. FLOWERS **large**, ±65mm diam, **glistening scarlet** (pink), tube ±30mm long, style split (Jan-Apr). GENERAL: This is a strikingly lovely plant in the wild. It is a popular garden plant, frost resistant and a good cut-flower. (see pg 30)

Hesperantha schelpeana (named after E.A.C.L.E. Schelpe, 1924-1985, well known SA plant ecologist, taxonomist, phytogeographer and plant collector)

Crocus-like flower, close to the ground. In short wet turf, seasonally waterlogged stony ground on the summit, 2750-3200m. EMR endemic. LEAF **produced after the flowers**, on a separate shoot. FLOWERS **solitary**, 20-30mm wide, tepals 14-22 ×6-9mm, pale pink to white inside, feathered red-purple outside, scented (Oct). **Similar species:** *Hesperantha crocopsis* (*crocopsis* - refers to the similarity to the N Hemis genus *Crocus* where the flower stalk elongates to bear the capsule well above ground) In marshy turf and silt along marshy streams, on the summit, 2870-3200m. EMR endemic. FLOWERS **small**, tepals 6-7×2-3mm, ± white inside, rosy or purplish outside, flower stalk lengthens to bear the capsule well above the ground (Nov).

Dierama (*dierama* - a funnel) - **Hairbells, Wand-flowers; Grasklokkies (A)** Popular garden plants. Afr, ±44, mostly SAfr summer rainfall region, ±8 in this region.

Dierama dracomontanum Drakensberg Hairbell; lethepu (SS) (see pg 30)

Dierama latifolium Broad-leaved Hairbell; lethepu (SS); ithembu (Z) (*latifolium* - broad leaves)

In large clumps, 1-1.8m tall. In open grassland, up to 2200m. KZN endemic. LEAVES up to 900×**8-13mm**. FLOWERS 22-33mm long, pale pink to wine red, **bracts white to very lightly speckled** (Jan-Mar). GENERAL: Used in traditional medicine. Leaves plaited into rope. Lovely garden plant. (see pg 30)

Dierama pauciflorum (*pauciflorum* - few flowers)

300-600mm tall. In clumps in marshy ground or forming tussocks in the water, singly on drier ground, 1500-2400m. E Cape to Mpum and E Zim. LEAVES 100-400×1-4mm. INFLORESCENCE **erect** with ±5 pendulous branches, **bracts bright rust-brown, 6-8 veins each side of midvein, nearly to margins**; FLOWERS 20-28mm, pink or reddish (Nov-Dec). GENERAL: Few flowers in each inflorescence but massed plants bloom profusely, a lovely sight.

Romulea thodei

Martin von Fintel

Hesperantha grandiflora

Pam Cooke

Hesperantha baurii

Martin von Fintel

Anne Rennie

Hesperantha schelpeana

Hesperantha coccinea

Charles Rostance

Hilliard & Burtt

Dierama pauciflorum

Dierama latifolium

Trevor Coleman

Hilliard & Burtt

Dierama pauciflorum

Dierama dracomontanum

David McDonald

187

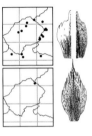

Dierama robustum lethepu (SS) *(robustum - strong, robust)*
1-2 m tall, solitary or in small clumps. Widespread at high altitude, in grassland, 1600-2900m. E Cape to EMR. LEAVES 400-1200×4-8mm. INFLORESCENCE pendulous with 3-7 branches, bracts 20-35(8-14mm, **whitish heavily flecked brown in upper parts**; FLOWERS large, 26-35mm long, creamy white to pale pink or mauve (Dec-Feb). **Similar species:** *Dierama pictum* *(pictus - painted or coloured, refers to bracts)* Solitary or in small clumps, up to 1m tall. In grassy, rocky places up to 2200m. Found only at Royal National Park in this region. FLOWERS 15-23mm long, **wine-red or magenta; bracts dark brown with conspicuous white shoulders (Nov-Jan)**. *Dierama cooperi* *(named after Thomas Cooper, a plant-collector who spent 3 years in SA, 1859-1862)* 0.6-1.4m tall. Solitary or in small tufts, in grassland, scattered in extensive colonies. E FS, Les, low Drak. FLOWERS **smaller**, bright pink, sometimes white, tepals up to 15×6.5mm, bract veins so crowded that colour is almost solid (Oct-Feb). GENERAL: Hybridises with *D. robustum* and *D. dissimile* (see pg 232).

Tritonia *(triton - a weathercock, refers to the variable direction of the stamens of the different species)* SAfr to Tanz, 28 species, mostly in coastal areas of S Cape, 2 in this region.

Tritonia disticha [= *T. rubrolucens*] **Red Tritonia; isidwi esibomvu (Z)** *(disticha - in 2 rows)*
Up to 300mm tall. In grassland, rock crevices, up to 2300m. SE Cape to Mpum. LEAVES 8-12mm wide, with strong midvein and marginal veins. FLOWERS 25-30mm, bright red or **pink** with small yellow blotch on 3 lower lobes (Jan-Feb). GENERAL: Used in traditional medicine to treat stomach complaints in babies. (see pg 30)

Gladiolus *(gladiolus – small sword, refers to leaf shape)* Hybrids created since the early 1800s have produced the cut-flowers and garden plants popular worldwide. Known as *itembu* (X) 'fruits of the earth' corms are dug up and eaten in rural areas. Afr, S Europe and Middle East, ± 260 species, ± 165 species in SAfr, ± 14 in this region.

Gladiolus crassifolius **Thick-leaved Gladiolus; khahla-e-nyenyane (SS); igulusha, ingangulazi (Z)** *(crassifolius - thick leafed, refers to the thick, leathery, strongly ribbed leaves)*
Up to 1m tall. In grassland, up to 1950m. E Cape to Trop Afr. LEAVES erect, ±700×12mm, **margins and veins heavily thickened**, forming a **sheathing fan**. INFLORESCENCE dense, **stem curving out from leaves**, with 1-3 branches, buds in two rows; FLOWERS **turned to one side, small**, 25-40mm long, mauve to pink, lower 2 lobes with dark blotch (Jan-Mar). GENERAL: Pollinated by long-tongued bees (*Amegilla* species). Used in traditional medicine to cure headaches and other ailments.

Gladiolus loteniensis **Loteni Gladiolus** *(named after the upper Loteni River Valley where the type specimen was found and described by Olive Hilliard and Bill Burtt)*
300-600mm tall. In grass around rocks, alongside river, 1800m. S EMR endemic. LEAVES slender, 4-8mm wide. INFLORESCENCE inclined, 6-12 flowers, **in two ranks**. FLOWERS 25mm long, **tepals pointed**, pale mauve with darker feathering on 3 lower tepals (Dec-Jan).

Gladiolus microcarpus *(microcarpus - with a small fruit, refers to small capsules)*
Stem slender, 0.4-1m long. Hanging from moist crevices in cliffs, 1800-2700m. N EMR endemic. LEAVES in a soft fan, forming a sheathing stem, with fine golden hairs on **prominent ribs**. INFLORESCENCE **pendulous**; FLOWERS pink or mauve with darker stripes on lower 3 tepals, **tube long, narrow, 35-40mm**, tepal lobes 25-40mm long, **tips narrowing to slender points** (Dec-Feb). GENERAL: Pollinated by long-tongued flies (*Prosoeca ganglbaueri*).

Gladiolus oppositiflorus [= *G. salmoneus*] **Salmon Gladiolus, Transkei Gladiolus; Transkei-swaardlelie (A)** *(oppositiflorus - opposite flowers; flowers facing in opposite directions, usual in Gladiolus)*
Deciduous, 0.5-1m tall. In clumps, on damp, rocky slopes, up to 2500m. E Cape to S KZN. LEAVES arranged in a fan, sheathing stem below, **velvety between the raised veins**. INFLORESCENCE erect; FLOWERS **in 2 ranks**, large, 65-110mm long, pale to deep **pink to deep salmon**, with dark lines on tepals, blotches in throat (Dec-Mar). GENERAL: The plant first described as *Gladiolus salmoneus*, collected near Kokstad, was later described as *G. oppositiflorus* subsp. *salmoneus*. It is the more common form of *G. oppositiflorus* found in this region, conspicuous when in salmon or pink flower in the foothills and on the face of the Drak. Pollinated by long-tongued flies. Very variable. It has been grown in Europe since late 1800s, and was one of the species used to create the popular *Gladiolus* hybrids.

Dierama pictum

David McDonald

John Grimshaw

Dierama robustum

Martin von Fintel

Gladiolus crassifolius

Martin von Fintel

Tritonia disticha

David McDonald

Gladiolus oppositiflorus

Anne Rennie

Gladiolus loteniensis

John Manning

Gladiolus microcarpus

David McDonald

Gladiolus oppositiflorus

Darrel Plowes

Gladiolus oppositiflorus

Auriol Baten

189

Gladiolus parvulus (*parvulus* - very small)
Up to 350mm tall. Often in colonies, in rocky grassland, in thin soil on sandstone pavements, up to 3300m. KZN to Mpum. LEAF **solitary**, sheathing stem. FLOWERS **small, funnel-shaped**, delicate, horizontal to nodding, ± 20mm long, **pale pink, tepals equal in size**, flowering stem slender, wiry (Oct-Dec). GENERAL: Pollinated by bees. The flowers do not resemble a typical *Gladiolus* becaue they are wide open.

Gladiolus sericeovillosus subsp. *sericeovillosus* Large Speckled Gladiolus; Bloupypie (A); udwendweni, isidwi esincane, umlunge (Z) (*sericeovillosus* - silky haired, refers to fine, whitish hairs on leaves and bracts)
0.35-1m tall, solitary or in small colonies. In grassland, up to 1750m. E Cape to Zim. LEAVES **form a stem at base**, ±6(35)mm wide, firm, margins prominent, ribs yellow. INFLORESCENCE crowded, ±20(40) flowers, erect, overlapping, **in 2 ranks**, stem sturdy, with **woolly white hairs, bracts woolly, inflated**; FLOWERS hooded, 25-40mm long, pale green, cream or pink, sometimes speckled pink or mauve, lower tepal lobes with dark edged yellow-green blotches (Jan-Mar). GENERAL: Pollinated by bees of the *Amegilla* species. Used in traditional medicine to treat dysentery, swollen joints, menstrual pain, help expel afterbirth and treat sterility in women, also as a charm to ensure a good harvest.

Watsonia (named after English scientist Sir William Watson, 1715-1787) Mostly SAfr, ±52 species, 1 in Madag, 5 in this region.

Watsonia confusa (*confusa* - refers to the species often being confused with other KZN species with similar dry bracts, especially *W. densiflora*)
Robust, up to 1m tall. **In small clumps, on moist grassy slopes**, 1525-1980m. E Cape, KZN. LEAVES 15-25mm wide, pale blue green. INFLORESCENCE with ±30 flowers, bracts dry brown, overlapping, clasping in lower two thirds; FLOWERS **large**, tube 30-40mm long, tepal lobes 25-30mm, **bright pink** (purple), often with dark pink line in middle of 3 lower tepals (Oct-Mar). GENERAL: A lovely garden plant.

Watsonia lepida khahla (SS) (*lepida* - attractive or pleasing)
Up to 500mm tall, **solitary**. Scattered in grassland, 1500-2400m. EMR and KZN/Mpum. LEAVES 2-3 basal, 5-15mm wide, margins and midrib strongly thickened, flowering stem leaves large, overlapping, sheathing. INFLORESCENCE crowded, **stem short, sturdy, erect, bracts ±25×12mm, narrow, only clasping stem near base, dry uniformly dark brown**; FLOWER tube 20-30mm long, tepals ±20×9mm, bright pink (Oct-Dec). GENERAL: Flowers sucked for nectar by children. Leaves plaited for rope. Used in traditional medicine to treat diarrhoea in calves.

ORCHIDACEAE - Orchid Family A very large family with highly specialised flowers. Cosmop, ±800 genera, ± 20 000 species, 52 genera in SAfr. **Stenoglottis** (*stenos* - narrow; *glotta* - tongue, possibly refers to the lobes of the lip) Terrestrial or epiphytic. Leaves in basal rosette. SAfr to EAfr, ±4 species in SAfr, 1 in this region.

Stenoglottis fimbriata Fringed Stenoglottis; Fraaiingstenoglottis (A) (*fimbriata* - fringed)
Up to 100mm tall. On mossy rocks and tree trunks in forest, up to 1950m. E Cape to Tanz. LEAVES firm, 15-70mm long, **margins wavy**, often purple spotted, in a small basal rosette. FLOWERS small, lilac-pink with darker markings, **lip 3-lobed** (Dec-Mar). GENERAL: A good container plant. The small EMR plant is sometimes described as a separate subspecies.

Satyrium (*Satyros* - refers to the 2-horned satyr, half man, half goat, the two spurs somewhat resemble a satyr's horns) Ovary not twisted. Lip forms a hood, 2 conspicuous spurs or 2 pouches. Used in traditional medicine, mixed with other medicines to help with illnesses that are difficult to cure. Afr, Madag, India, China, 88 species, 37 in SAfr, ±10 in this region.

Satyrium hallackii subsp. *ocellatum* (named after Russell Hallack, 1824-1903, businessman and amateur botanist; *ocellus* - eye, refers to the two coloured spots which look like little eyes)
Robust, 0.19-1m tall. Solitary or in large colonies, in marshy ground, up to 1600m. E Cape to Malawi. LEAVES large, long and narrow, 70-200mm long, sheathing stem, tips pointed. INFLORESCENCE dense; FLOWERS white to deep pink, spurs 15-30mm long, faintly scented (Dec-Jan). GENERAL: Pollinated by large hovering hawk moths. Subsp. *hallackii* does not occur in this region.

Lal Greene

Godfrey Symons

H J Venter

Wally Menne

Gladiolus parvulus   *Gladiolus sericeovillosus*   *Stenoglottis fimbriata*   *Watsonia confusa*

Wally Menne

Watsonia confusa

Rodney Moffett

Watsonia lepida   *Stenoglottis fimbriata*

H J Venter

Hilliard & Burtt

Godfrey Symons

Godfrey Symons

Watsonia lepida   *Satyrium hallackii*   *Satyrium hallackii*

191

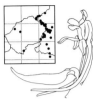

Satyrium longicauda Blushing Bride Satyrium; Langstert-trewwa (A); lekoesha (SS) (*longicauda* - long tailed)
Slender, 300-450mm tall. In small groups or large colonies. LEAVES usually flat on the ground, **on a separate shoot from the flowering stem**. INFLORESCENCE a crowded slender spike, up to 200mm long; FLOWERS white to pink or red, veins and tips of sepals and petals often darker, sweetly scented (Dec-Mar). GENERAL: Used as protective and love charms. **Var. longicauda** (*longicauda* - long tail) In moist uplands up to 2100m. W Cape to Trop Afr. FLOWERS large, side sepals 5-11mm long, spurs 22-46mm long (Dec-Feb). **Var. jacottetianum** (named after Mlle H Jacottet who, with her brother Rev E Jacottet, collected plants in the high mountains of Lesotho between 1905-14) In wet or dry rocky grassland, up to 3000m. E Cape to Mpum. FLOWERS **smaller, pink to red**, side sepals 4-7mm long, **spurs 15-26mm long** (Jan-Mar). (see pg 66)

Satyrium macrophyllum uklamkleshe, unoklamu, unokleshe (Z) (*macrophylum* - large leaves)
Robust, up to 1m tall. In groups or colonies, in moist grassland, up to 1800m. E Cape, KZN. LEAVES 2-3 at base, up to 400×70mm, erect, sheathing. INFLORESCENCE dense, ±400mm long; FLOWERS **held horizontally, well away from stem**, white to deep pink, tinged darker, **hood flattish, merging with broad based spurs**, 13-26mm long, tapering gradually, faintly scented (Feb-Mar). GENERAL: Tuberous roots eaten by people.

Satyrium neglectum subsp. **neglectum** Pink Candle Satyrium (*neglectum* - overlooked, insignificant)
Slender to robust, 150-950mm tall. On moist grassy mountain slopes, up to 3000m. E Cape to Tanz. LEAVES 1-2, **spreading**, on a separate shoot next to the flowering stem, absent or fully grown at flowering. INFLORESCENCE a dense spike; FLOWERS white to **dark or light pink**, 10mm wide, **spurs 6-19mm long**, sweetly scented (Jan-Feb).

Disa (origin unclear, possibly from *dis* - double, referring to the two large wings in the style or *dis* - rich or opulent, referring to the red of the spectacular *Disa uniflora*, the first species of the genus described) Median sepal hooded, prolonged into a spur or pouch. **The direction in which the spur points is useful in identification in the field.** Afr, Madag, Reunion, 1 in Arabian peninsula, ±162 species, 131 in SAfr, ±29 in this region.

Disa aconitoides Oumakappie (A); ihlamvu, umashushu (Z) (*aconitum* - like a monk's hood)
Slender, 250-500mm tall. On stony, grassy slopes up to 2000m. S Cape to Mpum. LEAVES overlapping. INFLORESCENCE a long slender spike; FLOWERS facing down, white to pale mauve with darker spots, **spur massive, almost as broad as the hood, upward pointing**, ±10mm long (Nov-Dec). GENERAL: An infusion of roots is used in traditional medicine to promote fertility in women.

Disa cephalotes subsp. **frigida** (*cephalotes* - a head; *frigida* - cold)
Robust, 150-200mm tall. In small or large colonies, on damp or dry grass slopes, 2400-3000m. EMR endemic. LEAVES **soft**, lower leaves often clustered at base, stem leaves clasping. INFLORESCENCE dense, compact; FLOWERS **deep pink, with purple speckles on tips of sepals**, spur ± horizontal, slender, 3-6mm long (Jan-Mar). GENERAL: This plant looks very different from the white flowering subsp. *cephalotes*. (see pg 66)

Disa cooperi ´mametsana-a-liliba (SS) (named after Thomas Cooper who collected plants in KZN and the Cape in the 1850s)
Robust, 400-600mm tall. Locally common, in stony mountain grassland, 1500-2200m. E Cape to Mpum. LEAVES on separate shoot, 50-100mm tall. INFLORESCENCE large, dense, stem leafy; FLOWERS facing downwards, ±15mm diam, white to pale pink (purple), **lip green, triangular**, spurs 35-45mm long, **pointing upwards, overlapping** (Dec-Jan). GENERAL: Pollinated shortly after dusk by hawk moths, the flowers producing a very strong scent at about that time. **Similar species: Disa scullyi** (named after William Charles Scully, 1855-1943, magistrate, author, collector, who came to Cape Town in 1867, died in Mbogintwini, KZN) In marshy ground, 1500-2100m. E Cape to KZN. INFLORESCENCE less dense; FLOWERS ±20mm diam, white to pale pink, **lip green, oblong, spur pointing upwards then curving down toward the tip** (Dec-Jan).

192

Satyrium longicauda

Martin von Fintel

Satyrium longicauda

Martin von Fintel

Satyrium macrophyllum

Martin von Fintel

Satyrium neglectum

David McDonald

Disa scullyi

Emile Plumstead

Disa cephalotes subsp. *frigida*

David McDonald

Satyrium neglectum

Martin von Fintel

Disa aconitoides

Martin von Fintel

Disa cooperi

David McDonald

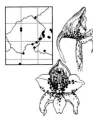

Disa crassicornis ´mametsana (SS) [= *D. jacottetiae*] (*crassus* - thick; *cornis* - horn, refers to spur)
Robust, up to 500mm tall (up to 1m at lower altitudes). Solitary or in small groups, on damp grassy slopes, up to 2200m. E Cape, Les, KZN. LEAVES sometimes on a separate shoot, stem leaves sheathing, usually withered at time of flowering. INFLORESCENCE large, 5-25 flowers, up to 300mm long, bracts papery, reddish brown; FLOWERS **large**, ±50mm diam, thick textured, creamy white to pink, mottled purple or pink, **spur 30-40mm long, curving out then down, tip slender, greenish**, with a strong, sweet scent (Nov-Feb). GENERAL: The flower shape and size varies according to altitude. Cultivated in Europe since the 1800s but difficult to maintain. Populations have been reduced by farming operations. (see pg 68) **Similar species:**

Disa thodei (named after Justus Thode, 1859-1932, pioneer plant collector in the Drakensberg) Slender, 150-350mm tall. In mountains in damp grassy places, along streams, 1800-3000m. E Cape to EMR. INFLORESCENCE smaller, 3-8 flowers; FLOWERS small, ± 20mm diam, white to creamy pink, blotched pinkish purple, **spur nearly horizontal**, 20-40mm long, smelling of cloves (Dec-Jan).

Disa dracomontana

Slender, 150-450mm tall. On grassy slopes, often among rocks, 2100-2900m. EMR endemic. LEAVES rigid, up to 180mm long, mostly near base. INFLORESCENCE loose, 40-100mm long, bracts dry; FLOWERS white to lilac-pink, striped with darker veins, **spur almost horizontal**, 2-5mm long (Dec-Feb).

Disa fragrans Fragrant Disa; Lekkerruik-disa (A) (*fragrans* - fragrant)

Robust, 150-500mm tall. In mountain grassland on rock sheets, around rock pools and on cliff ledges, 1800-3000m. E Cape to Tanz. LEAVES ±100mm long, folded, overlapping, **purple barred**. INFLORESCENCE dense, **cylindrical**, ±100mm long, bract tips dry; brown; FLOWERS small, ±8mm diam, white to deep pink, mottled darker pink, **spur slender, pointing down**, 5-10mm long, strongly scented (Jan-Mar). GENERAL: Leaves may be covered in purplish red spots or bars or these may be very faint to almost absent.

Disa montana (*montana* - belonging to the mountains)

Slender, 300-600mm tall. Rare, on dry rocky grassy slopes, 1000-2400m. E Cape, S KZN. LEAVES erect, overlapping, rigid, up to 120mm long. INFLORESCENCE loose, 100-200mm long, bracts dry; FLOWERS white to pale pink, spotted maroon, **spur horizontal, slender, 8-15mm long** (Nov-Dec).

Disa oreophila (*oreophila* - mountain loving)

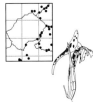

100-350mm tall. LEAVES **narrow**, ±200×1-3mm. INFLORESCENCE loose, 40-150mm long; FLOWERS white or pink, lightly or heavily spotted purple, **spur almost horizontal** (Dec-Feb). **Subsp. *erecta***, erect, in shallow soil over rock pavements and damp grassy slopes, 2100-2700m. Drakensberg endemic. FLOWERS **large**, sepals 6-10mm, spur 10-25mm (Jan-Feb). **Subsp. *oreophila*** Hangs or curves out from damp crevices and grass slopes. FLOWERS small, sepals 4-6mm, spur 5-10mm (Dec-Feb). (see pg 68)

Disa patula (*patulus* - spread out, extended)

Slender, 250-450mm tall. On rocky grass slopes, up to 1800m. E Cape to Zim. LEAVES ±100×15mm, erect, overlapping, sheathing stem. INFLORESCENCE slender, 50-250mm long; FLOWERS **held horizontally**, pale to bright pink, with purplish spots on tips of segments, **spur round, pointed, 5-12mm, ± horizontal** (Dec-Jan). GENERAL: Var. *transvaalensis* Widespread and locally common in this region. INFLORESCENCE narrow, less than 35mm diam. Var. *patula* Occurs in E Cape. INFLORESCENCE broad, usually 40-50mm diam; FLOWERS larger.

Disa crassicornis

David McDonald

Disa thodei

Hilliard & Burtt

Disa crassicornis

Clinton Carbutt

Disa oreophila

Hilliard & Burtt

Disa dracomontana

Hubert Kurzweil

Disa montana

Neil Crouch

Disa patula

Martin von Fintel

Disa oreophila

David McDonald

Disa fragrans

David McDonald

Disa fragrans

David McDonald

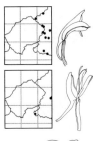

Disa pulchra (*pulchra - beautiful*)

Slender to robust, 250-600mm tall. In stony, grassy places, up to 2300m. E Cape, KZN, E FS. LEAVES up to 200mm long, rigid, folded, overlapping. INFLORESCENCE crowded, 100-280mm long; FLOWERS **large**, sepals 20-30mm long, **bright pink, parts spreading forward to form a false tube, lip broad at base**, spur slender, horizontal, 15-20mm long, curved down at tip (Dec-Jan). GENERAL: Conspicuous in bloom. **Similar species: *Disa nervosa*** (*nervosa - veins/nerves*) Robust, 400-800mm tall. In rocky grassland up to 2000m. E Cape to Mpum. INFLORESCENCE dense, 80-250mm long; FLOWERS **bright pink** with purple marks towards tips, **held horizontally, lip long and narrow**, spur horizontal (Dec-Mar).

Disa rhodantha (*rhodantha - bearing red flowers*)

Slender, 300-600mm tall. In marshy ground, 1500-2000m. E Cape to Zim. LEAVES well developed, on separate slender shoot 30-40mm long, those on stem sheathing. INFLORESCENCE crowded; FLOWERS **face down**, ±15mm diam, pink to red, lip yellow to pink, **spur slender, curving up**, 7-17mm long (Jan-Feb). GENERAL: Pollinated by long-tongued bees and long-tongued flies.

Disa sankeyi (*named after H.J. Sankey, 1885-1945, b. England, d. Kenya, a forester who collected specimens for Kew when working first at Harrismith and later in the E Cape*)

Robust, 150-300mm tall. In rocky grassland on ridges and slopes, 1800-3000m. EMR endemic. LEAVES overlap, up to 150×20mm. INFLORESCENCE a dense, thick, spike; FLOWERS **face down**, dull greenish white or yellow, spotted purple, spur ±3mm long, hanging down, fragrant (Feb-Mar).

Disa versicolor [= *D. macowanii*] **Apple-blossom Orchid; ihlamvu elibomvu (Z)** (*versicolor - variously coloured, changing colour*)

Robust, 300-600mm tall. In moist grassland, up to 2400m. Widespread, E Cape to Zim, Moz and Ang. LEAVES on separate shoot, folded, ±200×20mm, leaves on flowering stem few, usually thin, overlapping. INFLORESCENCE dense, bracts often dry; FLOWERS **small, rounded**, usually facing downwards, buds pink turning dull red to pink on opening, fading greenish brown, **spur hooked up then down**, 5-7mm long, vanilla scented (Jan-Feb). GENERAL: Plant used as a protective charm. Pollinated by bees (*Amegilla* spp.). The short, nectar producing spur looks like the mouthparts of the bees.

Brownleea (*named after Rev John Brownlee, early Scottish missionary who collected the type species of the genus, B. coerulea, in E Cape*) Median or odd sepal joins with two lateral petals to form trumpet-shaped hood which tapers gradually into curved spur, lip insignificant. Afr, 7 species, 5 in SAfr, all found in this region.

Brownleea macroceras **lefokotsoane (SS)** (*macroceras - large horns*)

Slender, 100-300mm tall. On damp rocky grass slopes and grassy cliffs, 1800-3000m. E Cape, Les, FS, KZN. LEAVES **1**(3), **narrow**, ±80×10mm. FLOWERS **1-3**(6), **large**, ±30mm diam, white to deep lilac-blue, **spur long, 25-40mm**, ± horizontal then curving downwards, sweetly scented (Jan-Apr). GENERAL: Cultivated as an alpine species. Pollinated by the long-tongued fly *Prosoeca ganglbaueri*. Plants in the north are mostly smaller, with a single leaf and single larger flower. Those in the south have up to six smaller flowers and up to 3 leaves.

Disperis - Granny Bonnet Orchids (*dis - double; pera - pouch, refers to spurs or pouches on side sepals*) Petals joined to median sepal to form a helmet-shaped hood, side sepals each with a noticeable spur or pouch. Afr, India, New Guinea, ±84 species, ±26 in SAfr, 13 in this region.

Disperis cardiophora (*cardiophora - bearing hearts, refers to the bracts*)

Slender 110-200mm tall. In moist grassland, up to 2700m. E Cape to Mpum. LEAF **solitary**, roundish, 10-30mm, **clasping base of stem**. INFLORESCENCE with 6-20 flowers, **all facing one way**, each supported by a **firm, kidney-shaped, horizontal bract**; FLOWERS small, white and green, tips of side sepals and petals magenta, sepals 5-7mm long, **outside of hood exposed**, speckled pink within, resembling a face with bulging, downcast eyes, spicy scent (Dec-Mar). GENERAL: Common but easily overlooked. Closely related to *D. renibractea*. Pollinated by the oil collecting bee *Rediviva neliana*. **Similar species: *Disperis renibractea*** (*renibractea - kidney-shaped bracts*) 150-300mm tall. In moist grassland, up to 2800m. E Cape to Mpum. FLOWERS larger than *D. cardiophora*, greenish, pinkish or brownish, **inside of hood visible, heavily spotted purple**, like a staring owlish face, pungent odour (Dec-Mar).

Brownleea macroceras   *Disa sankeyi*   *Disa nervosa*   *Disa pulchra*

Brownleea macroceras

Disperis cardiophora

Disa rhodantha

Disa versicolor   *Disperis cardiophora*   *Disperis renibractea*

197

Disperis concinna (concinna - pretty, neat, elegant)

Slender, 150-500mm tall. Rare, in damp or marshy grassland, up to 2400m. Rare in EMR, scattered records from Gaut, Mpum, Zim. LEAVES 2-3, 15-30×4-9mm, clasping the stem. FLOWERS 1-4, small, pale to deep pink, usually spotted green inside, **hood deep, top rounded, side sepals 6-7mm long, spreading, sharply pointed** (Jan-Mar). GENERAL: Pollinated by oil collecting bees (*Rediviva* species).

Disperis cooperi (named after Thomas Cooper, 1815-1913, English plant collector who visited SA in 1859)

Stout, 150-400mm tall. In damp or marshy grassland, 1200-2100m. KZN to Mpum. LEAVES 2-4, 25-35mm, clasping the stem. FLOWERS 5-12, creamy **white to pinkish purple**, tinged green, **hood deep**, rounded, 8-10mm tall, rim green and purple spotted, side sepals spreading, 7-10mm long, sharply pointed (Feb-Mar). GENERAL: Pollinated by oil collecting bees (*Rediviva* species).

Disperis oxyglossa (oxyglossa - pointed tongue)

Slender, 120-250mm tall. In damp grassland, up to 2700m. E Cape to KZN. LEAVES 3-4, clasping, 10-35×4-8mm. FLOWERS 2-4(6), bright purple-pink, petals cream with green spots, hood narrow, slightly compressed, less than 10mm tall, **side sepals 12-17mm long, reflexed, spreading, narrowing into a long narrow tip** (Jan-Mar). GENERAL: Pollinated by oil collecting bees (*Rediviva* species).

Disperis stenoplectron (stenoplectron - with narrow spurs)

Stout, 140-300mm tall. On grassy slopes, 1500-2850m. E Cape to Mpum. LEAVES 2-4, stem clasping, 20-35×8-12mm. FLOWERS 5-8, all facing one side, dark red, purple and green or pale white to pink, **hood ±10mm tall**, cone-shaped, side sepals 10-12mm long, spreading and pointing downwards (Jan-Apr). GENERAL: Pollinated by oil collecting bees (*Rediviva* species).

Disperis tysonii (named after William Tyson, b. Jamaica 1851, d. Grahamstown 1920, teacher and plant collector)

Slender, 150-300mm tall. In damp grassland, up to 3000m. E Cape to Mpum. LEAVES 3-6, clasping, 15-30×5-8mm. INFLORESCENCE with flowers all facing the same direction; FLOWERS 2-20, **small**, pink to magenta, spotted green, **hood tall**, cone-shaped, **inclined backwards**, 5-8mm long, side sepals 6-8mm long, spreading, sweetly scented (Jan-Mar). GENERAL: Pollinated by oil collecting bees (*Rediviva* species).

Eulophia (eu - well; lophos - crest, refers to the crested lip) Terrestrial herbs. **Lip ridged on upper surface.** Old and New World, most common in Afr, 42 in S Afr, 9 in this region.

Eulophia aculeata subsp. **huttonii** lekholela, ´mametsana (SS) (aculeata - thorny, or pointed; huttonii, named after Henry Hutton, 1825-96, a civil servant who collected plants in the E Cape and E Free State)

150-300mm tall. In short stony grassland, 1500-2600m. E Cape to Mpum. LEAVES stiff, pleated, ±600×17mm, partly to fully grown at flowering. INFLORESCENCE **short, crowded**; FLOWERS greenish-white, pink tinged green to dark reddish purple, sepals and petals the same colour, 9-16mm long, hardly spreading, lip crests yellowish green to white, **spur absent**, faintly scented (Nov-Dec). GENERAL: Subsp. *aculeata* Mostly in fynbos in W and E Cape. LEAVES narrower. FLOWERS **smaller**, ivory to greenish white, lip crest tinged purple, sepals and petals 6-8mm long (Nov-Jan).

Eulophia clavicornis lekholela, maholohanya, ´mametsana (SS); elihlaza, imfeyamasele (Z) (clava - club; cornis - horn)

Slender, 100-400mm tall. Widespread in grassland, up to 1700m. Cape to Trop Afr, Madag. FLOWERS few, widely spaced, sepals dark green to purplish brown, petals and lip white to purple or yellow, spur cylindrical, **lip crests fleshy, with peglike outgrowths** (not ridges), **almost reaching the tip of the lip** (Sep-Feb). GENERAL: Grazed by stock. Used as a protective charm. **Flower colour, size and leaf development very variable**, the varieties differing mostly in details of the lip. Var. *clavicornis* Leaves partly developed at flowering, 20-300mm long; flowers white, pale pink to pale blue, **lip as long as median sepal**, often distorted (Aug-Sep). Var. *inaequalis* (inaequalis - unequal, uneven) **Lip often shorter than median sepal** (Sep-Oct). Var. *nutans* (nutans - nodding) **Leaves fully developed at flowering**, 170-730mm long. Flowering stem sometimes branched; FLOWER petals white to pale or deep purple or tinged with blue or yellow, **midlobe crests often united at base** (Dec-Feb).

Neil Crouch

Disperis concinna

Martin von Fintel

Disperis cooperi

Clinton Carbutt

Disperis oxyglossa

Hendrelien Peters

Disperis stenoplectron

Martin von Fintel

Disperis tysonii

Martin von Fintel

Disperis tysonii

Martin von Fintel

Eulophia aculeata

Tony Abbott

Eulophia aculeata

Pam Cooke

Eulophia clavicornis

199

DICOTYLEDONS Two seed leaves, net veins, flower parts in fours, fives or multiples of these.
POLYGONACEAE - Rhubarb Family Base of leaf stalk often forms a sheath. Cosmop, ± 43 genera, ± 1100 species, 5 genera in SAfr. *Rumex* (culinary sorrel) Fruit 3-angled, enclosed within enlarged, persistent sepals. Cosmop, ±200 species, ± 18 in SAfr, some introduced, 6 in this region.

Rumex woodii Paper Hearts, Wood's Rumex; Tongblaar (A); bolila-ba-likhomo (SS)
(named after John Medley Wood, 1827-1915, botanist, founding curator of Natal Herbarium)
Perennial herb, up to 600mm tall. In grassland, up to 2250m. Cape to Mpum. Stems **erect, solitary** or 2-3 together. LEAVES ±15×34mm. FLOWERS **in few-flowered whorls** (Sep-Jan). FRUIT with **heart-shaped lobes**, ±12mm wide, coppery red. GENERAL: Very decorative. Leaves eaten raw. Used in traditional medicine.

Persicaria (*persicum* - leaves like those of a peach) Perennial (annual) herbs or shrubs. Cosmop, ±150 species, ±10 in SAfr, some introduced.

★*Persicaria lapathifolia* [= *Polygonum lapathifolium*] Spotted Knotweed; Hanekam (A); khamane-ea-noka, tolo-la-khongoana (SS); idolenkoynyane, umancibikela, umancibilika (Z) (*lapathifolia* - leaves like *Rumex lapathum* Dock)
Robust annual herb, up to 1m tall. In damp ground, up to 2400m. Widespread. Stem sheaths brownish. LEAVES ±100×20mm, marked with dark blotches. INFLORESCENCE branched; FLOWERS widely spaced (Nov-Mar). GENERAL: Used in traditional medicine.

MESEMBRYANTHEMACEAE - Vygie Family (see pg 72) *Delosperma* (*delos* - conspicuous; *sperma* - seed) (see pg 128)

Delosperma lavisiae [= *D. alticolum, D. obtusum, D. smythae*] Mountain Vygie; Bergvygie, Kransvygie (A); mabone (SS) (named after Miss Lavis, a friend of Louisa Bolus, who specialised in Mesems)
Succulent perennial herb. Forms mats, on rock sheets and outcrops, in stony places, up to 2650m. EMR endemic. Stems prostrate, ±1 mm diam, (in section when cut across). LEAVES spreading, 5-17×3mm, **round to 3-angled, blunt-tipped**. INFLORESCENCES much branched; FLOWERS ±20mm diam, magenta, stalks 5-15mm long (Nov-Mar).

Delosperma sutherlandii [= *D. galpinii, D. ashtonii*] (after Dr P.C. Sutherland, 1822-1900, surveyor general of Natal, keen plant collector)
Succulent herb, up to 120mm tall. In grassland, up to 2100m. KZN to Mpum. Stems roughly hairy. LEAVES **opposite, slightly joined at base, flat**, 50-80×15-20mm, tapering to slender point, **keeled beneath**, margins with short hairs. FLOWERS 1-3, in terminal clusters, 35-60mm diam, magenta fading to white at base, pink or white, stamens white, stalks 50-100mm long (Oct-Dec). GENERAL: Quick to flower after veld fires.

Ruschia (named after E. Rusch, farmer near Windhoek) Dwarf succulent shrubs, erect or spreading. Leaves 3-angled, often with dark transparent dots, smooth or hairy. Fruit with small hook-shaped closing bodies. SAfr, ±224 species, 1 in this region.

Ruschia putterillii (named after V.A. Putterill, mycologist, appointed government fruit inspector in 1917)
Hard, woody dwarf shrublet. Forms cushions or mats on north-facing summit basalt cliffs, basalt sheets and gravelly slopes, 2500-3000m. E Cape to KZN/Mpum. Young branches compressed, winged, internodes 5-25mm long. LEAVES 8-10×3-5mm, 3-4 mm thick, erect to spreading, with prominent dots at the recurved tips. FLOWERS **massed**, ±15mm diam, pale to dark magenta pink, stalks ±50mm long (Oct-Jan).

CARYOPHYLLACEAE - Carnation or Pink Family Leaves in opposite pairs, joined at base, nodes more or less swollen. Petal tips often notched, lobed or fretted. Mostly N temp, ±80 genera, ±2200 species, 22 genera in SAfr (11 exotic). *Silene* (see pg 72)

Silene burchellii Gunpowder Plant; Kruitbossie (A); ho-batla, kopane, lithokoano, motebane, molokolokoana, monyekane, tšoloane (SS); iyeza lehashe (X); igwayintombi elincane, injuju, umthusi (Z) (named after William Burchell, 1781-1863, great English naturalist)
Herb, up to 700mm tall. In grassland, up to 2400m. Widespread. Stems ± sticky hairy. LEAVES up to 60×8mm. FLOWERS open in the evenings ±10mm diam, white or pink inside, **all flowers held to one side**, calyx inflated, 10-25mm, green or red-veined, (Dec-Mar). CAPSULE seeds rattle. GENERAL: Used in traditional medicine.

Dianthus - Carnations and Pinks (*dios* - divine; *anthos* - flower, refers to the scent of some species) Tufted herbs. Leaves opposite, narrow. Petals entire, toothed or fringed, calyx tubular, base surrounded by bracts. Europe, Asia, Afr, ±300 species, 15 in SAfr, 4 in this region.

Dianthus basuticus subsp. *basuticus* Lesotho Dianthus, Lesotho Carnation; Lesothose grootblom-wilde-angelier (A); hlokoa-la-tsela, moqollo, tlokofiloane (SS)
Herb, flowering stems 150-300mm tall. Often **forms small mats** on rocky grass slopes, in crevices of rock sheets, cliffs, 1400-3050m. EMR to Mpum. LEAVES **basal**, ±100×15mm long, **densely tufted**, grasslike. FLOWERS solitary (1-7), ±30mm diam, white to pale or bright pink, petals toothed or long-fringed, stalks 110-450mm long (Dec-Mar). GENERAL: Used as a love charm and to increase fertility of bulls.

Rumex woodii   *Rumex woodii*   *Silene burchellii*   *Persicaria lapathifolia*

Delosperma sutherlandii   *Ruschia putterillii*

Delosperma lavisiae

Delosperma lavisiae

Dianthus basuticus   *Dianthus basuticus*

201

Dianthus mooiensis subsp. *mooiensis* Frilly Dianthus, Frilly Carnation; Wilde-angelier (A); utshanibezwe (Z) (*mooiensis* - from Mooi River, Natal, where the plant was first found)

Perennial herb, flowering stems 250-600mm tall. In grassland over Cave Sandstone, up to 2450m. Cape to CAfr. Stems straggling, **lower parts leafy.** LEAVES 25-45 ×3-5mm, **blue-green,** rigid, tapering to long point. INFLORESCENCE **branched**; FLOWERS 5-15, ±30mm diam, bright pink (Nov-Dec). GENERAL: Used in traditional medicine.

FUMARIACEAE Leaves tipped with a tendril. Mostly N Hemisp, ±17 genera, ±530 species, 4 genera in SAfr. *Cysticapnos* [= *Phacocapnos*] (*kystis* - bladder; *kapnos* - smoky, refers to capsules) Climbing herbs. Back petal spurred. SAfr endemic, 5 species, 1 in this region.

Cysticapnos pruinosa [= *Phacocapnos pruinosus*] Wild Fumaria; ´musa-pelo-oa-noka (SS) (*pruinosa* - waxy, powdery secretion on surface)

Tangled, climbing, soft shrubby herb, up to 600mm tall. In boulder beds, damp rocky places, damp grassy slopes, 1200-3000m. E Cape to KZN. LEAVES finely dissected, grey-green. FLOWERS 2-lobed, pink, **lower lip with narrow claw, pitted in the middle, upper lip expanded, spur wide, blunt, reflexed** (Nov-Mar). FRUIT a hanging pod, narrowed to tip. GENERAL: Used as a charm to comfort the sorrowing.

BRASSICACEAE (CRUCIFERAE) - Cabbage or Mustard Family (see pg 74) *Heliophila* (*helios* - sun; *philein* - to love) (see pg 74)

Heliophila formosa (*formosa* - beautiful)

Perennial herb, in **big leafy clumps, flowering stems pendulous,** 300-1000mm long. On damp rocky cliffs, streamside rubble or among large boulders, 1950-3350m. EMR endemic. LEAVES 70-130×10mm, **tufted,** in big clumps. INFLORESCENCE long, narrow, tips of flowering stems held erect, petals 10-14 mm long, light to deep violet, sweetly scented (Nov-Jan). FRUIT 40-60mm long.

DROSERACEAE - Sundew Family Small insectivorous herbs, in damp places. Leaves usually rolled in bud, covered in sticky, glandular hairs which trap small insects then secrete enzymes which dissolve the prey and absorb the fluid into the plant. Petals 5, free. Fruit a capsule. The family includes the famous Venus Flytrap (*Dionaea*). Cosmop, 4 genera, ±100 species, 2 genera in SAfr. *Drosera* (*droseros* - dewy, refers to the leaf glands) Tip of inflorescence bent over open flower. Cosmop, mostly S Hemisp, ±80 species, ±20 in SAfr, 3 in this region.

Drosera natalensis Sundew; Doublom, Sondou (A)

Small herb, flowering stems up to 150mm tall. In marshy ground around tarns, near streams, on damp earth terraces on grass slopes, up to 2400m. E Cape to Trop Afr. LEAVES in rosette, ±20×5mm, **soft, thin,** tips broad, rounded, tapering to base. FLOWERS ±10mm diam, **stem wiry, erect** or curved (Jan-Feb).

CRASSULACEAE - Crassula Family (see pg 74) *Crassula* (*crassus* - thick, refers to fleshy leaves) (see pg 74)

Crassula alba feko, khato (SS); isidwe, isikhelekhehlane (Z) (*alba* - white, inappropriate because most petals are red)

Succulent herb, flowering stem 100-500mm tall. On rocky banks, up to 1900m. E Cape to Ethiopia. Stem finely hairy, leafy. LEAVES in rosette at base, up to 150×40mm, in pairs on stem, often with reddish purple markings, hairless except on margins. INFLORESCENCE flat topped, ±150mm wide; FLOWERS cup-shaped, **petals erect,** 5-6 mm long, **blunt, with distinct appendage at the tip,** white inside, pink or red in bud (Mar). GENERAL: Used as a charm to make one invisible. Rewarding garden plant. (see pg 36)

ROSACEAE - Rose Family (see pg 130) *Rubus* (*ruber* - red, also the old Latin name for the plant) Prickly, mostly scrambling shrubs. Leaves simple or 3-5-foliolate. Fruits edible. Mostly N Hemisp, ±250 species, ±17 in SAfr, many of them introduced invasive plants, ±4 species in this region.

Rubus ludwigii Silver Bramble, Ludwig's Ample-bramble; Wildebraam (A); monokotsoai-oa-basali (SS); imencemence, itshalo, unomhloshane (Z) (named after Carl von Ludwig, 1784-1847, German born, pharmacist, businessman, patron of natural science who came to SA in 1805)

Shrub, up to 2m. In small colonies, in grassland, scrub, on rock tumbles and outcrops up to 2400m. E Cape to KZN. LEAVES mostly with 5-7 leaflets, upper surface green, hairless, margins deeply toothed, **lower surface white woolly,** stalks 12-40mm long. FLOWERS ±13mm diam, **pale pink** to red, sepals white woolly (Oct-Dec). FRUIT oval, 6-10mm diam, **purple with white down.** GENERAL: Crushed leaves used to make ink. Fruits edible. Used in traditional medicine to ease stomach ache, treat pain, fits and snakebite. **Similar species: *Rubus rigidus* White Bramble; Braam (A); monokotsoai-oa-banna (SS)** Scrambling shrub. In scrub at foot of Cave Sandstone cliffs and overhangs, up to 2100m. SW Cape to Ethiopia. LEAVES **densely woolly white beneath, 1-3(5) leaflets.** FLOWERS **small,** pink, petals slightly shorter than calyx lobes (Nov-Dec). FRUITS **orange.**

Cysticapnos pruinosa

Clinton Carbutt

Dianthus mooiensis

Lal Greene

Martin von Fintel

Crassula alba

Drosera natalensis

Lal Greene

Heliophila formosa

Hilliard & Burtt

Drosera natalensis

Simon Milliken

Clinton Carbutt

Rubus ludwigii

Rubus rigidus

Braam van Wyk

LEGUMINOSAE (FABACEAE) - **Pea or Legume Family** (see pg 130) *Hoffmannseggia* (named in honour of Johannes Centurius, Graf von Hofmannsegga) Herbs or low shrubs, often covered in dark scattered glands. C America, Afr, ±30 species, 3 in SAfr, 1 in this region.

Hoffmannseggia sandersonii (after J. Sanderson, 1820-1881, journalist, trader, plant collector in Natal)

Shrublet, up to 400mm tall. In grassland, up to 1600m. KZN endemic. **Stems covered in reddish hairs.** LEAVES 20-80mm long, leaflets 5-14×2-6mm, **dotted with dark glands.** INFLORESCENCES ±300mm long, including stem; FLOWERS ±20mm diam, red to salmon-pink, calyx with short tube, gland dotted (Aug-Nov). PODS oblong, slightly curved, ±45×16mm, **dark brown, covered in dense, shaggy, pinkish hairs.**

Trifolium - **Clover** (*tri* - three; *folium* - leaf) Herbs. Attracts butterflies. Cosmop, ±250 species, ±19 in SAfr, mostly introduced, 2 in this region.

Trifolium burchellianum Wild Clover; Wildeklawer (A); mokopshoe, moqoiqoi, moqopolla-thula, moqopshoe, moroko (flowerhead only), ´musa-pelo (SS); usithathi (Z) (after William Burchell, 1781-1863, great English naturalist, author of 'Travels in the Interior of SAfr')

Creeping, mat forming herb, up to 200mm tall. In damp grassland, around rocks, in marshy turf on the summit, up to 2800m. Cape to Trop Afr. **Plant ± hairless.** LEAFLETS **heart-shaped**, ±25×19mm, **stalks long**, **±25-70mm.** INFLORESCENCE compact, ±30mm diam; FLOWERS ±13mm, bright pink to red (Dec-Mar). GENERAL: Inflorescences eaten raw by people. Used in traditional medicine. Grazed by livestock.

Indigofera (produces indigo, a blue dye obtained from several species of this genus) (see pg 36)

Indigofera cuneifolia Wedge-leaved Indigo; Wigblaarindigobos (A) (cuneifolia - wedge-shaped)

Slender, shrublike herb, up to 1m tall. On streambanks, grassy hillsides, up to 1800m. LEAVES **3-foliolate**, hairy, grey-green; LEAFLETS 12-25×6-10 mm, **stipules broad based**, **prominent**, 9-12mm long, leaving collarlike scars on stems. INFLORESCENCE dense, bracts large, hiding buds; FLOWERS 6-10mm long, bright pink (Sep-Oct).

Indigofera dimidiata ´musa-pelo-oa-thaba, qoi-qoi (SS) (dimidiata - halved)

Low growing, perennial herb, 100-300mm tall. In grass, near streams, up to 2600m. E Cape to Malawi. Stems ± branched. LEAVES **3 foliolate**; LEAFLETS 25-35×8-10mm, stalks 10-25mm, **stipules large**, up to 4mm wide at base. INFLORESCENCES **compact**, stems ±250mm; FLOWERS ±6mm, pink, hairless (Sep-Feb). GENERAL: Used in traditional medicine to treat fevers, used in mourning rites and as a good luck charm.

Indigofera longebarbata (longebarbata - long-bearded)

Herb up to 1.2m tall, bushy with support of other plants or prostrate. On margins of scrub, streamsides, among rocks, up to 2500m. E Cape to Ethiopia. **Covered in soft white hairs.** LEAVES ±80mm long; LEAFLETS 9-13, stalkless, ±20×10mm. INFLORESCENCE ±80(250)mm long, **stem long, dark brown, hairy**; FLOWERS small, up to 5mm long, pink (Jan-Mar). PODS **inflated**, ±8×1.8mm, **with shaggy black hairs.**

Tephrosia (*tephros* - ashen, refers to grey-green or silvery leaves of many species) Herbs or shrubs (see pg 36)

Tephrosia diffusa [= *T. macropoda* var. *diffusa*] Creeping Tephrosia; intozane (X); ilozane, ugwengu (Z) (diffusa - spreading)

Trailing herb, stems up to 1m long. Forms dense mats, in rocky grassland, on rock outcrops, up to 1950m. E Cape to KZN. LEAFLETS 5-9, narrow, 8-20×3-6mm, **veins well marked**, stipules broadly clasping, **maturing dark brown, curling away from stems.** INFLORESCENCE **on long stem**; FLOWERS **crowded at tip**, ±20mm (Dec-Feb).

Lessertia (after J. Delessert, 1773-1847, notable French botanist) Pods papery, flat or slightly inflated. Afr, ±50 species, ±47 in SAfr, ±5 in this region.

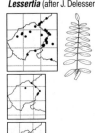

Lessertia perennans Lessertia; ´musa-pelo-o-moholo-oa-liliba (SS) (perennans - perennial)

Stiffly hairy, grey-green shrublet, up to 1.2m tall. Often in large stands in grassy streamlines, boulder beds, 1200-2400m. E Cape to KZN. LEAVES ±50mm long, leaflets in 8-10 pairs, silky hairy. INFLORESCENCES **large**, stems 75-150mm long; FLOWERS ±6mm, pale pink, buds deep pink (Nov-Jan). PODS 15-20×10-12mm, flat, papery.

Lessertia thodei (named after Justus Thode, 1859-1932, pioneer plant collector in the Drakensberg)

Perennial herb, **stems prostrate**, up to 200mm long. In moist, rocky grassland, 2100-2900m. EMR endemic. LEAVES **mostly hairless**; LEAFLETS 5-9×2-4mm, in 5-9 pairs, tips rounded. INFLORESCENCE 30-75mm long; FLOWERS **±10mm long** (Nov-Feb). **Additional species: *Lessertia depressa* ´musa-pelo (SS)** On dry ground under Cave Sandstone overangs, grassy places, above 2400m. Stems thinly hairy; LEAFLETS stiffly hairy, flowering stems shorter than leaves (Dec-Feb). Pods ±25×12mm, **inflated**.

Trifolium burchellianum

Hoffmannseggia sandersonii

Indigofera dimidiata

Indigofera longebarbata

Indigofera cuneifolia

Lessertia thodei

Lessertia depressa

Tephrosia diffusa

Lessertia depressa

Lessertia perennans

205

GERANIACEAE - Geranium Family Herbs or soft wooded shrubs, often aromatic. Leaves usually lobed or divided, with stipules. Flowers regular or slightly irregular, ovary superior. Fruit beaked, splitting into 5 1-seeded sections, each separating with part of the persistent dry style. Economically important for aromatic oils, horticulture, especially the garden plants known as 'Geraniums', which belong to the genus *Pelargonium* and not the genus *Geranium*. Temp, subtrop, 11 genera, ±800 species, 5 genera in SAfr. *Geranium* (*geranos* - a crane) Annual or perennial herbs, shrubs. Flowers symmetrical, solitary. Attracts butterflies. Mainly temp, ±300 species, 31 in SAfr, ±11 in this region.

Geranium drakensbergense

Perennial herb. Forms large clumps in moist shady places below cliffs, up to 2400m. EMR endemic. Stems sparsely branched. LEAVES **densely tufted**, blade up to 35m diam, 3-5 lobes cut almost to base, deep green above, paler beneath, stipules deeply dissected, stalks much longer than the blades. FLOWERS in 2s, stalks much longer than leaves, petals 13-18×10-12mm, shallowly notched, blue-purple (Nov-Feb).

Geranium multisectum hlapi-e-kholo, ngope-ea-setšoha, tlako (SS) (*multisectum* - many incisions)

Perennial herb. **Forming mats or cushions**, in open marshy places, along streamlines, below cliffs, 1400-3300m. E Cape to Limpopo Prov. Rootstock thick, woody, stems downy, well branched. LEAVES **densely tufted**, blade up to 50mm diam, **finely divided, lobes twice pinnate, segments 1-2mm broad, incurved, lower leaves on long stalks, up to 300mm**. FLOWER stems much longer than leaves, hairy, often gland tipped, petals ±17×13mm, violet, purple or magenta, calyx downy (Nov-Jan). GENERAL: At high altitudes leaves are usually smaller, with short, incurved lobes. At lower altitudes leaves are larger with longer, more spreading lobes. Used to make a herbal tea. Used in traditional medicine to treat dysentery and worm infestations and by diviners when throwing the bones. **Similar species: *Geranium magniflorum*** (*magniflorum* - large flowers) On damp grassy slopes, drainage lines, 1800-3200m. LEAVES **less divided** than *G. multisectum*, **lobes once pinnate**, up to 50mm diam, green above, white beneath. FLOWERS pink to purple (white) (Nov-Feb).

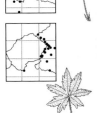

Geranium pulchrum (*pulchrum* - beautiful)

Robust subshrub, up to 1.2m tall. In damp or marshy ground, on streambanks, in drainage lines 1500-2285m, often forming large, pure stands at high altitudes. EMR endemic. STEMS woody at base, silky hairy. LEAVES large, 80-120mm diam, deeply 5-7-lobed, hairy above, **silvery silky beneath**, stalks longer than leaves. INFLORESCENCES **large, loose, ± leafless**; FLOWERS 20-35mm diam, light to deep pink, petals 17-22×11-19mm, stalks ±60mm, covered in white hairs (Dec-Mar). GENERAL: Attractive garden plant. **Similar species:** *Geranium robustum.* (see pg 236)

Geranium schlechteri Schlechter's Geranium (named after Friedrich Schlechter, 1872-1925, eminent German botanist and traveller)

Fragrant, straggling herb. In moist grassland, on forest margins, up to 2590m. LEAVES ±60mm diam, lobes cut to 4-10mm of base, **sparingly toothed**, thinly hairy above with long, spreading, **often gland tipped hairs** beneath, lower leaf stalks ±180mm long. FLOWERS small, pink fading white or white veined pink, petals **9-12×4-7mm, shallowly notched or entire, stalks with spreading gland tipped hairs** (Oct-Apr). GENERAL: Can be mistaken for *G. wakkerstroomianum.* (see pg 76)

Pelargonium (*pelargos* - stork's beak, refers to fruit) Perennial (annual) herbs or soft woody shrubs. Leaves usually lobed or divided, often aromatic. Flowers asymmetrical. Horticultural varieties, generally (incorrectly) known as Geraniums, have been popular garden and container plants since the 1700s. Attracts butterflies. Afr, Asia, Madag, Austr, New Zealand, ±270 species, ±219 in SAfr, mostly W Cape, ±13 in this region.

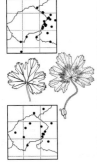

Pelargonium alchemilloides Pink Trailing Pelargonium; Wildemalva (A); bolila-ba-litšoene (SS); inkubele (X,Z); ishwaqa, umangqengqe (Z) (*alchemilloides* - resembles *Alchemilla*)

Sprawling, softly hairy perennial herb, stems few, ± prostrate, 200-900mm long. On grassy slopes, near streams, up to 2400m. SW Cape to Ethiopia. Stems with long, internodes, often reddish, with fine hairs ±20mm long. LEAVES 20-70mm diam, shallowly to deeply lobed, **sometimes with purplish brown mark in centre**, on long stalks, stipules large, oval. FLOWERS few (3-7), petals narrow, ±15mm long, white to pale pink, often veined, on long stalks, held above the leaves (Nov-Mar). GENERAL: Leaves aromatic. Used in traditional medicine. Grown from seed. **Similar species:** *Pelargonium ranunculophyllum* (*ranunculophyllum* - leaves like *Ranunculus*) Low growing herb. Smaller, more slender than *P. alchemilloides*. In shade, on steep rocky slopes, 1800-2400m. FLOWERS 2-3, white fading pink, petals ±12×3mm, upper two marked with a red spot, sometimes also on lower three (Feb).

Geranium pulchrum

David McDonald

Geranium magniflorum

David McDonald

Geranium drakensbergense

Clinton Carbutt

Geranium schlechteri

Lal Greene

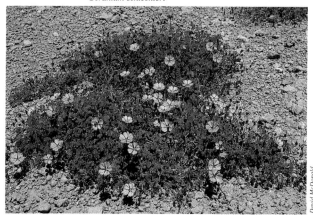

Geranium multisectum

Martin von Fintel

Geranium multisectum

David McDonald

Pam Cooke

Pelargonium alchemilloides

Lawrence Peacock

Pelargonium ranunculophyllum

Peter Linder

Tony Abbott

207

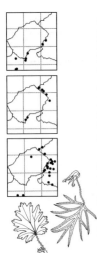

Pelargonium capituliforme (capituliforme - flowers in a head)

Softly hairy ± prostrate herb. On bare, damp, partly shaded ground, silty boulder beds, up to 2600m. E Cape to KZN. LEAVES almost round, 3-5 lobed, margins finely toothed, stalks long. FLOWERS very small, white, pink or purple, crowded in a head, on short stems, opposite leaves (Dec-Mar).

Pelargonium dispar (dispar - different, unequal)

Flowering stems 400-900mm, erect, simple or sparsely shortly branched. In grass at margins of forest or scrub, up to 2440m. LEAVES velvety, heart-shaped, on long stalks, **aromatic.** INFLORESCENCE 1-3-flowered, branched; FLOWERS dainty, 15-17mm wide, stalks very short, petals subequal, pink to white, veined dark reddish purple (Oct-Apr).

Pelargonium luridum Waving Pelargonium; Wildemalva (A); inyonkulu, isandla sonwabu, umsongelo, unyawo-lwenkuku, uvendle (Z) (luridum - smoky or drab, refers to flower colour)

Deciduous, low growing herb, flowering stems up to 600mm tall. Widespread in grassland, up to 2000m. E Cape to Tanz. Plant hairy throughout. LEAVES 1-3 at base, up to 250mm diam, young leaves shallowly lobed, mature leaves shallowly to deeply divided, stalks ±300mm long. INFLORESCENCE solitary, ±130mm diam, stem bare, erect; FLOWERS pink (cream) (Nov-Dec). GENERAL: Eaten raw as a vegetable. Grazed. Used in traditional medicine to treat dysentery, nausea, vomiting, fever and as a love charm. Easily grown from seed. **Similar species: Pelargonium schlechteri.** (see pg 38)

OXALIDACEAE - Sorrel Family Herbs. Leaves usually with 3 leaflets, simple, often folded at night. Petals clawed, often twisted. Fruit a capsule or berry. Trop, temp, 7 genera, ±900 species, 2 genera in SAfr. *Oxalis* (oxys - acid, sour; als - salt, refers to the sharp taste of the plant) Herbs, many with enlarged vertical or horizontal underground stems. Leaves in basal rosette. Flowers bell-shaped. Attracts butterflies. About 600 species, cosmop, centred in S America, Afr, mostly SAfr, ±270, mostly in winter rainfall area, ±4 in this region.

Oxalis obliquifolia Oblique-leaved Sorrel; Skuinsblaarsuring (A); bolila (SS) (obliquifolia - leaves unequal sided)

70-100mm tall, in small colonies. In damp grassland, up to 3000m. E Cape to Ethiopia. LEAFLETS 3-15mm, **broader than long**, tips broad, **stalks very slender with long hairs near base.** FLOWERS **solitary**, petals ±20mm long, bright pink, white in throat, tube yellow (Oct-Jan). GENERAL: Flowers visited by butterflies, honey-bees. **Similar species: Oxalis depressa bolila (SS)** Small perennial herb, 60-80mm tall. In grassland. **Hairless.** LEAFLETS often purple below, tips broad, with shallow notch. FLOWERS with 2 hairlike bracts at base, pink or white with yellow centre, **petals ±15mm long**, callus pale brown blobs on backs of sepals at top.

Oxalis smithiana Narrow-leaved Sorrel; Klawersuring (A); bolila, bolila-ba-lipoli (SS); zotho (X); umuncwane (bulb), inkolowane (X,Z); incangiyane (Z) (possibly named after J.E. Smith, founder of the Linn. Soc who bought Linnaeus's herbarium, end 18th century)

Herb up to 250mm tall. In damp grassland, on mossy rocks in forest, up to 2560m. Cape to Mpum. LEAFLETS **deeply divided, lobes narrow**, ±20×3mm. FLOWERS **solitary**, petals ±20 mm long, bright pink, throat white, stalk slender, ±120mm long (Nov-Jan). GENERAL: Grazed. Leaves, bulbs eaten by children. Used in traditional medicine as a tapeworm remedy.

POLYGALACEAE - Milkwort family Herbs, shrubs or small trees. Flowers superficially resemble 'pea' flowers, keel terminating in a brush. Cosmop, ±80 genera, ±900 species, 5 genera in SAfr. *Polygala* (poly - much; gala - milk, refers to the old belief in Europe that grazing certain species of these plants would increase the milk yield of cows) Herbs or shrubs. Seeds often distributed by ants. Many popular garden plants. Cosmop, ±600 species, ±88 in SAfr, ±14 in this region.

Polygala hottentotta Small Purple Broom; lehlokoa-la-tsela (SS); umanqandi, uzekane (Z)

(pertaining to the land of the Hottentots, the Khoikhoi, who occupied the SW Cape)

Slender, perennial, deciduous herb, 200-600mm tall. In grassland, on stabilised boulder beds, up to 2400m. SAfr to Zim, Moz. Stems erect, arching, wiry, sparsely branched. LEAVES few, slender, 10-40×0.5-2mm, stem hugging. INFLORESCENCE up to 200mm long; FLOWERS widely spaced, wings 5-8×3-6mm, pinkish mauve, conspiuously veined (Nov-Mar). GENERAL: Used in traditional medicine to treat abdominal complaints, anthrax and as charms. Roots and stems scented.

Pelargonium capituliforme

Mike Hirst

Pelargonium capituliforme

Mike Hirst

Pelargonium dispar

Martin von Fintel

Pelargonium luridum

Lorraine van Hooff

Oxalis depressa

Mike Hirst

Oxalis obliquifolia

Darrel Plowes

Oxalis smithiana

Lal Greene

Polygala hottentotta

Tony Abbott

209

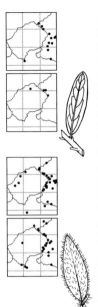

Polygala gracilenta [gracilis - slender]
Perennial tufted herb, 100-300mm tall. On grassy stony slopes, up to 1700m. E Cape to Mpum. Stems slender, erect. LEAVES 10-35×2-6mm. FLOWERS in crowded terminal clusters, large, 6-8mm, purple, blue, magenta (Oct-Jan).

Polygala myrtifolia September Bush; Septemberbossie (A); moomang-la-thaba (SS)
(myrtifolia - leaves like a myrtle)
Leafy shrub, up to 1m tall. In rough grass, on scrubby slopes and in valley bottoms, up to 2745m. LEAVES thin, ±20×8mm, bristletipped. FLOWERS large, pinkish mauve, in small clusters in leaf axils (Oct-Jan). GENERAL: Var. *cluytioides* was the name given to the plant in this region. The coastal form has become a popular garden plant, flowering for much of the year.

Polygala ohlendorfiana mahlaka-hlaka (SS)
Small, slender, tufted herb. In shade of rocks, in marshy ground, up to 2200m. E Cape to Trop Afr. LEAVES 10-24×5-14mm long, thin. FLOWER wings 6×5mm, pink (Oct-Dec).

Polygala rhinostigma (rhinos - a nose; stigma - pollen receptor)
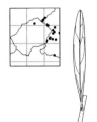
Erect or spreading, tufted herb, stems 150-200mm long. Common in moist grassland, 1800-2900m. Stems unbranched, leafy. LEAVES 7-15×2-4mm, ± overlapping, softly hairy. INFLORESCENCES **terminal, dense**, 50-150mm long; FLOWERS small, pale magenta pink, petals ±4×3 mm (Oct-Feb). **Similar species:** *Polygala hispida* bolao-ba-noka, mooa-nokeng (SS) (hispidus - long, straight) Spreading, cushionlike herb, stems 200-300mm long. In grassland, up to 2400m. Stems spreading to erect, branching towards tips, leafy. **Plant covered in long straight hairs.** LEAVES variable, 12-20×2.5-7mm, broader below, narrow above. INFLORESCENCES terminal, compact to elongating; FLOWERS pink, ±4×2.5mm (Nov-Dec). GENERAL: Used as a love charm.

Polygala virgata Purple Broom; Bloukappies (A); hlokoa-le-lelle, ntsebele-ea-moru (SS); ithethe, ujulwezinyosi, umphehlwana, unohlonishwayo obomvu (Z)

(virgata - slender branches)
Slender shrub, 1.5-2m tall. On forest margins, on stabilised boulder beds, up to 2000m. SAfr to Tanz, Congo. **Single main stem, branching in upper third**. LEAVES ±20-60×3-20mm, stalks short, usually dropping before flowering. INFLORESCENCE dense, drooping, 30-200mm long; FLOWERS large, wings 10-17×9-13mm, pink to magenta, with darker veins (Nov-Jul). GENERAL: Heavily browsed. Used in traditional medicine as a blood purifier. Popular garden plant, hardy, free flowering, attracts carpenter-bees (incorrectly called bumble-bees). A good cut-flower.

Muraltia (named after John von Muralt, Swiss botanist and author) Shrubs or shrublets. Leaves small, dense, sharp-tipped, often pungently scented. Flowers small, solitary, lower petal with two winglike lobes. Fruit a flattened capsule, often tipped with horns. Afr, ±115 species, mostly SW Cape, 4 in this region.

Muraltia flanaganii (named after Henry Flanagan, E Cape naturalist and plant collector, one of the first people to collect plants in the high N Drakensberg)
Erect to prostrate shrublet, stems up to 600mm long. In valley scrub, on steep rocky slopes, rock outcrops, in grassland on the summit, 1525-3000m. EMR to Tanz. LEAVES ±10×3 mm, **blunt tipped**. FLOWERS mauve-pink, white to purple, **forming long terminal inflorescence**s (Oct-Mar).

Muraltia saxicola (saxicola - rock loving)
Shrublet, up to 200mm tall. Often in tangled masses, among rocks, in scrub on steep slopes, up to 2650m. E Cape to KZN. Woody rootstock, stems densely tufted. LEAVES in clusters, small, up to 7×2mm, **tips hooked backwards, sharply pointed**, margins thickened. FLOWERS ±5mm, at tips of dwarf side shoots among leaves, mauve-pink (Sep-Feb).

Polygala gracilenta

Muraltia flanaganii

Muraltia saxicola

Lorraine van Hooff

Neil Crouch

Lal Greene

Polygala myrtifolia

Neil Crouch

Muraltia flanaganii

Neil Crouch

Polygala ohlendorfiana

Martin von Fintel

Polygala virgata

Lal Greene

Polygala rhinostigma

Tony Abbott

211

BALSAMINACEAE - Balsam Family Soft, often fleshy perennial herbs, usually in damp places. Flowers asymmetrical, 3-5 sepals, back sepal petal-like, extended into a spur, side petals 2-lobed. Fruit splits elastically. Popular ornamentals. Trop and subtrop, 2 genera, ±850 species, 1 genus in SAfr. *Impatiens* (*impatiens* - impatient, refers to bursting pod which forcefully scatters seeds) 4 species in SAfr, 1 in this region.

Impatiens hochstetteri [= *I. duthiae*] **Common Wild Impatiens; Kruidjie-roer-my-nie (A); ihlula, umadolwane (Z)** (after C.G. Ferdinand von Hochstetter, 1829-84, German geologist and anthropologist)
Bushy soft herb, 200-600mm tall. In colonies in damp shade of forest, on mossy rocks, up to 1800m. Cape to Trop Afr. LEAVES 30-80×25-40mm, margins toothed, each tooth tipped with a hair **tapering to long, narrow tip**, stalks slender, 15-40mm long. FLOWERS in groups of 1-3, **small**, front petal and spur ±10 mm, pale pink or mauve, stalks slender, ±50mm long (Jan-Apr). FRUIT explodes open. GENERAL: Used in traditional medicine. Attractive ground cover for moist shady areas.

MALVACEAE - Hibiscus Family Flowers often with epicalyx (leafy whorl below calyx), stamens partly united into tube around style, branched above. Economically important for cotton and ornamentals such as hollyhocks and hibiscus. Cosmop, ±90 genera, ±2000 species, 22 genera in SAfr (7 exotic). *Anisodontea* (*aniso* - unequal; *odon* - toothed, refers to leaves) Epicalyx with 3-5 bracts. SAfr, 21 species, 2 in this region.

Anisodontea julii subsp. *pannosa* [= *Sphaeralcea pannosa*] **Ilefeta, letjeane-la-noka (SS)** (*pannosus* - ragged, refers to leaf margins)
Coarse perennial, straggling shrub, up to 2.4m tall. In scrub, among boulders, on roadsides, 1200-2300m. Young parts velvety, stems very hairy towards base. LEAVES **3-7-lobed**, ±75mm long, coarsely toothed, hairy at first, stalks long. FLOWERS **2-3**, in axils of leaves, ±40mm diam, shiny deep pink to purple (Feb-May).

Pavonia (named after José Antonia Pavon, 1754-1840, Spanish botanist, traveller) Herbs or shrubs, epicalyx of 5 or more bracts, close to 5-lobed calyx. Attracts butterflies. Warm countries, ±150 species, especially in America, 11 in SAfr, 1 in this region.

Pavonia columella **Pink Pavonia; indola ebomvu (Z)** (*columella* - small pillar)
Hairy, perennial herbaceous shrub, 1-2m tall. On steep moist slopes, riverine scrub, in moist cracks in rocks, up to 1950m. E Cape to CAfr. LEAVES 25-120×20-150mm, heart-shaped at base, 3-5-lobed, margins toothed, stalks up to 60mm long. FLOWERS **solitary or in small stalked clusters**, ±50mm diam, palest pink, epicalyx of 5 narrow bracts, stalks short, ±10mm long (Jan-May). GENERAL: Attractive garden plant.

ONAGRACEAE - Evening Primrose Family Herbs or shrubs. Flowers with 4 petals, stamens 4 or 8, style 4-lobed. Cosmop, especially Americas, ±17 genera, ±674 species, 4 genera in SAfr (2 introduced, naturalised). *Oenothera* (name used by Theophrastus) Flowers usually open in evening, close before midday. Popular ornamentals. N,S America, naturalized in Old World, ±125 species, 14 in SAfr ±4 in this region.

★*Oenothera rosea* **Rose Evening Primrose; Pienkaandblom, Rooskleurige nagblom (A); moopeli-o-mofubelu (SS)** (*rosea* - rose coloured)
Slender, much branched perennial herb, 200-500mm tall. In damp, disturbed areas, up to 2500m. Naturalized in SAfr (from S America). LEAVES 20-50mm, stalks 4-30 mm. FLOWERS **small**, bright pink, ±15mm diam, nodding before opening, opening near sunrise (Sep-Feb). FRUIT a club-shaped capsule, ±20×4mm, narrowly winged.

ERICACEAE - Erica / Heath Family (see pg 82) *Erica* (*ereiko* - to rend, refers to the reputed ability of some species to break down gallstones) Leaves in whorls or 3-4, margins, recurved. Flowers in terminal inflorescences or clustered in upper leaf axils. Hardy, attractive garden plants and cut-flowers. Mainly Afr, Europe, ±650 species, 600 in SAfr, mainly SW Cape, ±30 in this region. Sterile specimens can be easily mistaken for *Passerina* which has stringy bark, and *Cliffortia* which has alternate leaves, never in whorls of 3 or 4, and conspicuous stipules.

Erica aestiva (*aestiva* - flowering in summer)
Low growing shrublet. Forms mats or depressed cushions in grassland, among rocks, at edge of rock sheets, 1700-2750m. EMR endemic. LEAVES 2-4mm long, fine, on short side shoots, spreading to erect, overlapping. FLOWERS **sticky**, in masses, 3mm, purplish pink, bell-shaped, **narrowing to mouth**, style protruding (Feb-Jul).

Erica algida **lekhapu-le-leynyenyane, sehalahala (SS)** (*algida* - cold loving, refers to habitat)
Dwarf shrub, up to 300mm tall. Often in conspicuous large stands, on grassy slopes, valley bottoms, 1800-3000m. EMR endemic. Stems erect, downy. LEAVES clustered, ±5mm, needlike. FLOWERS pale pink to whitish, downy (Oct-Feb). GENERAL: Grey-brown when dry. Favoured fuel plant.

Erica alopecurus **Foxtail Erica; chalebeke-e-nyenyane, chesa-litelu, molomo-oa-lekolukotaoane (SS)** (*alopex* - refers to the inflorescence that resembles a fox's tail)
Compact, tufted dwarf shrub, up to 300mm tall. In damp grassy streambanks, marshy grassland, 1370-3000m. E Cape to Mpum. LEAVES in 3s, erect, incurving, midrib visible beneath. FLOWERS pink, massed in **dense, cylindrical spikes** (Jan-Jul). GENERAL: Used as fuel.

Anisodontea julii

Hilliard & Burtt

Pavonia columella

Lorraine van Hooff

★*Oenothera rosea*

Lorraine van Hooff

Anisodontea julii

Lorraine van Hooff

Impatiens hochstetteri

Martin von Fintel

Erica aestiva

Simon Milliken

Erica algida

Martin von Fintel

Erica alopecurus

Cameron McMaster

Erica aestiva

Martin von Fintel

Erica algida

Peter Linder

Erica alopecurus

Peter Linder

213

Erica cooperi (named after Thomas Cooper, 1815-1913, English plant collector and cultivator who came to live SAfr in 1859, son-in-law of J Medley-Wood)

Stout, rigid, much branched shrub, up to 1m tall. In grassland, up to 1800m. EMR endemic. Branches rough, with spreading hairs. LEAVES in 4s, mostly spreading, rough-hairy, paler beneath. FLOWERS white to **pale pink**, hairy, lobes spreading in 4s, **held together in small round clusters by intermingling hairs** (Feb-Jul).

Erica dominans lekhapu (SS) (*dominans* - ruling, refers to its dominance in the summit heath)

Much branched, erect or prostrate shrub, 150-450mm tall on summit, up to 1.2m tall on steep slopes down to 1900m. Dominant on grass slopes, in large stands among rocks on summit plateau up to 3000m, also on steep rocky slops, near streams, on Cave Sandstone platforms down to 1900m. EMR endemic. LEAVES 2-3×0.75-1mm, olive-green, glossy, overlapping, held erect, close to the stem, margins with forked hairs on young leaves, tall specimens have larger leaves, 19-33mm long. FLOWERS **in nodding heads**, **very small**, 2-3mm long, funnel-shaped, **pink or red**, **stigma well exserted**, calyx conspicuous (Sep-Jan). GENERAL: A popular fuel plant in Les. **Similar species:** *Erica dissimulans* (*dissimulans* - dissimilar) Shrub up to 1.2m tall. **In rocky stream gullies**, **near water**, on wet cliffs, 1825-2600m. EMR endemic. LEAVES proportionally narrower than *E. dominans*, 3-7×0.5-0.75mm, margins with small glands. FLOWERS reddish, soon turning brown (Jul-Aug, Oct-Dec).

Erica frigida khoarai (SS) (*frigida* - refers to its liking for high altitudes)

Small, dense shrublet, up to 500mm tall or in mats. Frequent on cliffs and very steep slopes, 1900-3300m. EMR endemic. Branches slender, straggling, hairy. LEAVES ± recurved, covered in long hairs, spreading at right angles to stem. FLOWERS **sticky**, often **white**, sometimes **pink** (red) (Nov-Feb).

Erica schlechteri (named after Friedrich R.R. Schlechter, 1872-1925, botanist and traveller. Worked in the Cape from 1891 to1898, collecting plants widely in SA)

Erect shrub up to 1m tall. Often in conspicuous stands, on grassy slopes, in valleys near streams, on Cave Sandstone platforms, 1500-2600m. EMR endemic. LEAVES ±5mm long, in 4s, **erect**, **overlapping**, narrow, grooved, blunt tipped. FLOWERS **pink** or whitish, 5-7mm long, **sticky**, in terminal clusters of 3-4 (Nov-Feb).

Erica straussiana (named after Berlin gardener Obergartner Strauss)

Spreading, leafy shrublet, ±600mm tall (up to 1m). Often in conspicuous stands, on rocky grass slopes, valley bottoms, Cave Sandstone ridges and platforms, 1600-2560m. EMR endemic. LEAVES in 3s, ± leathery, 8-10×1mm. FLOWERS **pink** or white, ±6mm long, calyx conspicuous, **sepals as long or longer than corolla** (Nov-Jan).

Erica woodii Pienkheide (A); hlaha-hlaha, tlali-tlali (SS) (named after John Medley Wood, 1827-1915, botanist, founding curator of Natal Herbarium)

Spreading tufted shrublet, up to 600mm high, sometimes forming spreading mats. On rocky ground, up to 2560m. E Cape to Limpopo Prov. LEAVES crowded on short side branches, 2-4mm long, **with conspicuous long**, **white**, **pointed hairs**. FLOWERS in axils, **massed**, **± forming spikes**, ±2mm, white, cup-shaped, sepals dark red, stigma swollen, protruding, stalks dark red (Jan-Feb). GENERAL: *Subsp. woodii*, in grassland up to 2200m. FLOWERS white, stigmas just exserted. *Subsp. platyura*, on earth cliffs near watercouses, up to 2550 (2700)m. EMR endemic. FLOWERS deep pink (white), **stigma well exserted**.

GENTIANACEAE - Gentian Family (see p 140) *Chironia* (named after Chiron, a centaur who studied medicine, astronomy, music and arts) Leaves opposite, usually stalkless. Flowers in loose inflorescences, anthers sometimes spirally twisted. Fruit a capsule, dry or berrylike. Afr, Madag, ±30 species, ±15 in SAfr, ±3 in this region.

Chironia krebsii Kreb's Chironia; khomo-ea-sephatla, lehlapahali, ´mamorulane, mosia (SS); umanqunduswazi, umbangwangwa (Z) (Georg Krebs, 1792-1844, apothecary, naturalist, visited SA)

Herb, 400-700mm tall. In marshy places, up to 2450m. E Cape to Mpum. **Creeping rhizome**. STEMS unbranched, erect. LEAVES long, crowded at base, 90-300×6-17mm, stem leaves smaller. INFLORESCENCE narrow; FLOWERS crowded, ±26mm diam, lobes pointed, tube 10-20mm, deep pink, anthers twisted, **stigma 2-lobed** (Nov-Jan). GENERAL: Used in traditional medicine to treat colic and diarrhoea in children, uneasiness in pregnant women. Attractive plant in the garden in damp places.

Auriol Batten

Erica cooperi

Hilliard & Burtt

Erica dominans

David McDonald

Erica frigida

Peter Linder

Erica frigida

Neil Crouch

Erica straussiana

D Schumann

Erica schlechteri

David McDonald

Erica woodii

Martin von Fintel

Erica woodii

Neil Crouch

Chironia krebsii

215

ASCLEPIADACEAE - Milkweed Family (see pg 140) *Pachycarpus* (see pg 260, 268)

Pachycarpus vexillaris Mountain Pachycarpus / Thickfruit; leshokhoa (SS) (see pg 260)

Asclepias (named after the Greek doctor Aesculapius who was immortalised in ancient mythology as a god of medicine) Perennial geophytic herbs with milky latex. Stems annual, from a turniplike or deeply rooted cylindrical fleshy tuber. Flower lobes free to base, spreading or reflexed, corona lobes with a central cavity; fruits solitary (rarely paired), spindlelike, smooth, warty or with long spiny hairs. Genus undergoing revision at present.

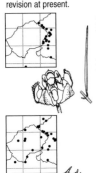

Asclepias cucullata [= *Trachycalymma cucullatum*] Hooded Meadow-star; udambisa, udelunina (Z) (*cucullatus* - hooded, refers to corona lobe shape)

Slender herb, stems reclining, 170-350mm long, tips erect. In open, often burnt grassland, amongst rocks, 1000-2400m. E Cape to Limpopo Prov. Leaves long, narrow, 7-10×**0.3-4mm**, margins rolled under, midrib prominent below, covered in short harsh hairs. Inflorescences **erect**, stems 20-80mm long; flowers **in 4s**, **starlike**, lobes creamy brown or pink, tips turned up, 6-7.5×3-5mm, **corona lobes helmet-shaped** (Sep-Feb). General: Visited by beetles. Used in traditional medicine.

Asclepias gibba Humped Turret-flower; montsokoane, montsoko, montsuku, motsoko, motsuku (SS); umanqanda (Z) (*gibbus* - humplike swelling, refers to the hump on the back of the corona lobe)

Herb, up to 300(450)mm tall. In grassland, up to 2500m. E Cape to Bots. Stems branched from base. Leaves 10-105×1-6mm. Inflorescences **terminal, solitary, erect**; flowers lobes reflexed 6.5-12×2.5-5mm, silvery grey, greeny mauve, **corona lobes clawlike, much taller than broad, 4.5-8.5mm tall, keel with humplike swellings, anther wing with distinct notch** (Nov-Feb). Fruit 50-105×6-12mm, with long pointed beak, smooth with pale stripes. General: Visited by bees. Rootstock eaten. Nectar laden flowers eaten by children as sweets. Used to treat snakebite.

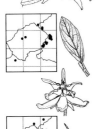

Asclepias humilis Drakensberg Meadow-star; sehoete (SS) (*humilis* - low growing, refers to habit)

Low growing, erect herb, 50-200mm tall. In mountain grassland, 1800-2900m. EMR endemic. Stems 1-2, branched at base. Leaves soft, **crowded near base, oblong,** 19-75×**4.5-18mm, spreading erect**, veins protrude beneath, **covered in long white hairs**. Inflorescences 1(2-4), erect, stems 12-25mm long; flowers **in 4s, large, slipper-shaped lobes**, white tinged brownish or reddish mauve, tips turned up, 8-11×4-5mm, **corona large**, white, lobes slipper-shaped, **6-8.5mm long**, anther appendages rounded to kidney-shaped (Oct-Jan). General: Rootstock eaten.

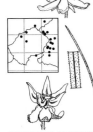

Asclepias stellifera Common Meadow-star; khola-ntja, mohola-ntja (SS) (*stellifera* - starlike, refers to flower shape)

Slender, erect or slightly reclining herb, branching from base, 120-300mm tall. In open grassland, on stony ground, up to 2200m. E Cape to Bots. Leaves long, narrow, 10-105×0.5-2mm, **midrib very prominent below**, margins rolled under, covered in short, harsh hairs. Flowers **in 4s**, stems up to 50mm long, **starlike, large, lobes reflexed**, tips turned up, 4.5-7×3-4mm, **corona lobes slipper-shaped, large, 4-7.5mm long** (Sep-Jan). Fruit erect, narrow, 60-100×5-12mm, tip narrowly beaked, smooth. General: Often appears in burned grasslands after first spring rains.

LABIATAE / LAMIACEAE - Sage/Mint Family (see pg 86) *Stachys* (Greek for spike, originally an ear of wheat) (see pg 86)

Stachys rugosa taraputsoe (SS) (*rugosa* - wrinkled)

Much branched shrub, 0.3-1.2m tall. Rocky mountain slopes, 2500-3000m. Stems densely white-hairy, greyish black with age. Leaves 13-80×3-20mm, thinly hairy above, whitish beneath, **conspicuously wrinkled**. Flowers in ±6-flowered clusters, well spaced, bracts leaflike below, pink to purple, tube 5-7mm long, upper lip 3-6mm, calyx densely hairy. General: Used for a herbal tea.

Satureja (Latin for savoury herb) Herbs or subshrubs. Leaves with minty smell. Cosmop, ±30 species, ±4 in SAfr, all in this region.

Satureja reptans (*reptans* - creeping and rooting)

Trailing perennial herb, 250-600mm. In grassland, 1500-2500m. EMR endemic. Stems slender, hairy. Leaves 16-24×12-20mm, margins toothed. Flowers 10-15mm long, white to pale blue, flushed pink in throat with a yellow stripe, **bracts small, slender**, stalks slender, 10-25mm (Dec-Apr). **Similar species: *Satureja compacta*** (refers to compact habit) Creeping, mat forming. On damp ground between grass tussocks, 1800-2300m. EMR endemic. Leaves **small, 5-11×4-10mm**. Flowers **small**, 6-7mm long (Nov-Mar). *Satureja grandibracteata* (*grandis* - large, *bracteata* - bracts) N Drak. Flowers **large, 18-20mm long, bracts leaflike**.

Hilliard & Burtt

Pachycarpus vexillaris

Martin von Fintel

Asclepias cucullata

Martin von Fintel

Asclepias stellifera

Peter Linder

Asclepias humillis

Lal Greene

Satureja compacta

Tom de Waal

Ashley Nicholas

Asclepias gibba

Peter Linder

Mike Hirst

Stachys rugosa   *Satureja reptans*   *Asclepias gibba*

217

Mentha (Latin for mint) Aromatic herbs. Flowers small, in congested inflorescences. Some grown for essential oils or as culinary herbs, such as peppermint, spearmint, pennyroyal. Mostly temp, ±25 species, 2 in SAfr, both in this region.

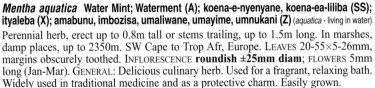

Mentha aquatica Water Mint; Waterment (A); koena-e-nyenyane, koena-ea-liliba (SS); ityaleba (X); amabunu, imbozisa, umaliwane, umayime, umnukani (Z) (*aquatica* - living in water)

Perennial herb, erect up to 0.8m tall or stems trailing, up to 1.5m long. In marshes, damp places, up to 2350m. SW Cape to Trop Afr, Europe. LEAVES 20-55×5-26mm, margins obscurely toothed. INFLORESCENCE **roundish ±25mm diam**; FLOWERS 5mm long (Jan-Mar). GENERAL: Delicious culinary herb. Used for a fragrant, relaxing bath. Widely used in traditional medicine and as a protective charm. Easily grown.

Mentha longifolia Wild Spearmint; Kruisement (A); koena-ea-thaba (SS); inxina, inzinziniba (X); ufuthane lomhlanga (Z) (*longifolia* - long leaves)

Perennial herb, up to 1.5m tall. On streamsides, in damp places, up to 2400m. Cape to Ethiopia, Europe, E Asia. LEAVES 45-100×7-20mm, margins with widely spaced teeth, **stalkless**, strongly aromatic. Subsp. *capensis* leaves velvety white beneath, dark green above. GENERAL: Used in traditional medicine. Easily grown.

Syncolostemon (*syn* - united; *kolos* - stunted; *stemon* - pillar, refers to the filaments) Herbs, rarely woody. Leaves on short leafy branchlets. Flowers in dense, branched infloresces, calyx 2-lipped, 5-lobed. SAfr endemic, 10 species, 1 in this region.

Syncolostemon macranthus Long-flowered Pink Plume (*macranthus* - large flowers)

Much branched, aromatic shrub, 1-2.5m tall. Along streams, on forest margins, in shrubby grassland, 1600-2200m. EMR endemic. LEAVES 20-45×12-20mm, **rough**, margins faintly toothed, stalks short, 2-8mm. INFLORESCENCE branched, 80-180mm long; FLOWERS in small clusters, 25-30mm long, pink to purple, calyx cylindrical, ±10mm, densely hairy, upper lobe larger than lower narrow lobes (Nov-May).

SCROPHULARIACEAE - Snapdragon Family (see pg 90) ***Diascia*** (*di* - two; *askion* - bladder, refers to the two flower pouches in first species described) Flowers usually with 1 or 2 translucent yellow patches (windows), forming shallow pouches behind, tube very short or absent, **twin spurs.** Cultivated as ornamentals in Europe, much hybridised. Pollinated by oil-collecting bees. Used as pot herbs. SAfr. ±60 species, ±11 in this region.

Diascia anastrepta Upturned Twinspur; Opswaai-diascia (A) (*anastreptos* - turned up)

Trailing, much branched herb, 150-350mm tall, **forming loose tangled masses**. In damp places at foot of basalt cliffs, in grass tufts along rocky watercourses, 1800-3000m. EMR endemic. Stems square, leafy. LEAVES 10-25×8-20mm, margins ± **toothed**. FLOWERS pink, with two patches of dark glands on palate, **window concave**, **spurs conspicuous, spread wide, tips upturned**, stalks 15-40mm (Nov-Mar).

Diascia barberae (after Mrs Barber, from E Cape, who, with her brother Col. Bowker, first sent it to Kew in 1869)

Tufted perennial herb, up to 450mm tall. On boulder beds, gravel patches in streams, damp banks and bases of cliffs, 1675-2900m. EMR endemic. Stems ± erect, leafy. LEAVES 10-25×5-20mm, margins toothed. INFLORESCENCE loose, leafy; FLOWERS large, bright pink, window yellow, marked maroon, with **two patches of dark glands** on the palate, **spurs conspicuous, incurved, calyx reflexed** (Dec-Feb).

Diascia cordata (*cordata* - heart-shaped)

Sprawling herb, stems up to 600mm long. In rank vegetation along streams, on damp slopes, 1400-2400m. LEAVES 12-30×8-20mm, **margins sharply toothed**. INFLORESCENCE slender, 50-200mm long; FLOWERS ±18mm wide, pink, central patch of dark glands on palate, **spurs blunt, conspicuous, diverging widely** (Nov-Mar).

Diascia integerrima Twinspur; Pensies (A); bolao-ba-litoeba, leilanenyana (SS) (*integerrima* - perfect)

Slender, erect, tufted herb, 200-500mm tall. In crevices of cliffs, rocky areas, loose or hard dry gritty soil, along streambanks, conspicuous along roadsides, up to 2865m. LEAVES **narrow**, 13-40×1-3mm. FLOWERS ±10×20mm, petal lobes rounded, keel raised, usually covered in dark gland dots on mouth, window yellow and maroon, **spurs incurved at tips, held straight down**, calyx lobes spreading (Dec-Mar). GENERAL: Hardy, long flowering garden plant.

Diascia purpurea (*purpurea* - purple)

Perennial herb, up to 450mm tall. On moist bare patches, in rough grassland, 1675-2440m. EMR endemic. Stems few. LEAVES 20-45×15-50mm, thick, dark green above, **deep purple below**, margins toothed. FLOWERS nodding, light to dark salmon-pink, **spurs very short, curved in** under bowl of corolla tube (Jan-Apr).

Syncolostemon macranthus

Simon Milliken

Mentha aquatica

Pam Cooke

Mentha longifolia

John Grimshaw

Diascia barberae

David McDonald

Diascia anastrepta

Mike Hirst

Diascia purpurea

Rodney Moffett

Diascia barberae

Peter Linder

Diascia integerrima

Mike Hirst

Diascia cordata

David McDonald

Diascia cordata

Pam Cooke

Diascia integerrima

Mike Hirst

219

Nemesia (from *Nemesion*, name used by Dioscorides for similar plant) (see pg 90)

Nemesia rupicola (*rupicola* - rock loving)
Well branched, 300-750mm tall. In boulder beds, rock tumbles, on mountains, 1800-2650m. KZN to Limpopo Prov. LEAVES 20-45×10-20mm, margins coarsely toothed, stalks 5-15mm long. INFLORESCENCE never becoming long and slender, **bracts large and leafy**; FLOWERS **clustered**, white, pink, pale mauve, **palate yellow, no humps/bosses at mouth of spur**, spur short, up to 3.5mm long (Nov-Apr).

Diclis (*diclis* - double folding, a reference to bilobed spur) (see pg 90)

Diclis rotundifolia (*rotundifolia* - round leaves) (see pg 90)

Graderia (anagram of *Gerardia*) Perennial herbs or subshrubs. Afr, 5 species, 3 species in SAfr, 1 in this region.

Graderia scabra Pink Ground-bells; impundu, isimonyo, ugweja, umphuphutho (Z)
(*scabra* - rough, refers to hairs on leaves and stem)
Tufted perennial herb, up to 300mm tall. In grassland, up to 2100m. E Cape to Zim. Stems ± hairy. LEAVES overlapping, ±50×15mm, margins entire or with a few teeth, stalkless. FLOWERS ±30mm, pink, deep mauve, reddish, whitish, thinly hairy, in upper leaf axils (Oct-Dec). GENERAL: Used in traditional medicine as love charm emetics.

Sopubia (Indian common name for this plant) Perennial herbs, root parasites. Leaves narrow or deeply dissected. Flowers regular, solitary in upper leaf axils, forming slender, elongate inflorescences. Trop Afr, Madag, Himalayas to Indo China, ±30 species, 4 in SAfr, 1 in this region.

Sopubia cana Silvery Sopubia; leilane, pulumo-tšoeu (SS) (*cana* - grey)
Velvety silvery grey perennial herb or shrublet, up to 450mm tall. In grassland, up to 2100m. E Cape to Trop Afr. LEAVES ±25×2mm. INFLORESCENCES dense, terminal; FLOWERS 8-20mm diam, pink, **petals delicate, crinkly**, plentiful nectar (Dec-Mar). GENERAL: Conspicuous after fires. Parasitic on grasses. Used in traditional medicine.

Buchnera (named after 18th Century German naturalist J. Buchner) Perennial herbs, often parasitic. Flowers regular, in axils of bracts, forming spikelike inflorescences. Trop, subtrop, mostly Old World, ±100 species, ±9 in SAfr, 2 in this region.

Buchnera simplex [= *B. glabrata*] umusa omkhulu (Z) (*simplex* - simple)
Slender erect perennial herb, up to 600mm tall. In damp grassland, up to 2400m. SW Cape to Limpopo Prov. Stems unbranched. LEAVES basal, ±70×15mm, 3-veined, margins with few small teeth, stem leaves few. INFLORESCENCE small, congested, (elongate in fruit); FLOWERS ±5mm diam, blue to lilac or white, **tube ± hairless outside** (Sep-May). GENERAL: Used as a love charm emetic.

Cycnium (*kyknos* - swan, probably refers to the slender, elongated, white flower tube) Perennial **parasitic herbs**. Flowers nearly regular, large, in axils, forming terminal inflorescences. Afr, ±15 species, ±4 in SAfr, 1 in this region.

Cycnium racemosum Large Pink Ink Plant; Berginkplant (A); injanga (X); uhlaba-hlangane (Z) (*racemosum* - inflorescence a raceme)
Erect, usually unbranched herb, up to 750mm tall. In grassland, among rock outcrops, up to 2600m. E Cape to Mpum. Stem ribbed, rough. LEAVES large, ±80×20mm, rough, margins purplish red, **prominent toothed**. INFLORESCENCE ± branched; FLOWERS **large, ±60mm** wide, tube ±25mm long, deep pink, **stalks short**, fragrant (Nov-Dec). GENERAL: Flowers turn black when bruised. Used in traditional medicine.

Striga (*striga* - harsh, refers to the hairs on stems and leaves) Parasitic herbs. Afr, Asia, Austr, ±40 species, ±7 in SAfr, ±4 in this region.

Striga bilabiata Small Witchweed; seona (SS); isinone esimhlophe, isona (Z) (*bilabiata* - divided into two lips)
Small, erect, tufted herb, up to 300mm tall. In grassland, up to 1800m. Widespread in SAfr. Stems sometimes branched, purplish at base, roughly hairy throughout. LEAVES erect or spreading, ±20×1mm. FLOWERS **2-lipped**, lilac, in dense terminal spikes (Dec-Jan).

Harveya (named after Dr William Harvey, 1811-1866, chief author of early volumes of Flora Capensis, Prof of botany in Dublin, Ireland) Parasitic herbs. Leaves reduced to scales. Mostly Afr, ±40 species, ±25 in SAfr, ±4 in this region.

Harveya pulchra (*pulchra* - beautiful)
Parasitic herb, about 200mm tall. In gritty soil on slopes, in gullies, 1900-3000m. EMR endemic. FLOWERS small, pink with **yellow throat, petals 8-12mm long**, calyx 17-23mm, teeth 4-5mm long (Jan-Mar). **Similar species:** *Harveya leucopharynx* (*leucopharynx* - white throat) 150-450mm tall. In damp grassy rocky places, damp scrub, 1800-2550m. EMR endemic. FLOWERS large, ±30-40mm, **throat white, petals 14-17mm long**, calyx 20-30mm, teeth 5-10mm long, scent fruity (Nov-Feb). (see dedication pg)

Diclis rotundifolia

Neil Crouch

Nemesia rupicola

Mike Hirst

Sopubia cana

David McDonald

Harveya pulchra

David McDonald

Buchnera simplex

Neil Crouch

Graderia scabra

Martin von Fintel

Graderia scabra

Pam Cooke

Cycnium racemosum

David McDonald

Striga bilabiata

David McDonald

221

LOBELIACEAE - Lobelia Family (see pg 242) *Cyphia* (*kyphos* - twiner) Perennial herbs, erect or twining. (see pg 100)

Cyphia tysonii (named after William Tyson, 1851-1920, teacher and plant collector)
Perennial twining herb, on grasses. In grassland, 1250-2300(1800)m. KZN to Mpum. Stems hairless. LEAVES 20-50×1-4mm, margins entire or with tiny, widely separated, teeth, narrowing to short stalk. INFLORESCENCES loose, **twining**; FLOWERS solitary (or in clusters of 2-5), ±18mm long, white or lilac (Jan-Mar).

COMPOSITAE (refers to the composite nature of flowerheads), also called **ASTERACEAE - Daisy Family** (see pg 144) *Aster* (see pg 144)

Aster ananthocladus (*ananthocladus* - with flowerless shoots)
Up to 300mm tall. In colonies, on damp, steep grass slopes, 1800-2500m. EMR endemic. STEMS **very slender**, simple or with 2-3 very slender branches that seldom bear flowerheads. STEM LEAVES up to 25×2mm, 1-veined, margins thickened, rough, **basal leaves hairy**, purple below. FLOWERHEADS **solitary**, ±25mm across, rays palest lilac, disc yellow (Dec-Jan). GENERAL: Conspicuous in green grass after late fires.

Aster bakerianus **phoa (SS); noxgxekana, umthekisana (X); udlatshana, umaqhunsula, umhlungwana (Z)** (see pg 100)

Aster erucifolius **mohantšoane-os-loti (SS)** (*erucifolius* - leaves like *Eruca*, Cruciferae)
Perennial herb with prostrate branching stems. In marshy ground, on damp, silty or gravelly patches among rock sheets, wet scree on summit plateau only, 2375-3050m. EMR endemic. Covered in sparse, harsh hairs. **Stems, flower stalks, bracts deep red**. LEAVES up to 30×10mm, **deeply lobed**. FLOWERHEADS 20-30mm diam, rays mauve, blue, purple or white, disc yellow, stalks short, leafy (Feb-Apr). GENERAL: Growth form varies from single rosette to a well branched plant up to 600mm across.

Aster perfoliatus **Grysblaar-aster (A); khotolia-ea-thaba (SS)** (*perfoliatus* - stem as if it were passing through the leaf)
Perennial herb, up to 600mm tall. In colonies, on stony grass slopes, around rock outcrops, 1500-2300m. E Cape, Les, KZN. **One to several stems from base, hairless throughout**, leaves mostly on lower half. LEAVES up to 50×40mm, **leathery, veins prominent, base of leaves encircle stem**. FLOWERHEADS ±40mm across, ray florets blue, mauve, disc florets yellow, bracts dark keeled, margins papery (Oct-Dec).

Felicia (after Herr Felix, died 1846, a German official at Regensburg) Herbs with hairy fruits. Afr, ±80 species, mainly SAfr, ±11 in this region.

Felicia quinquenervia [= *Aster quinquenervius*] (*quinque* - five; *nervia* - nerve or leaf vein)
Robust, perennial herb, up to 500mm tall, often in large colonies. In damp grassland, near streams (1200)1800-2500m. E Cape to KZN/Mpum. LEAVES **large, up to 150×30mm**, erect, mostly in basal tufts, **thin**, roughly hairy or hairless, **margins with peglike glands**. FLOWERHEADS 25-30mm diam, pink, mauve or magenta, disc yellow, **solitary or in branched inflorescence**, flowering stems hairy, glandular (Nov-Apr).

Denekia (after a Dutch botanist friend of Thunberg who described the genus) Perennial herb, greyish or white woolly. SAfr, Angola, 1 species.

Denekia capensis **toane-mohlaka (SS)** (see pg 102)

Helichrysum (*helios* - sun; *chrysos* - gold) Herbs, shrubs, sometimes dwarfed and cushion forming. Usually hairy or woolly. Flowerheads solitary or in compact or spreading inflorescences. Mainly Afr. a large genus.

Helichrysum caespititium **Speelwonderblom (A); phate-ea-ngaka, boriba, botsikinyane, lelula-phooko, mafole, moriri-oa-lefatse (SS)** (*caespitosa* - tufted, forming a carpet)
Prostrate, carpet forming perennial herb, ±10mm tall. On bare areas, up to 2400m. Widespread in SAfr. LEAVES 5-10×0.5mm, spreading, margins rolled under, with **silvery tissue-paperlike covering**. FLOWERHEADS ±5×2mm, bracts webbed together with wool, **tips white or pink**, disc florets yellow tipped pink (Aug-Dec). GENERAL: Used in traditional medicine to treat colds, nausea, roots used for virility.

Helichrysum spiralepis [= *Leontonyx squarrosus*] **mosuoane-oa-metsi, toane-ea-metsi (SS)** (*spiralepis* - spirally arranged bracts)
Tufted herb, up to 300mm tall. In grassland, up to 2500m. SW Cape to Zim. Stems simple or branched from near base. LEAVES in rosette, basal ones up to 70×15mm. FLOWERHEADS ±5×3mm, narrowly bell-shaped, **in small congested clusters surrounded by leafy bracts, in compact or spreading inflorescences**, bracts webbed to leaves, outer shorter woolly, inner longer, whitish cream or pinkish red, **tips often sharply pointed, recurved**, flowers sweetly or honey scented (Dec-Apr).

Neil Crouch

Cyphia tysonii

Wally Menne

Aster bakerianus

Hilliard & Burtt

Aster ananthocladus

Pam Cooke

Aster erucifolius

Lorraine van Hooff

Aster perfoliatus

Van Wyk & Malan

Helichrysum caespititium

Hilliard & Burtt

Felicia quinquenervia

Martin von Fintel

Denekia capensis

John Grimshaw

Helichrysum spiralepis

223

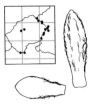

Helichrysum retortoides (resembling H. retortum)

Mat-forming, prostrate shrublet, flowering stems up to 200mm tall, closely leafy. On steep rocky slopes, among boulders, in crevices of rock sheets, dominant in places on the summit plateau, 2200-3350m. EMR endemic. Main stems thick, woody with age. LEAVES up to 10×3mm, with smooth **'tissue paper' covering above, white-felted below**. FLOWERHEADS solitary, **±20mm long**, 30mm across spreading bracts, bracts in ±9 series, outer much shorter and broader than inner, glossy brown tinged red, inner bracts much longer than florets, white or tinged deep pink to red (Sep-Dec).

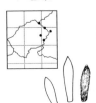

Helichrysum praecurrens (praecurrens - creeping)

Densely tufted, mat-forming herb. On bare or sparsely grassed areas, above 3000m. EMR endemic. Main stems prostrate, branching, bare, with **numerous erect, closely leafy branchlets up to 20mm tall.** LEAVES up to 7×2mm, closely overlapping, **appearing rosetted from above**, with tissue paperlike covering. FLOWERHEADS small, **±10mm long**, 20mm across spreading bracts, bracts in ±7 series, outer palest brown, inner white or tinged deep pink (Nov-Dec).

Helichrysum sessilioides (sessilioides - resembling H. sessile) (see pg 106)

Helichrysum adenocarpum   Pienk- of Rooisewejaartjie (A); senkotoana, toane-balingoana (SS); uhlambahloshane obomvu (Z) (adenocarpum - glandular fruits)

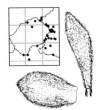

Perennial herb, flowering stems 40-450mm tall, reclining or erect. In grassland, on moist slopes, up to 3000m. E Cape to Zim, Moz. LEAVES prostrate, **roundish**, 20-40(140)×15-25(40)mm, **grey-woolly**. FLOWERHEADS solitary (rarely in branched inflorescence), 25-35mm across spreading bracts, **flowering stems produced from the side of the rosettes**, reclining or erect, **bracts glossy red, pink**, sometimes white (Jan-Sep). GENERAL: Size, shape, hairiness and colour very variable. Used in traditional medicine to treat diarrhoea and vomiting in children. Lovely garden plant.

Helichrysum ecklonis [= H. calocephalum, H. lamprocephalum, H. scapiforme] Ecklon's Everlasting; toane-balingoana-e-kholo, toane-ea-loti (SS); umthi wechanti (X) (named after Christian Ecklon, 1795-1868, apothecary, traveller and plant collector)

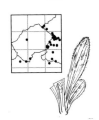

Tufted perennial herb, flowering stems up to 500mm tall. On grassy slopes, in large colonies, up to 2750m. E Cape to Mpum. BASAL LEAVES rosetted, up to 100(200)×20mm, upper surface loosely woolly cobwebby, sometimes hairless and then **3-5 veins visible, upper surface margins and lower surface downy wooll**y. FLOWERHEADS **large, solitary**, 50-60mm across spreading bracts, bracts in ±10 series, loosely overlapping, much longer than the flowers, **glossy white to deep pink** (Sep-Dec). GENERAL: Used in traditional medicine to treat diarrhoea. (see pg 108)

Helichrysum lingulatum (lingulate - tongue-shaped, refers to the leaves)

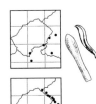

Mat-forming with crowded leaf rosettes, up to 180mm tall. In large mats on hard bare earth or stony turf, 1500-2200m. E Cape, KZN. LEAVES up to 35×8mm, **tonguelike**, tips rounded, **grey woolly**. FLOWERHEADS solitary, ±20mm long across spreading (radiating) bracts, bracts **glossy, delicate pink at first**, fading to white (Sep-Nov). (see pg 108)

Helichrysum vernum (vernum - of the spring, referring to the plants which are one of the first to flower in spring)

Mat-forming perennial herb. On stony grassy slopes, 1675-2560m. EMR endemic. LEAVES in crowded rosettes, up to 50×15mm, **thick, leathery**, loosely cobwebby above at first, becoming **hairless, margins woolly, usually only midvein visible**. FLOWERHEADS solitary, large, 50-60mm across spreading bracts, often stalkless or stalks up to 250mm tall (elongating only under good conditions), bracts pointed, longer than flowers, **rich glossy pink to almost red** (white) (Sep-Nov). GENERAL: Easily confused with *H. ecklonis* which does not form mats, leaf veins clearly visible.

Athrixia (a - without; thrix - hair) Erect perennial herbs or shrubs. Afr, Madag, ±14 species, 9 in SAfr, ±5 in this region.

Athrixia arachnoidea (arachnoidea - spidery, refers to the cobwebby indumentum on the involucre)

Stiffly erect, tufted perennial herb, up to 350mm tall. On rocky slopes 1800-2400m. EMR to Mpum. **Stems stout**, simple or ±branching above, leafy. LEAVES up to 30×3mm, spreading, **rigid**, white-felted below, margins rolled under. FLOWERHEADS stalkless, rays **mauve**, disc yellow, stalkless, **bracts bristle-tipped, recurved, cobwebby** (Jun-Sep). GENERAL: Winter flowering.

Helichrysum retortoides

Helichrysum lingulatum

Helichrysum retortoides

Helichrysum praecurrens

Helichrysum sessilioides

Helichrysum ecklonis

Helichrysum adenocarpum

Helichrysum vernum

Athrixia arachnoidea

225

Printzia Shrubs. SAfr endemic, 6 species, 4 in this region.

Printzia laxa [= *P. densifolia*] Giant Daisy Bush; sephomolo (SS) (*laxus* - loose)

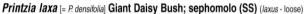

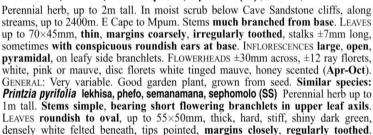

Perennial herb, up to 2m tall. In moist scrub below Cave Sandstone cliffs, along streams, up to 2400m. E Cape to Mpum. Stems **much branched from base**. LEAVES up to 70×45mm, **thin, margins coarsely, irregularly toothed**, stalks ±7mm long, sometimes **with conspicuous roundish ears at base**. INFLORESCENCES **large, open, pyramidal**, on leafy side branchlets. FLOWERHEADS ±30mm across, ±12 ray florets, white, pink or mauve, disc florets white tinged mauve, honey scented (**Apr-Oct**). GENERAL: Very variable. Good garden plant, grown from seed. **Similar species: *Printzia pyrifolia* lekhisa, phefo, semanamana, sephomolo (SS)** Perennial herb up to 1m tall. **Stems simple, bearing short flowering branchlets in upper leaf axils.** LEAVES **roundish to oval**, up to 55×50mm, thick, hard, stiff, shiny dark green, densely white felted beneath, tips pointed, **margins closely, regularly toothed**. INFLORESCENCE **oblong**; FLOWERHEADS with ±21 ray florets, sweetly scented (**Dec-Jun**). GENERAL: Used in traditional medicine to treat internal tumours.

Bidens - Black-jacks/Cosmos (*bidens* - 2-toothed, refers to hooks on fruits) Cosmop, ±233 species, ±6 in SAfr, including introduced weeds.

★*Bidens formosa* [= *Cosmos bipinnata*] Cosmos; Kosmos (A); moqhoboqhobo (SS) (*formosa* - beautiful)

Bushy annual herb, up to 2.5m tall, often seen in spectacular stands. A naturalised weed, on roadsides, disturbed places. Introduced in fodder in the late 1890s from USA. LEAVES opposite, ±100×50mm, deeply lobed. FLOWERHEADS large, ±90mm diam, solitary, on long bare stalks, ray florets **white, pink or deep red** (Feb-May).

Senecio (*senex* - old man, refers to whitish hairs of pappus) Herbs, shrubs, rarely trees (see pg 162)

Senecio macrocephalus ngoakoane-ea-loti, sebea-mollo (SS); ihlaba lenkomo (X)
(*macrocephalus* - large head)

Tufted, **glandular hairy** perennial herb, 150-600mm tall. In damp, open grassland, around wet rock sheets, up to 3200m. E Cape to Mpum. LEAVES mostly basal, up to 150×30mm, narrowed to base, thick, **margins entire or shallowly toothed**. FLOWERHEADS 30-40mm diam, rays and disc deep pink to purple, solitary or ± 8 on long stalks in flat topped inflorescence, bracts with shaggy, glandular, long, jointed hairs (Sep-Dec). GENERAL: Often flowers after a fire. Used in traditional medicine.

Senecio polyodon ihubo (Z) (*polyodon* - many toothed)

Perennial herb, up to 750mm tall. **In marshy or seasonally flooded grassland**, up to 3000m. Widespread. **Plant ± sticky hairy** or smooth. Leafy throughout. LEAVES **long, narrow**, up to 100(300)×10(40)mm. FLOWERHEADS var. *polyodon*, **no rays; var. subglaber** with **rays, mauve, magenta or bluish**, disc whitish to yellow (Oct-Jan). GENERAL: Whole plant sweet smelling.

Garuleum (corruption of *coeruleum* - refers to the blue colour of rays) Shrubs with sticky rough hairs. SAfr endemic, 8 species, 2 in this region.

Garuleum sonchifolium (*sonchifolium* - leaves like *Sonchus*, the Sow thistle)

Slender, leafy, softly woody shrublet, up to 2m tall. On margins of forest, up to 1860m. E Cape to KZN. Plants aromatic, with sticky (glandular) hairs on stems and leaves. LEAVES up to 90×35mm, stem clasping, **coarsely lobed, lobes sharply toothed**. FLOWERHEADS showy, ±30 mm diam, ray florets pink, blue (white), disc florets yellow, **bracts in two series, all ± the same length** (Nov-May).

Garuleum woodii mahloko-a-Baroa (SS) (named after John Medley Wood, 1827-1915)

Well branched shrublet, up to 600mm tall. On rocky slopes, cliffs, 1800-2000m. Cave Sandstone, Les/FS to KZN/Mpum. Stems, leaves rough with sticky hairs. LEAVES **pinnate**, up to 50×20mm, **segments narrow**. FLOWERHEAD showy, ±30mm diam, stalks long, rays pink, blue, white, **bracts in 4 series**, gland-dotted (Jan-May).

Dimorphotheca (*di* - two or twice; *morph* - shape; *theka* - a fruit, refers to two kinds of fruit found in the same fruiting head) Herbs, shrubs or subshrubs, hairless or hairy, often sticky (glandular). Afr, 19 species, 4 in this region

Dimorphotheca jucunda [= *Osteospermum jucundum*] Trailing Pink Daisy; Bergbietou, Bloutou (A); umasigcolo-nkonakazi (Z) (*jucunda* - lovely)

Perennial herb, stems up to 450mm long, erect or trailing. In moist rocky grassland, on broken cliffs, 1000-3200m. E Cape to Mpum. LEAVES 60-150×20mm. FLOWERHEADS solitary, ±60mm diam, **ray florets pink, coppery below, disc florets yellow tipped black** (Sep-Apr). GENERAL: Used in traditional medicine. Lovely garden plant.

★ *Bidens formosa*

Printzia laxa

Printzia pyrifolia

Dimorphotheca jucunda

Senecio macrocephalus

Senecio polyodon

Garuleum woodii

Senecio macrocephalus

Garuleum sonchifolium

Garuleum woodii

227

MONOCOTYLEDONS Single seed-leaf, parallel veins; flower parts in threes or multiples of three

AGAPANTHACEAE (*agape* - love; *anthos* - flower) Monotypic family, endemic to SAfr, 10 species, 2 in this region

Agapanthus campanulatus subsp. *patens* Bell Agapanthus; Bloulelie (A); Iera-laphofu (SS); ugebeleweni (X); ubani (Z) (*campanulatus* - bell-shaped)

Slender, deciduous perennial, up to 700mm tall. In colonies, on moist slopes, in valley bottoms, drainage lines and damp places on cliffs, 1800-2400m. EMR, Mpum, Gaut. LEAVES slender, 150-400×10-25mm, grey-green, narrowing to a purplish stemlike base. INFLORESCENCE dainty at higher altitudes; FLOWER **lobes widely spreading to reflexed**, less than 35mm long, light to dark purplish blue with darker blue stripe, **tube shorter than tepal lobes** (Jan-Mar). GENERAL: Used in traditional medicine to bathe newborn babies to make them strong, to treat 'cradle cap' and as a protective charm. Popular garden plant and a good cut-flower. Subsp. *campanulatus* is found at lower altitudes in KZN and E Cape (Transkei), flower tube longer, tepal lobes less spreading.

Agapanthus nutans (*nutans* - nodding)

Deciduous, up to 900mm tall. On steep slopes, up to 2000m. Scattered distribution from Mont-aux-Sources (N EMR) to Mpum. LEAVES 200-500×10-40mm, blue-green with whitish bloom, the overlapping bases forming a stem. INFLORESCENCE few to many flowered; FLOWERS **drooping, 35-60mm long**, tube 13-27mm, stalks spreading (Dec-Feb).

HYACINTHACEAE Afr, Eurasia, N America, ±46 genera, ±900 species, 27 genera in SAfr. Popular ornamentals. *Scilla* (*squilla* - the sea squill) Bulbous herbs. Afr, Europe, Asia, ±40 species, 6 in SAfr.

Scilla natalensis [= *Merwilla natalensis*] Large Blue Scilla; Blouslangkop (a); kherere (SS); ichitha, imbizenkulu, ubulika, inguduza (Z)

Up to 1m tall, often in large colonies. On cliffs and rocky slopes, up to 2000m. Widespread in eastern summer rainfall areas. BULB **large, half above the ground, covered in purplish brown papery sheaths**. LEAVES few, erect at first, broad at base, tapering to pointed tip, developing fully **after flowering**, becoming large and lax and coppery gold in autumn. FLOWERS ±10mm diam, pale to deep purplish blue (Sep-Nov).

GENERAL: Poisonous to sheep. Bulb used as soap. Used in traditional medicine to treat internal tumours, boils, fractures and for lung disease in cattle. Frost resistant garden plant, grown from seed. White 'sports' and hybrids with *S. dracomontana* can be found. **Similar species:** *Scilla dracomontana* [= *Merwilla dracomontana*] **Miniature Blue Scilla 60-110mm tall**. In colonies, on cliffs, rock platforms, 1675-2100m. EMR endemic. LEAVES **flat on ground**, 30-80×10-35mm, **produced with flowers** (Sep-Nov).

IRIDACEAE - Iris Family Temp regions, ±70 genera, ±1800 species, ±32 genera in SAfr ±12 in this region. *Moraea* (Linnaeus altered the original spelling from *Morea* to *Moraea* to associate the name with his father-in-law, J Moraeus, a physician in Sweden) End of style branches petal-like. Afr, Madag, Austr. ±200 species, ±180 in SAfr, mostly SW Cape, 15 in this region.

Moraea ardesiaca (*ardesiaca* - slate-coloured, refers to the dull slate-blue flower)

Slender, up to 700mm tall, solitary. In damp grassland, near streams, 1800-2350m. EMR endemic. LEAF solitary, 5-10(25)mm wide, usually longer than flowering stem. FLOWERS **large**, outer tepals ±75mm long, **slate-blue to purple**, brown beneath, nectar guides narrow, pale yellow (Nov-Jan).

Approach road to
Injasuti, northern
Drakensberg.

Lorraine van Hooff

Scilla natalensis

Scilla natalensis

Pam Cooke

Scilla natalensis

Pam Cooke

Moraea ardesiaca

Lal Greene

Scilla dracomontana

Neil Crouch

Agapanthus campanulatus

Simon Milliken

David McDonald

Agapanthus nutans

Agapanthus campanulatus

David McDonald

229

Moraea inclinata Nodding Wild Moraea; Knikkende wilde-iris (A) (*inclinata* - inclined, refers to the stem)
Up to 900mm tall, **flowering stem inclining**. Sometimes in scattered colonies, in damp grassland, 1525-2400m. E Cape to KZN. LEAF solitary, **round, much longer than flowering stem, inserted on upper part of the stem just below flowers.** FLOWERING STEM long, slender, with 2-4 branches; FLOWERS **large**, up to 25×10mm, **blue-violet** with yellow nectar guides (Dec-Feb). CAPSULE **round**.

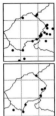

Moraea stricta Bloutulp (A) (*stricta* - very straight or upright)
Slender, 150-250mm tall. In grassland, up to 2400m.Widespread in Afr. LEAF **absent at flowering, round**, eventually up to 600×1.5mm. FLOWERING STEM erect with **3-6 short branches**; FLOWERS **small**, outer tepals 19-24mm long, pale lilac to blue-violet, ±3 flowers open at once, closing at sunset (Sep-Nov). GENERAL: Common on recently burnt grassland. **Similar species: *Moraea alpina*** Plants small, **40-120mm** tall. In shallow soil over rock, dry gravelly patches, 2680-3200m. EMR endemic. FLOWERS small, outer tepals 12-18mm long, blue to mauve (Oct-Dec).

Aristea (*aristos* - best, noblest) Flowers blue, **tepals twisted into tight spiral after blooming**. Afr, ±52 species, ±39 in SAfr, ±5 in this region.

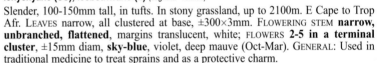

Aristea angolensis
450-600mm tall, in small clumps. In mountain grassland, up to 2200m, E Cape to Nigeria. LEAVES ±600×10mm. INFLORESCENCE **with short slender branches**, bracts ±6mm long; FLOWERS 15-20mm diam, in clusters, **bright sky-blue**, also mauve, dark purple-blue, open early, closing by midday except on overcast days. GENERAL: A hardy garden plant (Nov-Feb).

Aristea cognata [= *A. abyssinica*] **Blue-eyed Grass, Miniature Blue Aristea; lethepu-le-lenyenyane (SS); icebethwane (Z)** (*cognata* - related)
Slender, 100-150mm tall, in tufts. In stony grassland, up to 2100m. E Cape to Trop Afr. LEAVES narrow, all clustered at base, ±300×3mm. FLOWERING STEM **narrow, unbranched, flattened**, margins translucent, white; FLOWERS **2-5 in a terminal cluster**, ±15mm diam, **sky-blue**, violet, deep mauve (Oct-Mar). GENERAL: Used in traditional medicine to treat sprains and as a protective charm.

Aristea grandis (*grandis* - large, great)
Robust, 270-400(1000)mm tall. On grassy streambanks and moist grassy places around rock outcrops, up to 2250m. E Cape to KZN. LEAVES leathery, spreading, 180-445×5-14mm, stem leaves narrow, tips often rusty brown, base of lower leaves deeply keeled and sheatheing. INFLORESCENCE **unbranched**; FLOWERS **2-6 in well separated clusters**, 20-25mm wide, deep blue, each cluster with a **large leathery bract at base**, 15-25mm long, rusty brown (Nov-Jan). **Similar species: *Aristea montana*** In moist or marshy grassland, up to 2450m. E Cape to Mpum. Flowering stems unbranched or with 1-2 short branches, bracts ±15mm long **margins conspicuously white**.

Aristea woodii **Wood's Aristea; Blousuurkanol (A); khahla, lethepu-le-lenyenyane (SS); umluzi omncane (Z)** (named after John Medley Wood, 1827-19215, botanist, founding curator of Natal Herbarium)
Evergreen perennial, up to 600mm tall. In moist or marshy grassland, 1800-2450m. E Cape to Zim. LEAVES **in basal fan**, tips and margins translucent white, tips of leaves on flowering stem **fringed, translucent white**. FLOWERING STEM not flattened, with short branches, bracts ±10mm, oval, **dark brown, deeply torn, white-tipped**; FLOWERS 15-20mm diam, dark blue, pale blue or deep mauve (Dec-Feb). GENERAL: Variable in size, leaf width and shape of bracts. Used as a protective and good luck charm. Garden plant for semi-shady areas.

Auriol Batten

Darren Webster

Martin von Fintel

Aristea cognata   *Moraea alpina*   *Moraea stricta*

Martin von Fintel

Godfrey Symons

Martin von Fintel

Aristea woodii   *Aristea woodii*   *Moraea inclinata*

Rod Saunders

Martin von Fintel

Tony Abbott

Aristea grandis   *Aristea angolensis*   *Moraea inclinata*

231

Dierama - **Hairbells, Wand-flowers; Grasklokkies (A)** (*dierama* - a funnel) Popular garden plants. Afr, ±44, mostly SAfr summer rainfall region, ±8 in this region.

Dierama jucundum (*jucundum* - delightful)

In clumps, up to 950mm tall. On dry rocky slopes, **near the summit of basalt cliffs**. EMR endemic. LEAVES 450-650×4.5-7mm. INFLORESCENCES pendulous; FLOWERS **large, 25-28mm long**, tepals 8-12mm broad, usually **light mauve** (Sep-Oct). GENERAL: Similar to the more widespread *D. dracomontanum* (see pgs 30 & 186) which has smaller flowers, narrower tepals, usually pink to red (Nov-Feb).

Dierama dissimile (*dissimile* – dissimilar to *D. dracomontanum* with which it can be found growing)

Solitary or in small tufts, 500-700mm tall. In grassland, 1500-2150m. E Cape to KZN. LEAVES few, narrow, 300-600×**1.5-2-3.5-4mm**. INFLORESCENCES pendulous, **branches 50-100mm long**; FLOWERS 18-22mm long, tepals 13-15×5-6mm, pale pink to mauve to magenta (Oct-Nov). GENERAL: Similar to *D. dracomontanum* (see pgs 30, 186) which forms large clumps, has broader leaves, shorter branches, larger flowers, usually red to pink (Nov-Feb).

ORCHIDACEAE - Orchid Family A very large family with highly specialized flowers. Cosmop, ±800 genera, ±20 000 species, 52 genera in SAfr. *Brachycorythis* (*brachy* - short; *koros* - helmet, refers to the uppermost of the 3 sepals) Terrestrial herbs, densely leafy from the ground level, with large, leaflike bracts. Flower lip stretches forward. Afr, ±33 species, 7 in SAfr, 2 in this region.

Brachycorythis ovata **imfeyamasele yentaba (Z)** (*ovata* - egg-shaped)

Slender to robust, up to 400mm tall. In grassland up to 1800m. Widespread but not common, E Cape to Trop Afr. LEAVES **crowded, overlapping, stiff**, ±70×25mm, **hairless**. INFLORESCENCE **crowded**, lower flowers hidden within long bracts; FLOWERS **pale pink to purple**, fleshy, ±20×10mm, **lip spoon-shaped, longer than wide**, 8-16mm long, **keel white blotched purple**, 3-lobed at the tip, no spur, strongly scented (Dec-Jan). GENERAL: Used in traditional medicine to treat madness and as a protective charm. **Similar species:** *Brachycorythis pubescens* (*pubescens* - slightly hairy, downy) In grassland, up to 1500m. KZN to Trop Afr. LEAVES ±50×17mm, **finely hairy**, conspicuously veined. FLOWERS brownish purple, **lip as wide as long, pink to mauve with red spotted yellow patch at base** (Nov-Dec).

Disa (origin unclear, possibly from *dis* - double, referring to the two large wings in the style or *dis* - rich or opulent, referring to the red of the spectacular *Disa uniflora* the first species of the genus described) Median sepal hooded, prolonged into a spur or pouch. **The direction in which the spur points is useful in identification in the field.** Afr, 1 in Arabian peninsula, ±162 species, 131 in SAfr, ±29 in this region.

Disa baurii [= *Herschelianthe baurii, Herschelia baurii*] **Bloumoederkappie (A)** (named after Leopold Richard Baur, German pharmacist, missionary and botanical collector who worked in the Transkei in the 1800s)

Slender, 200-400mm tall. On damp grass slopes up to 2250m. E Cape to Tanz. LEAVES produced after flowers, slender, grasslike, ±300mm long. FLOWERS few (2-14), ±20mm wide, purplish blue, **lip deeply fringed**, 10-25mm long, spur greenish with slightly enlarged tip, ±5mm, pointing upwards (Sep-Dec).

Disa cornuta **Golden Orchid** (*cornuta* - horned or spurred) (see pg 264)

Disa stachyoides **ihlamvu elimpofu lasenkangala (Z)** (*stachyoides* - resembling *Stachys*)

Slender to robust, 100-400mm tall. Very common, scattered in grassland up to 2800m. E Cape to Limpopo Prov. LEAVES few, overlapping, ±80×10mm. INFLORESCENCE dense, 30-100mm long; FLOWERS **small, purple** with white lip, **spur 2-6mm long, broad, flat, almost horizontal** (Dec-Jan). GENERAL: Used by traditional healers to ward off evil spirits and storms.

Disa stricta (*strictus* - erect)

Slender, erect, 150-450mm tall. On grassy mountain slopes, damp floodplains, 1800-2450m. E Cape, KZN, Les. LEAVES folded, rigid, ±200mm long. INFLORESCENCE dense, 20-120mm long; FLOWERS small, pink to **lilac or bluish purple**, petals white, lip darker pink, **spur 2.5-5mm long, horizontal or pointing upwards** (Nov-Dec).

Eulophia (*eu* - well; *lophos* - crest, refers to the crested lip) Terrestrial herbs. Lip ridged on upper surface. Old and New World, most common in Afr, 42 in SAfr, 9 in this region.

Eulophia zeyheriana (named after Carl Zeyher, 1799-1858, botanical collector who came to the Cape in 1822)

Slender, up to 400mm tall. In stony or marshy grassland, up to 2000m, E Cape to Mpum. LEAVES stiff, erect, 200-400×3-7mm. INFLORESCENCE loose; FLOWERS, sepals and petals 7-10mm long, sepals green and purplish brown or dull red, **petals and lip pale blue tinged purple** or completely dull red, lip crests white, warty (Dec-Jan).

Hilliard & Burtt

Dierama jucundum

Trevor Coleman

Disa cornuta

Lal Greene

Disa stachyoides

Auriel Batten

Dierama dissimile

Eulophia zeyheriana

Clinton Carbutt

David McDonald

Disa stricta

Neil Crouch

Disa baurii

Charles Rostance

Brachycorythis ovata

233

DICOTYLEDONS Two seed leaves, net veins, flower parts in fours, fives or multiples of these.

BRASSICACEAE (CRUCIFERAE) - Cabbage or Mustard Family (see pg 74) *Heliophila* (*helios* - sun; *philein* - to love) (see pg 74)

Heliophila rigidiuscula Grassland Heliophila; Bloubekkie (A); ´musa-pelo-oa-mangope, semameloana, tloko-filoane-e-kholo (SS); uvemvane oluncane (Z) (*rigidiuscula* - rigid)

Slender, erect perennial herb, 250-750mm tall. In grassland, in stream valleys, up to 2800m. E Cape to Mpum. Stems unbranched, leafy, a few from rootstock. LEAVES few, very slender, 20-80×**1mm**. INFLORESCENCE slender, stem leafless; FLOWERS drooping, 10-20mm diam, pink, mauve, blue, purple, **petals often with white or light 'eye'** (Oct-Jan). POD 30-70×3-8mm. GENERAL: Leaves used as a spinach. Used in traditional medicine for chest complaints and by diviners to prepare the bones.

LEGUMINOSAE (FABACEAE) - Pea or Legume Family Second largest flowering plant family. (see pg 130) *Lotononis* (see pg 130)

Lotononis galpinii (named after Ernest Galpin, 1858-1941, banker, naturalist, 'prince' of plant collectors)

Much branched shrublet, prostrate or erect, 150-600mm tall, 300-600mm diam. Forming mats or low cushions in rocky streambeds, on steep rocky slopes, edges of wet gravel patches, rock sheets, 1980-3300m. EMR endemic. Very variable, silvery hairy. LEAFLETS small, 3-5×3mm. FLOWERS **solitary**, ±10mm long, deep violet-blue with white eye, yellow spot at base of standard (Dec-Feb). GENERAL: Heavily grazed.

Lotononis lotononoides [= *L. dieterlenii*, *Buchenroedera lotononoides*] **mosita-tlali (SS)**

Perennial shrublet, ±500mm tall. Sometimes in large colonies, in moist rocky grassland, 1500-2650m. EMR endemic. Stems tufted, mostly unbranched, leafy. LEAFLETS **oval**, ±20×8mm, grey-green, **sparsely hairy**, **tips recurved**, **hairlike**, stalks ±8mm. INFLORESCENCE **long, narrow**; FLOWERS ±10mm long, dark blue, in axils towards ends of branchlets (Dec-Feb).

Lotononis pulchella [= *Buchenroedera tenuifolia* var. *pulchella*]

Robust, woody, branches up to 1.2m tall (often much shorter). In stabilised boulder beds, rocky grass ridges and slopes, in scrub, 1800-2560m. EMR endemic. LEAFLETS ±13×8mm, stalk up to 10mm, silvery grey. INFLORESCENCES small, flattish, terminal; FLOWERS ±5mm long, pale blue-violet, bracts shorter than calyx (Nov-Jan).

Lotononis sericophylla [= *L. trisegmentata*] **khonyana-tšooana, motoaitoai (SS)** (*sericophylla* - silky leaves)

Slender, erect shrub, up to 1.5m tall. In boulder beds, along rocky streams and on riverbanks, 1525-2400m. EMR endemic. STEMS silky, **much branched**, bark greenish brown. LEAFLETS small, ±10×4mm, covered in silvery hairs. FLOWERS solitary, ±15mm long, pale blue, wings, keel pale greenish yellow or whitish (Dec-Mar).

Pearsonia (named after Dr Harold Pearson, 1870-1916, first Director of the National Botanical Gardens, Kirstenbosch) Perennial herbs or shrublets. Leaves 3 foliolate. Flower standard erect, **concave in the lower part**. Similar to *Lotononis* which has the standard reflexed and the keel ± boat-shaped. S Trop Afr, ±11 species, ±7 in SAfr, 1 in this region.

Pearsonia grandifolia Mauve Frilly Pea (*grandifolia* - large leaves)

Perennial herb, stems prostrate, forming small mats in short, stony grassland, up to 2100m. KZN to Zim. Stems zigzag, covered in short silvery hairs. LEAVES hairy, leaflets tapering to hairlike tip, very variable in size and shape. INFLORESCENCE terminal, 50-150mm; FLOWERS crowded, **crumpled**, ±20mm long, blue-mauve or white with purple centre, calyx densely hairy, scented (Nov-Feb).

Otholobium (*otheo* - to burst forth; *lobos* - pod, fruit of *O caffrum* seems to be 'pushing out of calyx') Leaflets entire, oval, tips hairlike, recurved. Flowers in 3s, with bract at base. Found in drier areas than *Psoralea* species. SAfr, ±40 species, 2 in this region.

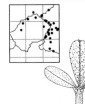

Otholobium polystictum [= *Psoralea polysticta*] **Vlieëbos (A); mohlonecha, mohlonep-shoa (SS)** (*polystictum* - many spots)

Perennial shrub, up to 1.5m tall. In boulder beds, on steep damp grass slopes, up to 2050m. E Cape to Limpopo Prov. Stems covered with short white hairs. LEAVES **stalkless**, leaflets 9-36×3-15mm, covered in gland dots, midrib ending in short, hard, recurved tip. FLOWERS **stalkless**, in clusters in axils of upper leaves, pale blue, ±8mm (Aug-Apr). GENERAL: Used in traditional medicine to treat head colds and as a body wash by chiefs.

Otholobium polystictum

Pearsonia grandifolia

Lotononis galpinii

Lotononis lotononoides

Lotononis galpinii

Lotononis lotononoides

Heliophila rigidiuscula

Lotononis sericophylla

Lotononis pulchella

235

Psoralea (*psoraleos* - scabby, refers to gland dots on leaflets) Mostly found in damp areas. Leaflets slender. 24 species in SAfr, 1 in this region.

Psoralea sp.

Slender subshrub, 1-2m tall. On streambanks, boulder beds, up to 2000m. Stems tufted, branching above. LEAFLETS **fine**, 20-35×**1.5-3mm**, grey-green, dotted with small gland dots. FLOWERS in axils of upper leaves, bright blue (Dec-Feb).

GERANIACEAE - Geranium Family (see pg 206) ***Geranium*** (*geranos* - a crane) (see pg 206)

Geranium brycei [= *G. thodei*] (James Bryce,1838-1922, jurist, mountaineer, who collected plants in SA in 1895)

Bushy shrub or perennial herb or herb, in clumps up to 1m tall (often much shorter). In damp, rocky places, drainage lines, 2225-3000m. LEAVES **crowded at branch tips**, blade 20-150mm diam, lobes 5(7), **thickly hairy**, not silvery, stipules deeply dissected, stalks 30-300mm long, shorter upwards. INFLORESCENCE ±2-flowered, mostly leafless; FLOWERS large, petals up to 20×13mm, pale to deep violet, sometimes with a white patch near the base, veins ± reddish (Nov-Apr).

Geranium robustum (*robustum* - big, strong)

Robust shrub, up to 1m tall. Often in large stands, on moist shrubby mountain slopes, streamsides, 1600-2590m. E Cape to Mpum. LEAVES ±50mm diam, ±5-lobed to base, **each lobe twice divided, silky silvery hairy above, thickly silvery beneath**, stalks long, ±100mm. FLOWERS ±35mm diam, light purple, in terminal clusters (Nov-Mar).

PERIPLOCACEAE - Periploca Family Now included in Apocynaceae as subfamily Periplocoideae. Herbs, twiggy shrubs or woody climbers. Corona only on corolla, not on stamens; translator consisting of a sticky gland, short arm and spoon carrying granular pollen. Old World, 62 genera, ±170 species, 8 genera in SAfr. ***Raphionacme*** (*rhaphis* - needle; *akme* - point) Afr endemic, ±39 species, 18 in SAfr, 2 in this region.

Raphionacme hirsuta [= *R. divaricata, R. velutina*] Khadiwortel (A); kherenchane (SS); intsema (X); umathangane, umathanjana (Z) (*hirsuta* - hairy, although many plants are hairless)

Much branched herb, 50-250mm tall. In grassland, up to 2600m. E Cape to Limpopo Prov. LEAVES 12-50×6-25mm. FLOWERS purple, lobes oblong, 4-9×1.5-3.5mm, corona lobes variable, white or purple (Sep-Dec). FRUIT 25-75×7-13mm. GENERAL: Said to be poisonous, though tubers are used to help brew beer.

BORAGINACEAE - Forget-me-not/ Borage Family ***Cynoglossum*** (*kyon* - dog; *glossa* - tongue) Fruit covered in small hooked spines. (see pg 86)

Cynoglossum austroafricanum (*austro* - southern; *africanum* - Africa)

Slender, erect, branching herb, up to 1m tall. On damp paths, disturbed places, 1370-2600m. EMR endemic. **Leafy throughout**, covered in short hairs. BASAL LEAVES up to 170×25mm, conspicuously veined, **harshly hairy**. FLOWERS blue, stalks short, crowded in large inflorescences (Dec-Apr). NUTLETS covered in small hooked spines.

Myosotis (*myos* - mouse; *otis* - ear) Corolla tube almost closed by 5 scales. Cosmop, mostly temp, ±100 species, 7 in SAfr, 1 in this region.

Myosotis semiamplexicaulis [= *M. afropalustris*] Forget-me-not; Vergeet-my-nie (A); sethuthu (SS) (*semi* - half; *amplexicaulis* - stem clasping)

Bushy herb, up to 600mm tall. In damp ground, scrub, among rocks, 1400-3000m. **Bristly hairy.** INFLORESCENCE much branched; FLOWERS small, 6-8mm wide, **blue, white or pink**, throat scales yellow (Nov-Mar). GENERAL: Used in traditional medicine and to train traditional healer initiates to develop memory.

LABIATAE / LAMIACEAE - Sage/Mint Family Aromatic herbs or shrublets. (see pg 86) ***Ajuga*** (*ajuga* - corruption of the apothecary's 'bugula', an obscure name with counterparts in German, French, Italian, Spanish) Flowers upper lip very short. Mostly N Hemisp, ±50 species, 1 in SAfr.

Ajuga ophrydis Bugle Plant; senyarela (SS) (*ophrydis* - resembles orchid genus *Ophrys*)

Perennial herb, 60-250mm tall. In stony grassland, up to 2700m. E Cape to Mpum. LEAVES mostly basal, 30-170×15-40mm, thick, usually hairy, **margins coarsely toothed**. INFLORESCENCE up to 200mm long; FLOWERS ±12×14mm, blue, bracts leaflike (Oct-Feb). GENERAL: Used in traditional medicine. Easily grown, by division.

SCROPHULARIACEAE - Snapdragon Family (see pg 90) ***Nemesia*** (see pg 90)

Nemesia caerulea Nemesia; Leeubekkie (A) (*caerulea* - sky-blue)

Robust, **tufted**, perennial herb, up to 600mm tall. On grassy slopes, amongst rocks, 1400-2900m. EMR endemic. Stems simple. LEAVES ±25×12mm, margins with thickened teeth, **stalkless**. INFLORESCENCE a terminal cluster, 25-75mm, **on long bare stems**; FLOWERS 8-10mm, **violet-blue**, mouth pale yellow to white, hairy, **2 raised orange-yellow humps/bosses inside mouth**, spur 2-3 mm, calyx hairy (Oct-Dec).

Psoralea sp.   *Ajuga ophrydis*   *Cynoglossum austro-africanum*

Martin von Fintel   *Darrel Plowes*   *Neil Crouch*

Geranium robustum   *Raphionacme hirsuta*   *Geranium brycei*

John Grimshaw   *Martin von Fintel*   *Mike Hirst*

Myosotis semiamplexicaulis   *Raphionacme hirsuta*   *Nemesia caerulea*

Pam Cooke   *Wally Menne*   *Auriol Batten*

Myosotis semiamplexicaulis   *Manulea florifera*   *Nemesia caerulea*

David McDonald   *Martin von Fintel*   *David McDonald*

237

Manulea (*manus* - a hand, refers to 5 spreading corolla lobes) Annual or perennial herbs, rarely shrubby. (see pg 90)

Manulea florifera (*florifera* - bearing many flowers) (see pg 90)

Jamesbrittenia (named after James Britten, 1846-1924, a British botanist, Keeper of Botany at British Museum of Natural History and editor of Journal of Botany) **Stamens hidden** inside corolla tube. Differs from *Sutera* which has stamens protruding. Mostly Afr, 83 species, 74 in SAfr, ±8 in this region.

Jamesbrittenia jurassica [= Sutera jurassica] (*jurassica* - refers to the old Jurassic landscape on the top of the Drakensberg, the only place where this plant is found)

Perennial **mat forming herb**, stems 60-120mm long. On bare gravelly ground on summit plateau, 2500-3230m. EMR endemic. LEAVES 10-20×7-12mm, **deeply lobed and divided**. FLOWERS ±14mm wide, **light violet** or pink with dark violet streaks, throat and base of lip yellow, **tube up to 9mm long**, stalks short, 4-10mm (Jan-Mar). GENERAL: This has become a popular alpine garden plant in Britain.

Jamesbrittenia pristisepala [= Sutera pristisepala] pokaetsi, phiri-ea-hlaha (SS); umahokwe (Z) (*pristisepala* - like a sawfish, refers to the ragged sepals)

Dwarf, **erect grey shrublet**, up to 350mm tall. On rock sheets and cliffs, rocky stream gullies and boulder beds, scree, 1500-3000m. EMR endemic. Very variable. LEAVES 10-30×5-17mm, **deeply lobed, lobes deeply cut**. INFLORESCENCE long, crowded; FLOWERS ±11mm wide, tube ±11mm long, mouth compressed, petals lilac, throat white to pale yellow, tube purplish outside, **calyx lobes strongly toothed** (Nov-Apr). GENERAL: Strongly aromatic. Hybridises with *J. breviflora*.

Sutera (named after Johan Suter, 1766-1827, Swiss botanist and physician, Prof of Greek and philosophy at Berne) **Stamens protrude**. SAfr, ±47 species, ±4 in this region.

Sutera patriotica (*patriotica* - from the type locality, Patriot's Klip in the Stormberg)

Erect, branching herb, 70-450mm tall. In grassland, disturbed places, up to 2950m. E Cape, FS, Les to Nam. Covered in glandular-pubescent hairs, densely leafy. LEAVES **thin**, opposite and **in tufts in axils**, 17-30×2-8mm, margins ± toothed, hairy. INFLORESCENCES **long, branching**; FLOWERS 8-14mm across, pink, mauve, tube yellow-orange, 3-4.5mm long (Nov-Apr).

Strobilopsis (*strobilos* - like a cone, refers to inflorescence) Inflorescence erect. Only one species in genus, EMR endemic.

Strobilopsis wrightii (named after F.B. Wright, veterinarian, nature conservationist, plant collector in the Kamberg/Giants Castle area of the Drakensberg and the top of the escarpment)

Perennial, tufted herb, stems up to 250mm tall. In damp places, silty patches on Cave Sandstone outcrops, 2000-2450m. EMR endemic. LEAVES thick, 15-25×2-4mm, stalkless, margins ± toothed, thick, margins running onto stem in two ridges. INFLORESCENCE erect, solitary or branched, flowers in tightly congested oblong or roundish heads; FLOWER upper lip cream to pale mauve, lower lip mauve with orange blotch and **hairs at base** of upper lobes, tube ±4mm long (Nov-Jan).

Selago (an ancient name, used by Linnaeus) Herbs or shrublets. (see pg 96)

Selago flanaganii lenyofane-khono-koane (SS) (named after Henry Flanagan, Eastern Cape farmer, naturalist, plant collector, one of the first people to collect plants in the high N Drakensberg. His garden, Flanagan's Arboretum was bequeathed to the nation and is now at the Union Buildings)

Handsome subshrub 1-1.5m tall, much branched from base. In colonies, in grassland, in shrub communities, 2200-3300m. EMR endemic. LEAVES 4-12×1-3mm, **in clusters**, margins entire or with 1-3 pairs small teeth in upper half. INFLORESCENCE large, dense, main branches 80-170mm long; FLOWERS 5-7mm wide, white to mauve (Nov-Jan).

Selago galpinii [= S. cooperi, S. sandersonii] tšitoanenyana, tšitoanyane (SS) (named after Ernest Galpin, 1858-1941, SA naturalist and 'prince' of plant collectors)

Perennial herb, 150-300mm. Rounded cushions, in rough, rocky grassland, 1500-2600m. EMR endemic. LEAVES in clusters, 7-23×1-2mm, midrib channelled above, raised below. INFLORESCENCE slender, dense, with small rounded heads ±10mm diam, on side branchlets, mostly on one side; FLOWERS ±5mm diam, blue-violet (Jan-May).

Selago trauseldii (named after William (Bill) Trauseld, 1911-89, game ranger in the KZN Drakensberg, photographer and amateur botanist, author of *Wild Flowers of the Natal Drakensberg*, 1969)

Perennial herb, up to 750mm tall. On moist, grassy slopes, 1500-2400m. EMR endemic. Stems few. LEAVES 4-10×1-2mm, margins entire, in clusters close to stem, thickened, finely hairy. INFLORESCENCE widely branched, flowers **in compact clusters 7-10mm diam**; FLOWERS ±5mm diam, white, buds flushed mauve (Jan-May).

Jamesbrittenia jurassica

David McDonald

Sutera patriotica

Peter Linder

Strobilopsis wrightii

Hilliard & Burtt

Strobilopsis wrightii

Hilliard & Burtt

Sutera patriotica

Peter Linder

Selago trauseldii

Martin von Fintel

Jamesbrittenia pristisepala

David McDonald

Jamesbrittenia pristisepala

Clinton Carbutt

Selago flanaganii

Martin von Fintel

Selago galpinii

Mike Hirst

239

GESNERIACEAE - African Violet Family *Streptocarpus* (*streptos* - twisted; *karpos* - fruit) (see pg 96)

Streptocarpus gardenii (named after Major Robert Garden, served in Natal, 1843-1859)

Perennial herb, 50-170mm tall. On mossy rocks in forest, up to 1800m. E Cape to KZN. LEAVES **in rosette,** ±300×70mm, margins scalloped, reddish purple beneath, softly hairy, stalks ±70×6mm. FLOWERS large, solitary, funnel-shaped, 35-50mm long, **lower lip very pale violet with deep violet broken lines,** tube narrow, greenish white (Jan-Feb). GENERAL: A popular container plant.

Streptocarpus polyanthus subsp. *dracomontanus* (*polyanthus* - many flowers)

Perennial herb, up to 80mm tall. On rocky outcrops, forest margins, up to 2000m. N EMR. LEAVES 2-3, up to 70×90mm, thick, upper surface grey-green, reddish purple beneath. INFLORESCENCE **short, stout;** FLOWERS few, **small, less than 20mm wide, upper lobes not strongly reflexed,** chalky pale violet to mauve, tube narrow, sharply deflexed then directed forwards, with keyhole opening.

LENTIBULARIACEAE - Bladderwort Family (see pg 144).

Utricularia livida Bladderwort; Blaaskruid (A); tlamana-sa-metsi (SS); intambo (Z) (*livida* - lead coloured)

Delicate, terrestrial herb, 50-150mm tall, in colonies. In marshy places, up to 2700m. Cape to Trop Afr, Madag. LEAVES 10-20×1-5mm, **main vein branched,** traps 1-2mm, on leaves and stems. FLOWERS 1-8, in terminal cluster, ±10mm mauve, ± yellow blotch on lower lip, spur short, equal to lip, blunt (Dec-Feb). GENERAL: Leaves not conspicuous at time of flowering. Used in traditional medicine to help babies keep milk down.

ACANTHACEAE - Acanthus Family Herbs, shrubs or climbers. Leaves opposite, without stipules. Inflorescence often with large leafy bracts, flowers irregular or 2-lipped, upper lip entire or 2-lobed, lower lip 3-lobed. Fruit an explosive capsule, ± club-shaped, seeds often with water absorbent hairs. Pantrop, ±350 genera, ±4350 species, 42 genera in SAfr. *Barleria* (named after Jacques Barrelier, 1606-1673, Dominican monk and French botanist) Herbs, shrubs. Leaves with 2 buds in axils, 1 sometimes developing into a spine, the other into a leafy branch or inflorescence. 2 small and 2 large calyx lobes. Fruit an explosive capsule. Cosmop, mainly trop, ±250 species, ±60 in SAfr 1 in this region.

Barleria monticola Berg Barleria (*monticola* - growing on mountains)

Cushionlike, tufted herb, 150-450mm. In colonies, in moist grassland. Stems hardly branching, plant covered with **long, silky golden hairs throughout.** LEAVES ±45×12-20mm, stalkless. FLOWERS ±30mm wide, calyx lobes overlapping, sharply pointed, ±20mm long (Aug-Dec). GENERAL: Beautiful when flowering after fires.

RUBIACEAE - Gardenia or Coffee Family (see pg 98) *Pentanisia* (*pente* - five; *anisos* - unequal) Perennial herbs. Afr, ±15 species, ±3 in SAfr.

Pentanisia prunelloides Broad-leaved Pentanisia; Sooibrandbossie (A); khatoane, setima-mollo (SS); icishamlilo (X,Z); isibunde, umakophole (Z) (*prunelloides* - resembles *Prunella*)

Perennial herb, up to 600mm tall. In grassland, up to 1980m. E Cape to Tanz. Rootstock thick, woody. LEAVES variable, 13-85×2-35mm, very hairy to ± hairless. INFLORESCENCE dense, ±45mm diam, stems 35-300mm long; FLOWERS ±8mm diam, pale to deep purplish blue (Oct-Dec). GENERAL: First to bloom after fires. Afrikaans name means 'heartburn shrublet', Zulu 'that which puts out the fire'. Used in traditional medicine to treat a range of ailments from stomach pains to haemorrhoids.

CAMPANULACEAE - Bell Flower or Canterbury Bell Family Herbs or shrubs. Cosmop, mostly temp and subtrop, ±35 genera, ±700 species, 12 genera in SAfr. *Wahlenbergia* (named after Dr Goran Wahlenberg of Uppsala, 1780-1851, Swedish author of 'Flora Lapponica') Herbs or shrublets. Flowers bell-like, 5-lobed. Fruit a capsule. Cosmop, ±200 species, ±150 in SAfr, ±15 in this region.

Wahlenbergia appressifolia moopetsane (SS) (*appressifolia* - leaves pressed against stem)

Perennial herb, 200-450mm tall. In colonies, in damp grassland, up to 2440m. EMR endemic. Stems often simple. LEAVES alternate, ± **erect, close to stem,** 8-25×3-6mm, margins wavy, ± toothed. FLOWERS on long, **hairless stalks, violet-blue,** bell-shaped, up to 22mm long, calyx lobes **up to 9×4mm long, hairless** (Dec-Apr).

Wahlenbergia cuspidata [= *W. dentifera*] (*cuspidata* - drawn out into a point, refers to calyx lobes)

Bushy herb, 300-600mm tall, sometimes in conspicuous stands. On damp grassy, often rocky slopes, damp cliff faces, 1525-3100m. E Cape to KZN. Stem branching just above base. LEAVES up to 35×12mm, spreading, margins wavy, toothed, **hairy, half clasping stem at base.** FLOWERS large, 18-32mm long, violet-blue, on long bare stems, **calyx lobes long, slender, pointed,** margins ± toothed (Dec-Mar).

Lal Greene

Streptocarpus gardenii

David McDonald

Streptocarpus polyanthus

Utricularia livida

Lal Greene

Lorraine van Hooff

Baleria monticola

Pentanisia prunelloides

Martin von Fintel

Hilliard & Burtt

Wahlenbergia appressifolia

Tony Abbott

Wahlenbergia cuspidata

Wahlenbergia cuspidata

Lorraine van Hooff

241

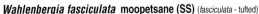

Wahlenbergia fasciculata moopetsane (SS) *(fasciculata - tufted)*

Slender erect herb, 100-300mm tall. In grassland, rocky places, 1500-2750m. EMR endemic. Stems usually solitary, unbranched. LEAVES **short, narrow,** ±5×0.3mm, crowded, **in tufts.** FLOWERS ±15mm, stalkless, crowded in upper axils, dark blue-mauve (Feb-Mar).

Wahlenbergia huttonii moopetsane (SS) [= *Lightfootia huttonii*]

Small, erect perennial herb, 100-350mm tall. In rocky grassland, on bare earth and crevices of rock sheets, up to 1950m. E Cape to Tanz. Stems simple or branched from base. LEAVES **stalkless,** 5-18×3-8mm, **crowded, spreading,** hairless to hairy beneath. FLOWERS **in small terminal clusters,** 6-10mm, blue or violet, **lobes long and narrow** (Dec-Apr).

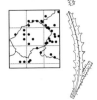

Wahlenbergia krebsii [= *W. zeyheri*] Fairy Bell-flower; moopetsane, tenane (SS) *(named after Georg Krebs, 1792-1844, apothecary, plant collector)*

Slender perennial herb, 200-700mm tall, in conspicuous groups. In grassland, often in damp places, up to 3000m. E Cape to KZN/Mpum. Stems slender, simple below, branched above. LEAVES **crowded towards base of stems,** ±55×10mm, margins wavy, toothed, **stalkless,** narrow and widely spaced up the stem. FLOWERS 10-15mm long, violet-blue, **stalks 2-25mm long,** in loose inflorescence (Nov-May) GENERAL: Used as a pot herb.

Wahlenbergia polytrichifolia subsp. *dracomontana* *(polytrichifolia - leaves like those of the moss, Polytrichum)*

Lovely, low growing perennial herb, forming small mats. In colonies, in bare sandy or gravelly soil over rock sheets (which can be seasonally waterlogged), up to 3300m. EMR endemic. LEAVES crowded, ±12×0.3mm. FLOWERS solitary, erect, ±10 mm long, sky-blue (whitish), **sometimes with darker blue markings in throat** (Jan-Feb).

Craterocapsa *(krateros - cup-shaped; capsa - capsule)* Prostrate, perennial herbs. Flowers ± stalkless, bell-like. Fruit a capsule dehiscing by an apical lid. SAfr, 4 species, all in this region.

Craterocapsa congesta *(congesta - congested, refers to leaves)*

Small prostrate perennial herb. In small colonies, in moist, stony grassland, 1500-3350m. Stems slender, simple, leafy. LEAVES up to 35×3mm in basal rosette, smaller on stems, margins fringed with hairs. FLOWERS **stalkless, several open at once, crowded together at tips,** bluish mauve (Dec-Mar).

Craterocapsa tarsodes Carpet Bell flower *(tarsodes - mat forming)*

Perennial herb. Forms small mats on rocky outcrops, in stony grassland, 1200-2500m. E Cape to Zim. Stems short, branching, **ending in rosettes of leaves.** LEAVES 15-25×5(12)mm, tapering to broad, stalklike base, margins hairy. FLOWERS **solitary, stalkless,** in axils of rosette leaves, ±20mm, **pale blue or white, opening one at a time,** soon overtopped by new shoots (Nov-Feb).

LOBELIACEAE - Lobelia Family Herbs, often with milky sap. Fruit a capsule. Includes some well known ornamentals. Cosmop, ±30 genera, ±1000 species, 5 genera in SAfr. *Lobelia* (named after Matthias de L'Obel, 1538-1616, Flemish nobleman, botanist, physician to King James I) Herbs or shrublets. Flowers 5-lobed, regular or 2-lipped. Fruit a capsule. Trop and subtrop, mostly American, ±300 species, ±70 in SAfr, ±5 in this region.

Lobelia flaccida subsp. *flaccida* motlapa-tsoinyana (SS); itshilizi, ubulawu (X); isidala esiluhlaza (Z) *(flaccida - limp)*

Annual herb, stems slender, erect or sprawling, 50-300mm long. Locally common, in grassland, often at foot of cliffs, rock outcrops or along streambanks, in moist, partly shaded places, up to 2450m. Widespread. Stems **angled, ± narrowly winged.** LEAVES stalkless, narrow, well spaced, 20-70×2-10mm, margins toothed. FLOWERS 10-15mm long, in loose inflorescence, sky-blue with white on palate, **two crests in mouth** of tube, lower lip 3-lobed, much larger than upper (Nov-Apr). GENERAL: Used as a pot herb in Les.

Wahlenbergia fasciculata   *Wahlenbergia huttonii*

Wahlenbergia krebsii

Wahlenbergia polytrichifolia subsp. *dracomontana*

Wahlenbergia krebsii

Wahlenbergia polytrichifolia subsp. *dracomontana*

Lobelia flaccida

Craterocapsa congesta

Craterocapsa tarsodes

243

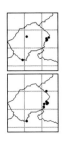

Lobelia galpinii (named after Ernest Galpin, 1858-1941, banker, SA naturalist and 'prince' of plant collectors)
Creeping herb, forming thick carpets. In marshy places, summit plateau, above 2800m. EMR endemic. LEAVES ±10-15×3-5mm. FLOWERS solitary in leaf axils, deep blue (Dec-Mar).

Lobelia preslii mahlo-a-konyana-a-loti (SS) (after K.B. Presl, 1794-1852, Prof of Botany, Prague Univ)
Perennial herb, 200-350mm tall. In tangled clumps or mats, in damp, partially shaded places, rocky gullies, on cliffs, 2100-2400m. Cape to KZN. LEAVES mostly crowded below in rosettes, **roundish**, 12-35mm diam, margins **bluntly** toothed, stalks 25-70mm long. FLOWERS 15-25mm long, 2-lipped, bright deep blue, palate white with pale yellow ridges in throat, **stems up to 240mm long** (Dec-Apr).

Monopsis (mon - one; *opsis* - appearance, flowers almost regular) Flowers regular or 2-lipped. Mainly SAfr, ±20 species, 1 in this region.

Monopsis decipiens [= *Lobelia decipiens*] **Butterfly Monopsis; Skoenlapperplant (A); mahlo-a-konyana (SS); isidala somkhuhlane (Z)** (*decipiens* - deceiving, a species that closely resembles another)
Slender, erect herb, 100-200mm tall. In marshy grassland, up to 2000m.Widespread. Stems wiry, branched. LEAVES 8-15×1-2mm. FLOWERS solitary, or few, ±18mm long, **upper lip violet, lower bright blue with yellow palate** (Oct-Feb). GENERAL: Used in traditional medicine. Needs damp places in garden.

COMPOSITAE also called **ASTERACEAE - Daisy Family** (see pg 144) *Vernonia* (named after William Vernon, died 1711, English botanist who collected in USA) Cosmop, over 1000 species, ±40 in SAfr, absent from winter rainfall area, ±7 in this region.

Vernonia hirsuta **Quilted-leaved Vernonia; Wildesonsoekertjie (A) hlele-hlele, phefo-e-kholo, sechee (SS); ijungitheka, ikhambi lenyongo, uhlunguhlungwana lwentaba, umhlazawentaba (Z)** (*hirsuta* - long-haired)
Herb, up to 1m tall. Occasional, **on dry grass slopes**, up to 1980m. Widespread. LEAVES ±100x50mm, **thick, stalkless, clasping the stem.** FLOWERHEADS **5-8mm diam**, in dense, flat, branched inflorescence; bracts **abruptly contracted to hairlike tips** (Sep-Jan). GENERAL: Used in traditional medicine. Hardy garden plant, grown from seed. **Similar species:** *Vernonia flanaganii* [= *V. hirsuta* subsp. *flanaganii*] (after Henry Flanagan, E Cape naturalist and plant collector, one of the first people to collect plants in the high N Drakensberg) Up to 800mm tall. Often in pure stands, **in moist, scrub filled gullies**, 1525-2100m. EMR endemic. LEAVES thick, ±80×50mm, shape variable, **tapered into short stalk.** FLOWERHEADS ±10mm diam, bracts **gradually narrowed to the tip** (Nov-Dec). GENERAL: Can be confused with *V. hirsuta* which is always found on drier sites.

Vernonia natalensis **Silver Vernonia; ileleva, isibhaha sasenkangala, umlahlankosi-omphlophe (Z)** (*natalensis* - from Natal, the province now called KwaZulu-Natal)
Silver shrublet, up to 1m tall. In clumps and sometimes colonies, on open grassy slopes, up to 1980m. Widespread. **Covered in silvery silky hairs.** LEAVES 35-60 ×4-10mm. FLOWERHEADS up to 10mm diam, in flat, branched inflorescences (Aug-Dec). GENERAL: Used in traditional medicine and as a charm against lightning. A popular garden plant, grown from seed, cuttings, division. **Similar species:** *Vernonia oligocephala* **Bicoloured-leaved Vernonia; Bitterbossie, Groenamarabossie, Maag-bossie, Wildetee (A); mofefa-bana (SS); ihlambihloshane, uhlungu-hloshana (Z)** (*oligocephala* - with few heads) Stems silvery hairy. LEAVES up to 40×25mm, **dark green above, silky white beneath, broadly rounded at base, margins wavy.** GENERAL: Used in traditional medicine. Leaves used for a tea. Good garden plant.

Felicia (after Herr Felix, died 1846, a German official at Regensburg) Herbs with hairy fruits. Afr ±80 species, mainly SAfr, ±11 in this region.

Felicia caespitosa (*caespitosus* - tufted mats)
Stems creeping, forming tufted mats, along streams at high altitude. EMR endemic. First collected by Galpin (1904) and then by Hilliard and Burtt (1983), otherwise unknown. LEAVES about 10×1mm, margins with long hairs, mature leaf blade hairless. FLOWERHEADS about 15mm diam, rays light purple, disc yellow.

Felicia drakensbergensis
Compact, dwarf shrublet. On basalt cliffs, among outcropping rocks, along streambanks on the summit plateau, 2800-3350m. EMR endemic. Stems and leaves thinly covered with coarse white hairs, leaves towards ends of branches. LEAVES up to 10×1mm, thick, **opposite, joined at base.** FLOWERHEADS 20-25mm diam, blue to mauve, solitary on stalks 15-40mm long (Jan-Feb).

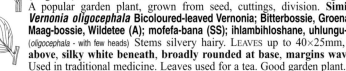

Lobelia preslii

Monopsis decipiens

Lobelia preslii

Darrel Plowes

Auriol Batten

David McDonald

Lobelia galpinii

Peter Linder

Felicia caespitosa

Hilliard & Burtt

Felicia drakensbergensis

David McDonald

Vernonia hirsuta

Darrel Plowes

Vernonia natalensis

Darrel Plowes

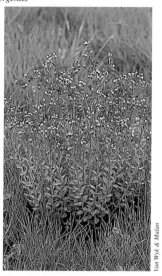

Vernonia oligocephala

Van Wyk & Malan

245

Felicia filifolia [= *Aster filifolius*] **Fine-leaved Felicia; Persbergdraaibos, Wilde-aster (A); leholo, sehalahala, sehalahala-se-seholo (SS)** (*filifolia* - thread leaved)
Much branched aromatic shrub, up to 1m tall. On broken cliffs, bare steep, rocky places, boulder beds of rivers, becomes a weed in overgrazed areas, up to 2400m. W Cape to Limpopo Prov. Twigs creamy brown. LEAVES **needlelike**, in clusters. FLOWERHEADS massed, ±20mm diam, ray florets mauve, blue (white), stalks up to 50mm long (Sep-Oct, all year). GENERAL: Poisonous to sheep. Used for firewood in Les. Hardy garden plant.

Felicia rosulata [= *F. natalensis, Aster natalensis*] (*rosulatus* - rosette, refers to leaf arrangement)
Perennial herb, 150(300)mm tall. In rocky grassland, valley bottoms, on edge of rock sheets, steep slopes below basalt cliffs, in loose scree, **2000-3200m.** Mountains, NE Cape to Mpum. LEAVES up to 90×25mm, in basal rosette, ± **flat on the ground, densely hairy, often purplish below, margins ± toothed.** FLOWERHEADS solitary, ±20mm diam, rays mauve (blue or white), stems with long shaggy hairs (Sep-Dec).

Felicia uliginosa [= *Aster uliginosus*] (*uliginosa* - swampy, marshy, moist, refers to the habitat)
Dwarf, mat-forming herb, up to 80mm tall. In marshy grassland on summit plateau, 2835-3350m. EMR endemic. Branches prostrate or reclining, rooting. LEAVES up to 25mm long, less than 1mm wide, closely overlapping, **margins with conspicuous hairs** on lower half. FLOWERHEADS 25-30mm diam, rays blue to mauve, stalks hairy (Jan-Mar).

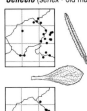

Felicia wrightii (named after F.B. Wright, veterinarian, nature conservationist, plant collector in the Kamberg / Giants Castle area and on the summit of the Drakensberg)
Mat-forming perennial herb, up to 250mm tall. In big colonies. On damp earth banks, **along incised streams, 1675-2100m.** EMR endemic. LEAVES up to 40×10mm, **thick, hairless except for stout hairs on margins**, in flat basal rosettes. FLOWERHEADS ±20mm diam, mauve (white), disc yellow, stem hairy (Sep-Oct).

Senecio (*senex* - old man, refers to whitish hairs of pappus) (see pg 162)

Senecio barbatus **Sticky-plume Senecio** (*barbatus* - bearded)
Perennial herb, up to 300mm tall, **all parts covered in long soft, shaggy, sticky, often purplish hairs**. In grassland, up to 3400m. E Cape to Mpum. LEAVES in rosette, up to 70×20mm, margins ± entire, stem leaves narrower, margins finely toothed. INFLORESCENCE **congested**; FLOWERHEADS ±12×10mm, bracts ±10mm long, florets purplish maroon, blue, whitish or yellowish (Nov-Jan).

Senecio discodregeanus [= *S. dregeanus var. discoideus*] **lehlomane-le-lenyenyane, mantoana, sebiloane (SS)** (*discodregeanus* - *S. dregeanus* without rays)
Slender, erect, perennial herb, up to 1m tall. In grassland, up to 2200m. KZN to Mpum. Stem simple, leafy below. All parts **white-woolly cobwebby at first, persisting in leaf axils and on bracts around the flowerheads**. LEAVES leathery, up to 400×40mm, tapering to long stalklike base. INFLORESCENCE small, branched; FLOWERHEADS ±15mm diam, bracts ±9mm long, red-edged (Dec-Mar). GENERAL: Used in traditional medicine.

Berkheya (after Dutch botanist Jan le Francq van Berkhey, 1724-1812) (see pg 176)

Berkheya purpurea **Purple Berkheya; Bloudisseldoring (A); sehlohlo (SS)**
Robust, very spiny perennial herb, up to 900mm tall. Often in large colonies, on steep grassy mountain slopes, in rough vegetation along streams, 1525-3050m. E Cape to KZN. Stem stout, cobwebby or with long, soft, spreading hairs, winged, leafy. BASAL LEAVES crowded, up to 250×100mm, **lobes coarsely toothed or lobed, spines 7-10mm long**, harshly hairy above, woolly white beneath. FLOWERHEADS few, 50-80 mm diam, on stalks up to 80mm long, **ray and disc florets pale to deep purple** (white), bracts up to 5mm wide, tips, margins spiny (Jan-Apr). GENERAL: Uppermost flower opens first.

Felicia filifolia

Felicia filifolia

Felicia uliginosa

Senecia discodregeanus

Felicia wrightii

Felicia uliginosa

Senecio barbatus

Felicia rosulata

Senecio barbatus

Berkheya purpurea

247

MONOCOTYLEDONS Single seed-leaf, parallel veins, flower parts in threes or multiples of three.

CYPERACEAE - Sedge family Grasslike herbs usually found near water or damp areas. Stems often 3-angled or occasionally cylindrical, solid, mostly without joints (grass stems jointed, often hollow). Leaves in 3 ranks or reduced to tubular sheaths. Flowers small, clustered in spikelets on upright or spreading branches, or in heads forming collectively an inflorescence. Fruit a nutlet. Cosmop, ± 104 genera, ± 5000 species, ±40 genera in SAfr, ±400 species. *Mariscus* (old name used by Pliny for a rush) Doubtfully distinct from *Cyperus*. More or less cosmop, ±200 species, ±32 in SAfr, 2 in this region.

Mariscus congestus qoqothoane (SS) *(congestus - crowded)*

Tufted perennial, 600-900mm (up to 1.2m) tall. In wet or moist hollows and damp streambanks, up to 2100m. SW Cape to Zim, also Europe, Middle East, Austr. LEAVES tough, about 10mm wide. INFLORESCENCE branched, spikes large, green streaked red, about 35mm diam; SPIKELETS 8-20mm long, bracts about 220mm long (summer). **General:** Grazed by cattle. Used to make ropes and baskets. (see pg 262)

Carex (*caric* - sedge) An old established genus, the fruits hardly differing at all from fossil remains identified from between 70-30 million years ago. Fairly cosmop in moist time climates, also Arctic and Antarctic regions. Mostly N Hemisp, ±1700 species, ±19 in SAfr, 8 in this region.

Carex austro-africana Nodding Sedge, Cat's Tail Sedge; Knikkende rietgras (A); lesuoane-le-lenyenyane (SS)

Leafy perennial, less than 1m tall. Often form dense stands in wet places, usually rooted in shallow, slow flowing water, up to 2250m. Mountains from KZN to Trop Afr. SPIKELETS dense, drooping or **nodding, brown**, up to 70mm long, on long, slender stalks, usually 5-6 per stem.

Juncus (*jungere* - to join, refers to ancient use in making mats, chair seats) Leaves closely resemble grasses and sedges. Cosmop, mainly in mild and cold conditions, ±250 species, ±22 in SAfr, at least 9 in this region.

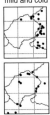

Juncus effusus *(effusus - spread out)*

Stiffly erect perennial, up to 1m tall. Found in wet places, up to 2400m. Cosmop. LEAVES reduced to glossy brownish black sheaths, stems green, 2-3mm diam, **stems and leaves do not have transverse joints** (do not feel knotty when grasped and run through the fingers). Cluster of flowers appears to be on one side of the stem because it is overtopped by a long sharp pointed bract that closely resembles the stem (spring flowering). **Similar species:** *Juncus inflexus* (*inflexus* - bent) In marshy ground, up to 2600m. Very similar to *J. effusus* but **central cavity interrupted by transverse plates** (stems and leaves feel knotty when grasped and run through the fingers).

HYACINTHACEACE (See pg 228) *Bowiea* (named after James Bowie, 1789-1869, plant collector) SAfr to CAfr, 2 species, 1 in this region.

Bowiea volubilis Bowiea, Climbing Lily; Knolklimop (A); umgaqana (X); iguleni, ugibisisila (Z) *(volubilis - twining)*

Deciduous, succulent climber, up to 3m high. On forest margins, among rocks, up to 1800m. E Cape to EAfr. BULB light green, large, ±150mm diam, on surface of the soil. Stems fleshy, **bright green, much branched, functioning as leaves**. LEAVES small, dropping early. FLOWRS starry, green, 16-24mm diam, stalks long, backward pointing (Jan-Mar). GENERAL: Bulb very poisonous. Extensively used in traditional medicine.

Galtonia (named after British scientist Sir Francis Galton, 1822-1911, who travelled widely in SA) Genus endemic to SAfr, 4 species, 3 in this region.

Galtonia viridiflora Green Berg Lily (see pg 52)

Dipcadi (*dipcadi* - oriental name originally used for the Grape Hyacinth) Afr, Madag, Medit, India, ±30 species, ±14 in SAfr, ±3 in this region.

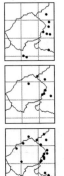

Dipcadi viride Dainty Green Bells, Green Dipcadi; Gifbolletjie, Grootslymuintjie, Skaamblommetjie (A); lephotoana, molubeli, morotoana-phookoana, theleli-moro (SS); ikhakhakha elihluza (Z) *(viride - green)*

Up to 1m tall. In grassland, on shallow stony soil, up to 2400m. Widespread. LEAVES 2-3, hairless, grey-green, 2-4mm broad. INFLORESCENCE long, slender; FLOWERS **all face the same way, outer tepal lobes with long 'tails' ±20mm**, green to reddish brown, unpleasant scent at night (Oct-Jan). GENERAL: Bulbs and leaves eaten as culinary herbs. Used as a protective charm against storms. **Similar species:** *Dipcadi gracillimum* (*gracillimum* - slender, thin) 250-400mm tall. Widespread, in grassland and on edges of rock sheets, up to 2400m. LEAVES threadlike. FLOWERS ±10mm long, **all tepals the same length** (Nov-Dec). *Dipcadi marlothii* Dronkui (A); morothoana-phookoana (SS) (named after H.W.R. Marloth, 1855-1931, analytical chemist, botanist) In grassland, up to 2285m. Widespread. LEAVES **spirally twisted above**, short hairs on margins. INFLORESCENCE **tip droops sharply in bud, tepal lobes without tails, spreading** (Oct-Feb). GENERAL: Used in traditional medicine and to induce good aim of hunters.

Tony Abbott

Mariscus congestus

Rosemary Wiliams

Juncus effusus

Tony Abbott

Carex austro-africana

Rosemary Wiliams

Juncus effusus

Neil Crouch

Boweia volubilis

Rosemary Wiliams

Dipcadi gracillimum

Neil Crouch

Boweia volubilis

John Grimshaw

Galtonia viridiflora

Braam van Wyk

Dipcadi marlothii

Jo Onderstall

Dipcadi viride

249

Eucomis - Pineapple lilies (*eucomis* - beautiful hair, topknot) Inflorescence topped with tuft of green leafy bracts. SAfr, ±10 species, ±4 in this region.

Eucomis autumnalis subsp. *clavata* [= *E undulata*] Common Pineapple Lily; Krulkop, Wildepynappel (A); khapumpu, khato, maboni, mathebethebale, mathethebale, moboni, mohale-oa-marumo, mothusi (SS); ubuhlungu becanti (X); umathunga, umakhondle (Z)

(*autumnalis* - autumn, flowering time; *clavata* - club-shaped, refers to shape of flowering stem)

Up to 300mm tall. In damp grassland, on slopes or at foot of cliffs, up to 2450m. LEAVES 150-450(600)×60-130mm, **margins crisped and wavy.** INFLORESCENCE 70-170×50-70mm, flowers tightly packed, **stem stout, club-shaped,** strongly tapered to base; FLOWERS creamy green (Dec-Feb). CAPSULE **hard,** angled. GENERAL: Three subspecies in SAfr. Widely used in traditional medicine. A popular garden plant.

Eucomis humilis Dwarf Pineapple Lily, Lowly Pineapple Flower; Beskeie Berglelie (A) (*humilis* - lowly, modest) (see pg 54)

ASPARAGACEAE - Asparagus Family Subshrubs or climbers. Leaves reduced to scales. Afr, Asia, Europe, 1 genus, ±120 species, ±81 in SAfr, ±5 in this region. *Asparagus* (*aspharagos* - after the name given to the edible *asparagus*) Description for family.

Asparagus asparagoides [= *Myrsiphyllum asparagoides*] Broad-leaved Asparagus; Breëblaarklimop, Krulkransie (A); khopananyane, likhopa, sethota-sa-mathuela (SS); isicakathi (X); ibutha, inkunzimbili (Z)

Scrambling climber, up to 2m high. In scrub and on forest margins, up to 2450m. S Cape to Trop Afr. Stems wiry. 'LEAVES' oval, 25-40× ± **8mm,** tips sharply pointed. FLOWERS ±15mm diam, greenish, **tepal lobes long, slender, curving back, stamens protruding,** sweetly scented (Nov-May). FRUIT ±10mm diam, black. GENERAL: Used in traditional medicine to treat sore eyes and as a charm to increase fertility of cattle. Popular with florists, known as Cape Smilax, and as a container plant. Introduced into gardens in Europe in the 1700s.

DIOSCOREACEAE - Yam Family (named after Pedanios Dioscorides, 1st century AD, a Greek herbalist) Climbers with tuberous or thick woody rootstock. Male and female flowers on separate plants. Cosmop, in trop and warm regions, 5 genera, ±600 species, SAfr 1 genus, ±16 species, 3 in this region.

Dioscorea rupicola impinyampinya, inkwa (Z) (*rupicola* -growing in stony places)

Slender climber, up to 3m high. On forest margins, in stream gullies, up to 1950m. E Cape to Mpum. Tuber buried below ground. LEAVES ±70×60mm, **heart-shaped, 5-7-lobed, margins wavy.** FLOWERS **in erect spikes** up to 80mm long (Nov-Jan). FRUITS ±30×20mm, 3-winged, glossy light brown, in hanging bunches. GENERAL: Tubers edible when boiled, eaten in times of famine. Used in traditional medicine.

Dioscorea sylvatica Forest Elephant's Foot, Wild Yam; Olifantsvoet, Skilpadknol (A); ingwevu, ufudu (Z) (*sylvatica* - growing in woods and forests)

Slender climber, up to 15m high. On forest margins and over bushes in stream gullies, up to 1900m. E Cape to CAfr. Tuber **large,** up to 300(1000)mm diam, flattened, ±120 mm thick, dark brown, corky with reticulate markings, **exposed above ground or buried.** LEAVES 50-80×60mm, **heart-shaped, 3-lobed or without lobes, very variable.** FLOWERS yellowish green, **in long hanging spikes** (Nov-Apr). FRUITS ±25×15mm, yellowish green, edged reddish brown. GENERAL: Rootstock contains diosgenin, used in preparation of cortisone. Used in traditional medicine to treat cuts, wounds, blood problems and chest complaints. Threatened through over exploitation. Decorative container or feature plant.

ORCHIDACEAE (see pg 232) *Habenaria* (*habena* - strap, thong; *aria* - possessing, refers to the long spur) Flowers mostly green and white, median sepal joined with whole or upper lobes of petals forming a hood, lip lobed, spur long. About 800 species, 35 in SAfr, ±12 in this region.

Habenaria clavata ´mametsana (SS) (*clavata* - club-shaped, refers to the spur)

200-700mm tall. In rocky grassland, up to 2000m. E Cape to Trop Afr. LEAVES sheathing at base, ±130×40mm. INFLORESCENCE loose, many flowered; FLOWERS green **with white stigmas,** hood 15-20mm, lower **petal lobes hornlike, 25-40mm long, slender, strongly curved upwards,** lip side lopes slender, **stigmatic arms white, long, 8-12mm, spur 30-50mm long,** slender with thickened tip (Jan-Mar). **Similar species:** *Habenaria cornuta* ´mametsana (SS) (*cornuta* - horned, refers to lower petal lobes) In damp or marshy grassland, up to 2100m. E Cape to Limpopo Prov. INFLORESCENCE **dense;** FLOWERS green, lower petal lobes long, **swollen at base,** strongly curved upwards, lip side lobes wide towards base, **stigmatic arms short, 3-8mm,** spur 15-25mm long (Feb-Mar).

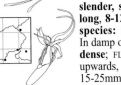

David McDonald

Lal Greene

Eucomis autumnalis

Eucomis humilis

Wally Menne

Martin von Fintel

Dioscorea rupicola

Dioscorea sylvatica

H J Venter

Hilliard & Burtt

Lal Greene

Habenaria clavata

Habenaria cornuta

Asparagus asparagoides

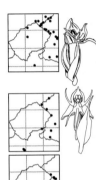

Habenaria dregeana Small Green Hood; ´mametsana (SS) (named after Johann Drège, German pharmacist, horticulturist and botanical collector who travelled widely in SA from from 1826-1834, Called the 'father of South African phytogeography')

Slender, 100-300mm tall. In rocky grassland, up to 2000m. Widespread. E Cape to DRC, Zim, Uganda. **Basal leaves flat on the ground**, ±85mm diam, fleshy. INFLORESCENCE dense, ±110mm long; FLOWERS yellowish green, petal lobes short, 1-4mm, **lip 3-lobed, midlobe twice as long as side lobes**, spur short, ±10mm long, **wide at the mouth** (Feb-Mar). GENERAL: Used as a protective charm against storms. Similar species: **Habenaria lithophila** (lithos - stone; philos - loving) Slender, 100-300mm tall. In rocky grassland, up to 2500m. W Cape to Tanz. Lower **petal lobes long, very slender**, 4-8mm, **lip lobes ± equal**, spur not wide at mouth (Jan-Mar).

Habenaria laevigata (laevigata - smooth, slippery)

Slender, up to 400mm tall. In grassland, up to 2100m. E Cape to Limpopo Prov. LEAVES clasping stem, 30-60×7-15mm, margins hard, **grading into bracts**. INFLORESCENCE **slender, bracts long**, ±32mm; FLOWERS green to yellowish green, **lip 3-lobed, midlobe erect, ±6mm, longer than side lobes**, spur long, slender, 16-25mm (Jan-Feb).

Satyrium (Satyros - refers to the 2-horned satyr, half man, half goat, the two spurs somewhat resemble a satyr's horns) Ovary not twisted, lip forms a hood, 2 conspicuous spurs or 2 pouches. Used in traditional medicine, mixed with other medicines to help with illnesses that are difficult to cure. Afr, Madag, India, China, 88 species, 37 in SAfr, ±10 in this region.

Satyrium microrrhynchum (mikros - small; rhynchos - beak or snout)

Slender, 150-250mm tall. Scattered, in grassland, 1600-3300m. E Cape to Mpum. LEAVES 2-3, at base of stem, 50-120mm, partly spreading, thick, smooth. INFLORESCENCE a dense spike, 30-150mm long; FLOWERS pale yellowish green to dull white, ± tinged pink around the hood, inner surface of the petals and lip **thick textured with short hairs, spurs absent or tiny** (Jan-Feb).

Satyrium parviflorum Devil Orchid; ´mametsana (SS); ilabatheka elikhulu elibomvu, impimpi enkulu (Z) (parviflorum - small flowers)

Slender and leafless to robust and leafy, 150-750mm tall. In damp or marshy ground near streams and in rank vegetation, up to 2300m. S Cape to Trop Afr. LEAVES 100-330mm long, sometimes on a side shoot, often withered at time of flowering. INFLORESCENCE crowded, ±300mm long; FLOWERS small, **yellowish green** to dark maroon, **petals drying brown soon after opening**, spurs ±15mm long, sweetly scented (Dec-Mar). GENERAL: Used as protective and love charms.

Eulophia (eu - well; lophos - crest, refers to the crested lip) Terrestrial herbs. **Lip ridged on upper surface**. Old and New World, most common in Afr, 42 in S Afr, 9 in this region.

Eulophia foliosa lekholela, loetsane, ´mametsana (SS) (foliosa - leafy)

Stout, 150-300mm tall. Frequent, on grass slopes, often around rock outcrops, up to 2000m. E Cape to Limpopo Prov. LEAVES pleated, stiffly erect, partly to fully grown at flowering. INFLORESCENCE dense, elongated, ±100×40mm; FLOWERS **fleshy, dull lime green**, sepals and petals 9-16mm long, lip tipped dark purple (white to pale purple), no spur, honey-scented (Nov-Dec).

Mystacidium (mystax - moustache; idium - diminutive, refers to rostellum lobes) Small epiphytes. Sepals and petals curved back, pointed at tip, spur mouth wide, tapering to long, narrow point. SAfr and EAfr, 9 species, 7 in SAfr, 5 of them endemic, 1 in this region.

Mystacidium gracile (gracilis - slender, refers to the slender roots and flowers)

Epiphyte with a **mass of slender, unbranched, bluish green roots**. In forest patches, up to 1900m. E Cape to Zim. **Usually leafless**, occasionally 1-2 leaves, ±20×3mm. INFLORESCENCES several, 30-50mm long; FLOWERS delicate, 9-14mm diam, **pale yellowish green, spur very slender, white**, 20-25mm long (Sep-Nov).

Habenaria dregeana

Habenaria lithophila

Eulophia foliosa

Satyrium parviflorum   *Satyrium microrrhynchum*   *Habenaria lithophila*   *Habenaria dregeana*

Satyrium parviflorum

Habenaria lithophila   *Habenaria laevigata*

Eulophia foliosa   *Mystacidium gracile*   *Mystacidium gracile*

253

DICOTYLEDONS Two seed leaves, net veins, flower parts in fours, fives or multiples of these.

PIPERACEAE - Pepper Family Slightly succulent herbs. Pantrop, ±2000 species, 15 genera, 2 in SAfr. ***Peperomia*** (*peperi* - pepper; *homoios* - like) Several species popular as container plants. Warmer parts of N and S Hemisp, mostly America, ±1000 species, 5 in SAfr, 1 in this region.

Peperomia retusa Wild Peperomia (*retusa* - rounded, shallowly notched end)
Perennial creeping herb, 50-200mm tall. In mats on mossy rocks in forest, up to 1900m. W Cape to Limpopo Prov. LEAVES slightly succulent, ±20mm long, **alternate**, dark green above, greyish beneath. FLOWERS tiny, green, in terminal spikes ±10mm long (Nov-Jan). GENERAL: Popular container plant, groundcover for shady areas.

CANNABACEAE *Cannabis* (*cannabis* - Greek noun from which 'canvas' was derived; *sativa* - cultivated) **Dagga or Marijuana** Robust annual herb. Central Asia, 1 species, widely cultivated both for fibre and for its drug properties.

★ *Cannabis sativa* Dagga, Marijuana, Hashish; matekoane, ˈmoana (SS); insangu (Z)
Herb up to 2m tall. From Central Asia, a naturalised weed in Les. LEAVES 3-7 foliolate, leaflets ±120×12mm. GENERAL: Widely cultivated for intoxicant drug properties.

SANTALACEAE - Sandalwood Family *Thesium* (a Greek word) Herbs or subshrubs or shrubs, hemiparasitic. (see pg 128)

Thesium alatum (*alatum* - winged)
Robust, dull yellowish green tufted perennial herb, up to 600mm tall. Often in large stands on steep grass slopes and short stony grassland on ridges, 1800-2285m. EMR endemic. STEMS **winged**. LEAVES ±15×1mm, few, widely spaced. FLOWERS dull yellowish green outside, white inside with **tufts of white hairs at tips of lobes**, in short racemes on the well branched upper part of the stems (Nov-Jan).

MOLLUGINACEAE Leaves often crowded into basal rosettes or false whorls on stems. Petals absent or small. Trop, subtrop, mostly SAfr, ±16 genera, ±120 species, 1 genus in SAfr. *Psammotropha* (*psammos* - sand; *trophos* - living) Mostlyt SAfr, ±11 species, 5 in this region.

Psammotropha mucronata bohomana, mothujoane, senama (SS) (*mucronata* - small hard tip)
Dwarf herb, stems sprawling, forming loose mats or sometimes in a compact cushion. On damp cliffs, boulder and earth banks above streams, bare ground, up to 3200m. LEAVES in compact tufts, 5-20mm long, thin, **nearly transparent, distinctly narrowed to base, midrib not projecting, often invisible**. INFLORESCENCES erect or spreading, 30-250mm long; FLOWERS in small groups at nodes, **bracts resemble leaves, tipped with small mucro** (Nov-Jan). GENERAL: Used in traditional medicine. **Similar species: *Psammotropha myriantha* impepho-tshani (Z)** (*myriantha* - numberless flowers) Composed of many leaf tufts, forming a cushion. On bare stony ground, up to 2400m. E Cape to Trop Afr. LEAVES up to 80mm long, **opaque, not narrowed to the base, midrib easily seen, slightly projecting on underside**. INFLORESCENCES erect, often well branched, ±20-100mm long, **bracts much narrowed to tip, resemble leaves**, strongly scented (Nov-Jan). GENERAL: Used in traditional perfumed ointment.

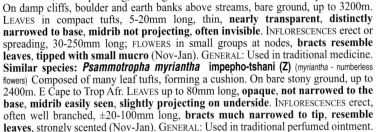

Psammotropha obtusa (*obtusa* - blunt)
Forming small mats. On bare wet gravelly patches or damp turf around rocks, on summit plateau. EMR endemic. LEAVES **crowded in rosettes** at branch tips, 2-3mm long, oval, blunt, **margins white**. FLOWERS in axils of terminal leaves (Nov-Jan).

RANUNCULACEAE - Buttercup Family (see pg 128) *Thalictrum* (refers to bright green colour of young leaves) Perennial herbs, widespread in cool, sheltered or shady localities. Mainly N Temp regions, ±85 species, 2 in SAfr, 2 in this region.

Thalictrum rhynchocarpum Kabousie (A) (*rhynchocarpum* - beaked fruit)
Perennial, much branched, herbaceous shrub, up to 1.5m tall. On forest floor, 1300-1800m. SAfr to Trop Afr. Stems very slender, much branched, hairless. LEAFLETS **thin, slightly greyish beneath, superficially resemble maiden hair fern**. INFLORESCENCE loosely branched, branches very slender; FLOWERS tiny, with a green to purplish tuft of stamens and an ovary (Oct-Dec). FRUITS **asymmetrical**, with a long beak.

ROSACEAE - Rose Family (see pg 130) *Alchemilla* (*alchemilla* - from its alleged value in alchemy) Annual or perennial herbs or low shrubs. Temp regions and trop mtns, about 250 species, ±16 in SAfr, ±6 in this region. Genus poorly understood in SAfr.

Alchemilla colura (*coluros* - truncated, refers to the leaf lobes)
Mat forming perennial herb. In damp grass or damp soil near streams, 1800-2900m. EMR endemic. LEAVES ±15×30mm, upper third divided into 5 **shallow, rounded lobes**, margins toothed, **stalks 20-30mm long**. INFLORESCENCE branched, up to 100mm long; FLOWERS creamy green, in axils of bracts (Dec-Feb). **Similar species: *Alchemilla woodii* Lady's Mantle; molalaphoka, morothetso, phokana (SS)** (after John Medley Wood, 1827-1915, founding curator of Natal Herbarium) Mostly in disturbed areas, 1500-2400m. KZN to Mpum. LEAVES **grey, very hairy** (Oct-Nov).

Cannabis sativa

Peter Linder

Thesium alatum

Hilliard & Burtt

Peperomia retusa

Olaf Wirminghaus

Psammotropha myriantha

Martin von Fintel

Psammotropha mucronata

Wally Mennee

Psammotropha mucronata

Pam Cooke

Psammotropha obtusa

Peter Linder

Alchemilla colura

John Grimshaw

Alchemilla woodii

David McDonald

Thalictrum rhynchocarpum

Lal Greene

255

EUPHORBIACEAE - Rubber or Euphorbia Family Herbs, shrubs, trees twiners, succulent or not, often with milky sap. Leaves simple, divided or absent. Flowers unisexual, male and female within a cuplike structure (cyathium) or in a regular inflorescence, petals absent or reduced to a rim or three lobes. Fruit usually a 3-chambered capsule. Economically important species produce rubber (*Hevea*), castor oil (*Ricinus*), cassava and tapioca (*Manihot*) and ornamentals such as poinsettia, crown-of-thorns (*Euphorbia*) and croton (*Codiaeum*). Cosmop, ±300 genera, ±5000 species, 50 genera in SAfr. *Clutia* (named after Outgers Cluyt, 17th century Dutch botanist, curator of Leiden Botanical Gardens) Shrubs, herbs. Flowers in leaf axils, male in small clusters, female solitary, on separate plants. Mostly Afr, ±70 species, ±35 in SAfr, ±5 in this region.

Clutia katharinae (named after Katharine Saunders, 1824-1901, botanical artist and plant collector, born England, lived and died on the farm Amanzimnyama, at Tongaat, KwaZulu-Natal)

Spindly shrub, 1-2m tall. In scrub, on boulder beds, streambanks and on forest margins, 1500-2440m. **Young stems and capsules with long, silky white hairs.** LEAVES 25-7×6-10mm, blunt tipped, narrowing to base, **covered in long silky white hairs at least when young**. FLOWERS small, white, male and female on separate plants (Sep-Dec). CAPSULES **silky hairy.**

Clutia monticola (monticola - growing on mountains)

Tuft of unbranched stems, up to 600mm tall. In montane grassland up to 1675m. E Cape to Limpopo Prov. Stems angular, leafy. Plant hairless. LEAVES ±50×30mm, firm, pale green, turning pink with age, with **translucent gland dots** when held up to the light. FLOWERS greenish white (Jul-Dec). FRUIT a capsule ±5mm diam.

Euphorbia (named after Euphorbus, 1st century physician to King Juba of Mauritania) Herbs, shrubs, trees, usually with milky sap, sometimes succulent. Flowers reduced, within a cyathium or 'cup' rimmed with petal-like glands. Cosmop, ±1600 species, over 300 in SAfr, ±7 in this region.

Euphorbia epicyparissias Wild Spurge; Melkbos, Pisgoedbossie (A); sehlakoana-se-senyenyane (SS); ikhanda lentuli (Z) (epi - upon; kyparissos - cypress)

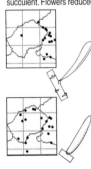

Perennial, spindly subshrub, 0.6-1.5m tall. **In large stands**, in moist grassland, on streambanks, up to 2300m. Stem simple at base, well branched above, rough with leaf scars, bark dark reddish. LEAVES **crowded**, 10-40mm, **blunt** tipped, spreading or curved up. INFLORESCENCES spreading or congested, 20-80mm diam; FLOWERS in cyathia with **2 large yellowish green** (tinged red) **bracts at base**, 10-20mm wide (Oct-Jan). **Similar species:** *Euphorbia natalensis* sehlakoana-se-senyenyane (SS); inkalamasane, inkamamasane, umnhlonhlo (Z) **Tufted perennial herb**, 150-600mm tall. **In dense stands** in coarse grassland in valley bottoms, or scattered on grassy slopes and dwarfed, up to 2440m. E Cape to Mpum. LEAVES crowded, 8-25×1-7mm, grey-green, **often deflexed, tapering to pointed tip**. GENERAL: Zulu names refer to its use to sour milk.

Euphorbia striata Milkweed, Spurge; Melkgras (A); mohlatsisa (SS) (striata - striped or furrowed)

Slender, **single stemmed herb**, up to 600mm tall. Scattered in grassland, up to 2500m. Stems branch at the top. LEAVES ±40×3mm, **erect**, widely spaced, tapering to **sharply pointed tip**, margins red. INFLORESCENCE loose, bracts ±10mm diam, greenish (Oct-Jan).

MELIANTHACEAE - Melianthus Family Trees or shrubs. Leaves simple or compound. Some species grown as ornamentals. Afr, 2 genera, ±14 species, 2 genera in SAfr. *Melianthus* (meli - honey; anthos - flower, refers to abundant nectar) **Honey Flowers** Shrubs or subshrubs, often strong smelling. Flowers greenish or reddish. Fruit a capsule. Attracts butterflies. SAfr, 6 species, 2 in this region.

Melianthus villosus Maroon Honey-flower; Kruidjie-roer-my-nie (A); ibhonya (Z) (villosus - shaggy)

Soft perennial shrub, up to 2m tall. In moist places, on forest margins, below cliffs, up to 1800m. EMR endemic. LEAVES large, compound, **densely hairy**; LEAFLETS in 5-7 pairs, ±140mm long, margins deeply toothed, stipules 20-25mm long. INFLORESCENCE terminal; FLOWERS pendulous, sepals large, brownish purple, veined green, petals small, pink to purplish brown (Nov-Feb). FRUIT **inflated, 4-angled**. GENERAL: Leaves have an unpleasant odour when crushed. Decorative garden plant.

ACHARIACEAE SAfr, 3 genera, 3 species. *Guthriea* (after Francis Guthrie, 1831-1899, Prof of Maths, SA College, Cape Town, who, with H. Bolus contributed Ericaceae to *Flora Capensis*) Stemless herb with fleshy roots. Leaves in rosette. Fruit a capsule. Monotypic genus, endemic.

Guthriea capensis Hidden Flower

Compact, stemless herb with rosette of beautiful leaves. In damp places on scree steep slopes below cliffs, under rocks, around grass tussocks, 2000-3000m. LEAVES 40-70×35-65mm, **glossy dark green above, veins deeply indented**, heart-shaped at base, margins scalloped, stalks 30-120mm long. FLOWERS bell-shaped, creamy green, ±15mm, male and female separate on same plant, hidden under leaves (Oct-Jan).

Clutia katharinae   *Clutia katharinae*   *Clutia monticola*

Tony Abbott   *Cameron McMaster*   *Lal Greene*

Euphorbia epicyparissias   *Euphorbia epicyparissias*   *Euphorbia striata*

Tony Abbott   *Lal Greene*   *Martin von Fintel*

Melianthus villosus   *Guthriea capensis*

Hilliard & Burtt   *David McDonald*   *Mike Hirst*

257

UMBELLIFERAE / APIACEAE - Carrot Family (see pg 80) *Dracosciadium* (*draco* - Drakensberg; *sciadium* - Greek for 'umbel') Perennial herb. Leaves palmate. SAfr endemic, 2 species, 1 in this region.

Dracosciadium saniculifolium (*saniculifolium* - leaves like genus *Sanicula*)

Tufted herb, flowering stems up to 450mm tall. Among boulders, at foot of basalt cliffs, 2100-2800m. EMR endemic. Flowering shoots sparingly branched from low down. LEAVES mostly basal, **palmate**, 50-90mm diam, divided into 7 main lobes, each lobed and sharply toothed, stalks ±150mm long. INFLORESCENCE very open; FLOWERS small, cream, clusters 10-20mm diam (Dec-Feb). FRUITS **drooping**.

Peucedanum (Greek name for Ferula, Fennel) - Perennial herbs. Leaves mostly basal, compound or finely divided. Flowers in compound inflorescence. Fruits flattened, ribbed and winged. Europe, Asia, Afr, ±120 species, ±31 in SAfr, genus much in need of revision.

Peucedanum thodei umphondovu (Z) (named after Justus Thode, 1859-1932, pioneer plant collector)

Robust perennial herb, up to2 m tall. On streambanks and gullies, open slopes, 1675-2600m. KZN to Mpum. Stems square, grooved, hollow, green to purplish red. LEAVES **3-pinnate**, ±600mm long below, leaflets lobed, lobes 20-60×10-20mm, irregularly toothed, stalks sheathing stem. INFLORESCENCES terminal, branched; FLOWERS tiny, yellowish green (Dec-Feb). FRUIT 5-6mm long, ridged. GENERAL: Used by diviners to bring rain, but only in times of extreme drought.

ASCLEPIADACEAE - Milkweed Family (see pg 140) *Xysmalobium* (see pg 266)

Xysmalobium involucratum Scented Xysmalobium; Hongersnoodbossie (A); udambisa omkhulu (Z) (*involucratum* - refers to reflexed petals that resemble involucral bracts)

Slender, erect herb, **150-360mm tall**. In well drained grassland, up to 2600m. All prov. except Limpopo. **Stems 1-3**. LEAVES **long, narrow**, 35-130×1-9mm. FLOWERS creamy green to greenish yellow, corolla **lobes completely reflexed to expose green corona and gynostegium**, anther wings with **distinct medial notch**, fragrant or sickly sweet scent, strong enough to induce a headache (Sep-Feb). FRUIT 60-170 ×5-15mm, smooth, tapering to sharp beak. GENERAL: Used as a charm against evil.

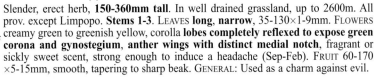

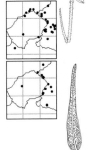

Xysmalobium parviflorum Octopus Cartwheel; leoto-la-khoho, ntsime, tsoetla (SS)
(*parvus* - small; *florus* - flower) (see pg 266)

Xysmalobium stockenstromense Mountain Uzura (named after Stockenstrom, town in E Cape)

Erect, stout herb, 100-800mm tall. In grassland, 1200-2590m. E Cape to NW Prov. Stem **usually solitary** or 1-2 branches from base. LEAVES lance-shaped, curved upwards, **closely clustered**, 60-200×15-45mm, **waxy, hairless, margins wavy**. FLOWER CLUSTERS surrounded by leaves; corolla lobes erect, tips slightly rolled under, covered in stout white hairs, musty or strong cinnamon smell (Nov-Jan). FRUIT 70-100×20-30mm, slightly inflated, shallowly ridged with **stout, blunt, recurved spines**. (see pg 266)

Xysmalobium undulatum Milkwort, Uzura; Bitterhoutwortel (A); leshokoa, poho-tšehla (SS); iyeza elimhlophe, nwachaba (X); ishongwane (fruit), ishongwe (plant) (X,Z) (*undulatum* - wavy, refers to leaf margins)

Robust herb, 0.1-1.8m tall. In open grassland, up to 2000m. Widespread, SAfr to Kenya. Stems annual. LEAVES **large**, 80-270×10-75mm, **hairy**. INFLORESCENCES dense, in axils; FLOWER lobes erect, tips recurved, with **stout white hairs at tips** (Oct-Jan). FRUITS large, 90-100×35-50mm, **inflated, covered in long, curly soft 'hairs'**. GENERAL: 'Parachute' hairs from seeds used to stuff pillows. Young leaves used as a pot herb. Used in traditional medicine to treat warts, corns, wounds, dysentery, colic and as a protective charm. Widely used in Africa and elsewhere, sold in Europe as an antidiarrhoeal under the name *Uzura*.

Miraglossum (*mira* - astonishing or miraculous; *glossa* - tongue, refers to ornate corona lobes) Perennial geophytic herbs. 2-8 flowers in stalkless inflorescences, lobes divided to base, reflexed, usually densely hairy, corona lobes thick, fleshy; often elaborate; pollinia without defined germination zone. Fruit erect, spindle-shaped, covered in soft bristles or thick down, stalk recurved. SAfr endemic, 7 species, 3 in this region.

Miraglossum verticillare [= *Schizoglossum verticillare*] Wreathed Miracle-tongue (*verticillus* - whorled)

Erect herb, 100-350mm tall. In rocky grassland, 1200-1980m. E Cape to KZN. LEAVES erect, never whorled below, **whorled and smaller at flowering nodes**, 17-45×1-2mm, hairy. FLOWERS greenish, lobes **reflexed**, 4.5-6.5×2.5-3.5mm, outer surface with brown hairs, inner surface with fine grey hairs, **corona lobe appendages white, curled round to the right to form a wreath over the style tip** (Nov-Feb).

Dracosciadium saniculifolium

Neil Crouch

Peucedanum thodei

Martin von Fintel

Xysmalobium involucratum

Martin von Fintel

Xysmalobium involucratum

Martin von Fintel

Xysmalobium parviflorum

Tony Abbott

Miraglossum verticillare

Martin von Fintel

Xysmalobium undulatum

Pam Cooke

Xysmalobium stockenstromense

Martin von Fintel

259

Pachycarpus (*pachy* - thick; *carpus* - fruit) Perennial geophytic herbs. Stems simple or sparsely branched, with latex. Leaves usually leathery. Flowers often very large, lobes free or fused for over two thirds their length, corona lobes flattened, usually tonguelike, usually with wings and/or appendages on upper surface. Fruit thick, often inflated, with stout spines or ridges. Afr endemic, ±30 species, 27 in SAfr, ±7 in this region.

Pachycarpus campanulatus Cluster bells; Trosklokkies (A); ishongwe (Z) (- bell-shaped)

Slender herb, 150-600mm tall. In grassland up to 2100m. **Stems unbranched.** LEAVES 60-165×2-10mm, **margins rolled under, midvein prominent below.** INFLORESCENCE terminal; FLOWERS usually **pendulous**, 10-50mm, **fused to over halfway**, lobes short, inflexed or reflexed, **corona lobes with large wings equaling erect apex in stature.** FRUIT **not inflated. Subsp.** *campanulatus* South of Tugela River. FLOWERS **3-5, large, 24-50mm**, corona lobes **9-17mm long** (Nov-Feb). **Subsp.** *sutherlandii* E Cape to Limpopo Prov. FLOWERS **5-18, smaller**, 15-30mm, corona lobes **2-8mm** (Dec-Jan).

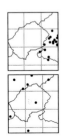

Pachycarpus dealbatus [= *P. ligulatus*] Tongued Pachycarpus, Tongued Thick-fruit; ishongwe, ukhatimuthi (Z) (*dealbatus* - whitewashed, refers to the colour of some plants)

Stoutish, erect herb, 150-500mm tall. On grassy slopes, up to 1800m. W Cape to Mpum. **Stems unbranched.** LEAVES spreading, erect, 40-110×10-42mm, margins ± wavy, sticky. FLOWERS 4-8 in clusters at nodes, greenish cream blotched dull purple, bell-shaped, **lobes erect**, 6-16×7-13mm, reflexed at tips, **corona spoon- shaped, without wings or flaps on upper surface**, dilated at erect tip (Nov-Mar). FRUIT solitary, 50-100mm, oval to spindle-shaped, surface with 6-toothed wings. (see pg 268) **Similar species:** *Pachycarpus rigidus* **phoma-metsu, leshokhoana, leraka-mpshane, maraca-mpshoane, mpshatle-ea-thaba, poho-tsehla, tsoe-nyaling (SS)** (*rigidus* - stiff) Up to 2000m. E Cape to Mpum. INFLORESCENCE, FLOWERS larger, **corona lobes variable, tip dilated to cross-shaped** (Nov-Feb). GENERAL: plant used as a vegetable in Les. (see pg 268)

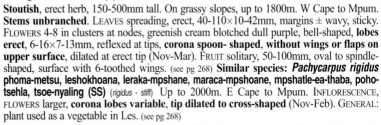

Pachycarpus macrochilus Large-lipped Pachycarpus, Large-lipped Thick-fruit; leshokhoa (SS) (*macro* - large; *chilus* - lips, refers to the corona lobe structure)

Erect herb, 140-330mm. In rocky, **high mountain grassland**, 1600-2600m. E Cape to Mpum. Stems slight hairy. LEAVES 30-150×17-43mm, margins ± wavy, harshly hairy, stalks 5-15mm long. FLOWERS 2-6 in clusters, **cup-shaped**, erect when young, pendulous when mature, 16-28mm, dull yellow blotched red, lobe **tips spreading to slightly reflexed**, 13-25×9-17mm, corona lobe with wings on upper surface, apex leaflike, ± inflexed, 11-14mm (Oct-Jan). GENERAL: Eaten by goats. **Similar species:** *Pachycarpus plicatus* Braided Pachycarpus (*plicatus* - braided, doubled up, refers to reflexed corona lobe tip) In rocky grassland, up to 2200m. E Cape to KZN. FLOWERS **bowl-shaped, greenish yellow to yellowish brown, anther wings subhorizontal** (Nov-Jan). *Pachycarpus vexillaris* leshokhoa (SS) (*vexillaris* - standard bearer, corona lobe resembles a pea flower) On rocky slopes, 1200-2600m. W Cape to KZN. FLOWERS with corona lobes crosslike, apex forked (Nov-Mar). GENERAL: Leaves, rootstock eaten in Les. (see pg 216)

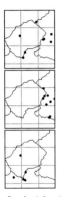

Brachystelma (*brachy* - short; *stelma* - crown, refers to the often extremely small corona) (see pg 268)

Brachystelma pygmaeum subsp. *pygmaeum* Pygmy Brachystelma (*pygmaeus* - pygmy)

Dwarf tufted herb, 40-80mm tall. On rocky ridges in grassland, up to 1900m. E Cape to Limpopo Prov. Stems shortly hairy. LEAVES 10-50×1.5-5mm, margins flat, thinly hairy below, ± hairless above, **not fully developed at flowering.** FLOWERS tubular, 1-3 at nodes, dull orange-yellow, lobes slender, 4.5-8.5mm long, **fused at tips to form a small cage**, tube up to 1.5mm long (Oct-Nov). FRUIT erect, 50-60×4-5mm.

RUBIACEAE (see pg 98) **Pygmaeothamnus** (*pygmaios* - dwarf; *thamnos* - bush) Perennial herbs. Trop Afr, ±4 species, 2 in SAfr, 1 in this region.

Pygmaeothamnus chamaedendrum var. *chamaedendrum* Pygmy Sand Apple; Goorappel (A) (*chamae*- on the ground; *dendron* - tree)

Dwarf herb, up to 250mm tall. On bare ground, in rocky places, up to 2130m. KZN to NW Prov. Underground parts woody. LEAVES clustered at top of stems, ± hairy, stipules scaly, with tuft of hairs. FLOWERS ±10mm, **greenish yellow** with white beard in throat, **petals curled back**, scented (Nov-Feb). FRUIT fleshy, ±15×8mm, edible.

Anthospermum (*anthos* - flower, *sperma* - seed, male flower may carry small ovary) Afr, Madag, ±40 species, 21 in SAfr, 4 in this region.

Anthospermum monticola (*monticola* - mountain dweller)

Much branched shrub, 0.3-1.5m tall. In scrub at mouth of Cave Sandstone overhangs, on moist slopes below cliffs, in boulder beds, up to 2450m. E Cape to KZN. LEAVES 3-10×1-2mm. FLOWERS tiny, 0.3-0.5mm long, up to 6 in a cluster, yellowish green, tinged reddish outside (Nov-Feb). FRUITS reddish brown. GENERAL: Heavily browsed.

Pachycarpus campanulatus subsp. *sutherlandii*

Pachycarpus campanulatus subsp. *campanulatus*

Pachycarpus campanulatus subsp. *sutherlandii*

Pygmaeothamnus chamaedendrum

Pachycarpus dealbatus

Brachystelma pygmaeum

Pachycarpus macrochilus

Pachycarpus plicatus

Pachycarpus macrochilus

Anthospermum monticola

261

MONOCOTYLEDONS Single seed-leaf, parallel veins, flower parts in threes or multiples of three.

CYPERACEAE - Sedge family (see pg 46) ***Cyperus*** (*cyperus* - sedge) Cosmop, ±650 species, ±70 in SAfr, 6 in this region.

Cyperus rupestris Russet Rock Sedge; taoane, taoanenyana (SS) (*rupestris* - rock dwelling)
Perennial, 60-150mm tall. In dense tufts, in shallow soil over rock or on rocky ground, up to 2300m. Widespread. LEAVES basal, wiry or succulent, ±17mm wide. INFLORESCENCE of shiny dark reddish brown spikelets, bracts ±70mm long, stem 3-angled at top with persistent brown leaf sheaths at base (summer).

Cyperus schlechteri roroana (SS) (named after Friedrich Schlechter, 1872-1925, eminent German botanist and traveller who collected plants widely in South Africa)
Slender perennials up to 250 mm tall. In shallow soil over rock sheets, in stony ground, often on sandstone, 1950-2570m. E Cape to KZN/Mpum. Stems thin. FLOWERHEADS **small, spiky**; SPIKELETS **closely packed**.

Cyperus semitrifidus hlohoana-ntso, ma-taoataoane, matobane (SS) (*semi* - half; *trifidus* - cut in 3 parts)
Erect, tufted, sparsely leafy perennial, up to 300mm tall. On rock sheets and stony ground on sandstone, up to 2600m. E Cape to Mpum. Rhizome woody, **stems bulbous, woody at base**. Variable. LEAVES curved outwards, ±250×1-4mm. SPIKELETS reddish to dark purplish black, stem 3-angled a top, rays ±30mm.

Mariscus (old name used by Pliny for a rush) Doubtfully distinct from *Cyperus*. More or less cosmop, ±200 species, ±32 in SAfr, 2 in this region.

Mariscus congestus (*congestus* - crowded) (see pg 248)

Ficinia (named after Heinrich Ficinus, 1782-1853, German botanist at Dresden) Afr, mainly SAfr, mostly S Cape, ±60 species, ±5 in this region.

Ficinia cinnamomea (*cinnamome* – cinnamon-coloured)
Loosely tufted, slender and straggling or erect leafy perennials, 100-310mm tall. On damp grass slopes or on rock, up to 2250m. Stolons well developed. LEAVES ±200mm. FLOWERHEAD solitary, with 5-10 spikelets, ±8mm, pale brown, upper sheath leafless, lower pale brown, long, bristly, bracts 2, lower 25-75mm, suberect.

Scirpus (*scirpus* - a rush, bulrush) Diverse genus with ±300 species worldwide. Presently undergoing breakdown into smaller genera.

Scirpus ficinioides (*ficinioides* - resembling *Ficinia*)
Robust, 450-600mm tall. On damp, marshy ground, up to 3000m. Fairly widespread in SAfr. Rhizome slightly elongate. LEAVES basal, inconspicuous. FLOWERHEAD compact, sometimes branched, stem firm rounded. GENERAL: Indicator of underground water.

Schoenoxiphium (*schoinos* - rush; *xiphos* - a sword) About 18 species in SAfr, ±13 in this region.

Schoenoxiphium burttii (named after B. L. Burtt, distinguished botanist)
Robust perennial, up to 1m tall. Along streambanks, on steep, rocky slopes, among grasses and small shrubs. EMR endemic. LEAVES up to 12mm wide. INFLORESCENCES up to 5 or more, **drooping with weight of dark brown spikelets**.

Carex (*caric* - sedge) An old established genus, the fruits hardly differing at all from fossil remains identified from between 70-30 million years ago. Fairly cosmop in moist temp climates, also Arctic and Antarctic regions. Mostly N Hemisp, ±1700 species, ±19 in SAfr, 8 in this region.

Carex zululensis
Robust perennial, up to 1m tall. Frequent amongst shrubs in rough grassland on forest margins, often on steep east and south facing slopes, in shade of forest, up to 1800m. E Cape to KZN/Mpum. LEAF margins and keel rough. SPIKES dense, 50-150mm long.

RESTIONACEAE - Cape Reed Family Resemble some sedges but leaf blades rarely present. Instead, at each node a split leaf sheath is tightly rolled round the stem. Flowers unisexual, male and female often on separate plants. S Hemisp, ±41 genera, ±420 species, mostly SW Cape in SAfr, ±28 genera, ±320 species. ***Ischyrolepis*** SAfr, ±49 species, mostly W Cape, 1 in this region.

Ischyrolepis schoenoides [= *Restio schoenoides, R. sieberi* var. *schoenoides*] mafielo-oa-thaba (SS) (*schoenoides* - resembles a rush)
Dense tufts of wiry stems up to 450mm tall. On rock sheets and in stony ground, 1950-2500m. W Cape to Limpopo Prov. Each stem ends in 1-4 spikes up to 15×5mm, flowers hidden by hard, brown, glossy, overlapping bracts from which anthers or style branches protrude (**2 style branches**). Male and female flowers on separate plants.

262

Cyperus rupestris   Tony Abbott

Cyperus semitrifidus   Tony Abbott

Cyperus schlechteri   Peter Linder

Ficinia cinammomea   Tony Abbott

Scirpus ficinioides   Tony Abbott

Mariscus congestus   Peter Linder

Mariscus congestus   Martin von Fintel

Carex zuluensis   Tony Abbott

Carex zuluensis   Tony Abbott

Ischyrolepis schoenoides   David McDonald

Schoenoxiphium burttii   Hilliard & Burtt

263

ORCHIDACEAE - Orchid Family (see pgs 190,232,252) *Satyrium* (see pg 252)

Satyrium bracteatum (*bracteatus* -refers to the bract-covered stem)
30-150mm tall. On wet grassy slopes, in tussocks in marshes, along streams, up to 2300m. W Cape to Limpopo Prov. LEAVES, 2 large ones, spreading at base, upper leaves sheathing. INFLORESCENCE a dense spike, **bracts large, dark maroon-brown, pitted**; FLOWERS yellowish, striped and mottled dark red along veins, spurs tiny, **smells of rotten meat** (Nov-Dec). GENERAL: Pollinated by small carrion and dung flies.

Disa The direction in which the spur points is useful in identification in the field. 131 species in SAfr, ±29 in this region. (see pgs 192,232)

Disa basutorum [= *Monadenia basutorum*] ´**mametasana (SS)** (*basutorum* - refers to the colonial name for Lesotho, Basutoland)
100-150(240)mm tall. In stony, damp grassland, above 2600m, frequent on summit. EMR endemic. LEAVES mostly basal, spreading, 15-45mm long, stem leaves sheathing, overlapping, merging into bracts. INFLORESCENCE dense, 15-80mm long, **bracts overtopping flowers**; FLOWERS **face downwards**, yellowish green or brown, **spur slender, straight, pointing out and upwards**, 5-6mm, strongly scented (Jan-Mar).

Disa brevicornis [= *Monadenia brevicornis*] (*brevicornis* - with short horns)
200-400mm tall. Common on rocky grass slopes and ridges up to 2500m. E Cape to Malawi, Madag. LEAVES clasping, 80-150mm long at base. INFLORESCENCE crowded, a slender spike; FLOWERS greenish or yellowish flushed dull dark red on back of the hood and at the base of the lip, **spur club-shaped, 7-11mm long** (Dec-Feb).

Disa cornuta Golden Orchid (*cornuta* - horned or spurred)
Robust, up to 600mm tall. In grassland, up to 2400m. Widespread, W Cape to Zim. LEAVES crowded, overlapping, **basal ones purple-spotted**. INFLORESCENCE dense, stout; FLOWERS silvery purplish red, yellowish inside the hood, lip yellow and green, **spur 10-20mm long, pointed backwards or upwards**, scent faintly spicy (Dec-Feb).

Disa hircicornis (*hircus* - goat; *cornis* - horn)
Slender to robust, 300-450mm tall. In marshy ground, up to 1800m. Rare in SAfr, widespread in Trop Afr. LEAVES overlapping, spotted and barred red. INFLORESCENCE dense, bracts large; FLOWERS overlapping, pale pink to deep purplish red, heavily spotted outside, lip whitish, **hood with dull purplish red spur 8-13mm long, hooked, pointing upwards at base** (Oct-Jan). GENERAL: Colour very variable.

Corycium (*korys* - helmet; *ium* - resembling, refers to shape of hood) Dorsal sepal and petals joined to form a deep globose hood, side sepals often fused at base, lip with appendage. SAfr endemic, ±14 species, 4 in this region.

Corycium alticola
Robust, up to 400mm tall. In damp mountain grassland, 1950-2400m. EMR endemic. LEAVES spreading, ±200×28mm. INFLORESCENCE dense; FLOWERS **large, ±20×7-10mm diam, sepals** white **turning black**, petals pale green, lip pale maroon, **lip oblong**, appendage shieldlike, ±5mm tall with 2 lobes, 8mm long (Feb).

Corycium nigrescens Black-faced Orchid; Moederkappie (A); umabelembuca (Z) (*nigrescens* - black)
Up to 550mm tall. In damp grassland, up to 3000m. E Cape to Limpopo Prov, S Tanz. LEAVES erect, overlapping, ±200×24mm. INFLORESCENCE up to 130mm long; FLOWERS small, round, ±16×6mm, sepals pale green soon **turning black and dry**, petals ±4mm long, with 2 downward pointing lobes, purple-brown to black, **lip purplish green, side arms of appendage tapering, pointing backwards**, maroon to purplish green (Dec-Feb). **Similar species: *Corycium dracomontanum*** Up to 220mm tall. Resembles *C. nigrescens* with similar distribution, **lip appendage bright green, side arms ± oblong, facing sideways**, not backwards (Nov-Mar).

Pterygodium (*pterygoides* - winglike, refers to side petals) Flowers with median sepal and petal joined to form a very shallow hood, lip with short or tall appendage, no spur. Mainly SW Cape (1 in Tanz), 18 species, 4 in this region.

Pterygodium magnum [= *Corycium magnum*] (*magnum* - large, strong)
Robust, up to 1.5m tall. In marshy grassland, on seepage lines and boulder beds, up to 1900m. E Cape to Mpum. LEAFY, leaves up to 250×60mm. INFLORESCENCE a large, dense spike, up to 500mm long, bracts long, slender, much longer than flowers, FLOWERS ±25×12mm, sepals green, **petals fringed**, yellowish **with red dots and darker veins**, lip white to pale green or mauve with darker veins, fringed (Jan-Feb).

Martin von Fintel

Peter Linder

Neil Crouch

David McDonald

Satyrium bracteatum   _Disa basutorum_   _Disa brevicornis_   _Pterygodium magnum_

Hubert Kurzweil

David McDonald

Pterygodium magnum

Disa cornuta   _Disa hircicornis_   _Dee Weeks_

Martin von Fintel

Auriol Batten

Neil Crouch

David McDonald

Corycium dracomontanum   _Corycium alticola_   _Corycium nigrescens_   _Corycium nigrescens_

265

DICOTYLEDONS Two seed leaves, net veins, flower parts in fours, fives or multiples of these.

GUNNERACEAE - Gunnera Family (after Johan Guner, 1711-1777, bishop of Trondheim who wrote a flora of Norway) Herbs of moist places. Leaves large, round, with long stalks. C & S America, Madag, Malaysia, Tasmania, New Zealand, Hawaian Is, 1 genus, ±40 species, 1 in SAfr.

Gunnera perpensa Wild Rhubarb; Wilderabarber (A); qobo (SS); iphuzi lomlambo (X); ugobho, imfeyesele, uklenya, uxobo (X,Z) *(perpensa* - hanging on)

Perennial herb, up to 500mm tall. In damp, marshy places, up to 2400m. Cape to Ethiopia. Covered in short hairs. LEAVES **large**, 40-250×60-380mm, margins lobed, teeth small, rough edged, stalks 250-450mm long. INFLORESCENCE spikelike, 200-900mm long; FLOWERS tiny, reddish brown, male flowers above, female below (Dec-Mar). FRUIT small, fleshy. GENERAL: Stems and roots peeled and eaten raw, also used to make beer. Used in traditional medicine to ease childbirth, assist in expulsion of the placenta in women and cattle and, with other plants, to treat kidney and bladder complaints. Attractive foliage plant for damp places, frost hardy.

ASCLEPIADACEAE - Milkweed Family (see pg 140) *Xysmalobium* (*xysma* - filings or shavings; *lobos* - lobes, refers to the small corona lobes that resemble cut slivers) Stout to delicate perennial geophytic herbs, sometimes ± shrubby, with milky latex. Stems produced annually from a tuber. Leaf margins rough, venation prominent. Corona lobes reduced to small lobules. Afr, 40 species, 21 in SAfr, ±7 in this region.

Xysmalobium parviflorum Octopus Cartwheel; leoto-la-khoho, ntsime, tsoetla (SS) *(parvus* - small; *florus* - flower)

Tufted herb, 120-320mm tall. In colonies, on very rocky slopes in short grassland, up to 2100m. E Cape to Limpopo Prov. **Stems much branched**. LEAVES 20-45 ×6-20mm, leathery, margins thickened, veins brown. INFLORESCENCES 1-4 per stem; FLOWERS **stiffly erect, small, ±3mm diam**, whitish green, corolla lobe tips inflexed, corona lobes brown, sickly sweet or 'oaty' scent (Oct-Feb). FRUIT 40-80×10-15mm, with parallel green stripes. GENERAL: Used in traditional medicine to treat colic. (see pg 258)

Xysmalobium stockenstromense Mountain Uzura (see pg 258)

Schizoglossum (*schizo* - cut or split; *glossa* - tongue, refers to the corona lobes that are often split into 2 or more parts) Perennial geophytic herbs. Stems annual from small carrotlike tuber, erect, usually solitary, with milky latex. Flowers lobed to base, corona lobes scalelike and with appendages, often complex. Fruit spindle-shaped, tip beaked, covered with long usually recurved bristles. Afr, ±80 species, 27 in SAfr, ±9 in this region.

Schizoglossum atropurpureum subsp. *atropurpureum* Basoetoraap, Melkwortel (A); sehoete-moru (SS); ishongwe (elincane elibomvu) (Z) *(atro* - blackish or very dark; *purpureum* - purple)

Erect herb, 0.6-1.3m tall. In unburned grassland or scrub near streams, especially amongst boulders, up to 2040m. E Cape to Mpum. Stems long, 1-2, **unbranched**. LEAVES 30-50×8-20mm. INFLORESCENCE stems sometimes **branched**. FLOWERS 8-15, **lobes almost black**, erect, oblong, **concave**, ±6×4mm, with a small oblique apical notch, caramel scented (Jan-Mar). GENERAL: Root eaten raw, sweet tasting. Roots bundled and preserved by smoke, used to ward off lightning.

Schizoglossum bidens subsp. *atrorubens* Variable Schizoglossum *(bi* - two; *dens* - tooth; *atro* - blackish; *rubens* - red)

Erect herb, 200-600mm tall, rarely branched. In grassland, up to 2600m. EMR endemic. LEAVES **in whorls or irregular**, 30-63×2-5mm. FLOWERS in small clusters above leaves in upper axils, corolla lobes ± erect, 4-4.5×2-2.5mm, brown and dull green, margins turned back, **corona lobes white marked dull purple**, appendages simple or forked (Nov-Jan). GENERAL: **Subsp.** *pachyglossum* In rocky grassland up to 2500m. INFLORESCENCES stalkless; FLOWERS yellowish green, **corona white** (Dec-Jan). **Subsp.** *bidens* A smaller plant, **90-220mm tall, often branched**. In grasslands up to 2600m. FLOWERS green or brown, corona white (Oct-Jan).

Schizoglossum hilliardiae Hilliard's Schizoglossum (see pg. 84)

Aspidonepsis (*aspido* - Aspidoglossoum; *anepsia* - cousin, refers to its relationship with this genus) (see pg 142)

Aspidonepsis reenensis [= *Asclepias reenensis*] *(reenensis* - Van Reenen's Pass, the type locality)

Slender herb with single stem up to 625mm tall. In dry mountain grassland, 1500-2100m. KZN to Mpum. LEAVES long, narrow, 10-55×0.7-2.5mm. FLOWERS **chocolate-brown or reddish purple**, 7-11mm wide, lobes reflexed, 5.5-6.5×2.5-3.8mm, **corona lobes clawlike with keel apex tailed**, 2-2.6mm tall, whitish, keel purple below, bright yellow above, **central cavity without an appendage** (Nov-Jan).

David McDonald

Schizoglossum bidens subsp. *atrorubens*

David McDonald

Gunnera perpensa

Peter Linder

Xysmalobium stockenstromense

Peter Linder

Xysmalobium stockenstromense

Pam Cooke

Xysmalobium parviflorum

Aspidonepsis reenensis

Ashley Nicholas

Schizoglossum atropurpureum
subsp. *atropurpureum*

Lal Greene

Peter Linder

Schizoglossum bidens subsp. *bidens*

Tony Abbott

Schizoglossum bidens subsp. *pachyglossum*

Martin von Fintel

Schizoglossum hilliardiae

Miraglossum (*mira* - astonishing or miraculous; *glossa* - tongue, refers to ornate corona lobes) (see pg 258)

Miraglossum pulchellum [= *Schizoglossum pulchellum*] Horned Miracle-tongue; mpulutsoane, sehoete-mpulutsoane (SS) (*pulcher* - beautiful)

Erect herb, 200-550mm tall. In grassland, near streams, up to 2300m. KZN to Limpopo Prov. LEAVES erect or close to stem, 20-50×1-5mm, margins rolled under, hairy. FLOWERS in clusters, greenish, lobes oval, ±8×4mm, **reflexed**, lower surface densely covered in brown hairs, **corona erect, appendage tips relaxed away from flower centre, like a rhino horn** (Oct-Jan).

Miraglossum superbum Crucifix Miracle-tongue (*superans* - rise above, refers to magnificent corona lobes which not only rise above the style tip but are superb)

Erect herb, 250-500mm tall. In grassland, near streams, 1500-2100m. EMR endemic. LEAVES erect, 15-40×0.5-2mm, margins rolled under, ± hairy. FLOWERS green striped brownish purple, lobes oval, 6-9×4mm, **reflexed**, hairless, **corona lobes erect, appendage tip large, crosslike**, chocolate-brown to dark maroon (Jan-Feb).

Pachycarpus (*pachy* - thick; *carpus* - fruit, refers to the thick-skinned fruits) (see pg 260)

Pachycarpus dealbatus [= *P. ligulatus*] Tongued Pachycarpus (see pg 260)

Pachycapurs rigidus phoma-metsu, leshokhoana, leraka-mpshane, mpshatle-ea-thaba, poho-tsehla, tsoenya-ling (SS) (*rigidus* - stiff) (see pg 260)

Asclepias (named after the Greek doctor *Aesculapius* who was immortalised in ancient mythology as a god of medicine) (see pg 216)

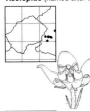

Asclepias cultriformis Satellite-dish; ishongwe elimpofu (Z) (*cultratus* - curved like a scimitar)

Erect herb, **covered in long white hairs**, 150-300mm tall. In grassland, on stony slopes, up to 2380m. KZN to Limpopo Prov. Stem solitary. LEAVES 25-50 ×6.5-16mm. INFLORESCENCE terminal, ± drooping; FLOWERS greenish brown, lobes spreading, tips turned up, 12-14×8-11mm, **densely hairy on outer surface**, margins fringed with long white hairs, corona large, lobes laterally compressed, ± **square in outline and hooked on inner, much extended tip, cavity with a small tongue**, white tipped purple (Nov- Jan). GENERAL: Dry roots burnt to ward off lightning.

Asclepias macropus Tailed Cartwheels (*macro* - large; *pous* - foot, refers to large corona lobes)

Reclining herb, 150-400mm tall. In grassland, up to 2000m. E Cape to Mpum. Stems several, **forking from near base**. LEAVES spreading, broadly triangular, 25-65 ×22-35mm, leathery, veins prominent below, harshly hairy, stalks 4-11mm long. FLOWERS yellowish brown, in **roundish, dense, erect, terminal clusters**, up to 60mm diam, stems 75-150mm long; **lobes extremely reflexed**, tips turned up, ±8×4.5mm, corona lobes square, compressed sideways, **upper outside end extended into a very long, pointed, tail-like appendage** (Dec-Mar).

Anisotoma (*aniso* - unequal; *tomos* - slice or piece) Perennial geophytic herbs. Stems many, trailing. Leaves ± heart-shaped, corona lobes 5, fixed only at base, free above, tip entire to forked. SAfr endemic, 2 species, 1 in this region.

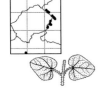

Anisotoma pedunculata Common Spiderweb; morarana-oa-letlapa (SS) (*pedunculatus* - peduncle, flower stalk)

Prostrate to trailing herb, stems 150-600mm long, sparsely branched at base. In grassland, 1200-2100m. E Cape to Limpopo Prov. Sap clear. LEAVES spreading, lying flat on ground, 8.5-38×6-35mm, stalks 4-19mm. INFLORESCENCE **held erect, stem 12-50mm long**; FLOWERS 2-10, corolla lobes reflexed, ±4.5×1.5mm, brown and hairy inside, whitish at base, **margins rolled back**, corona white, lobes ± oblong, entire or toothlike with a hairy pointed or forked appendage (Oct-Jan). FRUIT not yet known.

Brachystelma (*brachy* - short; *stelma* - crown, refers to the often extremely small corona) Perennial geophytic herbs, often dwarf. Corolla lobes shortly or longly fused but tube usually shorter than lobes, corona in 2 series. Fruits erect, spindle-shaped, smooth. Widely cultivated. Tubers of most species eaten by people and animals. Afr. Asia, Austr, over 100 species, most diverse in SAfr, ±70 species, ± 8 in this region.

Brachystelma perditum (*perditum* - lost or destroyed)

Dwarf herb, up to 50mm tall. Habitat unknown, 1800-2000m. EMR endemic. LEAVES 15-20mm long, oval, shortly hairy beneath and on margins. FLOWERS starlike, 18-25mm long, brown mottled, divided 3/4 to base, tube bell-like, 3-4.5mm deep; lobes tapering from base, margins recurving towards tip, finely wrinkled, ± long fine hairs near base of lobes (Oct/Dec). GENERAL: Little known about this plant. Rediscovered in 1976, almost 70 years since it was first collected, the second collection was made from plants obtained from herd boys in Lesotho who had collected bulbs to eat!

Miraglossum pulchellum

Martin von Fintel

Miraglossum superbum

Martin von Fintel

Brachystelma perditum

Auriol Batten

Asclepias macropus

Pam Cooke

Asclepias cultriformis

Tony Abbott

Anisotoma pedunculata

Neil Crouch

Pachycarpus dealbatus

Ashley Nicholas

Pachycarpus dealbatus

Lal Greene

Pachycarpus rigidus

David McDonald

269

MONOCOTYLEDONS Single seed-leaf, parallel veins, flower parts in threes or multiples of three.

POACEAE/GRAMINEAE – Grass Family Grasses have hollow, usually cylindric, jointed stems with slightly swollen nodes. Leaves in three parts - a narrow blade separated from the basal sheath by a ligule. Inconspicuous flowers (florets) grouped in spikelets. Cosmop, ±688 genera, 194 in SAfr (29 exotic); ±9500 species, ±912 in SAfr. Much work is still being done on the classification of grasses.

This page serves as a very small but beautiful example of the rich grass flora of the region, representing the second largest family after Compositae/Asteraceae. Grasses are notoriously difficult to photograph, especially in the field. For excellent field guides to the grasses of this region refer to *Grasses of the Eastern Free State, their description and uses* by Rodney Moffett, *Grasses, Sedges, Restiads & Rushes of the Natal Drakensberg* by Olive Hilliard and the colour illustrated *Guide to Grasses of South Africa* by Frits van Oudtshoorn.

Monocymbium (*monocymbium* - single boat, refers to inflorescence spathe) Trop Afr and SAfr, ±4 species, 1 in this region.

Monocymbium ceresiiforme **Boat Grass, Wild Oatgrass; Bootjiegras, Wildehawer-gras (A); ´meseletso, mobeseletso (SS)** (*ceresiiforme* - grain-shaped, resembling a crop) Loosely tufted perennial, 300-600mm tall. On open slopes up to 2400m, often locally dominant. Also in the Caprivi and Trop Afr. Stems yellow. SPIKELETS 1-sided, spathe boat shaped, turns red (Jan-Apr). GENERAL: Lovely in flower. Burnt by the Basotho in the grain fields in autumn to hasten ripening. Useful for grazing when young. Favoured by Oribi antelope.

Themeda (Arabic for a depression filled with water after rain) Trop and Subtrop regions of the Old World, ±18 species, 1 in SAfr.

Themeda triandra **Red Grass; Rooigras (A); seboku (SS); insinde (X,Z)** (*triandra* - three anthers)

Tufted perennial, 300-900mm tall. Often dominant on mountain slopes, up to 2900m. Widespread in undisturbed areas of SAfr, also in Old World trop and subtrop. Leaf blade flattened, tips pointed, bright green turning conspicuous red or bright brown when old (autumn/winter). SPIKELETS clustered in triangular units supported by conspicuous bracts flushed red, purple and brown (Sep-Mar). GENERAL: Valuable pasture grass, particularly when young. Sometimes used for a poor quality thatching.

Merxmuellera (named after German botanist and taxonomist H. Merxmüller, who made extensive collections SAfr, mostly in Namibia/South West Africa between 1957 and 1977). The genus is easily recognized by the tufts and fringes of hairs on the lemmas and the wiry, sharp-tipped leaves. SAfr, ±17 species which are difficult to classify, ±9 in this region.

Merxmuellera aureocephala [= *Danthonia aureocephala*] (*aureocephala* - golden-yellow head, refers to inflorescences)

Densely tufted perennials, up to 600(900)mm tall. Dominant on steep ridges below the summit cliffs at 2150-2500m, locally common (Giants Castle and Cathkin Peak). N EMR endemic. LEAF blade up to 400×1.5mm. SPIKELETS tawny gold, colouring the ridges, **winter flowering** (Jul-Aug).

Merxmuellera macowanii **moseha, mohlaba-pere (SS)** (named after P MacOwan, 1830-1909, plant collector, appointed government botanist in the Cape, eminent scientist)

Tufted perennial, up to 1.3m tall. Common on streambanks, 1500-3000m. LEAF blade 1-2 mm wide, **tightly folded with age**, persistent bases only slightly recurved. INFLORESCENCE plumelike, 170-270mm long, yellowish to golden brown; SPIKES show up yellow against green of grassland. GENERAL: Leaves used for making food and grain baskets and hats. Mats using other grasses (*Eragrostis plana* and *Hyparrhenia hirta*) are usually bound together with a thin, flat, plaited rope of this species or *M. drakensbergensis*. Both species are exported for 'yard brooms'.
Similar species: *Merxmuellera drakensbergensis* [= *Danthonia drakensbergensis*] Broom grass; Besemgras (A); mohlaba-pere, molalahlolo, mosea, moseha, mosikanokana, mosua (SS) Tussock forming perennial, up to 1m tall. Prominent on top of escarpment, also on streambanks and in high mountain grassland, 2100-3000m. Endemic to the EMR and the high mountains of Mpum. LEAF blade **very stiff, tightly folded, old leaf blade breaks off near the base and the remaining part splits and curls back**. INFLORESCENCE loose, 80-180mm long (Oct-Mar).

270

Themeda triandra

Colin Everson

David McDonald

Grasses

Merxmuellera aureocephala

Bill Bainbridge

Merxmuellera macowanii

Monocymbium ceresiiforme

Bill Bainbridge

Merxmuellera macowanii

David McDonald

271

CYCADOPSIDA Cone-bearing plants with naked seeds and large, compound leaves

ZAMIACEAE - Cycad Family Represents plants once dominant about 200 million years ago. About 8 genera, ±100 species. ***Encephalartos*** (*en* - within; *kephalos* - head; *artos* - bread, refers to a kind of bread made from trunk pith) Afr, ±45 species, ±30 in SAfr, 2 in this region.

Encephalartos ghellinckii Drakensberg Cycad; Drakensbergse-broodboom (A); isidawu (Z); isigqikisomkhovu, umphanga, umguza (X) (Eduard de Ghellinck de Walle, 19th century plant collector of Ghent)

Up to 3m tall. Among boulders in grassland, on steep south and east facing slopes, 1600-2400m. E Cape to KZN. MAIN STEMS burnt black by fire, 300-400mm diam. LEAF STALKS yellow, twisted, leaflets narrow, **margins rolled back**; NEW LEAVES greyish, covered in wool at first; MATURE LEAVES bright green. CONES 2-5, densely woolly, pale lemon. GENERAL: Fleshy outer covering of seeds eaten by baboons.

PINOPSIDA - CONIFERS Cone-bearing plants with naked seeds and small, simple leaves

PODOCARPACEAE - Yellowwood Family Mainly S Hemisp, ± 17 genera, 1 genus in SAfr. ***Podocarpus*** (*podos* - foot; *karpos* - fruit) Male and female cones on separate trees, female bracts develop into woody or fleshy base (receptacle). Over 100 species, 4 in SAfr, 3 in this region.

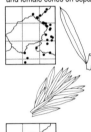

Podocarpus latifolius Broad-leaved Yellowwood, Real Yellowwood; Opregte Geelhout (A); umcheya (X); umkhoba, umsonti, umgeya (Z) (*latifolius* - broad, refers to the leaves)

Evergreen, 8-25m tall. Often dominant in montane forest, up to 1900m. Widespread in SAfr. BARK **longitudinally fissured in mature trees, peeling in strips.** LEAVES **thick, leathery, blue-green** (dark green), 60-160×5-13mm, **tapering abruptly near tip,** new leaves creamy mauve. FEMALE CONES 1-2, **seeds blue-grey to dark purple,** ±10mm diam, **on fleshy pink or reddish purple receptacle** which swells as the seed ripens (Dec-Feb). GENERAL: Juvenile leaves can resemble those of *P. henkelii*. Fruit eaten by birds and animals. Bark used in traditional medicine. Hardy garden tree.

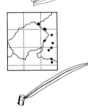

Podocarpus henkelii Henkel's Yellowwood, Drooping-leaved Yellowwood; Henkel-se-geelhout (A); umsonti (X, Z) (named after Dr J.S. Henkel, Conservator of Forests in Natal in the 1930s)

Up to 20m tall. Locally common in montane forest of N EMR. Cape to Tanz. BARK deeply fissured in a spiral pattern, flaking in long strips or in sheets, underbark reddish. LEAVES **long, drooping, widest in the middle, tapering gradually to a long pointed tip,** glossy dark green, 60-300×13mm. FEMALE CONES, **oval, olive green, up to 25×20mm,** ripen in winter (Apr-May). GENERAL: Fruit eaten by birds. Bark used in traditional medicine. Very ornamental, tolerates frost and some drought.

CUPRESSACEAE - Cypress Family Cosmop, ± 16 genera, 1 in SAfr. ***Widdringtonia*** - African Cypress (named after Edward Widdrington, navy captain and traveller who studied conifers and published a book on European pines in 1843) 3 species in SAfr, 1 in this region.

Widdringtonia nodiflora [=*W. cupressoides, W. dracomontana*] Mountain Cypress; Bergsipres (A); unwele-lwe-entaba (Z) (*nodiflora* - bare flowered, refers to fynbos species with which the type was confused)

Small, slender, **columnlike** tree, 3-6(10)m tall. On exposed mountain slopes, above Cave Sandstone cliffs. SW Cape to Limpopo Prov. BARK grey brown, **flaking in long narrow strips.** MATURE LEAVES scalelike, 2mm, dark green. FEMALE CONES dark brown, woody, up to 25mm diam, 4-valved. **General:** Used in hut construction. Easily damaged by fire, coppices freely. Slow growing, hardy ornamental plant.

MONOCOTYLEDONS Single seed-leaf, parallel veins, flower parts in threes or multiples of three.

GRAMINEAE (POACEAE) - Grass Family ***Thamnocalamus*** (*thamnos* - shrub; *calamus* - reed) 6 species, 5 in Himalayas, 1 endemic to SAfr.

Thamnocalamus tessellatus [= *Arundinaria tessellatus*] Drakensberg Bamboo; Drakensberg-bamboes (A); leqala (SS) (*tessellatus* - mosaic of small cubes, refers to conspicuous square veined leaf blade)

In dense clumps, 1-5m tall. In gullies, on damp rocky slopes below cliffs, forest margins, 1450-2700m. E Cape to KZN. 'CANES' up to 20mm diam, **much branched.** LEAF BLADE flat, 8-15mm wide, up to 120mm long, **conspicuously square veined.** FLOWERING sporadic, after which plants die. GENERAL: Easily grown in cooler areas. Used as an under layer for thatch, hut poles and screens.

DICOTYLEDONS Two seed leaves, net veins, flower parts in fours, fives or multiples of these.

SALICACEAE - Willow Family ***Salix*** (*salic* - the willow) Mostly N temp, ±400 species, 1 indigenous species with 5 subspeices in SAfr.

Salix mucronata subsp. *woodii* [= *S. woodii*] Flute Willow; Fluitjiewilger (A); moluoane, lebelete (SS); umnyezane (Z)

Small tree, 2-5m tall. Along rivers, streams, often bent by force of water. BARK dark brown, deeply fissured, young twigs red, branches drooping. LEAVES long, narrow, shiny green above, pale whitish beneath, **margins toothed, stalks 4-14mm long.** FLOWERS in short spikes (Aug-Sep). FRUIT splits to release woolly seeds (Jan-Apr).

Trevor Coleman

Trevor Coleman

Encephalartos ghellinckii

Encephalartos ghellinckii

Tony Abbott

David Johson

Geoff Nichols

Podocarpus latifolius

Podocarpus latifolius

Podocarpus henkelii

David Johnson

Martin von Fintel

Darrel Plowes

Trevor Coleman

Simon Milliken

Widdringtonia nodiflora

Thamnocalamus tessellatus

Salix mucronata

Trees

273

MYRICACEAE - Waxberry Family One genus in SAfr. *Morella* [= *Myrica*] Species often have aromatic leaves, male and female flowers on separate plants, fruit with waxy covering. Old and New Worlds excluding Austr, ±53 species, 9 species in SAfr, 3 in this region.

Morella serrata [= *Myrica serrata*] Lance-leaved Waxberry; Smalblaarwasbessie (A); maleleka (SS); isibhara, umakhuthula (X); umakhuthula, ulethi, iyethi (Z) (*serrata* - saw toothed)
Shrub or slender small tree, 1-6m tall. Along rocky streambanks up to 2000m, Cape to Mal. BARK smooth, pale grey with lines of raised dots when young, brown to black in mature plants. LEAVES 100-150×13-25mm, margins entire to deeply serrated, **tiny yellow gland dots beneath, aromatic**, lovely pinkish yellow flush on young leaves. FLOWERS in short, dense spikes (Aug-Sep). FRUITS small, pealike, in masses, dark blue or black with waxy white covering (Oct-Nov). GENERAL: Fruit sometimes eaten. Leaves, if chewed, produce burning in the throat and a severe headache. In the past, fruiting branches were boiled and 'berrywax' skimmed off to make candles and soap. Rootbark used for colds, coughs and headaches. Traditionally, branches burned in fields in Les as fertility charm to ensure good crops. **Similar species:** *Morella*

pilulifera [=*Myrica pilulifera*] Broad-leaved Waxberry; Breeblaarwasbessie (A) Big shrub or small tree, 3-4m tall. Among rocks at forest margins or on open mountain slopes up to 1850m. E Cape to Trop Afr. LEAVES 30-70×10-28(40)mm, margins smooth to coarsely toothed, stalk hairy. GENERAL: Leaves shorter and broader than *M. serrata*.

MORACEAE - Fig and Mulberry Family A large family, widespread in trop and subtrop. Milky sap, often conspicuous terminal bud sheaths (stipules), **which fall to leave a scar round the stem.** Leaves simple, alternate. Fruit either in berrylike clusters (mulberry) or enclosed in a receptacle (fig). Blue and copper butterflies (Lycaenidae) breed on plants of this family. *Ficus* - **Figs** A variable genus of beautiful and ecologically important trees or shrubs, occasionally climbers. About 750 species, cosmop, about 25 in SAfr, 1 in this region.

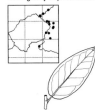

Ficus ingens Red-leaved Fig; Rooiblaarvy (A); uluzi, umthombe (X); umdende-obomvu, isigondwane, inkokhokho, umgomswane (Z) (*ingens* - large, remarkable)
Deciduous tree, 3-12m tall, often less than 1m high in cold areas where it spreads its canopy low over a rock face. On Cave Sandstone cliffs in N EMR; E Cape to Trop Afr. BARK yellowish grey, pitted, **stipular scars encircle the twigs.** LEAVES leathery, green, 60-150×30-100mm, yellow veins protrude beneath, stalk 10-25mm, shape variable. FIGS 10-13mm diam, smooth or furry, dull red when ripe, usually in pairs in leaf axils (Sep-Mar). GENERAL: **Spectacular spring flush of wine red leaves.** Figs eaten by birds and animals. Good garden plant, frost hardy if north facing, on rocks.

PROTEACEAE - *Protea* Family The scientific name *Protea* refers to Proteus, Greek sea god of legend who continually changed his shape, a reference to the many different growth forms of the Proteaceae. Flowers in dense inflorescences usually surrounded by showy bracts, sepals petal-like, petals absent or reduced to scales, stamens fused to sepals, ovary with long style. Mostly Austr, Afr, ±75 genera, ±1350 species, ±18 in SAfr, including 2 exotic genera. *Protea* - **Sugarbushes** Shrubs, small trees. Flowers massed in heads surrounded by coloured bracts. Fruits woody, hairy. Proteas are usually fire resistant with very thick bark or have well developed underground stems from which they resprout. They often require fire for germination of seed. Mostly W Cape, ±112 species in Afr, ±83 in SAfr, 6 in this region.

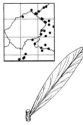

Protea caffra [= *P. rhodantha*, *P. multibracteata*] Common Protea/Sugarbush; Gewone Suikerbos (A); sekila (SS); isiqwane, indlunge (X); isiqalaba (X,Z); uhlikihlane (Z) (*caffra* - from Kaffraria, an old name for part of the E Cape)
Small to medium tree, 3-8m tall. On grass slopes, dominant or co-dominant in *Protea* savanna in montane and subalpine belts, up to 2300m. The most widespread *Protea* in SAfr, also E highlands of Zim. BARK very thick, black, reticulately fissured. LEAVES long, narrow, stalkless, 80-150×8-25mm, **light green**, yellowish compared to *P. roupelliae*. FLOWERHEADS up to 80mm diam, bracts pink or cream, flowers white, scented, nectar abundant (Dec-Jan). FRUIT a hairy nutlet. GENERAL: Nectar attracts birds, beetles. Good firewood. Grown from seed. Common name 'sugar bush' refers to the copious nectar which is rich in sugar. Bark is used in traditional medicine.

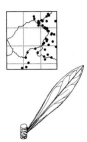

Protea roupelliae Silver Protea/Sugarbush; Silwersuikerbos (A); seqalaba (SS); isiqalaba (X,Z); uqhambathi (Z) (after Mrs Arabella Roupell who painted plates for a book of Cape flowers in 1840)
Small tree, 3-7m tall. On grass slopes, dominant or co-dominant in *Protea* Savanna in montane and subalpine belts, more common, up to 2400m. SAfr endemic. BARK thick, black, fissured. LEAVES **dark bluish green**, 60-160×15-45mm, held erect in terminal rosettes, young leaves silvery, hairy, mature leaves hairless. FLOWERHEADS 80-120mm diam, outer bracts brownish, **inner bracts spoon-shaped**, deep pink, edged with silvery hairs, **longer than the densely hairy flowers**, pale pink to red, brown, purple black (Feb-Apr). GENERAL: Gurney's Sugarbirds and Malachite Sunbirds probe the flowers, the sunbird nests in this species. Seeds and dry flowering heads provide food and nesting material for birds and small mammals. Wood used for fuel. Bark used in traditional medicine. Grown from seed, withstands some frost.

Morella pilulifera   Simon Milliken   *Morella pilulifera*   Simon Milliken   *Ficus ingens*   Lal Greene

Morella serrata   Simon Milliken   *Morella serrata*   Simon Milliken   *Ficus ingens*   David Johnson

Protea caffra   Neil Crouch   *Protea roupelliae*   David McDonald   *Protea roupelliae*   David McDonald

Trees

275

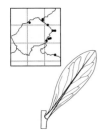

Protea dracomontana Drakensberg Dwarf Protea/Sugarbush; Drakensbergse dwerg-suikerbos (A); qaphatsi (SS) (*dracomontana* - from the Drakensberg)
Dwarf shrub, up to 1m tall and 1m diam. In very large colonies, very common on grassy slopes, over Cave Sandstone, 1600-2600m. EMR to Inyanga, Zim. Rootstock large, woody. STEMS **stout, 5-10mm diam**, bark often deep pinkish red. LEAVES 80-140×25-45mm, **thick**, leathery, with horny margins. FLOWERHEADS 40-60mm diam, creamy yellow, pink or light red, shallowly cup-shaped, **bracts rounded** hairless (**Nov-Feb**, Mar). GENERAL: Flowering time related to frequency of fire.
Similar species: *Protea simplex* Dwarf Grassveld Protea/Sugarbush (*simplex* - simple, refers to stems) Dwarf shrub, up to 1m tall. Often in huge stands in grassland over Cave Sandstone, up to 2000m. E Cape to Mpum. STEMS **slender, 2-5mm diam**. LEAVES 60-120×7-30mm, **thin**. GENERAL: Hybridises with *Protea caffra*.

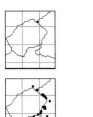

Protea nubigena Cloud Protea/Sugarbush; Wolkesuikerbos (A) (*nubigena* - living in the clouds)
Erect shrub, up to 1.1m tall. Forming clumps on very steep south facing slopes, about 2300m, EMR endemic. STEMS numerous, much branched, 5-25mm diam. LEAVES **small**, 40-60×7-13mm, pale blue-green, held erect. FLOWERHEADS 40-50mm diam, bracts green to coppery pink (Apr-May). GENERAL: Stems burnt off by fire.

Protea subvestita Lip-flower Protea/Sugarbush; Lippeblomsuikerbos (A); seqalabase-se-soeu (SS); isiqalaba (X,Z) (*subvestita* - not completely clothed, refers to soft hairs on leaves which rub off)
Shrub or small tree, 2-4m tall. On boulder beds, rocky stream gullies, rocky slopes and ridges, forming colonies where protected from fire, 1800-2440m. E Cape to KZN. BARK thin, smooth, grey, **young stems covered in dense woolly hairs**, smooth with age. LEAVES **grey**, up to 110×35mm, densely covered with shaggy to woolly hairs which rub off in patches, hairless with age. FLOWERHEADS **narrow**, 50-75 ×30-40mm, bracts creamy white, pink or carmine, **edged with long silky hairs, tips of inner bracts fold backward forming a 'lip'**, styles bend outwards, protruding beyond bracts (Dec-Mar). GENERAL: Gurney's Sugarbirds and Malachite Sunbirds feed on nectar of the flowers. Larval food plant for the butterfly *Capys alphaeus*.

SANTALACEAE - Sandalwood Family About 36 genera, 5 in SAfr. *Osyris* Shrubs, Afr and S Asia, 9 species, 3 in SAfr, 1 in this region.

Osyris lanceolata Rock Tannin-bush; Bergbas (A); ´masa, mofetola (SS); intekeza (X); intshakasa, ingondotha-mpete, umbulunyathi (X,Z) (*lanceolata* - lancelike)
Evergreen shrub or small tree, 2-6m tall. On forest margins, rocky places below cliffs, up to 2000m. Widespread. BARK dark, smooth, branchlets square. LEAVES small, up to 35×17-27mm, alternate (or opposite), thick, leathery, margin rolled, tip sharp. FLOWERS tiny, male and female on separate trees (Oct-Feb). FRUIT oval, ±15x10mm, fleshy, yellow ripening red to purplish black, crowned with persistent calyx (May-Sep). GENERAL: Bark use for tanning. Special pointed sticks from this plant used to stir meat in cooking pots. Dotted border butterfly breeds on this plant.

The Amphitheatre, Royal Natal National Park, northern Drakensberg with *Protea savanna* in the foreground

Pam Cooke

Clinton Carbutt

Protea nubigena

David McDonald

Protea dracomontana

Rob Scott-Shaw

Protea nubigena

David McDonald

Protea dracomontana

Piet van Wyk

Osyris lanceolata

Hilliard & Burtt

Protea subvestita

Olaf Wirminghaus

Protea subvestita

Trees

277

PITTOSPORACEAE - Cheesewood Family A small family found in warm countries. One genus with 1 tree species found in SAfr. *Pittosporum* (*pitta* - resin; *spora* - seed, refers to resinous coating of seeds) Trees or shrubs, ±200 species, Old World, Austr, Pacific, 1 in SAfr (2 introduced).

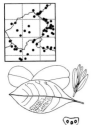

Pittosporum viridiflorum Cheesewood; Kaasuur (A); mohatollo, mofusafa, monkhanku, phuku-e-nyenyane, seteatea (SS); umkhwenkwe (X,Z); umfusamvu (Z) (*viridiflorum* - green flowered)

Evergreen tree (± deciduous at higher altitudes), 3-15m tall. On forest margins, streambanks, rock outcrops, up to 1800m. Widespread. BARK smooth, pale grey when young, with dark horizontal markings when mature. LEAVES alternate, 30-100 ×20-40mm, shiny dark green, paler beneath, resinous smell when crushed, **three small dots** (vascular bundles) **in a triangle are clearly seen in the cross section of a broken off leaf stalk.** FLOWERS small, creamy green, in dense terminal clusters, sweetly scented (Sep-Nov). FRUIT a **woody brown capsule, seeds shiny red, sticky, fleshy,** 6-10mm diam (Nov-Apr). GENERAL: Seeds attract birds. Bark bitter, smells like liquorice. Widely used for medicinal purposes. Grown from seed, frost hardy.

ROSACEAE - Rose Family (see pg 130) *Leucosidea* (*leucosidea* - with a white appearance) Small tree or shrub, 1 species, SAfr to Zim.

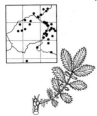

Leucosidea sericea Oldwood; Ouhout (A); cheche (SS); isidwadwa (X); umtshitshi (Z) (*sericea* - silky)

Shrub or small tree 2-7m tall. Common along streambanks, in boulder beds, on forest margins, often dominant in scrub, forming pure stands in sheltered places, 1800-2500m, E Cape to Zim. BARK **very rough, flaking.** LEAVES alternate, 30-100mm long, 2-3 pairs leaflets, sometimes with smaller pairs in between, dark green above, silky greyish white beneath, stipules silky. FLOWERS small, yellowish green, in terminal spikes up to 80mm long (Aug-Dec). GENERAL: Invades overgrazed, eroded areas. Young shoots, flowers browsed. Used in traditional medicine. Good firewood, burning slowly. Used to make the framework of sleighs. Fast growing, frost hardy.

Cliffortia (after George Clifford, 1685-1760, who grew the plants which Linnaeus described) Stipule joins onto the petiole/leaf stalk. Often the entire stalk is joined to the stipule and leaflets appear to come directly from the stipule. Afr, mostly SW Cape, ±112 species, 9 in this region.

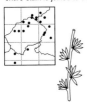

Cliffortia nitidula subsp. *pilosa* Starry Rice-bush; Sterretjierysbos (A); lenyofane (SS); untswabantswava, unwele (X); umhlahlahla (Z) (*nitidula* - shiny, refers to leaves; *pilosa* -hairy, branches)

Shrub, occasionally a small tree, 1-3m tall. Common along rocky watercourses, in boulder beds, on forest margins, open slopes, 1800-2500m, E Cape to Zim. LEAVES crowded on branchlets, in tufts of 3, very small, rolled, becoming **needlelike**, 10-30×1-2mm, dark green, margins revolute, leaflet tip blunt, **stalks very short,** hairy. FLOWERS small, inconspicuous amongst leaves (Sep-Oct). FRUIT very small, nutlike, hidden within leaves (Oct-Dec). GENERAL: Superficially resemble treelike Ericas but *Cliffortia* **leaves are always alternate not whorled**.

FABACEAE / LEGUMINOSAE - Pea family (see pg 130) *Calpurnia* - **African Laburnum Trees** (refers to similarity of genus *Calpurnia* to genus *Virgilia* as Calpurnius was considered to imitate the work of Virgil, the ancient Roman poet!) The leaves have insecticidal properties. A small genus, mainly in eastern parts of SAfr, also in Trop Afr, ±16 species, ±7 in this region.

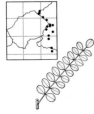

Calpurnia sericea [= *C. intrusa*] Mountain Calpurnia; Berg-geelkeur, Kleingeelkeur (A); tloele (SS) (*sericeus* - pertaining to silk)

Shrub up to 2.5m tall. Along streams, in grassland, amongst rocks, up to 2000m. SAfr endemic. LEAVES erect, 60-120mm long, leaflets in 3-13 pairs plus terminal one, 7-21×4-13mm. FLOWERS small, yellow, **in erect terminal bunches**, 60-130mm long (Nov-Jan). PODS 10-50×3-10mm. GENERAL: Used to wash maggot infested wounds in animals. **Similar species:** *Calpurnia reflexa* [= *C. robinoides*] Sotho/Free State Calpurnia; Sotho/Vrystaatse Geelkeur (A); motsohlo (SS) Shrub, 1-3m tall with 7-9 leaflets. In scrub, mountain ravines. GENERAL: Used for building purposes and fuel.

RUTACEAE - Citrus or Buchu family Economically important family. Leaves oil gland dotted (translucent dots when held against the light), often strongly scented when crushed. *Clausena* (after Peder Clausson, 1545-1614, Danish priest and naturalist) About 50 species, 1 in SAfr.

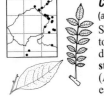

Clausena anisata Horsewood; Perdepis (A); isifudu(X); umnukambiba, umsaga; isifudu (Z) (*anisata* - like anise)

Small tree, 3-5m tall. In forest understorey. E Cape to Trop Afr. LEAVES in clusters towards ends of branches, compound, up to 300mm long, 10-60×6-25mm, gland dotted, asymmetrical at base, lowest leaflets much smaller. **Leaves smell very strongly of aniseed.** FLOWERS creamy yellow, in branched sprays, sweetly scented (Aug-Nov). FRUIT 7mm diam, fleshy, red ripening black (Oct-Feb) GENERAL: Birds eat the fruit. Used for medicinal and magical purposes throughout Africa.

278

Pittosporum viridiflorum

Hilliard & Burtt

Pittosporum viridiflorum

Geoff Nichols

Pittosporum viridiflorum

Trevor Coleman

Clausena anisata

Roy Wise

Leucosidea sericea

Neil Crouch

Leucosidea sericea

Pam Cooke

Clausena anisata

David Johnson

Cliffortia nitidula

Peter Linder

Calpurnia sericea

Hilliard & Burtt

Cliffortia nitidula var. pilosa

Peter Linder

Trees

279

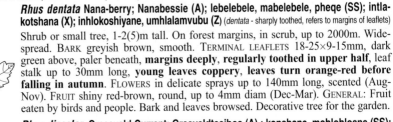

ANACARDIACEAE - Mango Family Large family. ***Rhus* - Wild Currant or Karree Trees** (*rhus* - from flow, refers to the resinous secretions or, to leaves turning red in autumn) **Male and female plants separate.** Leaves trifoliolate. About 200 species, ±75 in SAfr, ±10 in this region.

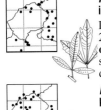

Rhus dentata Nana-berry; Nanabessie (A); lebelebele, mabelebele, pheqe (SS); intlakotshana (X); inhlokoshiyane, umhlalamvubu (Z) (*dentata* - sharply toothed, refers to margins of leaflets)

Shrub or small tree, 1-2(5)m tall. On forest margins, in scrub, up to 2000m. Widespread. BARK greyish brown, smooth. TERMINAL LEAFLETS 18-25×9-15mm, dark green above, paler beneath, **margins deeply, regularly toothed in upper half**, leaf stalk up to 30mm long, **young leaves coppery, leaves turn orange-red before falling in autumn.** FLOWERS in delicate sprays up to 140mm long, scented (Aug-Nov). FRUIT shiny red-brown, round, up to 4mm diam (Dec-Mar). GENERAL: Fruit eaten by birds and people. Bark and leaves browsed. Decorative tree for the garden.

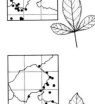

Rhus discolor Grassveld Currant; Grasveldtaaibos (A) ; kopshane, mohlohloane (SS); inkobesehlungulu, intlokotshane, umnungamabele (X) (*discolor* - of different colours)

Dwarf deciduous shrub, 0.5-1(2.5)m tall. In grassland, often in large colonies, up to 2258m, SAfr endemic. LEAFLETS about 82×18mm, grey-green above, **velvety white or cream beneath, tips sharply pointed**, stalks ±11mm long. FLOWERS in terminal sprays extending beyond leaves (Nov-Feb). FRUIT shiny yellowish brown ±5mm diam. GENERAL: Fruit eaten by birds and people. Ritually burnt to ensure a good crop.

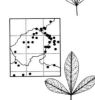

Rhus divaricata Rusty-leaved Currant, Mountain Kuni-bush; Roesblaartaaibos, Bergkoeniebos (A); kolitšana (SS) (*divaricata* - spreading, refers branching)

Multi-stemmed deciduous shrub, up to 3m tall, in scrub among rock outcrops and at foot of cliffs, **reaching the highest altitude of any *Rhus* species, up to 2750m.** E Cape to Gaut. LEAVES slightly leathery, dark olive green above with grey-green to **red-brown hairs beneath.** GENERAL: Good wood for knob sticks. Dried crushed leaves smoked to cure coughs and colds. One of the plants used in rain making.

Rhus montana Drakensberg Karree; Drakensbergkaree (A); kolitšana (SS)

Shrub or small deciduous tree, 1-5m tall. At foot of cliffs, rock outcrops, scrub forest, 1800-2400m. KZN. Single stemmed with weeping habit. LEAVES **3-5-7 foliolate, very variable**; **turn orange red in autumn**; TERMINAL LEAFLET 27-68×8-16mm, **parchmentlike texture**, dark green above, pale olive beneath, margin deeply serrated in upper half or entire, tapering to a fine pointed tip, stalk slender, up to 35mm long. FLOWERS (Oct-Feb). FRUIT round, ±3.5mm diam, smooth, shiny pale brownish red (Nov-Jun). GENERAL: Wood used for hut building. Frost hardy garden tree.

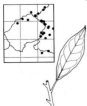

Rhus pyroides Common Currant; Gewone Taaibos (A); kolitšane, leroana (SS); inhlokoshiyane (Z) (*pyroides* - resembling the *Pyrus* or pear tree)

Shrub or small tree, 1-6m tall, on rock outcrops, rocky margins of forest patches, up to 2100m. Spineless or with **sturdy spines** up to 60mm long. LEAFLETS leathery, olive green, smooth above, hairy below. FLOWERS in hanging bunches up to 100mm long (Aug-Mar). FRUIT round, shiny dull yellowish red (Oct-May). GENERAL: Birds eat the fruit. Wood used for axe handles, fence poles. Decorative shrub for the garden.

Rhus tomentosa Bi-coloured Currant; Korentetaaibos (A) (*tomentosa* - thick covering of hairs)

Much branched shrub or small tree, 2-5m tall. In rocky places, on edge of scrub forest in foothills. BRANCHLETS **red, hairy.** LEAFLETS, leathery, dark green above, **creamy white, velvety to woolly beneath.** FLOWERS in **dense, furry, conspicuous terminal inflorescences**, male ones strongly scented (Jul-Sep). FRUIT **roundish, densely covered with creamy greyish furry hairs.** GENERAL: Bark used for tanning, twine.

AQUIFOLIACEAE - Holly Family *Ilex* (the holm oak *Quercus ilex*) Male and female flowers on separate trees. About 400 species, 1 in SAfr.

Ilex mitis African Holly, Cape Holly; Without (A); mollo-oa-phofu, phukhu (SS); umduma, umduduma (X); iphuphuma (Z) (*mitis* - soft, without thorns)

Evergreen, 8-20m tall. Usually **near streams in forest**, up to 1800m. Cape to Trop Afr. BARK whitish, **branchlets silvery white, young stems smooth, reddish.** LEAVES alternate, 60-80×19-45mm, shiny dark green, margin entire or with a few teeth on upper third, **conspicuously sunken midrib above, stalk short, pinkish purple.** FLOWERS small, white, in profusion, sweetly scented (Oct-Feb). FRUIT bright red, ±7mm diam, in profusion (Mar-Apr). GENERAL: Fruit attracts birds. Leaves used to for a soaplike lather. Used in traditional medicine. Handsome, frost hardy tree.

Neil Crouch

Rodney Moffett

Rhus dentata

Rhus divaricata

Simon Milliken

Rhus discolor

Simon Milliken

Rhus tomentosa

Rodney Moffett

Rhus montana

David Johnson

Rhus pyroides

Simon Milliken

Ilex mitis

Braam van Wyk

Ilex mitis

Piet van Wyk

Ilex mitis

Trees

281

CELASTRACEAE - Spike-thorn Family A large family. Mainly trop, ±65 genera, ±1000 species, ±19 genera in SAfr. *Maytenus* (from Chilean common name *maiten*) **Spineless.** Leaves never in clusters. Flowers always bisexual. Seeds ± covered by aril. About 150 species, ±11 in SAfr.

Maytenus acuminata Silky-bark; Sybas (A); tšikane (SS); umnama, umzungulwa (X); isinama, umlulama (Z) (*acuminata* - drawn out into a long point, refers to leaves)

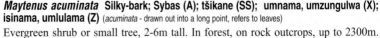

Evergreen shrub or small tree, 2-6m tall. In forest, on rock outcrops, up to 2300m. SW Cape to E Afr. BARK mottled brown with white and orange patches. LEAVES 13-120mm, margins and stalks reddish, twigs purplish, **silky elastic threads in broken leaf.** FLOWERS creamy green (Nov-Mar). FRUIT orange-red, **1-3-lobed capsules**, ±10mm diam, seeds covered in **orange aril** (Mar-Jun). GENERAL: Birds eat arils of seeds. Leaves browsed by game. Bark used medicinally and for ties for hut building, wood for fighting sticks. Frost hardy garden plant.

Maytenus peduncularis Cape Blackwood; Kaapse Swarthout (A); umnqayi (X,Z)

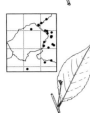

Small evergreen tree, 5(20-25)m tall. In forest, bush clumps around boulders, up to 1800m. BARK dark grey brown. Main branches erect, **young stems with weeping, willowlike habit.** LEAVES alternate, 13-90×8-40mm, with velvety golden brown hairs beneath when young, almost hairless when mature, **stalk short, with golden brown hairs.** FLOWERS **on slender stalks up to 30mm long** (Oct-May). FRUITS yellow, oval, 10mm diam, **2-lobed capsule**, seed almost completely covered by whitish yellow aril (Dec-Jul). GENERAL: Wood used for walking, fighting sticks. Survives severe frost.

Maytenus undata Koko-tree; Kokoboom (A); moqai (SS); inqayi-elimbomvu (X,Z); umnqayi-mpofu, umgora (X); idohame (Z) (*undata* - undulate, refers to wavy leaf margins)

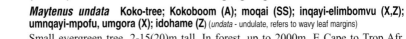

Small evergreen tree, 2-15(20)m tall. In forest, up to 2000m. E Cape to Trop Afr. BARK smooth, dark grey, New growth angular, purplish red. Spineless. LEAVES **alternate, very variable in size**, 20-130×10-90mm, glossy dark green above, **white waxy bloom below** (which can be wiped off), conspicuous reticulate veining beneath the bloom, stalks short, 10mm. FLOWERS small, in dense clusters (Sep-May). FRUIT small, whitish yellow to red-brown, seeds covered by shiny yellow aril (Oct-Jun). GENERAL: Bark used in traditional medicine. Wood used for fuel, fighting sticks.

Gymnosporia (gymno - naked; *sporia* - seed) Trees and shrubs, **with spines.** Unisexual, male and female separate. Fruit a capsule, seed covered in fleshy aril. Afr, Madag, Spain, S Europe, India, ±80 species, ±30 in SAfr.

Gymnosporia buxifolia [= *Maytenus heterophylla*] Common Spike-thorn; Gewone Pendoring (A); sefea-maeba (SS); umqaqoba (X); usala, ingqwangane, isibhubhu, isihlangu (Z) (*buxus* - box tree; *folia* - leaves)

Multi-stemmed shrub, small tree, 2-6m tall. In dripline of Cave Sandstone overhangs, at foot of cliffs, on forest margins, up to 1980m. Widespread. BARK rough, deeply grooved, branches arching, spines sharp, 13-50(240)mm. LEAVES **often in tufts**, on short side branchlets, 10-90×4-50mm, thinly leathery. FLOWERS **white**, massed, scent strong, unpleasant (Aug-Mar). FRUIT whitish pink, capsule **±5mm diam**, seeds partly covered by whitish yellow aril (Dec-May). GENERAL: Fruit eaten by birds. Leaves browsed. Widely utilized medicinally, and for fuel. Survives severe frost.

Gymnosporia harveyana [previously part of *Maytenus mossambicensis* complex] Black forest-spike-thorn; Swartbospendoring (A); ingqwangane, umqaqoba (X); ingqwangane-yehlathi (Z)

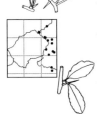

Straggling shrub or small tree, 2-4m tall, in **forest understorey** up to 2000m. E Cape to Trop Afr. Main stems slender, BARK smooth, spines **slender**, up to 80mm long. LEAVES alternate or **in tufts**, 10-65×6-40mm, **thin**, shiny bright green above, paler beneath, stalk short, ±6mm long. FLOWERS small, white to pink (Oct-Mar). FRUIT a semi-fleshy capsule, white ripening brown to bright red, up to 13mm diam, **hanging on long stalk**, seeds covered with orange-red aril (Dec-May).

Lauridia Endemic to SAfr, 2 species, 1 in this region.

Lauridia tetragona [= *Cassine tetragona*, *Allocassine tetragona*] Climbing Saffron; Rank-saffraan (A); umbovana (X) (*tetragona* - 4-angled, refers to twigs)

Scrambling shrub or small tree, 3-5(15)m tall. In forest understorey, on steep scrubby slopes, up to 1950m. E Cape to Swaz. **Branchlets 4-angled, short side branchlets form reverse hooks to assist in climbing.** LEAVES opposite, leathery, **stalk very short.** FLOWERS creamy white (Oct-Apr). FRUIT ± 8mm diam, fleshy, purplish black (Dec- Jun). GENERAL: Fruit eaten by children, birds. Leaves browsed by stock.

Maytenus acuminata

Simon Milliken

Maytenus acuminata

Piet van Wyk

Maytenus peduncularis

Geoff Nichols

Maytenus undata

Tony Abbott

Maytenus undata

Geoff Nichols

Gymnosporia harveyana

Piet van Wyk

Gymnosporia harveyana

Roy Wise

Lauridia tetragona

Tony Abbott

Gymnosporia buxifolia

David Johnson

Gymnosporia buxifolia

Braam van Wyk

Trees

283

ICACINACEAE - White Pear Family Three genera with trees in SAfr. *Cassinopsis* Small trees or shrubs. 6 species, 2 in SAfr, 1 in this region.

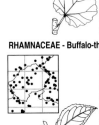

Cassinopsis ilicifolia Lemon Thorn; Lemoentjiedoring (A); motale (SS); icegceya (X); ikhumalo (X,Z); imamba eluhlaza, isihlokolozane (Z) (*ilicifolia* - leaves like *Ilex*)

Evergreen **scrambling shrub** or small tree, 2-5m tall. In forest, E Cape to Trop Afr. Branches in **zigzag pattern**, spines **single, green, slender, sharp**. LEAVES opposite, 40-60×20-25mm, very shiny, thinly leathery, margin with **sharp serrations** or entire, stalk short. FLOWERS small, greenish white, opposite spines (Sep-Nov). FRUIT orange, **fleshy**, roundish, 13mm long (Mar-May). GENERAL: Used for hut building.

GREYIACEAE - Wild Bottlebrush Family A family endemic to SAfr. One genus, *Greyia*, with 3 species.

Greyia sutherlandii Glossy Berg Bottlebrush; Blinkblaarbaakhout, Natalse Baakhout (A); indalu, umberebere, usinga-lwamaxhegokazi (X); indulo, umbande (Z) (named after P.C. Sutherland, 1822-1900, medical doctor, Surveyor General in Natal, sent parcels of plants to Kew)

Deciduous tree, 2-7m tall. On cliffs, rocky slopes, up to 1900m. E Cape, Free State to Swaz. BARK rough, dark. LEAVES up to 100×110mm, rough, green above, smooth paler beneath, **stalks almost sheathing stem**. INFLORESCENCE densely packed, mostly horizontal, up to 120mm long; FLOWERS scarlet, **petals spreading** (Aug-Oct). GENERAL: Nectar laden flowers attract birds. Dry capsules and seeds provide nesting material and food for birds. Red leaves in autumn. Frost hardy garden plant.

RHAMNACEAE - Buffalo-thorn Family Cosmop, 9 genera in SAfr. *Rhamnus* (Greek for prickly shrubs) ±200 species, 2 in SAfr, 1 in this region.

Rhamnus prinoides Glossyleaf, Shinyleaf, Dogwood; Blinkblaar (A); mofifi (SS); umnyenye (X,Z) (*prinoides* - like the holm-oak, possibly because of the similarity of the wood)

Scrambling shrub, 2-6m tall. On forest margins, streambanks, in scrub, up to 2150m. Cape to Ethiopia. BARK smooth, grey-brown with raised white dots on young stems. LEAVES alternate, 30-100×15-40mm, **conspicuously shiny, very dark blackish green** above. FLOWERS small, greenish, in clusters (Nov-Jan). FRUIT small, round, 5mm diam, fleshy, red to purplish black (Dec-Jun). GENERAL: Fruit attracts birds. Used in traditional medicine. Frost resistant garden plant, a good hedge in cold areas.

Phylica (*phylikos* - leafy) Shrubs or subshrubs. Leaf margins rolled under. Attracts butterflies. Afr. Madag, ±188 species in SAfr, 2 in this region.

Phylica paniculata Northern/Common Hardleaf; Noordelike/Gewone hardeblaar (A); umhlalamithi, umdidi (Z) (*paniculata* - tuft)

Evergreen, 1-6m tall. On rocky forest margins, in stream gullies, Cave Sandstone sheets, 1800-2300m. SW Cape to Zim. BARK whitish grey, young stems grey woolly. LEAVES overlapping, very small, 10-15×2-6mm, hard, dark green above, whitish beneath, margins rolled under. FLOWERS very small, in clusters, ±100×40mm, strongly scented, (Dec-Mar). FRUIT reddish brown woody capsule, ±6mm diam (Apr-Jul). GENERAL: Fruit eaten by birds. Frost hardy, decorative shrub, grown from seed.

VITACEAE - Grape Family Climbing shrubs with tendrils. Includes the grape vine *Vitis vinifera*. Trop, temp, 14 genera, ±1000 species, 5 genera in SAfr. *Rhoicissus* (*rhoicus* - of *Rhus*; *cissus* - ivy, refers to the climbing habit) Scramblers, climbers. Afr, ±10 species, 7 in SAfr, 2 in this region.

Rhoicissus tridentata Bushman's Grape, Northern Bushman's Grape; Boesmansdruif, Bobbejaantou (A); morara-oa-thaba (SS); isaqoni (X); isinwazi, umthwazi (Z) (*tridentata* - three-toothed)

Deciduous shrub or climber, 1-3(10)m tall. On margins of forest, scrub, up to 1800m. E Cape to Trop Afr. Young stems **velvety greyish or rusty hairy**. LEAVES 3 foliolate, 50-90×25-70mm, **side leaflets usually asymmetrical**, leathery. FLOWERS in tight clusters (Nov-Jan). FRUIT red to black, fleshy, ±18mm diam (Feb-Jun). GENERAL: Fruit eaten by birds and people. Leaves browsed by game. Lovely garden plant.

FLACOURTIACEAE - Wild Peach Family About 89 genera, 13 in SAfr. *Kiggeleria* (after Francois Kiggelaer, 1648-1722, Dutch botanist) 1 species.

Kiggelaria africana Wild Peach; Wildeperske (A); lekhatsi (SS); umkhokhokho (X); isiklalu(Z)

Evergreen tree, 4-13m tall. In forest, scrub, up to 2100m. Cape to Kenya. BARK flaky and fissured. LEAVES alternate, 35-170×20-50mm, **bluish grey and velvety brown or white beneath, hairy pockets in axils of main veins showing as small bumps on upper surface, very variable shape and size**. FLOWERS male and female on separate trees (Aug-Jan). FRUIT ± to 20mm diam, **rough, knobbly**, seed shiny black in sticky red coating (Feb-Jul). GENERAL: Fruits attract many birds. *Acraea* butterflies breed on the tree, the caterpillars attracting birds. Decorative, very frost hardy.

Cassinopsis ilicifolia

David Johnson

Greyia sutherlandii

Martin von Fintel

Rhoicissus tridentata

David Johnson

Greyia sutherlandii

Tom de Waal

Phylica paniculata

Tony Abbott

Phylica paniculata

Geoff Nichols

Kiggelaria africana

Geoff Nichols

Kiggelaria africana

Pam Cooke

Rhamnus prinoides

Geoff Nichols

Trees

285

Scolopia (*scolopia* - 'pointed stick' refers to the spines) Shrubs or trees. Afr, Madag, Malaysia, Austr, ±37 species, 5 in SAfr, 2 in this region.

Scolopia mundii Red-pear; Rooipeer (A); qoqolosi (SS); umnqanqa, iqumza (X); uloyiphela, ihlambahlale (Z) (J.L.L. Mund, 1791-1831, Prussian pharmacist, botanist who collected in the Cape)

Small to medium tree, 6-10(30)m tall. In forest, at foot of damp Cave Sandstone cliffs, up to 1950m. Cape to Swaz. BARK smooth, grey-brown becoming rough and flaky, coppice shoots with spines up to 20mm long. LEAVES alternate, 35-70 ×20-40mm, leathery, **stiff, glossy green** above, dull beneath, margin sharply serrated, mature leaves with blunt tip, young leaves tapering to a point, stalks short, pink, sapling leaves very large and shiny. FLOWERS in small clusters, sweetly scented (May-Aug). FRUIT 10mm diam, yellowish orange, in profusion (Oct-Jan). GENERAL: Fruit eaten by people, birds, wild pigs. Wood hard, heavy, used for furniture. Bark used in traditional medicine. Good garden plant, very frost hardy, fruit attracts birds.

Trimeria (*trimeria* - in three parts, refers to flowers) Shrubs or trees, Afr, ±5 species, 2 in SAfr, 1 in this region.

Trimeria grandifolia Wild-mulberry; Wildemoerbei (A); igqabi, ilitye, igqabela, umnqabane (X); idlebenlendlovu (X,Z) (*grandifolia* - large leaves)

Scrambling shrub, small tree (4-10)m tall. In forest, about 1800m. E Cape to Zim. Bark grey brown, flaky. LEAVES **large, almost round,** 70-130mm diam, **3-5(7) veins from base,** stalks up to 30mm long. FLOWERS very small, male and female separately (Nov-Dec). FRUIT a small red capsule, 5×3mm, seed black with red aril (Feb-Apr). GENERAL: Birds eat the fruit. Used in traditional medicine. Graceful small garden tree.

OLINIACEAE - Hard Pear Family Afr, 1 genus, 8-10 species. *Olinia* (named after Johan Hendrik Olin, 1769-1824, Swedish botanist) 4 species in SAfr, 1 in this region.

Olinia emarginata Mountain Olinia, Mountain Hard-pear; Berghardepeer (A); umngana-lahla, iqudu (X); unquthu (Z) (*emarginata* - notched, refers to the notched tip of the leaves)

Evergreen, 10-15(20)m tall. Common in montane forest, along streams, up to 2150m; E Cape to Zim. Main stem straight, branches upward growing. BARK **pale brownish yellow,** flaking off in patches, **young twigs 4-angled,** branchlets smooth, pale creamy white. LEAVES opposite, small, 20-50×7-20mm, **glossy dark green** above, paler, dull beneath, **tip rounded, notched, stalk very short, pink to red.** FLOWERS small, **pink, borne profusely, in loose branched spray,** faintly scented (Oct-Nov). FRUIT deep pink, 10mm diam, berrylike with **circular scar,** massed in **dense clusters** (May-Jul). GENERAL: **Crushed leaf faintly almond scented.** Fruit eaten by birds. Wood hard and heavy. Very decorative, frost resistant.

THYMELAEACEAE - Gonna Family (see pg 136) *Passerina* (*passer* - a sparrow, refers to black seeds that are beaked) Ericoid shrubs. Sterile material can be distinguished from related Ericas by breaking a twig to reveal stringy bark. SAfr, mainly SW Cape, ±20 species, 3 in this region.

Passerina montana Mountain Passerina, Mountain Gonna; Berg-gonna (A); lekhapu (SS) (*montana* - mountains)

Shrub, up to 3m tall. Common in scrub, boulder beds, on rock sheets, 1800-3000m. E Cape to Zim. Young stems woolly, tips of branchlets drooping. LEAVES very small, up to 4mm, lying flat against stem, **wider at base.** FLOWERS small, creamy pink, **in terminal clusters, in profusion** (Oct-Dec). GENERAL: On rock it forms a low, dense bush with erect branchlets. In valleys it forms a spreading shrub, tips of branchlets drooping. Favoured fuel. **Similar species:** *Passerina drakensbergensis* Drakensberg

Passerina Up to 2m tall. One of the dominants in subalpine fynbos between (1500)2100-2450m. N EMR endemic. Young stems white, woolly. LEAVES shiny, 3-10mm, slightly keeled. FLOWERS **towards ends of branches** (Nov-Dec).

Dais (*dais* - a feast or, a torch, both names referring to the flowers) Small trees, Afr and Madag, 2 species, 1 in this region.

Dais cotinifolia Pompon Tree; Kannabas, Basboom (A); tohotsoane (SS); intozane (X); intozane-emnyama (Z) (*cotinifolia* - with leaves resembling those of the genus *Cotinus*)

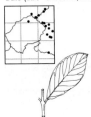

Tree 2-7m tall. In forest, on streambanks. E Cape to Zim. BARK smoothish grey with pale raised corky streaks, branches flattened at nodes. LEAVES opposite, smooth with slightly waxy texture, bluish green above, lighter beneath, **translucent yellow midrib and side veins.** FLOWERS pink, in dense, **round pomponlike terminal clusters up to 40mm diam,** dry brown flowers remain on tree long after flowering (Oct-Feb). GENERAL: Bark stripped and plaited into rope, used for whips and for binding. Popular garden plant, cultivated in Europe since the 1700s.

Olinia emarginata

Olinia emarginata

Olinia emarginata

Trimeria grandifolia

Passerina montana

Scolopia mundii

Passerina drakensbergensis

Scolopia mundii

Dais cotinifolia

Passerina montana

Trees

287

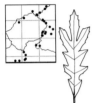

ARALIACEAE *Cussonia* - Cabbage Trees (after P. Cusson, 1727-1783, French prof of botany) Afr, 25 species, ±10 in SAfr, 2 in this region.

Cussonia paniculata var. *sinuata* Mountain Cabbage Tree; Berg/Hoëveldkiepersol (A); motšetše (SS); umsenge (X,Z) (*paniculata* - arranged in panicles, branched inflorescences; *sinuata* - crooked)

Evergreen, 4-6m tall. On cliffs, among boulders, 1800-1980m. Cape to Swaz. BARK corky, fissured. LEAVES **grey- to blue-green**, ±600mm diam, leaflets deeply lobed, **never cut to midrib**. FLOWERS in **long sprays**, forming **branched inflorescence or panicle** (Jan-Mar). FRUITS 6mm diam, purplish (Apr-Aug). GENERAL: Fruits eaten by birds. Leaves browsed. A hardy feature plant. **Similar species:** *Cussonia spicata* Cabbage tree; Gewone-kiepersol (A); umsenge (X,Z) Deciduous, 4-10m tall. LEAVES **dark green, leaflets cut to midrib.** FLOWERS in **thick spikes in double umbel.**

UMBELLIFERAE / APIACEAE (see pg 80) *Heteromorpha* (heteromorpha - different forms) Afr; ±5 species, 3 in SAfr, 1 in this region.

Heteromorpha arborescens var. *abyssinica* [= *H. trifoliata*] Parsley-tree; Pietersieliebos (A); ´makatlala, monkhoane (SS); umbangandlala (X,Z) (*arborescens* - treelike)

Deciduous small tree, 2-6m tall. Forest margins, scrub patches, 1800-2000m. Cape to Trop Afr. **Bark satiny smooth, peeling horizontally in dark copper to purplish brown paper flakes, older stems segmented.** LEAVES 3 foliolate to pinnately compound, thin, **stalk broad based, stem clasping, parsley smell when crushed.** FLOWERHEADS ±50 mm diam, strong smelling (Jan-Apr). FRUIT flattened (Apr-May). GENERAL: Used in traditional medicine. Withstands severe frost.

MYRSINACEAE - Cape Myrtle Family Large family. *Myrsine* (Myrtus - Greek name for myrtle) Afr to China, 7 species, 2 in S Afr.

Myrsine africana Cape myrtle; Vlieëbos, Mirting (A); moroka-pheleu, semapo, sethakhisa, thakisa (SS)

Evergreen shrub 1-2m tall. On forest margins, in scrub, fynbos, 1800-1980m. Cape to Trop Afr, Asia. BRANCHLETS with fine rusty hairs, new growth purple. LEAVES **very small, 20-50×10mm**, glossy, leathery, very dark green, with **fine teeth in upper half**, new growth red. FLOWERS very small, **protruding anthers pinkish red**, in leaf axils (Sep-Nov). FRUIT **pink to purple**, 4-8mm diam (Nov-Mar). GENERAL: Fruit eaten by birds. Very decorative, frost-hardy garden shrub, grown from seed.

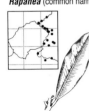

Rapanea (common name for a species in Trop America) Trees. Trop, ±100 species, 2 in SAfr, 1 in this region.

Rapanea melanophloeos Cape Beech; Kaapse boekenhout (A); isiqwane sehlathi (X); umaphipha (Z) (*melanophloeos* - dark bark)

Evergreen, 3-8(20)m tall. In forest, on streambanks, about 1800m. S Cape to Zam. BARK pinkish grey with raised dots on young stems, rough grey-brown on mature stems. LEAVES clustered towards ends of branches, 50-130×40-50mm, thick, dark green above, dull paler beneath, margin rolled under, **stalks usually purple**, up to 15mm long. FLOWERS clustered on stem (May-Jul). FRUIT **small, fleshy, purple, in profusion** (Aug-Nov). GENERAL: Flowers attract bees and flies. Fruit eaten by birds and animals. Decorative tree, grown from seed, withstands slight frost.

EBENACEAE - Ebony Family Two genera. *Euclea* - Guarrri Trees (eukleia - beautiful evergreen leaves) Characterized by translucent veins, clear when held against the light. Male and female flowers on separate trees. Afr, Arabia, Comoro Is; ±20 species, 16 in SAfr, 2 in this region.

Euclea crispa Blue Guarri; Bloughwarrie (A); mohlakola (SS); umtsheki-sane, umgwali (X); umshekisane, idungamuzi, umnqandane (Z) (*crispa* - curled)

Evergreen, 3-10m tall. On forest margins, at base of cliffs, in shelter of large boulders, 1800-2000m. Widespread. Young branchlets **rusty brown**. LEAVES, **hard, leathery, bluish green**, 40-100mm long, margins wavy or flat. FLOWERS in branched sprays, sweetly scented (Dec-May). FRUIT **black, hard**, 5mm diam (May-Dec). GENERAL: Fruit eaten by birds, animals, people. Used in traditional medicine. Frost hardy.

Diospyros (diospyros - 'divine wheat', refers to edible fruit) Afr, Asia, America, ±425 species, 20 in SAfr, 3 in this region. '

Diospyros austro-africana var. *rubriflora* Firesticks Star-apple; Kritikom, Vuurmaak-bossie (A); liperekisi-tsa-makhoaba, senokonoko (SS)

Small tree, 1-6m tall. On rock outcrops, boulder beds 1800-2450m. EMR endemic. LEAVES **small, 4-25×2-5mm**, stiff, leathery, bluish green, **densely velvety grey** below, **red** in winter, after frost. FLOWERS **pinkish red**, 4-9mm long, **solitary** (Aug-Nov). FRUIT red to black, ±15mm diam, velvety (Jan-Jun). GENERAL: Fruits eaten by birds and people. Used for fuel. Neat garden plant, survives severe frost.

288

Cussonia paniculata

Cussonia paniculata

Myrsine africana

Myrsine africana

Heteromorpha arborescens

Heteromorpha arborescens

Euclea crispa

Diospyros austro-africana

Rapanea melanophloeos

Rapanea melanophloeos

Diospyros austro-africana

Trees

289

Diospyros whyteana Bladder-nut; Swartbas (A); umanzimane (Z)

Evergreen, 2-7m tall. In forest understorey, in rocky places, about 1800m. S Cape to Tanz. LEAVES 25-50×10-20mm, **glossy dark green** above, **margins wavy, fringed with soft ginger hairs**. FLOWERS creamy yellow, sweetly scented (Jul-Oct). FRUITS red, up to 20mm long, **completely, loosely enclosed in inflated, papery, angled calyx** (Nov-Jun). GENERAL: Birds eat the fruit. Leaves browsed. Hardy garden shrub.

BUDDLEJACEAE (see pg 84). *Buddleja* (named after Rev Adam Buddle, 1660-1715, English botanist) ± 100 species, 7 in SAfr, ±6 in this region.

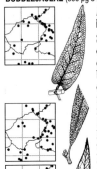

Buddleja salviifolia Quilted Sagewood; Saliehout (A); lelothoane (SS); ilothane, igqange (X); iloshane (Z) *(salviifolia - leaves like a salvia or sage)*

Small tree, 3-8m tall. On forest margins, rocky streambanks, near Cave Sandstone overhangs, 1800-2435m. Cape to E Afr. Twigs 4-angled, densely woolly. LEAVES opposite, 30-140×7-40mm, soft, **heavily textured above, velvety white beneath**, base deeply lobed, **stalkless, stipules leaflike**. FLOWERS white to mauve, throat orange, in **long dense spikes** ±120mm, sweetly scented (**Aug-Oct**). GENERAL: Used for a herbal tea. Leaves browsed. Wood used for spear shafts, fuel and to decorate reed fences around courtyards in Les. Frost hardy garden plant. **Similar species: *Buddleja loricata*** [= *B. corrugata*] Mountain Sagewood; Bergsaliehoud (A); lelora (SS); umngane (Z) Frequently dominant at higher altitudes, 1800-2400m. LEAVES 15-90 ×2-20mm, wrinkled above, rusty hairs beneath, stalk short, **ridge between leaves** (no stipules). FLOWERS creamy white with orange centre, in **short spikes**, sweetly scented, **summer flowering (Oct-Dec)**. ***Buddleja auriculata*** Weeping Sagewood; **Treursaliehout (A)** *(auriculata - earlike appendage)* 2-4m tall. On forest margins; E Cape to Zim. **Branches slender, arching, willowlike**, stipules leaflike, drop early. LEAVES drooping, **thin, shiny to dark green above, velvety white beneath**, stalk up to 10mm long. FLOWERS in dense **long spikes**, strongly scented, **winter flowering (May-Aug)**.

SCROPHULARIACEAE (see pg 90) *Halleria* (after Albrecht von Haller, 1708-1777, Swiss naturalist) Afr, ±10 species, 3 in SAfr, 1 in this region.

Halleria lucida Halleria, Tree Fuchsia; Notsung (A); lebetsa (SS); uminza (X,Z) *(lucida - shining)*

Tree 2-10(20)m tall. In forest, on rock outcrops, 1800-2100m. Cape to Trop Afr. BARK **finely fissured**. LEAVES opposite, 25-70×10-40mm, **base asymmetrical, square** or broadly tapering. FLOWERS ±40mm long, in **dense clusters on old wood** (Apr-Aug). FRUIT black, ±10mm diam (Jan-Feb). GENERAL: Leaves browsed. Wood used for spear shafts and to start fire by friction. Frost tolerant. Nectar and fruit attracts birds.

Bowkeria (after J.H. Bowker, 1822-1900, SA naturalist and plant collector) Shrubs or small trees, SAfr, 3 species, 1 in this region.

Bowkeria verticillata Southern Shell-flower; Suidelike Skulpblombos (A); isiduli, igqabi-lesiduli (X); umbaba (Z)

Evergreen, 3-5m tall. On forest margins, sometimes dominant on boulder beds of rivers, 1800-2135m. E Cape, FS, KZN. Very variable. LEAVES **usually 3-whorled**, 25-130×6-65mm, firm, dark green, **corrugated, with sunken veins above**, slightly hairy to velvety, stalk short or absent. FLOWERS in pairs, **white, sticky**, up to 20mm long, strongly scented (Nov-Jan). GENERAL: Leaves browsed. Flowers pollinated by oil collecting *Rediviva* sp. bees. Decorative, frost resistant garden shrub

RUBIACEAE - Gardenia Family (see pg 98). *Burchellia* (after William Burchell, great naturalist and writer in 1800s) 1 species, SAfr endemic.

Burchellia bubalina Wild Pomegranate; Wildegranaat (A); ithobankomo, umfincane (X); isigolwane (Z) *(boubalos - buffalo, refers to the hard wood)*

Evergreen tree, 3-6m tall. In forest. S Cape to Swaz. LEAVES opposite, 50-180 ×25-80mm, soft to thickly leathery, dark green, quilted above, **stalk short, thick, hairy**. FLOWERS **in dense terminal clusters** (Sep-Dec). FRUIT with **5 enlarged calyx lobes** (Nov-Apr). GENERAL: Birds feed on nectar and fruit. Ornamental shrub.

Canthium - Turkey-berry Trees (from Malabar name, *canti*) Shrubs or trees. Trop of the Old World, 52 species, 13 in SAfr, 3 in this region.

Canthium ciliatum Fringed/Hairy Turkey-berry; Harige Bokdrol (A); seeqoane (SS); umnyulushube (X) *(ciliatum - fringed)*

Small tree, up to 5m tall. **In forest understorey**, in scrub, rocky places, up to 1950m. E Cape to Mpum. Twigs with **paired straight spines**. LEAVES 6-30×4-18mm, **soft, finely hairy, margins fringed with fine hairs**. FLOWERS small, **on long stalks** (Oct-Feb). FRUIT black, 1-2-lobed, ±13mm long (Feb-May). **General:** Birds eat the fruit.

Diospyros whyteana
Martin von Fintel

Buddleja auriculata
David Johnson

Buddleja salviifolia
David Johnson

Buddleja loricata
John Grimshaw

Halleria lucida
David Johnson

Bowkeria verticillata
Hilliard & Burtt

Burchellia bubalina
Auriol Batten

Halleria lucida
David Johnson

Canthium ciliatum
Tony Abbott

Canthium ciliatum
Tony Abbott

Trees

291

PTEROPSIDA Ferns are ancient and primitive plants. They are widespread and reproduce by spores, not by seed.

LYCOPODIACEAE - Club Mosses *Lycopodium* (*lycos* - wolf; *pous* - foot, refers to the similarity in appearance of the densely leafy branches to a wolf's furry paw). Worldwide, over 45 species, 9 in SAfr, 4 in this region.

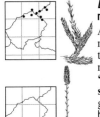

Lycopodium clavatum Club Moss, Toad's Tail; boriba-boboholo, moriri-oa-lilomo, moriri-oa-mafika (SS); inwele (Z) (*clavatum* - club-shaped, refers to arrangement of sporophylls)

A neat, evergreen creeping herb. Often in large colonies, in light shade on forest margins, on steep streambanks, at foot of Cave Sandstone cliffs, 1600-2300m. S Cape to trop Afr. MAIN RHIZOME creeps above ground. STEMS **erect,** branching. LEAVES needlelike, tipped with a fine hair, **fertile branches with two narrow cylindrical 'cones'.** GENERAL: Used in traditional medicine to treat a variety of ailments. **Similar species:** *L. carolinianum* (*carolinianum* - from Carolina, SE USA) **Stems prostrate,** in marshy ground at edge of rock sheets, up to 2000m. Cones held erect. *L. saururus* boriba-boboholo, moriri-oa-lilomo, moriri-oa-mafika (SS) (*saururus* - resembles a reptile or lizard) Robust, erect, up to 320mm tall. In crevices of cliffs and rock sheets, 1800-2590m. Afr mountains. STEMS unbranched. No 'cones'; sporangia hidden within leaves.

SELAGINELLACEAE *Selaginella* - **Lesser Clubmoss (Staghorn Mosses)** (*selaginella* - small *selago*, refers to *Lycopodium selago*) Mainly trop, ±700 species, 9 in SAfr, 4 in this region.

Selaginella caffrorum Staghorn Clubmoss; boribo, moriri-oa-matlapa, phate-ea-balimo (SS) (*caffrorum* - belonging to caffraria, a name loosely used to refer to SA, especially E Cape)

Mosslike plant, creeping, mat-forming. **On vertical cliff faces** and rock outcrops, 1800-2300m. S Cape to Sudan. LEAVES deep rich green (pale coppery brown when dry), branch tips bend inwards when dead. Dries out in dry periods but revives quickly with rain. GENERAL: Used in traditional medicine to drive away fevers caused by ancestral spirits, mixed with *Lycopodium clavatum* and smoked to cure headaches.

Selaginella imbricata Fish-scale Clubmoss (*imbricata* - overlapping, leaves look like fish scales)

Fronds erect, 50-300mm tall, branched. Found only on **basalt rock,** up to 2990m. Drak to Trop Afr. RHIZOME creeping. LEAVES very dark green, pale brown beneath. GENERAL: Shrivels in dry periods, regains green state within 12 hours of rain.

ISOETACEAE *Isoetes* - **Quillworts** (*isos* - equal; *etos* - year) About 75 species, ±9 in SAfr, 1 in this region.

Isoetes transvaalensis Quillwort

Aquatic herb, 30-160mm tall. In shallow pools in Cave Sandstone outcrops, on fallen boulders, 1600-2600m. SAfr endemic. Submerged in summer, dry in winter.

OPHIOGLOSSACEAE *Ophioglossum* - **Snake or Adder's Tongue Ferns** (*ophis* - snake; *glossa* - tongue, refers to the slender sometimes forked tip above the fertile spike) Temp and trop, ±50 species, 12 in SAfr, 4 in this region.

Ophioglossum vulgatum Common Adder's Tongue (*vulgatum* – common, widespread)

Up to 200mm tall. Sometimes in large colonies, in short grass, and wet earth up to 2500m. Palaearctic, south to Afr. LEAF **solitary, tip pointed, tapering to base,** stalk up to 140mm long above ground. GENERAL: Used to heal wounds in traditional medicine. *Ophioglossum* oil is a potential drug for treatment of cancer.

Mohria (named after Dr M Mohr, German botanist, Prof of Philosophy at University of Kiel) Six species in SAfr, 3 in this region.

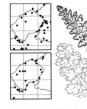

Mohria vestita [= *M. caffrorum* var. *vestita*] Scented Fern; Brandbossie (A); lehorometso, mahorometso (SS)

Closely packed, erect fronds, **up to 500mm tall.** On damp shady banks, at foot of cliffs and overhangs, on rock outcrops, up to 3000m. Widespread, S Cape to Kenya and Madag. FRONDS soft, hairy. GENERAL: Fronds smell strongly of turpentine when crushed. Used in traditional medicine to relieve colds, burns, nightmares, also to treat worms. **Similar species:** *M. rigida* Small, 50-280mm tall. Singly or in small groups, in seasonally moist, often exposed rock crevices, 1800-2480m. EMR endemic.

SCHIZAEACEAE *Schizaea* - **Cockscomb Ferns** (*schizein* - to split or divide) Trop and temp, ±30 species, 2 in SAfr.

Schizaea pectinata Cockscomb Fern (*pectinata* - comblike, refers to fertile portion of frond)

Wiry, grasslike, up to 300mm tall. Around rocks, in damp grassland, up to 2700m. SW Cape to Tanz, Madag. RHIZOME brown, creeping with densely crowded fronds. FERTILE FRONDS with **vertical comblike sori** up to 12mm long. FERTILE SEGMENTS up to 9mm long, not tapering significantly; **rachis recurved** when mature.

Lycopodium carolinianum

Neil Crouch

John Burrows

Lycopodium clavatum

John Burrows

Ophioglossum vulgatum

Neil Crouch

Selaginella caffrorum

John Burrows

Mohria vestita

John Burrows

Selaginella imbricata

Neil Crouch

Isoetes transvaalensis

Neil Crouch

Mohria rigida

Neil Crouch

Schizaea pectinata

293

GLEICHENIACEAE *Gleichenia* (named after Baron W. von Gleichen-Ruswurm, a microscopist 1717-1783) Fronds repeatedly forking into equal pairs. Trop and subtrop, ±10 species, 2 in SAfr and this region.

Gleichenia umbraculifera **Umbrella Coral-fern** (*umbraculum* - umbrella, refers to the fronds)
Robust creeping or climbing plant. Below cliffs and on steep slopes at forest margins, up to 2100m. S Afr, south of Zambezi. Stalk up to 1m tall. FRONDS **divided into 4-5 forks.** STIPE **covered with thick pale brown 'hairs'.** PINNULES **entire, silvery beneath.**

CYATHEACEAE - Tree Fern Family *Cyathea* (*kyatheion* - little cup) About 600 species, 2 in SAfr, 1 in this region.

Cyathea dregei [= *Alsophila dregei*] **Common Tree Fern; Gewone Boomvaring (A); umphanga, ishihi, isikhomankoma (Z)** (named after Johan Drège, 1794-1881, German pharmacist, horticulturist and botanical collector who travelled extensively in SA between 1826 and 1834)
Tree fern, 2-5m tall, with compact crown of arching fronds. In full sun, on streamlines, in sheltered gullies, up to 2300m. S Cape to Trop Afr. MAIN STEM thick, up to 450mm diam. STIPE **brown, woolly and prickly at base.** GENERAL: Main stem withstands frost and fire. Used in traditional medicine. A popular garden plant.

DENNSTAEDTIACEAE *Pteridium* (*pteris* - fern, resembles the fern, *Pteris*) Monotypic, cosmop.

Pteridium aquilinum subsp. *aquilinum* **Bracken; Adelvaring (A); umbewe, umhlasho-shana (Z)** (*aquilla* - 'of an eagle', meaning unclear)
Erect, up to 1.5m tall. Sometimes in large colonies, in grassland and on forest margins, up to 2500m. FRONDS **very stiff, hard,** arising from a **much branched creeping rhizome.** GENERAL: Rhizome rich in starch. Used to treat worms, mixed with other plants to treat menstrual problems, sap used to tread septic sores.

ADIANTACEAE Terrestrial ferns. Cosmop, ±40 genera, ±10 000 species, 11 genera in SAfr. *Adiantum* - Maidenhair Ferns (*adiantos* - dry, untouched by water - refers to the water repelling pinnules) Cosmop, ±200 species, 10 in SAfr, 2 in this region.

Adiantum poiretii **Fine Maidenhair Fern; Fyn Vrouehaarvaring (A); lehorometso, lepata-maoa, pata-leoana (SS)** (named after J.L.M. Poiret, 1755-1834, French botanist and clergyman)
Deciduous fern, up to 600mm tall. On forest floor, on floor of Cave Sandstone overhangs, up to 2600m. Pantrop, **montane in the tropics.** STIPE thin, wiry, shiny black. PINNULES semi-circular to kidney-shaped, **veins end between** rounded teeth. SORI **kidney-shaped, green.** GENERAL: Used in traditional medicine.

Cheilanthes (*cheilos* - lip; *anthos* - flower, refers to marginal sori) About 180 species, ±31 in SAfr, 8 in this region.

Cheilanthes eckloniana **Resurrection Fern; lehorometso, mathomeng (SS)** (named after CF Ecklon, 1795-1868, apothecary, plant collector and traveller who collected widely in the Cape with Carl Zeyher)
Up to 450mm tall. Among boulders and on rock sheets, up to 2700m. SAfr endemic. STIPE 70-260mm long, covered in creamy brown scales. LAMINA **lower surface covered in densely felted, soft, creamy brown hairs.**

Cheilanthes quadripinnata [= *Pellaea quadripinnata*] **Four-pinnate Lip Fern; Vierveelip-varing (A); lehorometso (SS)** (*quadripinnata* - 4-pinnate, frond divided 4 times)
Tufted, **up to 1m tall.** Among rocks, in shady places, up to 3300m. Cape to Ethiopia. STIPE **shiny, dark brownish black,** similar to bracken but not as hard or robust (bracken has a pale brown stipe). LAMINA hairless, 3-5 pinnate, soft or leathery depending on exposure. SORI **continuous along margins of ultimate segments.**

Pellaea (*pellos* - dark coloured, refers to the dark stipe) Trop and subtrop, 11 species in SAfr, 1 in this region.

Pellaea calomelanos **Blue Rock Fern, Hard fern; lehorometso, lepata-maoa, pata-leoana (SS); phaladza (Z)** (*calo* - beautiful; *melanos* - black, refers to stipe, rachis)
Tufted, up to 550mm tall. Around and in crevices of rocks in grassland, up to 2000m. One of the commonest ferns in SAfr. PINNULES **grey-green,** thickly leathery. GENERAL: Used in traditional medicine and as a protective charm.

Pteris (*pteron* - wing, refers to symmetrical fronds like wings) Cosmop, about 250 species, 6 in SAfr.

Pteris cretica **Avery Fern; lehorometso, lesira (SS)** (*cretica* - Isle of Crete)
Tufted fronds, leathery, up to 1m tall. In large clumps, on moist overhangs, among boulders, up to 2700m. SW Cape to E Afr, Medit, China, Japan. FERTILE FRONDS **almost twice as long as sterile fronds,** basal pair of pinnae bear subpinnae. GENERAL: Used as a protective charm. Attractive container and garden plant.

294

Gleichenia umbraculifera

Neil Crouch

Cyathea dregei

Neil Crouch

Adiantum poiretii

Neil Crouch

Pellaea calomelanos

Neil Crouch

Pteris cretica

Neil Crouch

Pteridium aquilinum

Neil Crouch

Cheilanthes eckloniana

John Burrows

Cheilanthes quadripinnata

Neil Crouch

295

GRAMMITIDACEAE Small to very small epiphytic or lithophytic plants. Widespread in the trop, S Hemisp. *Grammitis* (*gramma* - line, refers to parallel lines of sori) 5 in SAfr, 1 in this region.

Grammitis rigescens [= *G. flabelliformis, Xiphopteris flabelliformis, X. rigescens*] (*rigescens* - rather stiff, probably refers to the fronds)

Fronds stiffly erect, up to 220mm tall. On basalt cliffs, not below 2000m in this region. High mountain peaks of Zim, Moz, Trop Afr. RHIZOME widely creeping. STIPE dark brown. LAMINA **deeply incised to the midrib**, midrib dark brown/black. SORI **round, 1-4 per lobe**.

POLYPODIACEAE *Pleopeltis* (*pleon* - more, *pelta* - small shield, refers to scales) About 40 species, 3 in S Afr, 2 in this region.

Pleopeltis macrocarpa Scaly Lance-fern; Lansvaring (A); lehorometso, tsee-tsa-muthla (SS) (*macros* - large; *karpon* - fruit, refers to the large sori)

Up to 200mm tall. In shade, on mossy rocks or tree trunks, up to 2170m. Cape to Trop Afr, Trop America, India. RHIZOME widely creeping. STIPE **brown**. LAMINA **leathery**, margins slightly wavy, **speckled with pale scales beneath**. SORI **in top third to half of the frond**.

Polypodium (*poly* - much, many; *pous* - foot, refers to long the creeping rhizome) Cosmop, ±75 species, 2 in SAfr, this region.

Polypodium vulgare Common Polypody (*vulgare* - common)

Up to 350mm tall. In crevices of cliffs, on mossy rocks in forest, up to 2900m. Rare in SA, then to Europe, N America. RHIZOME creeping. STIPE pale, straw coloured; LAMINA thick, rigid, **smooth on both surfaces**. SORI round, in single row on each side of midrib. GENERAL: Tolerates snow, shrivels in drought but resurrects with moisture. Small in more exposed places.

ASPLENIACEAE A very large family, sori elongated. *Asplenium* - Spleenworts (*a* - without; *splen* - spleen, possibly refers to the fact that plants had once been used to treat enlarged spleen) Cosmop, ±650 species, ±44 in SAfr, 10 in this region.

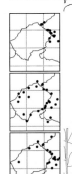

Asplenium aethiopicum Common Spleenwort

Up to 350mm tall. On tree trunks in forest patches, crevices of cliffs and rock outcrops, up to 2000m. SW Cape to Trop Afr. RHIZOME creeping. FRONDS tufted. STIPE **dark brown, 'hairy'**. PINNAE **sharply tapering, margins irregularly serrate**. SORI linear.

Asplenium adiantum-nigrum Black Spleenwort; lehorometso (SS) (*adiantum-nigrum* - black, *Adiantum* (maidenhair fern) because of its vague resemblance to some species of that genus)

Widespread fern, 120-450mm tall. Under outcropping rocks, along streambanks, up to 2500m. Cape to Trop Afr, Europe, N America. RHIZOME **shortly creeping with closely packed fronds**. STIPE shiny, black, **prominently swollen at base underground, semi-succulent, pale green**. FRONDS thinly leathery. PINNA LOBES triangular to ovate, more dissected toward the base.

Asplenium splendens subsp. drakensbergense Splendid Drakensberg Spleenwort

Small, 10-350mm tall. Found in rock crevices, on rocky banks or screes, 1600-2800m. EMR endemic. STIPE **equal to or longer than lamina**. FRONDS narrow, green above, dark green below. RACHIS green. PINNULES straight-sided.

Asplenium trichomanes Delicate Maidenhair Spleenwort; lehorometso (SS)

(*trichoma* - growth of hair, Dioscorides believed it was a hair restorer)

Closely tufted fronds, up to 300mm long. In moist, shady rock crevices, up to 3300m. N & S Hemisp, on **high mountains in the tropics**. FRONDS with no gemmae (little plantlets). RACHIS shiny, black. LAMINA with widely spaced rectangular pinnae. SORI in **2-6 pairs**. Similar species: *Asplenium monanthes* Single-sori Fern; lehorometso (SS) (*monanthes* - single flower, refers to single sorus per pinna) Firm, tufted fronds, up to 600mm long. In shade on forest floor, near shaded streams, usually on boulders, in crevices on Cave Sandstone up to 2500m. SORI **solitary on each pinna**; gemmae (plantlets) **on the stipe**.

Ceterach (probably Arabic, refers to European species, *C. officinarum* which had great medicinal value in ancient times) Old World, 3 species, 1 in SAfr and this region.

Ceterach cordatum Scaly Fern, Resurrection Fern; lehorometso (SS) (*cordatum* - heart-shaped)

Hardy, tufted fern, up to 300mm tall. In crevices of moist cliffs up to 2700m. Widespread in SAfr. STIPE **short**, up to 20mm long, **densely covered below with soft pale brown 'hairs'**. GENERAL: During dry spells, the fronds curl up, drying to half their size and unfolding when wet. Fire resistant.

296

Ferns

Grammitis rigescens

Pleopeltis macrocarpa

Polypodium vulgare

Asplenium adiantum-nigrum

Asplenium aethiopicum

Asplenium splendens subsp. *drakensbergense*

Ceterach cordatum

Asplenium monanthes

Asplenium trichomanes

John Burrows

John Burrows

Neil Crouch

Neil Crouch

Neil Crouch

Neil Crouch

Neil Crouch

Neil Crouch

Neil Crouch

297

ATHYRIACEAE About 650 species. ***Athyrium*** (*athurein* - variable, refers to sori) Cosmop, ±180 species, 2 in SAfr, this region.

Athyrium schimperi Grassland Lady-fern (named after Wilhelm G. Schimper 1804-1878, renowned German traveller and collector who visited Ethiopia and Eritrea where he collected this fern)

300-1000mm tall. In crevices of damp cliffs or around rock outcrops, **not a forest species**, up to 3000m. Widespread in mountains of E Afr. RHIZOME **shortly creeping**. FRONDS closely spaced. STIPE pink on new fronds, turning pale green, with long pale brown 'hairs'. BASAL PINNAE reduced. SORI 'j' shaped.

Cystopteris (*kystos* - bladder; *pteris* - fern) Temp and subtrop mountains, ±18 species, 1 in SAfr and this region.

Cystopteris fragilis Brittle Bladder Fern; lehorometso (SS) (*fragilis* - fragile)

Delicate, small fern, 170-400(600)mm tall. **Always in moist places**, in shady overhangs and cliffs, near waterfalls, up to 3300m. Cosmop, most widely distributed of all ferns, only above 1000m in SAfr. STIPE slender, **brittle**. FRONDS pale green. SORI **round**. GENERAL: Fronds shrivel in dry conditions. Rhizomes used to treat worms.

LOMARIOPSIDACEAE Trop, ±10 genera, over 500 species, 3 genera in SAfr, 1 in this region. ***Elaphoglossum*** (*elaphos* - stag; *glossis* - tongue, refers to lamina) Trop, subtrop, especially trop America, ±400 species, 14 in SAfr, 4 in this region.

Elaphoglossum acrostichoides Common Buck-tongue Fern; lehorometso, tsete-tsa-'mutla (SS) (resembling *Acrostichum*)

60-500mm long. In crevices of moist Cave Sandstone cliffs, in large freestanding blocks, up to 2800m. SW Cape to Trop Afr, Madag. **Very variable**. RHIZOME creeping, 5-8mm thick, dark brown. STERILE FROND: STIPE 30-150mm; LAMINA shape variable, 30-350×10-30mm, dark green above, **base tapering**, paler beneath with dark dots. FERTILE FROND: STIPE longer; LAMINA smaller, SORI **cover the whole undersurface**.

Elaphoglossum drakensbergense

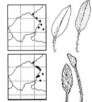

Small creeping fern 25-160mm tall. In crevices of cliffs, 1800-3200m. High mountains of SA. RHIZOME dark brown, fronds spaced. STERILE FROND: STIPE 10-100mm; LAMINA 15-60×7-12mm, upper surface covered in pale brown hairlike scales, only on midrib beneath. FERTILE FROND: LAMINA covered with sporangia beneath. **Similar species: *Elaphoglossum spathulatum* Very small, 28-70mm** tall. Earth cliffs along streams, rock ledges, up to 2400m. Montane to Tanz, Trop America. FRONDS clustered, **hairy on both surfaces, margins very hairy, new fertile fronds folded in half.**

ASPIDIACEAE Ten genera in SAfr. ***Woodsia*** (named after Joseph Woods) Alpine, Arctic, S America, ±40 species, 2 in SAfr, this region.

Woodsia montvidensis var. *burgessiana* (Montevideo, Uruguay, type from S America)

Deciduous fern, 85-400mm tall. In montane grassland or scrub, in shelter of boulders, in rock crevices and ledges on cliff faces, 1500-3000m. EMR endemic. RHIZOME **covered in dark brown scales.** STIPE straw coloured. LAMINA 65-300×20-60mm, covered in tiny round golden spots. SORI circular. GENERAL: Fire resistant.

Dryopteris (*drys* - oak; *pteris* - fern, refers to habitat of some species) Cosmop, ±150 species, ±9 in SAfr, 4 in this region.

Dryopteris athamantica koma-koma, lehorometso (SS); inkomkomo (Z) (*athamantica* - brightness, perhaps refers to this fern's preference for sunny habitats)

Narrow, erect fronds, light green, 500-950mm tall. **In full sun**, on drainage lines, on grass slopes, up to 2200m. E Cape to Trop Afr. STIPE with long brown 'hairs' at base. LAMINA 250-680×80-260mm. GENERAL: Used in traditional medicine. Attractive garden plant. **Similar species: *Dryopteris inaequalis* Lop-lobed Wood-fern; lehorometso (SS)** (*inaequalis* – unequal) **Fronds larger, more spreading, dark green**, 450-1800mm tall. **Shade loving**, up to 2400m. Widespread. PINNAE less angled, tips more blunt.

Dryopteris dracomontana Drakensberg Wood-fern (after the Drakensberg, home of this fern)

Tufted, 150-340mm tall. Under overhangs, among basalt boulders in short grassland, ericoid scrub, 2000-3000m. EMR endemic. FERTILE FRONDS **erect**, longer, narrower than **semi-prostrate sterile fronds**. SORI **round, covering the lamina beneath.**

Athyrium schimperi

Cystopteris fragilis

Woodsia montividensis

Dryopteris acrostichoides

Dryopteris athamantica

Elaphoglossum drakensbergense

Elaphoglossum spathulatum

Dryopteris dracomontana

Dryopteris inaequalis

299

Polystichum - Shield Ferns (*polys* - many; *stichos* - row, refers to rows of sori on pinnae, pinnules or lobes) Cosmop,±140 species, 9 in SAfr, ±7 in this region.

Polystichum dracomontanum Drakensberg Shield Fern

Erect to arching, tufted fronds up to 1m long. **Forms large colonies**, in damp shady ground at foot of cliffs, around rocks in forest patches, in understorey of montane scrub forest, 1600-3000m. EMR endemic. STIPE almost smooth with age. LAMINA **thickly leathery, ovate**, about 340×140mm, **glossy very dark green above, pale matt green beneath**. GENERAL: Withstands snow, frost and fires. **Similar species:** *Polystichum monticola* lehorometso (SS) **Arching fronds**, up to 800mm long. In exposed situations, against rocks in stream gullies and in *Leucosidea* scrub, in large colonies, 2000-2400m. SW Cape to EMR, SAfr endemic. RHIZOME **creeping**. STIPE hairy, with **large reddish brown scales** towards base.

Polystichum wilsonii [= *P. alticola*] lehorometso, mokubetso (SS)

Tufted, **compact fronds**, up to 750mm long. In damp shady ground at foot of cliffs, around rock outcrops, in stream gullies, mostly in fairly exposed situations **at high altitude**, 1800-2600m. Distribution scattered in Afr, also N India, Bhutan, China and Taiwan. STIPE pale with **large pale cream scales**. FRONDS up to 520×150mm, **pronounced reduction of the basal pinnae**. GENERAL: Smoke from burning fronds used as a protective charm. A good garden subject, survives snow and frost. Burning has little or no damaging effect on the rhizomes.

BLECHNACEAE *Blechnum* (*blechnon* - used by Dioscorides to define a certain fern) Cosmop, mainly S Hemisp, ±220 species, 7 in SAfr, 5 in this region.

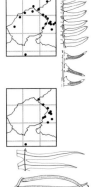

Blechnum australe Southern Hard-fern (*australe* - of the south)

Tuft of fronds, 350-700mm long. In damp earth under Cave Sandstone overhangs, damp shady side of outcrops, in *Leucosidea* thickets, often forming colonies, 1800-2450m. S Afr, Madag, Mascarenes, South Atlantic Islands. RHIZOME thin, creeping widely. FRONDS **stiff**, rough, sterile frond slightly larger than the fertile frond. PINNAE **narrowing to pointed tip**. SORI in long bars along margins of pinnae. GENERAL: There is a dwarfed form in dry rock crevices.

Blechnum giganteum [= *B. attenuatum* var. *giganteum*] Giant Hard-fern (*attenuatum* - narrowly tapering, refers to pinnules)

Fronds tufted, up to 1.9m long. In deep narrow clefts in Cave Sandstone cliffs or under damp shady overhangs, along streambanks in montane grassland or in forest, 1800-2000m. E Cape to Zam. RHIZOME **thick, creeping** (to suberect), dark brown. STERILE FROND: 45-360mm wide; PINNAE with prominent veins, fused to the rachis. FERTILE FROND: PINNAE very narrow, about 3mm wide; SORI linear along margins. GENERAL: **New unfurling fronds a lovely coppery colour**. A very decorative fern for cool moist gardens.

Blechnum inflexum (*inflexum* – bent inwards)

Up to 600mm tall. In sinkholes in streamlines, rock crevices in shady hollows, up to 2200 m. SW Cape to Zim, SAfr endemic. PINNAE **blunt-tipped**; FERTILE FRONDS **compact, much smaller**. SORI appear to cover the undersurface.

Near Drakensberg Gardens,
southern Drakensberg

Martin von Fintel

Polystichum dracomontanum

John Burrows

Neil Crouch

Blechnum inflexum

Neil Crouch

Blechnum giganteum

Neil Crouch

Polystichum wilsonii

John Burrows

Blechnum australe

Neil Crouch

Blechnum giganteum

Ferns

301

GLOSSARY PLATE 1

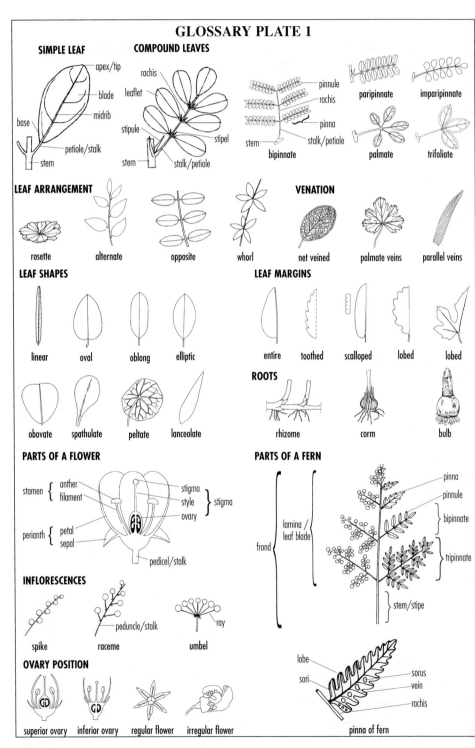

SIMPLE LEAF
apex/tip
blade
midrib
base
petiole/stalk
stem

COMPOUND LEAVES
rachis
leaflet
stipule
stipel
stem
stalk/petiole

pinnule
rachis
pinna
stem
stalk/petiole
bipinnate

paripinnate
imparipinnate
palmate
trifoliate

LEAF ARRANGEMENT
rosette   alternate   opposite   whorl

VENATION
net veined   palmate veins   parallel veins

LEAF SHAPES
linear   oval   oblong   elliptic

obovate   spathulate   peltate   lanceolate

LEAF MARGINS
entire   toothed   scalloped   lobed   lobed

ROOTS
rhizome   corm   bulb

PARTS OF A FLOWER
stamen { anther
         filament
perianth { petal
           sepal
stigma
style
ovary
} stigma
pedicel/stalk

PARTS OF A FERN
pinna
pinnule
bipinnate
lamina / leaf blade
frond
tripinnate
stem/stipe

INFLORESCENCES
spike   raceme   umbel
peduncle/stalk
ray

OVARY POSITION
superior ovary   inferior ovary   regular flower   irregular flower

lobe
sori
sorus
vein
rachis
pinna of fern

GLOSSARY PLATE 2

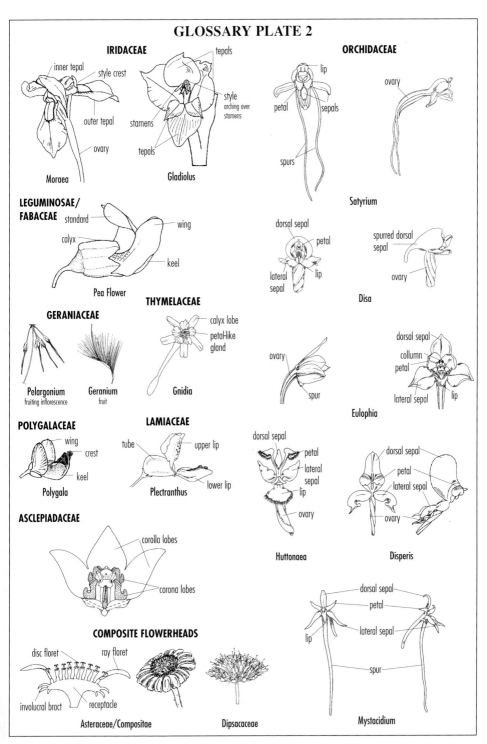

IRIDACEAE

inner tepal
style crest
outer tepal
ovary
stamens
tepals
tepals
style arching over stamens

Moraea

Gladiolus

ORCHIDACEAE

lip
petal
sepals
spurs
ovary

Satyrium

dorsal sepal
petal
lateral sepal
lip

spurred dorsal sepal
ovary

Disa

LEGUMINOSAE/ FABACEAE

standard
calyx
wing
keel

Pea Flower

THYMELACEAE

calyx lobe
petal-like gland

Gnidia

ovary
spur

dorsal sepal
collumn
petal
lateral sepal
lip

Eulophia

GERANIACEAE

Pelargonium
fruiting inflorescence

Geranium
fruit

POLYGALACEAE

wing
crest
keel

Polygala

LAMIACEAE

tube
upper lip
lower lip

Plectranthus

dorsal sepal
petal
lateral sepal
lip
ovary

Huttonaea

dorsal sepal
petal
lateral sepal
ovary

Disperis

ASCLEPIADACEAE

corolla lobes
corona lobes

COMPOSITE FLOWERHEADS

disc floret
ray floret
involucral bract
receptacle

Asteraceae/Compositae

Dipsacaceae

dorsal sepal
petal
lateral sepal
lip
spur

Mystacidium

303

GLOSSARY

achene   a small, dry, non-splitting, one seeded fruit
annual   a plant which germinates from seed, flowers, sets seed and dies in the same year
appendage   a secondary part attached to a main structure
aquatic   growing in water
aril   fleshy outer covering of a seed

achene

berry   fleshy, pulpy fruit without a stone
bract   a reduced leaf or leaflike structure at base of flower or inflorescence
bulbils   a small bulb arising from the base of a larger bulb

appendage

capsule   a dry, splitting fruit
cataphylls   membranous scale leaves
caudex   the persistent swollen stem base of certain herbaceous perennials
cladodes   a flattened stem with the form and function of a leaf
composite flowerhead   an apparently simple flower made up of many small flowers
corymb   short, broad, more or less flat-topped inflorescence, outer flowers opening first
cyathia/cyathium   the flowering head in genus *Euphorbia*, cuplike with a single pistil and male flowers with a single stamen

aril

deciduous   not evergreen, leaves falling at the end of one season of growth

cladodes

endemic   naturally found only in a particular and usually restricted geographic area or region
epicalyx   a whorl of bracts below a flower which resembles an outer calyx
epiphyte   a plant growing on another which does not draw food or water from it
ericoid   having narrow, needlelike, rolled leaves like *Erica* or heather

composite flowerhead

gynostegium   a structure formed from the fusion of the anthers with the stigmatic region of the gynoecium (as in Asclepiadaceae)

cyathia/cyathium

herb   a plant without an above ground woody stem, the stems dying back to the ground at the end of the growing season
herbaceous   not woody, soft branches before they become woody
hybrid   offspring produced from genetically different parents

inflorescence   a flowering shoot bearing more than one flower; the arrangement of flowers on the flowering shoot

lenticel   a small raised pore developing in woody stems when epidermis is replaced by cork

epicalyx

nectary   an organ which produces nectar, often appears as a scale, pit or protuberance

papillae   minute pimplelike bumps or protuberances
pappus   modified (much reduced) calyx of Compositae/Asteraceae made up of scales or bristles at the tip of the achene
parasite   plant or animal living in or on another, drawing food and water at least partly from it

latex

perennial   a plant that lives 3 or more years
pod   a dry, splitting fruit
pollinia/pollinium   a mass of waxy pollen grains (sticking together) transported as a unit during pollination

radial   spreading from a common centre
ranks (leaves)   a row, especially a vertical row
rosette   a dense, radiating cluster of leaves (or other organisms) at or near ground level
rostellum   a small beak; an extension from the upper edge of the stigma in orchids

pappus

scale   any thin, flat, dry, membranous body, usually a degenerate leaf
sessile   without a stalk, attached directly
simple   undivided ie leaf not divided into leaflets; inflorescence not branched
sinus   space or recess between 2 lobes or divisions of an organ, ie leaf or petal
sorus, sori (pl)   cluster of sporangia or spore cases
spadix   a thick fleshy spike or column with tiny flowers crowded on it
spathe   a large bract or modified leaf surrounding a flower cluster or spadix, sometimes coloured and petal-like eg *Zantedeschia*

pollinia/pollinium

spadix/spathe

spike	an unbranched elongated inflorescence with stalkless flowers
sporangium, sporangia (pl)	spore-bearing case
spores	fern equivalent of a seed, but much smaller
spur	a hollow, tubelike extension of a petal or sepal
succulent	juicy and fleshy eg leaves and stems of *Aloe*
tarn	small mountain lake
tendril	a modified leaf, leaflet, branch or inflorescence of a climbing plant that coils around suitable objects and helps support and elevate the plant
tepal	a segment of a perianth which is not differentiated into a calyx and corolla (sepals and petals)
trichomanes	a hair or hairlike outgrowth of the epidermis (outermost cellular layer of a non-woody plant)
umbel	usually a flat-topped inflorescence with the stalks arising more or less from a common point like an umbrella
whorls/whorled	arrangement of similar parts in a circle at the same level

tepal

ABBREVIATIONS

A	Afrikaans	Les	Lesotho	SAfr	Southern Africa
Afr	Africa(n)	Madag	Madagascar	SS	South Sotho
Austr	Australia	Medit	Metiterranean	sp.	species
Bot	Botanic(al)	Moz	Mozambique	spp.	species (plural)
CAfr	Central Africa	Mpum	Mpumalanga	subtrop	subtropical
cosmop	cosmopolitan	N	north(ern)	Tanz	Tanzania
diam	diameter	NW Prov	North West Province	temp	temperate
E	east(ern)			Trop/trop	tropics
EAfr	East Africa	Nam	Namibia	USA	United States
EC	Eastern Cape Province	Old World	Europe, Asia, Africa		(of America)
EMR	Eastern Mountain Region	pg	page	W	west(ern)
		paleotrop	paleotropic(al)	X	Xhosa
FS	Free State	pantrop	pantropical	Z	Zulu
Hemisp	Hemisphere	pp	pages	Zam	Zambia
Is	island(s)	prof	professor	Zim	Zimbabwe
KZN	KwaZulu-Natal	Prov	Province		

PLANT DESCRIPTIONS

Family and genus descriptions are written in full in at least one of the colour sections
Often they draw attention to characters useful for identification
Scientific names are given in *italics*
Synonyms in square brackets [ ]
Measurements are always length × breadth unless otherwise stated
When only one measurement is given, it is always length or height
Unusual or exceptional records, whether size, colour or form, are given in brackets
Flowering times are given in brackets after the flower description.
Similar species: Under this heading, the typeface conveys certain information eg
Aagapanthus campanulatus - the plant has a description and photograph in the book
Agapanthus campanulatus - the plant has a description but no photograph in the book
Agapanthus campanulatus (see pg 10) - the plant is described and illustrated elsewhere in the book

A QUICK GUIDE TO IDENTIFICATION

Don't pick the plant. 'Take the book to the plant, not the plant to the book'
Make careful observations on the following:
  • Height and shape of plant
  • Shape of leaves, arrangement on stem, length of stalk
  • Shape and colour of flowers, number of petals, stamens and styles
  • Arrangement of flowers
  • Shape and colour of fruits
  • Hairiness
  • Habitat and abundance

(with acknowledgement to *'The Wild Flowers of Britain and Northern Europe'* by Richard Fitter & Alastair Fitter, Collins 1974)

SELECTED BIBLIOGRAPHY

A number of scientific journals and books have been referred to when researching this field guide. Some of those that are accessible to the general public are listed.

ARNOLD, T.H & B.C. de Wet (1993) *Plants of southern Africa: names and distribution*. Mem Bot Survey of SA No: 62. National Botanical Institute
BATTEN, A., J. Manning & H. Bokelmann (2001) *Eastern Cape South African Wild Flower Guide 11*. Botanical Society of SA / National Botanical Institute.
BATTEN, A. (1988) *Flowers of Southern Africa*. Southern Book Publishers
BURROWS, J.E. (1990) *Southern African Ferns and Fern Allies*. Frandsen Publishers.
COATES-PALGRAVE, Meg (2002) *Keith Coates Palgrave Trees of Southern Africa*. 2nd revised edition. Struik
CODD, L.E. (1968) *The South African species of Kniphofia*. Bothalia 9
FOX, F.W. and M.E. NORWOOD YOUNG (1982) *Food from the Veld*. Delta Books
GIBSON, Janet (1975) *Wild Flowers of Natal (coastal region)* Wildlife Society (Natal Branch)
GIBSON, Janet (1978) *Wild Flowers of Natal (inland region)* Wildlife Society (Natal Branch)
GOLDBLATT, Peter (1986) *The Moraeas of Southern Africa*. Annals Kirstenbosch National Botanic Gardens 14
GOLDBLATT, Peter (1989) *The Genus Watsonia*. Annals Kirstenbosch National Botanic Gardens 18
GOLDBLATT, Peter and John MANNING (1998) *Gladiolus in Southern Africa*. Fernwood Press
GORDON-GRAY, K.D. (1995) *Cyperaceae in Natal*. Strelitzia 2, National Botanical Institute
GUNN, M.D. & Codd, L.E. (1981) *Botanical exploration of Southern Africa*. A.A. Balkema, Cape Town
JACOT-GUILLARMOD, Amy (1971) *Flora of Lesotho*. Lehre. Cramer
HENDERSON, Lesley (1995) *Plant Invaders of Southern Africa*. Plant Protection Research Institute Handbook No.5. Plant Protection Research Institute.
HILLIARD, O.M. (1977) *Compositae in Natal*. University of Natal Press
HILLIARD, O.M. (1985) *Trees & Shrubs of the Natal Drakensberg*. Ukhahlamba Series, no 1. University of Natal Press.
HILLIARD, O.M. (1987) *Grasses, Sedges, Restiads & Rushes of the Natal Drakensberg*. Ukhahlamba Series, No. 2 University of Natal Press
HILLIARD, O.M. (1990) *Flowers of the Natal Drakensberg - The lily, iris and orchid families and their allies*. Ukhahlamba Series No. 4, University of Natal Press
HILLIARD, O.M. and B.L. BURTT (1971) *Streptocarpus. An African plant study*. University of Natal Press
HILLIARD, O. M. and B. L. BURTT (1987) *The Botany of the Southern Natal Drakensberg*. National Botanic Gardens
HILLIARD, O.M. and B.L. BURTT (1991) *Dierama, The Hairbells of Africa*. Acorn Books
HUTCHINGS, Anne et al (1996) *Zulu Medicinal Plants*. University of Natal Press
KILLICK, Donald (1990) *A Field Guide - The Flora of the Natal Drakensberg*. Jonathan Ball & Ad Donker
LINDER, H.P. & H. KURZWEIL (1999) *Orchids of Southern Africa*. A.A. Balkema, Rotterdam.
MOFFETT, R.O. (1993) *Rhus*. Flora of Southern Africa vol. 19, Part 3, Fascicle 1. National Botanical Institute.
MOFFETT, Rodney (1997) *Grasses of the Eastern Free State, their descriptions and uses*. Uniqwa.
PAROZ, R.A. (1962) *A list of Sotho plant names*. Supplement to Lesotho: Basutoland Notes & Rcords 3 (1962)
PEARSE, R.O. (1973) *Barrier of Spears*. Howard Timmins, Cape Town
PEARSE, R.O. (1978) *Mountain Splendour*. Howard Timmins, Cape Town.
PHILLIPS, E.P. (1997) *A Contribution to the flora of the Leribe Plateau and environs*. Annals of the South African Museum 16(1), 1-379.
POOLEY, Elsa (1993) *The Complete Field Guide to Trees of Natal, Zululand & Transkei*. Natal Flora Publications Trust
POOLEY, Elsa (1998) *A Field Guide to the Wild Flowers of KwaZulu-Natal and the Eastern Region*. Natal Flora Publications Trust.
REBELO, Tony (1995) *Proteas, A field guide to the Proteas of Southern Africa*. Fernwood Press
RUBBRIGHT (1995) *Field manual: non-forage biological monitoring in the Mosafeleng/Tsasta-lemeno Range Management Area (RMA 5)*. Maseru: USAID
SCHMITZ, M. (1982) *Wild Flowers of Lesotho*. Roma, Lesotho: ESSA
TRAUSELD, W.R. (1969) *Wild Flowers of the Natal Drakensberg*. Purnell & Sons SA
VAN DER WALT, J.J.A. & P.J. Vorster (1977-1988) *Pelargoniums of Southern Africa*. Vols 1-3. National Bot. Gardens
VAN OUDTSHOORN, Frits (1999) *Guide to Grasses of S.A*. Briza. (2nd Edition)
VAN WYK, A.E. & Gideon F. SMITH (2001) *Regions of Floristic Endemism in Southern Africa*. Umdaus Press. SA.
VAN WYK, Ben-Erik, Gideon SMITH (1996) *Guide to the Aloes of South Africa*. Briza Publications
VAN WYK, Braam & Piet VAN WYK (1997) *Field Guide to Trees of Southern Africa*. Struik
VAN WYK, Braam & Sasa MALAN (1997) *Field Guide to the Wild Flowers of the Highveld* (2nd edition) Struik
VON BREITENBACH, Jutta et al (2001) *Pocket List of Southern African Indigenous Trees*. Briza/Dendrological Foundation.

INDEX

Current scientific names printed in **bold** type.　　　Synonyms in *italic*　　★Indicates alien invasive plants.
Page numbers in **bold** refer to where the full species, genus or family description occurs.

307

313

317

NOTE

A permit is required from the local Nature Conservation authority
or the landowner to collect plants in the wild.

CONTACT ADDRESSES

Bews Herbarium, University of Natal
    P Bag X01, Scottsville 3209 KwaZulu-Natal, South Africa
Botanical Society (KZN Branch)
    Pietermaritzburg: PO Box 21667, Mayor's Walk 3208
    Coastal: PO Box 30544, Mayville 4058
Donald Killick Herbarium
    Ezemvelo KZN Wildlife, P O Box 13053, Cascades Pietermaritzburg 3202
Ezemvelo KwaZulu-Natal Wildlife
    P O Box 13053, Cascades Pietermaritzburg 3202
Free State National Botanical Garden
    PO Box 29036, Bloemfontein 9300
Katse Botanical Garden
    c/o Lesotho Highland Development Authority, P O Box 7332, Maseru 100 Lesotho
Maloti-Drakensberg Transfrontier Conservation and Development Project
    website: www.maloti.org
    Co-ordinator (Lesotho)
        c/o Ministry of Tourism, Environment and Culture
        P O Box 10933, Maseru 100, Lesotho
    Co-ordinator (South Africa), Ezemvelo KZN Wildlife
        P O Box 13053, Cascades, Pietermaritzburg 3202
Natal National Botanical Gardens
    PO Box 21667, Mayor's Walk, Pietermaritzburg 3208
Natal Herbarium
    National Botanical Institute, Botanic Gardens Road, Durban 4001
Selmar Schonland Herbarium
    PO Box 101, Grahamstown 6140
National University of Lesotho, Herbarium, Biology Dept,
    PO Roma 180, Lesotho
National Herbarium
    NBI, Private Bag X101, Pretoria 0001

Tourism information
E Cape Dept of Economic Affairs, Environment & Tourism
    Private Bag X3513, Kokstadt 4700
E Cape Drakensberg: Information, Publicity and Tourism
    Municipal Buildings, Stockenstroom Street, Cradock 5880
E Free State: Tourism and Information
    Market Street, Clarens 9707
East Griqualand: Information and Tourism
    Museum, Municipal Buildings, 75 Hope Street, Kokstad 4700
Free State Tourism
    Municipal Buildings, 20 Muller Street, Bethlehem 9701
Southern Drakensberg: Sani Saunter
    Clocktower Centre, Main Street, Underberg 3257
Northern and Central Drakensberg:
    KZN Tourism, Library Building, Tatham Road, Bergville 3350
Lesotho: Ministry of Tourism, Environment and Culture
    P O Box 10933, Maseru 100, Lesotho
Tourism KwaZulu-Natal
    303 Tourist Junction, 160 Pine Street, Durban 4001